"Ryan Lister knows more about the biblical [t]... [the] world than anyone else I know. And there is n[o] ...[im]portant to our relationship with God. Lister's book is a great antidote to the temptation to see God only as a concept, doctrine, or formula, or to regard him only as a force in the world outside ourselves. This book shows that God is our friend and Father, and that in him we live and move and have our being."

John M. Frame, J. D. Trimble Chair of Systematic Theology and Philosophy, Reformed Theological Seminary, Orlando

"We need more biblical theologies like this one! Ryan Lister has identified a central biblical theme that we easily take for granted. With the unity of Scripture to the fore, he has provided us with a diligently researched study of one of the golden threads that highlight the glories of Christ's person and work. This is thematic biblical study at its best."

Graeme Goldsworthy, Former Lecturer in Old Testament, Biblical Theology, and Hermeneutics, Moore Theological College

"Ryan Lister provides a great service to the people of God by tracing the theme of God's presence from Genesis to Revelation, showing that it is not only central to the Christian eschatological hope, but also the gracious means by which God moves fallen sinners to that glorious beatific vision."

Steven B. Cowan, Assistant Professor of Philosophy and Religion, Lincoln Memorial University

"The whole of the Bible, from soon after the entrance of sin in Genesis 3 to Revelation 22, can be read as the story of God coming nearer. *The Presence of God* is filled with insight that unpacks the fullness of Scripture's development on this theme, but also shows how precious the concept of God's presence with his people is for our lives. Lister has been very careful to represent clearly and appropriately the development of this beautiful biblical theme, and he has done this in a way that is highly relevant for Christian identity and Christian living. Do yourself a favor—read this book and rejoice that God has chosen to come near."

Bruce A. Ware, Professor of Christian Theology, The Southern Baptist Theological Seminary

"The much misunderstood notion of the presence of God is central to the Bible's story from beginning to end. Ryan Lister explains how it is both God's goal for us and the means by which God accomplishes his redemptive mission. This fresh approach to biblical theology presents it as an unfolding drama, with many practical and pastoral implications. In particular, it shows that a sound and scripturally mature analysis of the presence of God can help answer this world's deep-seated spiritual desires."

David Peterson, Former Principal, Oak Hill College; Senior Research Fellow and Lecturer in New Testament, Moore Theological College

"Ryan Lister provides an exegetically grounded theology of relational divine presence that is traced along the Christ-centered storyline of the Bible. This work is an outstanding model of evangelical scholarship, and Lister's conclusions invade every square inch of our lives as we seek to fulfill the primary reason for our existence—knowing the holy God who mercifully draws near to his people."

> **Erik Thoennes,** Professor and Department Chair of Biblical and Theological Studies, Talbot School of Theology, Biola University; Pastor, Grace Evangelical Free Church, La Mirada, California

"God's presence is fundamental to God's story. It is a profound reality. While we have access to this reality in part through our experience of it, the reality is even more than what we experience—it is deep theology grounded in what God has said in his Word about himself. Lister's work examines this fertile soil of God's self-revelation, out of which our experiences can flourish with renewed vigor."

> **Mike Wilkerson,** author, *Redemption: Freed by Jesus from the Idols We Worship and the Wounds We Carry*

The Presence of God

THE
PRESENCE
OF
GOD

ITS PLACE IN THE STORYLINE OF SCRIPTURE
AND THE STORY OF OUR LIVES

J. RYAN LISTER

FOREWORD BY THOMAS R. SCHREINER

::: CROSSWAY

WHEATON, ILLINOIS

Cover design: Faceout Studio

First printing 2015
Printed in the United States of America

Trade paperback ISBN: 978-1-4335-3915-2
PDF ISBN: 978-1-4335-3916-9
Mobipocket ISBN: 978-1-4335-3917-6
ePub ISBN: 978-1-4335-3918-3

Library of Congress Cataloging-in-Publication Data
Lister, J. Ryan (John Ryan), 1978–
    The presence of God: its place in the storyline of
Scripture and the story of our lives / J. Ryan Lister; foreword
by Thomas R. Schreiner.
      pages cm
    Includes bibliographical references and indexes.
    ISBN 978-1-4335-3915-2 (tp)
    1. Presence of God. I. Title.
BT180.P6L57   2015
231.7—dc23   2014009495

Crossway is a publishing ministry of Good News Publishers.

VP		26	25	24	23	22	21	20	19	18	17	16	15
15	14	13	12	11	10	9	8	7	6	5	4	3	2	1

To Chase Elizabeth,
one of God's greatest
testimonies to me
that he is
still present
to bless his people

Psalm 16:11

Contents

Foreword

The goal of theology is to get us back to the garden of Eden. Actually, the goal of theology is to bring us into the heavenly city, for the heavenly city of Revelation 21 and 22 is even better than the garden. God's presence in the garden was lost because of the sin of Adam and Eve. But God will never abandon the New Jerusalem, the heavenly Jerusalem, the new heavens and new earth. John tells us that there is no night there, and there isn't any need for the sun or the moon because the light of the city comes from the Lord and from the Lamb. What makes the New Jerusalem new, what makes it heavenly and glorious, what makes it more desirable than anything you have ever experienced is the presence of God.

Sin is so painful and terrible because it separates us from God. He is our light and salvation. He is our sun and shield. He gives us grace and glory. When we think of the tabernacle and temple in Israel, we might think of a moveable shrine or of a stunningly beautiful building. What filled the Israelites with awe when they thought of the tabernacle and the temple was not fundamentally their structure or beauty, though the second temple was beautiful indeed. Still, the tabernacle and temple were awesome because God dwelt in them, because his glory filled the tabernacle and temple. The tabernacle and temple point us to something greater, to someone greater, for ultimately God's true temple is Jesus Christ. The apostle John tells us that in Jesus the Word became flesh and tabernacled among us. Paul says that the fullness of deity dwelt in Jesus bodily. Jesus said to Philip that the one who had seen him, Jesus, had seen the Father. God walked among Israel through and in Jesus Christ.

That is not the end of the story of course. The crucified and risen

Jesus sent the Holy Spirit upon his people. Now the people of God—the church of Jesus Christ—are the true temple. The Father has not left us as orphans and has not abandoned us. He is with us and in us. He abides in us through the Holy Spirit.

Theologians have tackled many subjects, but it is rather surprising how few have written about God's presence with his people, especially when we realize how central and important this theme is in the Scriptures. In this illuminating work, Ryan Lister helps us see the presence of God in the storyline of the Bible. Hence, we have a better understanding about how the Bible fits together. Lister doesn't appeal to a few proof texts. He shows us how God's presence is stitched into the biblical narrative so that it is clearly part of the warp and woof of the story.

We have an important contribution here, then, from the standpoint of biblical theology. But as readers we don't want to stop there, for the aim of the story is the knowledge of God. We should grow in understanding and in love, for we were created to know God, to see God, to love God, to experience God, and to enjoy his presence forever.

Thomas R. Schreiner

Acknowledgments

I would like to begin by acknowledging that without my wife, Chase, this book would not have been written. God blesses us beyond our imaginations, and my wife is the one through whom I am consistently reminded that the grace and mercy bought at the cross overflows into all aspects of our lives. Chase, you are the one who has been with me every step of the way, from the pontoon boat (see the first chapter), to our dysfunctional basement on Springdale Road, into the teeth of Louisiana, to the Holy City of Charleston, South Carolina, and now Portland, Oregon. You finally get your A+. I know it has been quite some time since you received a report card; and I know the trauma that this can cause someone of your disposition. But please know that it has been my honor, privilege, and joy to walk—and, at times, stumble—with you on this journey. I thank you for every spreadsheet you've done; every tax season you've suffered; every budget line you've cut; every diaper you've changed, dinner you've made, spool of thread you've sewn, book on tape you've listened to; every "smart aleck" response to your questions you've endured; every anxiety you've prayed over; every tear you've shed; and every time you've petitioned your "Lord God Almighty" on my behalf. Though they may seem mundane, these are the true testimony of your love for me—and more importantly the testimony of God's grace to me through his provision of you. So thank you, Chase, for all you have laid down for this little dream of mine—but, even more, for making my dreams yours.

Along with Chase, four of the greatest gifts the Lord ever gave me were my children, Jude and Silas, and Abby Kate and Asher. Books are always being published; every year more and more are churned out by much more skilled and qualified authors. But none of them are able to say they have four precious and mischievous children just like you! My prayer, as you well know, is that you would have eyes to see God's glory, ears to hear the gospel, a heart for God to dwell in, hands to serve him and be obedient to him, and a mouth to sing his praises. May it be so. And this, too, is my hope for each of you: that you will live in the presence of God and long for an eternity where you will be with him forevermore.

There are so many others I am indebted to. To begin, I would like to thank my mom and dad, Jane and Glenn Lister. Thank you for your responsiveness to the Spirit and your God-fearing parenting. I know it was tough at times, but I appreciate your willingness to give sacrificially not only to bring me to obedience, but, more importantly, to bring me to your Lord. I pray that your love for God will continue to grow and that the unconditional love you have for your boys will be directed toward the Lord's church and toward the families with whom you come in contact every day through your ministry of adoption. The Lord has been gracious in giving you to me as parents. Thank you for your love, attention, care for my family; the free babysitting; your support in prayer and finances; and, as always, your encouragement and cheerleading.

Next, I would like to thank my older brother, Rob, and his wife, LuWinn. For all my life, outside of the three years I was in junior high, when he would have nothing to do with me, Rob has been my closest friend. At times it is a struggle having a big brother as a best friend because the lines get a little blurred. For Rob, this manifests itself in his seeing me less as a peer and more as his oldest son (though LuWinn has helped this process quite a bit). But even in this I cannot complain; for it is this part of his nature that opened him to read and edit every single chapter of this book. Over the span of my life, Rob has always been one step before me clearing the way. And though at times I have questioned why my life has followed his so closely, the answer is, very simply, that I find it a great honor to be like my big brother in any way I can.

Like my own, Chase's family has played a substantial role in this project. I know full well that Chase's siblings—Taylor, with his wife, Elizabeth; Abby, with her husband Richard; and Laura Kate—have been holding me up in prayer. They have all been extremely generous in their time and care for us. Each of them has been a constant source of encouragement through their phone calls, conversations, and opening their lives to us.

Their generosity finds much of its source in the love their parents have shown them. From the time I met Charley and Kathy I knew that they would make wonderful in-laws—a difficult thing to find these days. And they have not disappointed. In fact, I have been overwhelmed by their generosity. Their love for us has expressed itself in many ways: financially, spiritually, in sharing their time, and in giving of their hearts. Kathy has proved to be invaluable to this project, for it is through her constant trips to the places where we lived to care for Jude, Silas, Abby Kate, and Asher that I have been able to finish this book (though it appears to be more a joy and less a chore for a grandmother). Charley, too, has given much to the completion of this work, as well as numerous Tennessee football tickets, dinners, and, most importantly, consistent questions about my walk with the Lord and growth in Christ. It is Charley and Kathy's desire to know the deep things of God that I have found encouraging and, simultaneously, challenging. So, to the Lindseys, I say thank you for all that you have done but, most importantly, for loving me as one of your own.

Along with family, there are those friends who have been gracious enough to walk this journey with me. At the Southern Baptist Theological Seminary and even beyond its walls, the Lord has given me great friends, but none has been greater than Oren Martin. Oren has been a help in many ways. He has been a wonderful confidant and has assisted in the formulation of my thesis in ways he probably does not even know. Our Tuesday conversations over chips, salsa, and fajitas have done wonders for my theology, worldview, and personal walk with Christ— though they have been slightly detrimental to my physical health.

I would like to offer a special thanks to my doctoral supervisor and one of my heroes, Dr. Bruce Ware. The rare combination of strength, passion, and theological tenacity, along with compassion and tenderhearted care for God's people, is something I aspire to in my own life. Thank you, Bruce, for your kind words and kind critiques. You have been a wonderful professor, elder, teacher, example, and friend. Thank you for your faithfulness and your wisdom.

I also want to thank Tom Schreiner for interacting with this book and graciously writing the foreword. If there ever were a scholar who could take pride in his own intellect and accomplishments, it would be Tom Schreiner. But instead of boasting in himself, Tom is one of the most humble and God-centered men I know. One of his greatest strengths is his ability to uncomplicate the complicated. I have benefited from his clarity time and time again in his classroom, through his writings, and in his sermons. But of all his gifts, Tom Schreiner's greatest gifts may be his love for God's church and enduring friendship.

I want to show my appreciation for the great team at Crossway. Without them, this book would not have become a reality. I would especially like to recognize two members of this team who have been wonderful sources of help and encouragement. First, I would like to thank Justin Taylor for being open to this project and for being a friend during the process. Second, I need to give credit to Thom Notaro, who, with great skill, edited this volume and, with great patience and grace, treated every word as if it were his own. Thank you both for your expertise and your kindness.

In the end though, all credit is ultimately the Lord's, for it is he who has brought these wonderful people into my life to minister to me, and it is he who opened my eyes to this central theme in his Word. Most significantly, it is God who has justly dealt with my sin and graciously opened up access to his presence for all eternity. My hope with this book, then, is to make much of our limitless God. To this end, I pray this work brings glory to the Lord and benefits his people. I hope that it will challenge each of us to make the presence of God our passion and our pursuit in this world and the next.

Abbreviations

BECNT	Baker Exegetical Commentary on the New Testament
BSac	*Bibliotheca Sacra*
CBQ	*Catholic Biblical Quarterly*
CCT	Contours of Christian Theology
HTR	*Harvard Theological Review*
ICC	International Critical Commentary
JBL	*Journal of Biblical Literature*
JSOT	*Journal for the Study of the Old Testament*
JSOTSup	Journal for the Study of the Old Testament—Supplement Series
LXX	Septuagint
MT	Masoretic Text
NAC	New American Commentary
NICNT	New International Commentary on the New Testament
NICOT	New International Commentary on the Old Testament
NIDOTTE	*New International Dictionary of Old Testament Theology and Exegesis*. 5 vols. Edited by Willem A. VanGemeren. Grand Rapids: Zondervan, 1997.
NIVAC	NIV Application Commentary
NSBT	New Studies in Biblical Theology
PNTC	Pillar New Testament Commentary
TOTC	Tyndale Old Testament Commentaries
TynBul	*Tyndale Bulletin*
VT	*Vestus Testamentum*
WBC	Word Biblical Commentary
WTJ	*Westminster Theological Journal*

1

Introduction

A Forgotten Storyline

It is everywhere. We hear about it all the time. It is alluded to in the sermon. We call for it in our prayers. We sing about it in our hymns and choruses.

For Christians, it is hard to escape. As I write this paragraph, I have just returned from a Christian college's chapel service where I counted seventeen references to it in a fifty-minute service while, of course, paying full attention to the sermon, prayers, and songs. In fact, I think you would be hard pressed to leave your own sanctuary this Sunday without at least one reference to it as well.

What is this refrain we hear over and over again in our churches, small groups, and devotionals? It is the presence of God.

Take a minute to listen to the Christian-speak and, even at times, yourself. How many of us have heard or spoken a prayer that starts like this: "Lord, we come into your *presence* now to lay our needs before you, asking you to *be here with us* as we cry out to you"?

Sound familiar?

And this is only the beginning. The vocabulary of divine presence weaves its way through our hymnals and PowerPoint slides:

I need *Thy presence* every passing hour.
What but Thy grace can foil the tempter's power?

Who, like Thyself, my guide and stay can be?
Through cloud and sunshine, Lord, abide with me.[1]

As I stand here in your *presence*,
Of your beauty I will always stand in awe,
I reach my hands out to the heavens,
And I will lift my voice to you alone, to you alone.[2]

Be Thou my Vision, O Lord of my heart;
Naught be all else to me, save that Thou art.
Thou my best Thought, by day or by night,
Waking or sleeping, *Thy presence* my light.[3]

This is the air I breathe
Your holy *presence* living in me.[4]

Surrounded by your glory, what will my heart feel? . . .
Will I stand in your *presence*, or to my knees will I fall?[5]

These examples—along with our sermons and other Christian teaching—reveal that the language of God's presence is, well, omnipresent in our churches and in Christendom at large.[6]

But there is a problem. As we constantly hear these vague references to God's presence, the concept remains just that: vague. So as our churches sing the chorus of divine presence, many of us simply do not have ears to hear what it means. So how do we tune our ears to hear the beautiful melody of God's presence?

To begin, we must understand the reasons for the theological dissonance surrounding this biblical reality. First, many of us are too busy or too overwhelmed to pick up on the overused references to God's presence in our worship. We are just happy if we can get out of church with all the kids we came with, with all their limbs intact, and with the nursery or education classrooms still standing. Between keeping

---

[1] Henry F. Lyte, "Abide with Me," 1847.
[2] Jeremy Camp, "In Your Presence," 2002.
[3] Ancient Irish Poem, "Be Thou My Vision," trans. Eleanor Hull, 1912.
[4] Michael W. Smith, "Breathe," 2001.
[5] MercyMe, "I Can Only Imagine," 2002.
[6] The notion of divine presence has even leaked into the culture at large. Take the stirring song of guitar icon Eric Clapton, "Presence of the Lord." Through the gospel roots of the blues, Clapton, unbeknownst to himself, penned a refrain that marks the future trajectory of many people when he sings: "I have finally found a place to live just like I never could before. / . . . I have finally found a way to live in the presence of the Lord—in the presence of the Lord."

our son's restless legs from kicking the seat in front of him and running to the car for a sippy cup every seven minutes, we have limited time to reflect on the sermon, much less a threadbare Christian expression touched on by the associate pastor praying between worship songs.

Second, we can easily become too passive in our worship. Granted that reading Scripture and hearing it preached is a noncontact sport, but our minds should be engaged. We should be asking questions and pursuing truth vehemently in these small windows of study and prayer. I think this is part of what Anselm was getting at with his maxim "faith seeking understanding."[7] For some of us, we stop at the first word and forgo the last two. We talk much of faith but we must also talk about pursuing the Lord in an intellectually informed and spiritually vibrant understanding of him. In other words, we must *seek* God. And not only that, we must seek to *understand* him relationally as he discloses himself to us through his Word and revelation.

Finally, and possibly the most significant concern, we have simply grown too accustomed to the jargon. Talk of God's presence is part of the white noise of evangelicalism, a catchphrase that means as little to the one saying it as to the one hearing it. This is typical for many of us. The more we hear something, the less we tend to contemplate its meaning and significance. Unfortunately, this is quite dangerous—especially for the church.

True Christianity is by nature repetitious—and that is a good thing. It is repetitious because God knows exactly who we are and what we need. We bear God's image and Adam's sin. So while the gospel shows us that we are the image of God and can know him as he reveals himself, it also reminds us that, at one point, we rejected God and continue to struggle with neglecting him. For this reason, true Christianity points us to Christ and his work on the cross over and over *and over* again. Scripture tells us that we are broken cisterns, cracked and chipped, needing minute by minute to return to the well of the gospel to be refilled and refreshed.

---

[7] Anselm's petition is extremely helpful here as it helps us see that our intellectual life and our spiritual life are connected, not at odds with one another. He writes: "I acknowledge, O Lord, with thanksgiving, that thou hast created this thy image in me, so that, remembering thee, I may think of thee, may love thee. But this image is so effaced and worn away by my faults, it is so obscured by the smoke of my sins, that it cannot do what it was made to do, unless thou renew and reform it. I am not trying, O Lord, to penetrate thy loftiness, for I cannot begin to match my understanding with it, but I desire in some measure to understand thy truth, which my heart believes and loves. For I do not seek to understand in order to believe, but I believe in order to understand. For this too I believe, that 'unless I believe, I shall not understand.'" Anselm, "Proslogion," in *A Scholastic Miscellany: Anselm to Ockham*, ed. Eugene R. Fairweather (Philadelphia: Westminster, 1961), 73.

As I hope to show in the pages ahead, the presence of God is more than a mere buzzword of evangelicalism; it is a strong, fresh current of living water that fills jars of clay like you and me. It is central to the hope-filled message of Scripture. This is what I want to make clear: beneath the cacophony we have made of this biblical theme is a deep, beautiful melody vital to God's song of salvation that is there only because of the presence of God. In short, I want to show just how intrinsic this theme is to the story of Scripture and to our story.

A King's Treasure

Part of the rationale behind this book is that it is part of *my* story. All the busyness, passivity, and familiarity you read about above, well, that was me. I grew up in the church, so I was well versed in Christian-speak and employed such phrases quite compellingly too—especially at church and other opportune times.

I remember the day when the games stopped and the concept of God's presence became more than just spiritual jargon; it was now the attention-arresting theme of Scripture that God intended us to see. It was the summer of 2000, and I was sitting on a pontoon boat in the middle of the Tennessee River. And though before me was a pristine view of the countryside and the beautiful girl who would soon become my wife, I was blind to it all because of King David's words:

> You make known to me the path of life;
>> in your presence there is fullness of joy;
>> at your right hand are pleasures forevermore. (Ps. 16:11)

Joy and pleasure were what I was looking for—things we all want, I think it safe to say—and here David was telling me exactly where I could find them. All that I sought, all this world relentlessly pursues in all the wrong places, is found in the presence of God.

Needless to say, this was a game changer. David had handed me a biblical treasure map for life.

But mixed in with the happiness of this discovery was the nagging feeling of doubt. "Okay, so the fullness of joy and eternal pleasures are found in the presence of God; but I am no closer to that goal than I was before I was hit with all of this." Where was I supposed to begin?

To my chagrin, there was no "You Are Here" sticker in Psalm 16. All I had to go on was the virtually meaningless understanding of God's presence I had misused and misunderstood up to this point. But I knew the best way forward was to follow David's lead and let Scripture direct my steps.

Since that day on the Tennessee River, I have been on an expedition to understand the biblical motif of God's presence. In the past years, as I have been blessed to examine and study it in depth, the Lord has graciously directed me to a better grasp of God's presence and helped me see the way to the promises of Psalm 16:11.

This book, in a sense, is part travelogue and part key to David's treasure. My desire is that it can be simultaneously the "You are Here" and "You Want to Be Here" stickers of Psalm 16. Hopefully, then, this work can help us move beyond the stagnant notions of God's presence to the joy and everlasting delight that marks those who truly understand, biblically and experientially, the presence of God. To get us there, I hope to walk with you through the vistas and valleys of God's mighty acts in redemptive history to show where God reveals his presence and, to the best of our ability, help us understand why he does so.

The Way Ahead

Once we step out beyond the initial overgrowth of confusion and obscurities surrounding this theme, we actually find that the biblical path ahead is well worn. Yahweh is the present God, and the biblical Canon is a beautiful and creative story of how he fulfills his promise to be in the midst of his people. Scripture's narrative suggests that the past, present, and future realities of redemption are inextricably tied to God's drawing near to a people.

What I hope to help impress upon us all is that the presence of God is not about mere intuitions and platitudes. It is not a mystical feeling or emotional charge. It is first and foremost a theme of Scripture; and even more, it is a theme on which the story of Scripture hinges.

To demonstrate this, I want to make one major argument in this book that rests on two very simple but very significant biblical truths. The first truth is this: the presence of God is a central *goal* in God's redemptive mission. The second truth follows: the presence of God is the *agent* by which the Lord accomplishes his redemptive mission. God's presence, then, is both *eschatological* (it is the end-of-time aim of the Lord's mission) and *instrumental* (it is ultimately what fulfills the Lord's mission). So to put our argument in its simplest terms, the presence of God is a fundamental objective in our redemption and, simultaneously, the means by which God completes this objective.

That is a lot to take in, so to consider this further, let's think first about the eschatological (the future goal-oriented) emphasis. The restoration of God's presence—or we could say his relational nearness—once lost in the fall is one of the most pivotal acts in the story of redemption. As John shows us, the final hope of history is that "the dwelling place of God is with man" and that God "will dwell with them, and they will be his people, and God himself will be with them as their God" (Rev. 21:3). Seen from a redemptive-historical standpoint, this text is essentially a summary of the eschatological purposes driving God's mission of salvation.

This objective, though, is not only prevalent at the story's end, but also woven throughout Scripture's plotline. From the beginning, the *goal* of God's presence affects the Creator-creature relationship. In Eden, God charges the first couple to expand the garden-sanctuary, the locus of God's presence, both geographically and genealogically (Gen. 1:28–30). The temple of God's presence found in the garden is meant to cover all of creation. From this perspective, we see that the Lord, in his divine wisdom, ties Adam's role to the administration of his presence to the entire world.

However, as the familiar story goes, in his sin Adam breaks this bond in pursuit of arrogant self-idolatry. The much-deserved curses add up—each levied against the couple's role in disseminating God's presence throughout the cosmos. By God's mercy, the story does not end here. God shines the light of his promises into the darkness of Adam's sin. Where Adam has failed, God succeeds, for God pledges to complete his own purposes and spread his own presence to the world.

Outside the garden, the eschatological purposes of God's presence remain front and center in God's redemptive story. From Genesis to Revelation, God's covenant voice calls a people to relationship, a call that reverberates throughout the Scriptures until it crescendos in John's prophetic vision (e.g., Gen. 9:1–15; 12:1–3; 15:6ff.; 17:19; Ex. 19:1ff.; 24:3–8; 2 Sam. 7:12–13; Jer. 31:31–34; Matt. 26:28; Luke 22:20; Heb. 8:6; Rev. 21–22). This covenant picks up where Adam left off, with God's creating a people and place for the enjoyment of his presence. This divine purpose pervades every covenant ratified and culminates in the new covenant arrival of Christ, the new and better Adam, the one who accomplishes what Adam could not. These covenantal promises of God's presence line the story of Scripture like mileposts pointing the way to the New Jerusalem, the city where God will dwell with his people forever.

As we will see, redemption moves forward. It has an objective. God is working to establish a people and a place for his presence. This is our guarantee and our hope. But this story is also our story, and regrettably, it is a story that we often forget.

Remarkably, though, the presence of God is not only a future prom-ise awaiting fulfillment; it is also the way God will fulfill his future promise of being with his people. Just as the waters of the rivers and tributaries flow into and fill the waters of the ocean, the presence of God is what brings humanity to the final source of God's eschatological presence. Our first point—God's goal to bring his people into his pres-ence eternally—therefore, actuates our second point—God is present to redeem. And, of course, the reverse is true as well. They feed one another in a great collaborative act rooted in God's glory. So while the presence of God is an end of redemption, it is simultaneously the means by which the Lord reaches this end. The presence of God, then, is es-chatological *and* instrumental: the Lord becomes present in redemption to direct his people to his eschatological presence.

As you can imagine, this theme floods the pages of Scripture. It ties together all of the major plot points found in redemptive history. As we see at the beginning, God walks with Adam in the cool of the day (Gen. 3:8). He stoops low to care for Adam, speak with him, and simply relate to him. He draws near to judge and discipline him as well. Likewise, God confronts Abraham and his offspring. He reveals himself to Israel. God becomes manifest to deliver his people (marked by his presence) from exile, to display his glory atop Sinai, and direct them to the Land of Promise. He is present to orchestrate Israel's history, bringing the nation to its pinnacle in David's reign and to its depths in the Assyrian and Babylonian exiles. Into the darkness of this dispersion God shines the light of Jesus Christ, the true Immanuel, the ultimate expression of "God with us." And now, in the time between Christ's first and second comings, the presence of God comes in the Holy Spirit to indwell and prepare his people for that treasure David heralds in Psalm 16. Even in such a brief catalog as this, Scripture makes it abundantly clear that the Lord is manifest in history. He is the active agent of salvation. He is the one who brings his people to enjoy his presence in redemption now and forever in glorification.

Who Needs This Trip?

Unfortunately, many have forgotten this storyline, and this has had massive consequences. First it steals glory from God. It should be clear from the outset that the story of Scripture is first and foremost about the author of that story. God speaks a drama of suspense, intrigue, wonder, hope, tension, and anticipation all the while the main character is God himself. This is his autobiography, not ours.

Second, forgetting this storyline has given us delusions of grandeur. We are not the lead actor and certainly not the author. Instead our bit parts in this drama are about God as well. What the theme of God's presence shows us is that this is God's story, and we are simply a part of a grand narrative that surpasses anything we can imagine on our own. In his grace he includes us in his story through his drawing near. Because divine presence is integral to the theological message of Scripture, the presence of God helps us understand our world, our own lives, and our relationship with the God who draws near. Know the author, know the story. Know the story, know your place in the story.

Third, neglecting this part of the story has kept the church from speaking boldly to the world's *ultimate* issues. Contemporary society— whether it knows it or not—needs to hear about God's presence. Though our world scorns and scoffs at any hints of a self-sufficient, holy God who manifests himself to save sinners, this same world constantly asks questions that only this God can answer *and has answered* in his Holy Word.

For example, today's postmodern is restless in his search for "meaningful" community.[8] Even while living, breathing, and participating in a world rampant with religious cynicism, the postmodernist remains fascinated with the prospect of some type of spiritual community (one obviously defined by the individual). As Stanley Grenz observes, people today have become increasingly aware of "the spiritual dimensions of life" as they have "grown dissatisfied with what they consider to be the truncated, materialist focus indicative of the modern world."[9] Out of the ashes of the modernist's isolated individualism arises the postmodernist's ubiquitous pursuit for true, relevant, and spiritual community. It seems to follow that today's Christian should be able to answer the question, What—if anything—can provide the *telos* of the spiritual quest for the postmodernist, and all others for that matter?[10] It is only the story of Scripture, with its emphasis on the presence of God, that can answer these concerns.

Unfortunately, many scholars and pastors have exchanged a biblically responsible model of God's relational fellowship for models that are more culturally palatable.[11] To appease the masses, some theologians attempt to pull the Lord down and make him look like the rest of the world. They exploit the doctrine of God's immanence (nearness),[12] por-

---

[8] It should be noted that I am not advocating postmodernism as the best approach to apologetics or evangelism. All I intend to maintain is that the desire for relationship with peers and, more specifically, with the divine is God-given, and it is also God-answered. My appeal is that a biblically based evaluation of the presence of God should be a more definitive theme within evangelicalism in order to contend with an inappropriate theological embrace of this philosophical climate and address the shortcomings of the church in dealing with the culture at large.

[9] Grenz argues that at the center of modernism coming out of the Enlightenment was the idea that "what it means to be human is reason and rationality." Furthermore, this rationality was tied to "the ability to disengage from one's own natural environment and social context so as to be able to objectify the world . . . forming the Modernist ideal: individual autonomy, understood as the ability to choose one's own purposes from within oneself apart from the controlling influence of natural and social forces." As a result, the world became an assortment of independent selves. In response, postmodernism is the rejection of this modernistic position of autonomy and independence and replaces it with the desire for community. Stanley J. Grenz, "Belonging to God: The Quest for Communal Spirituality in the Postmodern World," *Asbury Theological Journal* 54 (1999): 43.

[10] Ibid., 45.

[11] The desire for community and relationship has caused the recent influx of spiritual pursuits among postmodernists. Evangelicals as a whole, however, have been caught off guard. That is why the reality of the presence of God is important. If the world is captured by the truth of God's being with and for his people as it is presented biblically, then the longings of postmodern thinkers can be answered appropriately.

[12] In order to answer the desires of the world, the advocates of process theism replace the God of Scripture, who is separate but involved in creation, with one who is progressing with, learning through, and obtaining from the world. It is also important to see that the influence of process thought not only is felt outside orthodox Christianity but affects evangelicalism as well. For examples of process text, see, e.g., Charles Hartshorne and W. L. Reese, *Philosophers Speak of God* (Chicago: University of Chicago Press, 1953); John B. Cobb and David Ray Griffin, *Process Theology: An Introductory Exposition* (Philadelphia: Westminster, 1976); Alfred N. Whitehead, *Process and Reality* (New York: Macmillan, 1929); Charles Hartshorne, *The Divine Relativity* (New Haven, CT: Yale University Press, 1948). For examples of modern theological approaches utilizing process theology, see, e.g., Michael Vertin, "Is God in Process?," in *Religion and Culture: Essays in Honor of Bernard Lonergan*, ed. Timothy Fallon and Philip Riley (Albany: State University of New York Press, 1987), 45–62; William Dean, "Deconstruction and Process Theology," *Journal of Religion* 64 (1984): 1–19; John B. Cobb Jr., "Two Types of Postmodernism: Deconstruction and Process," *Theology Today* 47 (1990): 149–58; Nancy R. Howell, "Feminism and Process Thought," *Process Studies* 22 (1993):

traying him as not only intimately related to the world but partially—and for some even fully—reliant on the world.[13]

At the other end of the spectrum, there are those who push God beyond the reaches of knowledge, revelation, and relationship. These theologians contend that God, in his transcendence (separation), is too distant and distinct from creation to be known in any true or significant way.[14] And so it goes in our world's understanding of God and our relationship to him. We continue to sacrifice good theology for cultural vacillations when what we need is a biblically grounded theology to stabilize us and our culture, and to conform us to the image of God.

This is where the biblical drama of God's presence helps. On the face of it, biblical Christianity seemingly provides a vibrant and thoughtful countercultural answer to these large existential questions.[15] It tells the true story of the God who covenants with his people and overcomes sin for the purposes of his glory and their relational closeness to him. In a society longing for relational and spiritual closeness, a sound and scripturally mature analysis of the presence of God can help answer this world's deep-seated spiritual desires.[16]

69–106. For an explanation of the influence of process theology on contemporary evangelicalism, see Randall Basinger, "Evangelicals and Process Theism: Seeking a Middle Ground," *Christian Scholar's Review* 15 (December 1986): 157–67. Cf. Greg Boyd, *Trinity and Process: A Critical Evaluation and Reconstruction of Hartshorne's Di-Polar Theism Towards a Trinitarian Metaphysics* (New York: Peter Lang, 1992); R. A. McGrath and A. Galloway, *The Science of Theology*, vol. 1 (Grand Rapids: Eerdmans, 1996); Hans Frei, *Types of Christian Theology* (New Haven, CT: Yale University Press, 1992); Collin Gunton, "A Rose by Any Other Name? From Christian Doctrine to Systematic Theology," *International Journal of Systematic Theology* 1 (1999): 4–23.

[13] Such a view is open theism, in which God's foreknowledge and immutability have been questioned and, in many cases, rejected or redefined. According to the open view, God knows all things that can be possibly known, which thereby prohibits his knowledge of his free creatures' actions and decisions. Thus, the Lord does not have an exhaustive understanding of the future and is reliant upon and, in particular, related to his creation. See, e.g., Gregory A. Boyd, *God of the Possible: A Biblical Introduction to the Open View of God* (Grand Rapids: Baker, 2000); John B. Cobb Jr. and Clark H. Pinnock, *Searching for an Adequate God: A Dialogue between Process and Free Will Theists* (Grand Rapids: Eerdmans, 2000); Clark Pinnock et al., *The Openness of God: A Biblical Challenge to the Traditional Understanding of God* (Downers Grove, IL: InterVarsity, 1994); John Sanders, *The God Who Risks: A Theology of Providence* (Downers Grove, IL: InterVarsity, 1998).

[14] See, e.g., Rudolf Otto, *Das Heilige*, trans. J. Harvey (New York: Oxford University Press, 1950); John Whitaker, "Literal and Figurative Language of God," *Religious Studies* 17 (1981): 39–54. For a helpful summary and critique of the ineffability of God, see Harold Netland, *Dissonant Voices: Religious Pluralism and the Question of Truth* (Grand Rapids: Eerdmans, 1991), 133–41.

[15] Christianity can speak to the postmodernist without succumbing to the postmodernist's disdain for metanarrative (the big-picture story that attempts to explain everything). After all, Christianity is the greatest and one true metanarrative.

[16] I would argue that responding to the pertinent issues in contemporary culture is one of the major purposes of systematic theology. As Frame contends, we should "define theology as the application of the Word of God to all areas of life." John M. Frame, *The Doctrine of the Knowledge of God* (Phillipsburg, NJ: P&R, 1987), 81. Wayne Grudem also asserts, "Systematic theology focuses on summarizing each doctrine as it should be understood by present-day Christians"; systematic theology as "'what the whole Bible teaches us today' implies that application to life is a necessary part of the proper pursuit of systematic theology. Thus a doctrine under consideration is seen in terms of its practical value for living the Christian life." Wayne A. Grudem, *Systematic Theology: An Introduction to Biblical Doctrine* (Grand Rapids: Zondervan, 1994), 23. Furthermore, as John Franke concludes, "The unending

I am convinced that it is only through God's drawing near—on his own terms and for his own glory—that the demands of this lonely world can be met in full. To appropriately answer the world's ultimate concerns, we need not rewrite the script of Scripture to accommodate the philosophical assumptions, desires, and commitments of sinners. Instead, we need a biblically formed theology emphasizing the Lord's relational nearness as it is progressively revealed in the Christian plotline.[17] As we do this, we mitigate many of the aforementioned concerns, both practical and theological. A clearer grasp of the presence of God sheds light on the mystical and cultural misconceptions often affiliated with this critical theme, while also underscoring its significance for our theology and, subsequently, our lives.

Fourth, knowing the presence of God as it is expressed across the pages of the biblical script transforms the way we understand and live our Christian lives. The presence of God is more than theoretical; it lives. It enriches, expands, and even emends our faith at times.

This is important for all of us because to know salvation is to know God's presence. God's presence practically influences the way we live out our salvation, assemble with fellow believers, and hope in God's future promises. In our salvation we need to see that our atonement (the work of Christ on the cross that clears the rebel to enter into relationship with the holy God) *demands* the presence of God. Christ *came into this world*, into human history, in order to give his life as a ransom for many (Matt. 20:28; Mark 10:45). The substitutionary death of God's Son is inextricably tied to the divine being present with *and for* man. For salvation to be efficacious, God must be with us; God must be one of us. Immanuel came to dwell among his people and substitute

---

task of theology is to find ways of expressing and communicating the biblical story in terms that make use of the intellectual and conceptual tools of a particular culture without being controlled by them." John R. Franke, *The Character of Theology: A Postconservative Evangelical Approach* (Grand Rapids: Baker, 2005), 119.

[17] Unfortunately, the significant role God's presence plays in and for redemptive history has historically been largely overlooked or been relegated to some ethereal form of "mysticism" or numinous "experience." For examples of works that do highlight the importance of the biblical theological motif of God's presence, see John M. Frame, *The Doctrine of God* (Phillipsburg, NJ: P&R, 2002); Samuel Terrien, *The Elusive Presence: Toward a New Biblical Theology* (New York: Harper and Row, 1978); J. Lanier Burns, *The Nearness of God: His Presence with His People* (Phillipsburg, NJ: P&R, 2009). For examples of the emphasis on the mystical, see Brother Lawrence, *The Practice of the Presence of God*, trans. John J. Delaney (New York: Doubleday, 1977); Richard Woods, *Christian Spirituality: God's Presence through the Ages* (Chicago: Thomas More, 1989). Woods argues that the divine presence is spirituality, and there is, therefore, "in the depths of all experience, a sense of God as the compassionate origin, unfailing guide, and infinite destiny of the whole human tribe." Woods, *Christian Spirituality*, 1. For a historical survey of this experiential emphasis, see also Bernard McGinn, *The Presence of God: A History of Western Christian Mysticism*, 3 vols. (New York: Crossroad, 1991–1998).

himself for the lost. In his atoning work on the cross, Christ reconciled us to God by being present with man. He became man in this world to reopen access to the Lord so that those exiled from Eden may draw near to God once again (Heb. 4:16; 7:19, 25; 10:1, 19, 22; 11:6). Christ's presence in this world is a strong indicator that the vicarious nature of Jesus's work—that which leads to his becoming manifest in human history—is at the heart of the atonement and the heart of our salvation.

The presence of God also has implications for the way we understand the community of believers. The New Testament shows us that the church is the temple of God (1 Cor. 3:16–17; 2 Cor. 6:14–7:1; Eph. 2:13–22). The church, according to Paul, is where God dwells. This is a formative work of the Holy Spirit.[18] The community of Christ, therefore, is—in this time of waiting for Christ's return—the institution the Lord creates and uses to represent and perpetuate his divine presence in a lost and sinful world. In a lesser way, the church plays a role in bringing about God's redemptive mission. It tells others about God's presence to save and helps prepare believers to enter into God's presence once and for all in the new heaven and new earth.

This should change our understanding of the church's role in the world and in our lives. Think about what would happen if the church understood herself to be the reflection of God's presence to a lost world. How would this affect the way the body of Christ does ministry and views the other working parts of that body?

Finally, neglecting the presence of God impairs our thinking about eschatology. Some have been caught up in the seemingly endless debates swirling around the interpretation of Daniel, Revelation, and other end-time prophetic passages. And though many of these discussions are important and helpful (and some not so helpful), the eschatological nature of God's purposes has often been lost in the details of our apocalyptic flow charts and diagrams. The discussion of the presence of God helps us see that eschatology is not only the last chapter

---

[18] Please note that I do not intend to state that the Holy Spirit dwells at a physical address or in a certain building. Often the church is assumed merely to be a place where people gather on Sundays. Though this can be an aspect of the church, the reality of this institution should not be limited to this type of expression. Instead, the notion of the church is connected to what these metaphors reveal about it, namely, that it is a relational community. Thus, I agree with Everett Ferguson, who states, "The New Testament puts no emphasis on the place of worship—house, synagogue, or temple—because wherever the community is gathered that is the place of worship." Everett Ferguson, *Church of Christ: A Biblical Ecclesiology for Today* (Grand Rapids: Eerdmans, 1996), 219.

in our systematic theology textbooks or even the last few chapters of our Bibles. Instead, eschatology pervades the whole message of Scripture. Like our own circulatory system, eschatology helps the promises, plans, and purposes of God flow throughout the body of Scripture. What biblical theology helps us see is that God has Revelation 21–22 in his divine mind before breathing out Genesis 1:1, and he paints Genesis 1:1 with the same palette he uses in Revelation 21–22. The beginning is rooted in the end, and vice versa. And this helps our faith. The eschatological vein pervading Scripture reinforces our assurance in things hoped for and our conviction of things unseen (Heb. 11:1). The Lord will accomplish his purposes no matter how hard spiritual and fleshly powers work against him. All of the promises and purposes of God that fall between these bookends of redemptive history express his perfect will. The end is his purpose and it will be accomplished. For God, there is no "Plan B." There are no "audibles." God's story works out the end from the beginning, and we are the beneficiaries of this providential power, control, and authority.[19]

Clearing the Way

Seeing the redemptive-historical story of this magnitude is no easy undertaking, though it is a necessary one. Covering a biblical theme in a comprehensive manner while seeing its implications for our lives is a big project, hence our need for parameters. Accordingly, I want to acknowledge from the outset that it is not feasible to evaluate every text of Scripture that touches on the concept of divine presence (there are so many!). The principal purpose of this project is to bring glory to God by seeing the presence of God within a redemptive-historical perspective. As a consequence, I will address all theological issues within this context, thereby limiting the extent of Scripture and doctrinal reflection to how it informs the biblical emphasis on the presence of God as means and ends of God's redemptive activity.

Before we set out, let me also speak to the theological assumptions

---

[19] As J. V. Fesko summarizes: "Eschatology has an irrefragable connection to the beginning, or protology. This connection becomes even clearer when one considers that the categories of the beginning are embedded in eschatology, the creation of the heavens and earth become the *new* heavens and earth (Isa. 65:17; 66:22) and the garden of Eden reappears in the book of Revelation (2:7; cf. Isa. 51:3; Zech. 1:17)." J. V. Fesko, *Last Things First: Unlocking Genesis 1–3 with the Christ of Eschatology* (Fearn, Ross-shire, UK: Mentor, 2007), 34–35.

undergirding this project. There is no neutral approach to theology; there never was and there never will be. Understanding this helps us be honest, and it also helps us with what is essential. Instead of demanding neutrality, we need to be aware of our presuppositions and constantly evaluate them in light of the biblical text. To be sure, this project is not void of theological assumptions; and again, to try and defend each one is itself beyond the scope of this particular work. Yet, by no means are these presuppositions unjustifiable. These broader theological assumptions include my commitment to the authoritative, inspired, inerrant, and infallible Scripture as divine revelation;[20] human *and* divine authorship of the biblical Canon;[21] the possibility of "whole Bible" theology;[22] the unity and continuity of Scripture within the Bible's textual diversity;[23] Nicene Trinitarianism and Chalcedonian christology;[24] the epistemic ability to truly know God, in a finite sense, through his revelation;[25] and Christ's penal-substitutionary atonement as the Christian's point of access to reconciliation and God's eternal relational presence.[26]

Setting Out

With this in mind, the following chapters will seek to demonstrate that the presence of God is essential to understanding Scripture's theological message and our lives as Christians. To prepare the way for our discussion, I will use chapter 2 to set the theological context for our

---

[20] See, e.g., James M. Boice, ed., *The Foundations of Biblical Authority* (Grand Rapids: Zondervan, 1983); D. A. Carson and John D. Woodbridge, eds., *Hermeneutics, Authority, and Canon* (Grand Rapids: Zondervan, 1986); Paul Feinberg, "Bible, Inerrancy and Infallibility of," in *Evangelical Dictionary of Theology*, ed. Walter Elwell (Grand Rapids: Baker, 1999), 141–45. Norman Geisler, ed., *Inerrancy* (Grand Rapids: Zondervan, 1980); John D. Woodbridge, *Biblical Authority: A Critique of the Rogers/McKim Proposal* (Grand Rapids: Zondervan, 1982).

[21] See, e.g., D. A. Carson and John D. Woodbridge, eds., *Scripture and Truth* (Grand Rapids: Baker, 1992); E. J. Schnabel, "Scripture," in *New Dictionary of Biblical Theology*, ed. T. Desmond Alexander et al. (Downers Grove, IL: InterVarsity, 2000), 34–43.

[22] See chap. 2 for further description of "whole-Bible" theology.

[23] See, e.g., Craig L. Blomberg, "The Unity and Diversity of Scripture," in Alexander et al., *New Dictionary of Biblical Theology*, 64–72; D. A. Carson, "Unity and Diversity in the New Testament: The Possibility of Systematic Theology," in Carson and Woodbridge, *Scripture and Truth*, 65–95.

[24] See, e.g., Herman Bavinck, *Reformed Dogmatics*, vol. 2, *God and Creation*, ed. John Bolt, trans. John Vriend (Grand Rapids: Baker, 2006), 256–334; Robert Letham, *The Holy Trinity in Scripture, History, Theology, and Worship* (Phillipsburg, NJ: P&R, 2004).

[25] See, e.g., John S. Feinberg, *No One Like Him: The Doctrine of God* (Wheaton, IL: Crossway, 2001), 37–80; Frame, *Doctrine of God*, 199–207; Frame, *Doctrine of the Knowledge of God*; Ronald H. Nash, *The Word of God and the Mind of Man* (Grand Rapids: Zondervan, 1982).

[26] See, e.g., Steve Jeffrey, Michael Ovey, and Andrew Sachs, eds., *Pierced for Our Transgressions: Recovering the Glory of Penal Substitution* (Wheaton, IL: Crossway, 2007); Thomas Schreiner, "Penal Substitution View," in *The Nature of the Atonement: Four Views*, ed. James Beilby and Paul Eddy (Downers Grove, IL: InterVarsity, 2006), 67–98.

discussion while also defining a relational understanding of God and his presence. Chapter 3 will begin the first of two major sections that form the core of this book. It is here that I will work out my thesis through a biblical-theological assessment. With this in mind, I will use part 1 (chaps. 3–5) to show how the presence of the Lord is a central eschatological purpose in the Lord's redemptive mission. It will follow then that parts 2 and 3 (chaps. 6–10) will address the presence of God as the means of the divine mission. Here, we will trace the importance and impact of the Lord's redemptive presence through both the Old and New Testaments, revealing that God accomplishes his promises, first and foremost, by becoming present. The last chapter will show how such an understanding of the presence of God really changes the way we understand and live the Christian life. Here we will see just how important this theme is not only to Scripture's story but also to our own. In the concluding part we will look specifically at how God's presence informs the way we think about our redemption, the covenant community of the church, and God's eschatological promises. I will try to show just how the presence of God transforms the way we live, move, and have our being (Acts 17:28).

We do all this to provide a biblically based conception of the presence of God—demonstrating it to be both a means and a goal of God's redemptive activity—in order to show its central place within the storyline of Scripture and in our lives as those redeemed by the God who draws near.

So with our destination set and our itinerary ready, let us begin our journey. Let us discover what God's presence means. Let us see the story of Scripture and our Christian life in light of the presence of God. May we follow that story to its promises of fullness of joy and pleasures forevermore—and may we be wise enough not only to know that story, but to enter into it as well.

2

Of Storyboards and Location Scouts

A Biblical and Theological Foundation
for the Presence of God

We know that good stories do not begin at the theater or on the book-shelves. Instead they begin with the difficult (often tedious) yet necessary jobs of research, location scouting, and storyboard preparation. Likewise, a proper grasp of the biblical drama demands comparable legwork—though theological in nature and never tedious! This is what we will set out to do in this chapter. We want to do that ground-level work that will provide the theological parameters *and* theological clarity necessary to help us understand who God is and what it means for him to be present.

Let me be clear: establishing such foundations is difficult work and work that, given our focus, will be limited in scope.[1] Still, time spent in theological cultivation is necessary. It helps us worship God on his

---

[1] Understanding God completely is an unattainable goal. As Bavinck rightfully concludes: "Mystery is the lifeblood of dogmatics. . . . The knowledge that God has revealed of himself in nature and Scripture far surpasses human imagination and understanding. . . . For it does not deal with finite creatures, but from beginning to end looks past all creatures and focuses on the eternal and infinite One himself. From the very start of its labors, it faces the incomprehensible One." Still, this should not deter us from pursuing God in any way. The gift of revelation, through which the Lord has disclosed himself to creation using speech and words that can be studied and parsed, shows us that God has made a knowledge of him available, which, when pursued, often results in worship and his being glorified. Again, Bavinck sums this up well: "While Holy Scripture affirms [the qualitative difference between God and man] in the strongest terms, it nevertheless sets forth a doctrine of God that fully upholds his knowability." Herman Bavinck, *Reformed Dogmatics*, vol. 2, *God and Creation*, ed. John Bolt, trans. John Vriend (Grand Rapids: Baker, 2004), 30.

terms and understand ourselves in light of redemption. This particular type of theological spadework will begin with the doctrine of God, especially his relationship with creation. The thought of an infinite God stooping low to relate to and redeem a broken people rightfully leaves our minds reeling—or at least it should. When we meditate on the mysteries of God's relational pursuit of his creation, we are bombarded with theological questions that will ultimately determine our concept of God, the gospel, and ourselves. Why does the God of Christianity draw near to sinners in the first place? What does it mean for the transcendent God to engage, interact with, and even enter this fallen world and its people? My hope is to use this chapter to address these important questions by showing that God's free decision to be with his people finds its source in his transcendence, and most fundamentally in his self-sufficiency. That which makes the Lord distinct from creation is what leads him to draw near to creation.

But our questions do not end here. Trying to understand the presence of God confronts us with the most fundamental question: what *is* the presence of God? In fact, our story will only go as far as our definition of the presence of God will allow it to go. We need a biblical definition of God's presence to ground our understanding not in the thin air of today's mystical-spiritual conceptions but in the bedrock of Scripture's story. As a result, we will devote the second part of this chapter to the advancement of such a biblical definition. I will attempt to excavate our definition directly from Scripture's own emphases, specifically that the Lord's presence is redemptive and eschatological. The presence of God is the reward of redemptive history and the way God secures this reward for us. The answer to the question will play out organically in our analysis of the story of Scripture in the chapters ahead, but offering this definition from the outset will help organize our thinking and pave the way for a proper discussion of God's presence that is to come.

Who Is This God Who Becomes Present?

Let us begin with the doctrine of God: specifically, how we can account for his relational nature. When we pull back to see the big picture, we quickly realize that the personal nature of God grounds our salvation

and makes the gospel possible. It is only because of his relational nature that we—his reliant and finite creations—have life, delight, hope,
grace, mercy, and love available to us.[2] It is only because he has *chosen*
to be present that we are afforded the opportunity to experience the
glories of his presence.

Transcendence and Immanence

To understand the relational nature of God in a biblically faithful manner demands that we first come to grips with what theologians call
God's divine transcendence (the attribute that describes God as the one
who is distinct and separate from his creation) and God's immanence
(the attribute that describes him as the one who freely draws near to
and is involved in his creation).[3] In maintaining the balance between

---

[2] It is safe to say that most religions outside of the Judeo-Christian worldview, if not all, do not maintain that their divinity, "power," or god is simultaneously personal and absolute. In contrast, one characteristic is usually overemphasized to the denial or neglect of the other. For example, D. A. Carson catalogs the difference between the Christian claim and other religions when he writes: "The transcendent and the personal are separated in most of the world's religions. In animism and polytheism there are many personal spirits or gods, but none is absolute. Sometimes these religions supplement their gods as it were by appealing to fate—an impersonal absolute. Pan-theistic religions adopt an absolute, but it is not personal. World religions are sometimes so internally diverse that they fit into more than one of these categories. At one level Hinduism is clearly polytheistic, but much of Hindu outlook is finally pantheistic. Buddhism in its various branches is particularly difficult to label, but at no point does it adopt a vision of God as both absolute and personal. Contemporary science, with a frequent balance toward philosophical materialism, constantly tilts toward an impersonal absolute. In other words, persons are finally explained on an impersonal basis—bouncing molecules, statistically organized motion, chemical reactions in one's brain, and so forth." D. A. Carson, *The Gagging of God: Christianity Confronts Pluralism* (Grand Rapids: Zondervan, 1996), 223–24. To be fair though, in recent Christian theology, Christianity's distinct approach, in several cases, has been overshadowed by theological trends that allow a lack of balance and accuracy to creep into its own doctrine. This has resulted in theological error and, in some cases, new religious perspectives or even systems (e.g., process theology and open theism). Again, Carson goes on to argue that many of modern-day theological problems arise out of those within Christian circles who have divided God's absolute and personal nature. He contends that contemporary religious thought leaves us with "a God not clearly personal, and if absolute, sufficiently remote to be of little threat and of little use." He goes on to show the work of process theo-logians and their attempt to "emphasize God's personhood while dismissing his absoluteness. Process theology, in its plethora of forms, argues that God may be personal, but is certainly mutable and changing, himself (or itself) in process" (ibid., 224–25). This same critique applies to open theism, a theological movement that under-scores God's relationality to the point that it undermines his control. Needless to say, there is much confusion surrounding the nature of God's relationality and much to be sifted through before a biblical conceptualization of divine presence can be proposed.

[3] Millard Erickson reveals the consequent errors that arise when the proper tension between these two qualities of God is lost: "Where either is overemphasized at the expense of the other, the orthodox theistic conception is lost. Where immanence is overemphasized, we lose the conception of a personal God. Where transcendence is overem-phasized, we lose the conception of an active God." Millard J. Erickson, *Christian Theology*, 2nd ed. (Grand Rapids: Baker, 2000), 328–29. By this he means that when the balance is gone, divine immanence can be assimilated into a form of pantheism, and the divine becomes less personal and more a part of creation. With transcendence, the issue of separation arises. Excessive emphasis on God's transcendence ultimately conforms Christian theism into some degree of deism. Grenz and Olson, in their book on contemporary theology, describe our current theological crisis as stemming from "instability introduced when transcendence and immanence are not properly balanced." They continue, "As if in the ongoing course of theological history the twin truths of the divine transcendence and divine immanence are seeking their own proper equilibrium, twentieth-century theology illustrates how a lopsided emphasis on one or the other eventually engenders an opposing movement that attempts to redress the imbalance and actually moves too far in the opposing direction." Stanley J. Grenz and Roger E. Olsen, *Twentieth-Century Theology: God and the World in a Transitional Age* (Downers Grove, IL: InterVarsity, 1992), 12.

these dual realities, we see one of the emphases that makes Christian theology explicitly Christian, especially within the doctrine of God.[4]

I am sure that for some of us, the entry point to our understanding of the Lord is his transcendence. God is "other than." He is distinct from his creation in nature, action, and being. He is greater than all that is not God. We surmise that, at a fundamental level, God's transcendence is a corollary of other attributes, such as his majesty, holiness, and infinitude.

This transcendence has huge implications for God's relationship with his creation, for it is his transcendence that gives rise to his self-sufficiency and self-existence. God is self-sufficient in that he is reliant upon nothing outside of himself, out of his own being, and is in no way dependent on what he has made. Similarly, he is eternally self-existing, meaning that he draws his existence solely from himself; or, to put it another way, God *is* because God is God. In describing the transcendent God who is wholly other, Scripture articulates a Lord who is distinct from creation, existing solely in himself eternally, absolute in nature, without nonintrinsic limitations, and fully infinite.

Interestingly, Scripture most often depicts God's transcendence in spatial terms.[5] The biblical authors time and time again put physical, albeit metaphorical, distance between God and his creation. As the psalmists describe, God is the "most high" (Ps. 97:9), the God "above the heavens" (Ps. 8:1), and the one "over all the earth" (Ps. 57:5). This distance, though, is much more than physical or spatial; it is first and

---

[4] Historically speaking, the failure to balance these characteristics has resulted in many, if not most, of the doctrinal predicaments over the past century and beyond. In fact, Grenz and Olson use the distinction of transcendence and immanence to organize and structure their whole study of twentieth-century theology. They argue that the back-and-forth shifts in emphasis between these two aspects of God's nature are responsible for the drastic theological changes defining modern theology. The goal of our discussion is to maintain a proper theological symmetry between the Lord's transcendence and his immanence. Thus Bruce Ware holds that God is "both *transcendent*, as existing in the fullness of his infinitely glorious tri-Person unity and apart from the finite spatio-temporal created reality he freely brings into existence, but also as one who chooses to relate *immanently*, as he freely enters into the realm of the creaturely existence that he designed and made." Bruce A. Ware, *God's Greater Glory: The Exalted God of Scripture and the Christian Faith* (Wheaton, IL: Crossway, 2004), 35, emphasis original.

[5] I agree with John Frame, who argues that the biblical references to divine transcendence in spatial terms are not tied exclusively to heaven but instead point to a much larger reality. Frame asserts: "It is not biblical, therefore, to interpret God's transcendence to mean merely that he is located somewhere far away, in heaven. That may be part of the thrust of the terms 'Most High,' 'exalted,' and 'lifted up,' but there must be more to it. . . . We should, I think, see these expressions primarily as describing God's royal dignity. He is 'exalted,' not mainly as someone living far beyond the earth but as one who sits on a throne. The expressions of transcendence refer to God's rule, his kingship, his lordship." Frame's critique of many theological positions on divine transcendence sees this characteristic of God in light of the genre and purposes of Scripture itself. The imagery of Scripture is duly noted, and the focus of the spatial requirements is brought under the intent of the author. John M. Frame, *The Doctrine of God* (Phillipsburg, NJ: P&R, 2002), 105.

foremost moral. It is true that God is transcendent in his essence, but Scripture places its primary emphasis on his holiness. This is why biblical authors periodically describe God as a far off, elusive, and hidden.

We see this especially when sin enters the picture. The prophet Isaiah categorizes God's righteous response to mankind's sin as divine-human separation when he announces,

> Because of the iniquity of his unjust gain I was angry,
> I struck him; I hid my face and was angry. (Isa. 57:17)[6]

Probably the most famous example of this moral focus of God's transcendence is found in Eden. What is the culminating consequence of Adam's sin? God removes the first man from the garden-sanctuary of his presence, a theme we will return to in the next few chapters (cf. Gen. 4:14).[7]

The God who is gloriously separate from and over all things is the same God who has freely chosen in his grace to be *with* humanity. He is not constrained by his own creation, loneliness, or need to draw near to the world; rather, the divine-human relationship germinates out of the sheer beauty of his grace and the relational nature of the Trinity. This is the delicate and necessary balance struck in Scripture: God is transcendently self-sufficient and self-satisfied while simultaneously free to be relationally immanent. As one scholar observes:

> The OT never conceives of God's transcendence in opposition to his immanence, as if that which makes God wholly other is different from that which allows him to be a personal God who lovingly acts

---

[6] God's elusiveness can also describe his providential ways. We see this when the prophet declares, "Truly, you are a God who hides himself, / O God of Israel, the Savior" (Isa. 45:15). The context of this verse is the Gentiles' entering Jerusalem with great goods and treasures. God has seemingly reversed the fortunes of Israel by bringing beauty out of the conquering work of King Cyrus. God works in ways that finite man cannot foresee or understand. So although we know him, we do not know him in full. For further discussion, see J. Alec Motyer, *The Prophecy of Isaiah: An Introduction and Commentary* (Downers Grove, IL: InterVarsity, 1993), 364.

[7] Cain acknowledges his guilt when he announces: "Behold, you have driven me today away from the ground, and from your face I shall be hidden. I shall be a fugitive and a wanderer on the earth, and whoever finds me will kill me" (Gen. 4:14). What is illuminating in this passage is that Cain understands the weight of his actions and what it means to sin before a holy and transcendent God; yet, even in these bloody circumstances, Yahweh is graciously immanent, as is evidenced in his provision of the city of refuge, vengeance upon the people who stand against his purposes and his people, and the reestablishment of a dynastic line in Seth. Other examples of this tension include God's decision to be present in the temple but still be hidden behind the veil, the separation established in Adam's first sin, the allowance of judgment during the time of the judges and the prophets, and his concealment during the whole exilic period. The most important biblical example, though, is the person of Christ, who is himself both fully God yet veiled in human flesh. In Christ, the balance of transcendence and immanence is perfectly expressed (Phil. 2:5–11).

in time and history. For the Bible, transcendence and immanence do not describe two divine modes of being or two sets of distinguished qualities.[8]

The Lord is one who is simultaneously transcendent and immanent, separate and yet personal.[9] As Scripture helps us see, "He is God in the heavens above and on the earth beneath" (Josh. 2:11). But we must be reminded that his immanence stems from his transcendence, rather than vice versa. As Colin Gunton puts it:

> Transcendence cannot be won at the expense of God's immanence precisely because it is the ground of immanence. . . . God is transcendent in that he is able to become immanent. . . . The happening of God in time is not a negation of what God really is. It is his affirmation. . . . If God were not so supremely transcendent of reality that is other than he, he would not be the God who does the things that he does.[10]

It is his nature that provokes God's relational manifestation, not some internal or external deficiency. He is wholly other and he entered history and acted among his people.[11] Almost every word of Scripture (including the very fact that we have the words of God in written form), exhibits God's desire to reveal himself and relate personally to his creation in redemption and judgment.[12]

Numerous passages substantiate the importance of holding the dual realities of divine transcendence and immanence in concert.[13] Take Psalm 113 for example. Here the psalmist writes:

---

[8] Thomas G. Weinandy, *Does God Suffer?* (Notre Dame, IN: University of Notre Dame Press, 2000), 56.

[9] God's personal and relational character extends from the intra-Trinitarian relationship that characterizes the immanent Trinity, a topic that will be developed later in this chapter.

[10] Colin E. Gunton, *The Promise of Trinitarian Theology* (Edinburgh: T&T Clark, 1991), 56.

[11] As the Dutch theologian Herman Bavinck states, "Not only does Scripture ascribe to God . . . an array of human organs and attributes; but also it even says that he walked in the Garden (Gen. 3.8), came down to see Babel's construction of a tower (Gen. 11:5, 7), appeared to Jacob at Bethel (Gen. 28:10ff.), gave his law on Mount Sinai (Ex. 19ff.), dwelt between the cherubim on Zion in Jerusalem (1 Sam. 4:4; 1 Kings 8:7, 10–11). Scripture also therefore calls him the God of Abraham, Isaac, and Jacob, the king of Zion, the God of the Hebrews, the God of Israel." Bavinck, *Reformed Dogmatics*, 2:30.

[12] Cf. James M. Hamilton Jr., "The Glory of God in Salvation through Judgment: The Centre of Biblical Theology?," *TynBul* 57 (2006): 57–84.

[13] In a broader sense, each of these verses should be understood to be what Ware terms a "spectrum text." By this we mean that these passages proclaim two truths about the nature of God that are often assumed to be contradictory in some way. These texts, however, reveal them not to be in conflict but rather to be harmonious realities in the doctrine of God. For our purposes here we find that these texts show that God's transcendence and immanence are to be held in equilibrium. For more on "spectrum texts" and their theological impact, see Bruce A. Ware, *God's Lesser Glory: The Diminished God of Open Theism* (Wheaton, IL: Crossway, 2000), 150, 191–216.

> The Lord is high above all the nations,
>   and his glory is above the heavens!
> Who is like the Lord our God,
>   who is seated on high,
> who looks far down
>   on the heavens and the earth?
> He raises the poor from the dust
>   and lifts the needy from the ash heap,
> to make them sit with princes,
>   with the princes of his people.
> He gives the barren woman a home,
>   making her the joyous mother of children.
> Praise the Lord! (Ps. 113:4–9)

Here the complementary truths of the Lord's transcendent otherness and immanent closeness bring joy to the psalmist. The Lord is "high above," and yet he is also the one who stoops low and "raises the poor from the dust."

Similarly, the prophet Isaiah captures both of these divine realities:

> Thus says the One who is high and lifted up,
>   who inhabits eternity, whose name is Holy:
> "I dwell in the high and holy place,
>   and also with him who is of a contrite and lowly spirit,
> to revive the spirit of the lowly,
>   and to revive the heart of the contrite." (Isa. 57:15)

According to the prophet, where should Israel find its comfort? It is found in the God who "is high and lifted up," "inhabits eternity," and "dwell[s] in the high and holy place," the One who comes to restore the broken, needy, and repentant.[14] For Isaiah, the Lord's transcendence is the *source* of healing for broken humanity because only the Holy One who is greater than this world can placate the anxieties and despair of this fallen world.

---

[14] Notice how both verses (Ps. 113:4–9 and Isa. 57:15) have used the transcendence of God to heal and comfort the weak and oppressed. This shows that in order for the immanence of God to mean anything and/or affect our lives it must have his transcendence as its origin. If not, then the Lord is not able to affect our standing in the world. But if he is over all things, then he is over everything including our hardships and all our circumstances and worthy of faith, trust, love, and hope.

The New Testament holds the same tension. One clear example is Acts 17, where Paul delivers his theological treatise before the pagan Greeks.[15] God's transcendental self-sufficiency is on full display in Paul's argument: "The God who made the world and everything in it, being Lord of heaven and earth, does not live in temples made by man, nor is he served by human hands, as though he needed anything, since he himself gives to all mankind life and breath and everything" (17:24–25). At times overlooked is the emphasis on immanence that follows. Paul does not stop with God's self-existence but links it to God's relational pursuit of his creation. Paul challenges the misconceptions of an aloof, selfish, and reliant deity within the Greco-Roman world by portraying the God of Scripture to be a holy and separate God who graciously draws near to his people.[16] He advises his listeners to "seek God" in the hope that they might "feel their way toward him and find him" (Acts 17:27a). The Lord is near and can be found. Paul deepens the relational closeness of God, testifying that God

is actually not far from each one of us, for

"In him we live and move and have our being";

as even some of [the Greek] poets have said,

"For we are indeed his offspring." (Acts 17:27b–28)

So Paul's God is transcendently immanent. The Lord is beyond creation and distinct from it, while he has also chosen, on his own volition, to be intimately involved in creation and active in human history.[17]

---

[15] See also Ephesians 4:6, where Paul describes the Lord as "one God and Father of all, who is over all and through all and in all." This verse and its appeal to the spatial location of God being both "over" as well as "through" and "in" is another example of Paul's tying together the transcendent and immanent divine qualities. See also Wayne A. Grudem, *Systematic Theology: Introduction to Biblical Doctrine* (Grand Rapids: Zondervan, 1994), 267.

[16] This is theologically significant because Paul is speaking to a polytheistic culture that divided divine power throughout a panoply of gods. It is to this ignorance that the apostle speaks. He shows the foolishness of these deities by revealing the all-encompassing realities of God's transcendence and immanence.

[17] Again, Bavinck summarizes this balance when he writes: "The same God who in his revelation limits himself, as it were, to certain specific places, times, and persons is at the same time infinitely exalted above the whole realm of nature and every creature. Even in the parts of Scripture stressing this temporal and local manifestation, the sense of his sublimity and omnipotence is not lacking. The Lord who walks in the garden is the Creator of heaven and earth. The God who appears to Jacob is in control of the future. Although the God of Israel dwells in the midst of his people in the house that Solomon built for him, he cannot even be contained by the heavens (1 Kings 8:27). He manifests himself in nature and sympathizes, as it were, with his people, but he is simultaneously the incomprehensible One (Job 26:14; 36:26; 37:5), the incomparable One (Isa. 40:18, 25; 46:5), the one who is infinitely exalted above time, space, and every creature (Isa. 40:12ff.; 41:4; 44:6; 48:12), the one true God (Ex. 20:3, 11; Deut. 4:35, 39; 32:19; 1 Sam. 2:2; Isa. 44:8)." Bavinck, *Reformed Dogmatics*, 2:33–34.

God in Himself, God in Relationship

So if this is the case, why does God enter into his creation? If he is completely self-sufficient and requires nothing outside himself, then why create and relate? As hinted above, the answer to this question lies in his divine self-sufficiency. Though at first glance this may appear contradictory, the Lord's self-satisfaction is, in fact, the seedbed for the God-world relationship. Rooted in the Lord's transcendence, the doctrine of divine aseity describes God as "independent, self-existent, and fully self-sufficient."[18] So when we say that God is *a se*,

> we say that (as manifest and eternally actual in the relationship of the Father, Son, and Holy Ghost) He is the One who already has and is in Himself everything which would have to be the object of His creation and causation if He were not He, God. Because He is God, as such He already has His own being. Therefore this being does not need origination and constitution.[19]

In other words, the Lord is ontologically "uncaused, without beginning, not dependent on an external person, principle, or metaphysical reality for his existence."[20] Moreover, as Yahweh is ontologically (in his being) *a se*, he is also internally *a se*, indicating that he is in himself completely self-satisfied, for neither his happiness nor his fulfillment is contingent upon anything external to himself, since he does not need anything outside himself to be content or satisfied.[21]

This doctrine has obvious ramifications for God's relationship with the world. Because Yahweh requires nothing "outside of himself to exist, be satisfied, [or] be fulfilled,"[22] he in no way needs creation for anything, either for some deficiency within himself or for his own personal satisfaction. As a result, God's aseity emphasizes that his decision to create and relate to that creation does not come from a specific need or insufficiency

---

[18] James Beilby, "Divine Aseity, Divine Freedom: A Conceptual Problem for Edwardsian Calvinism," *JETS* 47 (2004): 648.

[19] Karl Barth, *Church Dogmatics*, ed. G. W. Bromiley and T. F. Torrance, vol. 2, *The Doctrine of God*, pt. 1, trans. T. H. L. Parker et al. (Edinburgh: T&T Clark, 1957), 306. Through this type of being, Barth affirms God's freedom from (transcendence) and freedom for (immanence). He writes, "Freedom in its positive and proper qualities means to be grounded in one's being, to be determined and moved by oneself" (ibid., 302). In short, out of his aseity, God has the freedom to be transcendent and immanent, separate and near. For citations and further interaction, see Michael S. Horton, *Lord and Servant: A Covenant Christology* (Louisville: Westminster John Knox, 2005), 28–52.

[20] Beilby, "Divine Aseity," 649.

[21] Ibid.

[22] Ibid.

within himself but *derives from his nature instead*. In other words, it is out of an abundance of his self-sufficient and independent nature that the desire and means to relate to the world arises.[23] The doctrine of divine aseity clarifies that the source of the God-world relationship is the independent, self-sufficient, self-existing, and transcendent nature of God.

So, we see that God's transcendence grounds his immanence, but we still need to understand how this "other than" God can, in any real sense, also be the God who is with us without contradicting his transcendent nature. Thus George Eldon Ladd asks, "How can the Infinite be known in the finite, the Eternal in the temporal, the Absolute in the relativities of history?"[24] His answer helps: "From a purely human perspective, this seems impossible; but at precisely this point is found perhaps the greatest miracle of biblical faith. God is the living God, and he, the Eternal, the Unchangeable, has communicated knowledge of himself through the ebb and flow of historical experience."[25]

Ladd shows us that the testimony of Scripture reveals that the infinite can work beyond the "normal" and conventional ways of "everyday" experience—the ways and experiences humans understand—because God *in his transcendence* is beyond our limitations. In other words, the contradictions of a transcendent God becoming immanent are *not* contradictions, because God's infinite nature transcends our finite limitations—the limitations that lead to contradictions for us. Again, Ladd, pointing to God's acts in his creation, helps us see that

> the Lord of history is transcendent over history yet is not aloof from history. He is therefore able to bring to pass in time and space events that are genuine events yet are "supra-historical" in their character. This merely means that such revelatory events are not produced by history but that the Lord of history, who stands above history, acts within history for the redemption of historical creatures.[26]

Ladd helps us see the very evident and very important doctrine of the Creator-creature distinction. This distinction reminds us that

---

[23] See John Piper, *God's Passion for His Glory: Living the Vision of Jonathan Edwards* (Wheaton, IL: Crossway, 1998), 165.
[24] George Eldon Ladd, *A Theology of the New Testament*, rev. ed., ed. Donald Hagner (Grand Rapids: Eerdmans, 2001), 23.
[25] Ibid., 25.
[26] Ibid.

God is the ruler of time and space. He is able to act in his creation and history in ways that surpass typical procedures of such events—the typical procedures and laws that God established. God stands above history but also uses history to bring about his redemptive purposes. John Frame explains:

> God (the Son, as well as the Father and the Spirit) has an experience that transcends all physical limitations. God is not, therefore, to be defined as a physical being. (Even the incarnate Son of God had a divine sovereignty over space and time.) But as Lord of all things that are material and physical, he is supremely able to understand the world from the perspective of every physical being, to reveal himself in any physical form that he chooses, and even to take human flesh, so that he has his own body, without abandoning his transcendent existence. I argued that it is better to say that God is Lord of time and Lord of space than to say merely that God is atemporal and nonspatial. Although he does have atemporal and nonspatial existence, he is also temporally and spatially omnipresent. His sovereignty does not mean that he is excluded from time and space; rather it means that he acts toward them as Lord, not as the one who is limited by them. The same point can be made about God's incorporeality. This doctrine does not exclude God from physical reality. Rather, it teaches that he relates himself to physical reality as the Lord, transcending it and using it as he chooses.[27]

Because the transcendent "Lord of history" created, rules, and sustains time and space, he is not limited in his nature from being immanently present in that time and space. The aseity of God shows us that the restrictions we feel are not restrictions for him. He is free to be distinct from his creation while simultaneously drawing near to his creation. Simply put, it is precisely his transcendence that leads to his immanence.

Solomon speaks to this very idea at the dedication of the temple. The king of Israel, fully anticipating the glory of God to enter the physical building he, Solomon, has built, calls upon the king of heaven to come and be present in the new temple (1 Kings 8:10–21, 28–30).

---

[27] Frame, *Doctrine of God*, 587.

Yet, even in full expectancy, Solomon qualifies the residence of God in the temple, announcing the utter inability to limit God to one location (8:27). God enters the temple because he can. He is not limited by his transcendence to remain distant; rather his transcendence is what allows him to fill the temple with his glory while simultaneously transcending the physical walls of the temple, the national borders of Israel, and any other finite limitation to his presence.

Like Solomon, we should recognize Scripture's need to strike a balance between God's transcendence and his immanence and apply this balance within our own doctrinal formulations. Yes, God chooses to be immanent in history, but clearly transcends history as well. Likewise, he draws near to people in time and space but still transcends any sense of literal and physical manifestation of the incorporeal God.

It is the absolute nature of God that allows him the freedom to be personal with the world.[28] In other words, "that which makes [God] divine, and thus wholly other and so transcendent, is that which equally allows him to be active within the created order and so be immanent."[29] To deny God's self-existence would, then, be what denies the very foundation for his immanent activity in human history. It is because of his being "high above all nations" that the Lord is able to raise the poor from the dust (Ps. 113:4–9). It is because the Lord dwells in the high and holy places that he is able to bring respite to the contrite and lowly spirit (Isa. 57:15). Through the knowledge of the transcendent realities of God's nature we appreciate what it means for God to be in relationship with the world, and, in particular, his people.[30] When we see that our holy and righteous God extends himself relationally, not out of need, but out of his transcendent nature, we are compelled to worship and bring glory to the transcendent and

---

[28] Among biblical texts that express the corresponding truths of transcendence and immanence, there is a consistent pattern. The transcendence of God is habitually mentioned first and is then followed by an expression of immanence. This order in no way eradicates the necessary balance between God's personal and absolute nature. Instead, I argue, it discloses that the source of divine immanence is in fact the transcendence of the Lord. Or, to say it another way, divine immanence is a result of transcendence. God's transcendence provides the possibility of his being relational with his creation in the first place, especially for the purpose of redemption.

[29] Weinandy, *Does God Suffer?*, 56.

[30] Bruce Ware argues, "Divine transcendence must be conceived first in order for the beauty and glory of the divine immanence likewise to be apprehended correctly." Ware continues to express the importance of transcendence for immanence when he maintains that "yes God is both transcendent and immanent. But marvel that the God who is fully and infinitely transcendent would choose to become immanent. Marvel that the One who stands eternally independent of the world should choose to relate so intimately with those of this world." Ware, *God's Greater Glory*, 46.

immanent one. Yet when we fail to do so, God quickly becomes an idol made in our image.

The Trinity and God's Relational Nature

God's transcendence and immanence both exist because of his Trinitarian nature. The eternal intra-Trinitarian relationship that exists between the Father, Son, and Holy Spirit reveals that God is self-fulfilled relationally and needs nothing outside of this fellowship (e.g., John 3:35; 5:20; 10:38; 14:10–20, 31; 15:9; 17:20–26). Here there is a perfect relationship between the persons of the Godhead. It can be said that "not only is the personal reality of each member of the Trinity discernable, but the divine persons also appear in unique relationship to one another."[31] Biblically, the interrelations between the persons of the Godhead are exemplified in the Son and the Spirit being with the Father by way of "seeing," "hearing," and "doing," as well as their "knowing" and "testifying" of each other.[32]

This intimacy between the members of the Trinity forms the basis of God's immanent relationship with the created order.[33] This relational nature of God in himself, first expressed and established in his transcendent self-fulfillment among the persons of the Trinity, is graciously conferred—in a limited sense—to the world. So just as "the three divine persons act in freedom to create and relate, they likewise manifest in their economic dealings with the world what is true of their logically prior and intrinsic relations."[34] In other words, the relations between God and the world emanate directly from the relations between the persons of the Trinity.

---

[31] J. Scott Horrell, "Toward a Biblical Model of the Social Trinity: Avoiding Equivocation of Nature and Order," *JETS* 47 (2004): 405.

[32] Ibid., 407. For examples of the Son's and the Spirit's being with the Father, see John 1:18; 3:11, 32; 5:19–20, 30; 6:38; 8:38; 12:49–50; 16:13–15; 1 Cor. 2:10–13. Also their knowledge and testimony of each other is seen biblically in John 1:32–33; 3:11, 34; 5:36–37; 7:29; 10:15; 14:26; 15:26; 16:7–11; 17:6; 18:37; 20:22; Rom. 8:9; Gal. 4:6; Eph. 2:18.

[33] I hold to differences of roles and positions among the persons of the Godhead as well. I also believe that God is singular in nature and plural in person. As Bruce Ware contends: "The Father is supreme in authority, the Son is under the Father, and the Spirit is under the Father and the Son. Yet there is also full harmony in their work, with no jealousy, bitterness, strife, or discord." Bruce A. Ware, *Father, Son, and Holy Spirit: Relationships, Roles, and Relevance* (Wheaton, IL: Crossway, 2005), 131.

[34] Bruce A. Ware, "How Shall We Think about the Trinity?," in *God Under Fire: Modern Scholarship Reinvents God*, ed. Douglas S. Huffman and Eric L. Johnson (Grand Rapids: Zondervan, 2002), 257. It is important to show that God's relation to his created order is not required for his existence, because that would ultimately deteriorate the distinction between the economic and immanent Trinity. If this distinction were erased and the aseity of God abandoned, then our only option would be something consistent with Rahner's rule, which argues that the economic Trinity *is* the immanent Trinity and the immanent Trinity *is* the economic Trinity. To avoid this problematic supposition, John Frame clarifies that "there is a difference between what God is necessarily and

In Scripture, Jesus models his love for the world after his relationship with the Father (John 17:24–26). When Christ declares, "As the Father has loved me, so have I loved you" (John 15:9), we catch a glimpse into the source and origin of the spiritual intimacy available to believers. Clearly, any relationship with God (as well as Christ and the Holy Spirit) derives from the perfect fellowship and communion that typifies the union between the first and second persons of the Trinity. It would seem, then, that our relationship with God is based on, or born out of, the interrelationship that exists between Father, Son, and Spirit (see, e.g., John 13:34–35; 14:10; 17:5, 21–26).

The Presence of God Defined

Based on his transcendent lordship and intra-Trinitarian relationality, God most high has chosen to be God most near. God covenants with fallen man precisely because he is transcendent (and gracious) and has the authority and control to do so. God is a "personal, powerful, self-existent being who is creator of the world and of humankind, *and* who is concerned about humanity."[35] He is the one who "commits himself to us, to be our God and to make us his people. He delivers us by his grace and rules us by his law, and he rules not only from above, but also with us and within us."[36] Emanating from God's transcendence is his immanence, and in particular, the manifest and relational presence of God in the midst of his creation. The immanence of God as expressed through his divine presence is certainly emphasized in Scripture, is imperative for the Bible's own theological message, and is personally applicable for our salvation and sanctification. In order to set the stage for our consideration of the power and purpose of God's manifest immanence, let us first define what Scripture means by the presence of God.

The Difference between "God Is Everywhere" and "God Is Here"

We begin with what the presence of God is not. There is a difference between God's relational nearness and his being everywhere. This latter

---

what he freely chooses to do in his plan for creation," which includes his choice to be relational with humanity. Frame, *Doctrine of God*, 629.

[35] Ladd, *A Theology of the New Testament*, 21, emphasis added.

[36] Frame, *Doctrine of God*, 96.

idea is what theologians call divine omnipresence (or immensity) and is, no doubt, the default category for the way many of us conceptualize God's presence. And though these concepts are by no means at odds, it is important to clarify the differences between them.

To be sure, divine omnipresence is evident throughout Scripture (1 Kings 8:27; Ps. 139:5–12; Prov. 15:3; Jer. 23:23–24; Ezek. 8:12; Amos 9:2–4; Acts 17:27–28; Rom. 10:6–8). God reveals himself to be one who "transcends spatial limitations and so is present at all places at once in his total being."[37] The Lord is ontologically everywhere at once along with each point in space in the totality of his being. More specifically, Yahweh's omnipresence, or what John Feinberg calls his "ontological presence" (meaning the presence of his being/nature), allows him to be "actually present at a given place in space"; yet, because of his immaterial nature, God "can still actually be somewhere (ontological presence) but [not] present physically."[38] God in his omnipresence, therefore, "is not limited to being present in just one place at a time . . . he is simultaneously everywhere ontologically."[39] Scripture describes God's omnipresence as an "essential universal generality of divine presence,"[40] an attribute that reveals God to be nonphysical, beyond localization, and seemingly impersonal.

While it is true that God is unlimited spatially and that he also fills all space, biblical revelation focuses more on his being relationally and redemptively present with man. The biblical text shows us that there is consistent tension between these two realities of God's presence. Along with the philosophical details of his immensity, Scripture more often than not stresses the special and specific manifestation of God as he reveals himself to his people for communion and salvation. It is this particular presence that is detailed in God's being in the midst of his people in Eden (e.g., Gen. 3:8, 10; cf. Revelation 21–22), in the tabernacle/temple (e.g., Ex. 25:8; 1 Kings 8:1–13), in the incarnation of Christ (e.g., Matt. 1:23; John 1:14; 2:21), and, ultimately, in the new heaven and the new earth (e.g., Isa. 66:22–23; Rev. 21:1–5, 22–27).

---

[37] John S. Feinberg, *No One Like Him: The Doctrine of God* (Wheaton, IL: Crossway, 2001), 249.
[38] Ibid.
[39] Ibid., 250.
[40] Daniel Strange, "A Little Dwelling on the Divine Presence: Towards a 'Whereness' of the Triune God," in *Heaven on Earth: The Temple in Biblical Theology*, ed. T. Desmond Alexander and Simon Gathercole (Waynesboro, GA: Paternoster, 2004), 212.

Scripture does not highlight "the divine presence as a general immanence" but rather as "the special realization of his presence in salvation and the final acceptance of the justified believer in his eternal presence."[41] The presence of God detailed in Scripture, therefore, expresses not only the classical doctrine of divine omnipresence—in no way are we wanting to undermine this biblical truth—but also, and I would argue more centrally, a relational-redemptive presence of God.[42] As the Canon of Scripture will show in the chapters ahead, this type of divine presence receives most of the attention because, as I will contend, it is the relational-redemptive presence of God that is both a goal of redemptive history and the means to that goal.

Definition of the Presence of God

This leads us to the definition of the presence of God that will guide the rest of our journey through Scripture together. To really understand the meaning of the presence of God in Scripture, I have tried to excavate our definition from the Bible's own structure and substance. When we listen to the rhythms of Scripture regarding this biblical theme, we hear the biblical writers accent two emphases: the eschatological presence of God and the redemptive presence of God.

Regarding the first, we find an unmediated and fully relational manifestation of God's presence at the beginning and end of redemptive history. As we will see in detail in the next chapter, God is relationally present to Adam and Eve in ways that those this side of the fall cannot comprehend. Interestingly, John the Seer appropriates this same Edenic presence to describe the new creation available to the redeemed in Christ. John goes as far as to depict our new heavenly/earthly home as a place similar to, yet still surpassing, the first garden, with the future reality of the presence of God, unmediated and fully relational, at its center (Revelation 21–22). This is the eschatological presence of God

---

[41] G. W. Bromiley, "Divine Presence," in *Evangelical Dictionary of Theology*, 2nd ed., ed. Walter Elwell (Grand Rapids: Baker, 2001), 873.

[42] Jim Hamilton provides a helpful example of the distinction between the general immanence of God and his relational presence extended to his people. Hamilton writes: "Consider, for instance, the statement that God was with Ishmael (Gen. 21:20), which immediately follows God's assertion to Abraham that the covenant would be kept through the line of Isaac (21:12; cp. Rom. 9:7). This shows that God's presence with Ishmael did not carry the same benefits as His presence with Isaac (Gen. 26:3)." James M. Hamilton Jr., *God's Indwelling Presence: The Holy Spirit in the Old and New Testaments* (Nashville: Broadman & Holman, 2006), 161.

that bookends the biblical story and formulates a central goal for all of God's redemptive purposes.[43]

It is the getting to this wondrous future experience of God's relational presence that is the hard part. To do this, God's eschatological presence gives rise to the redemptive function of his presence. In his providence and for his glory, Yahweh becomes present to restore and re-create his broken world and a broken people. We see that the redemptive aspect of God's presence differs from the relational aspect of God's presence in that it is mediated (thereby limiting the experience of divine-human relations in a way that the eschatological presence does not) and is predominantly defined by its purpose to enter time and space to redeem and reconcile. The redemptive presence of God serves the Lord's own eschatological agenda by saving and preparing a people for the full experience of God's presence that is to come.[44] The redemptive presence of God is the means to the goal of God's eschatological presence.

With this in mind, I want to provide a convenient and succinct definition of the presence of God. Through the excavation of Scripture, we find that the presence of God is *the manifestation of God in time and space—mediated in some sense—working to bring forth redemption and redemption's objectives and, simultaneously, the unmediated, fully relational, and eschatological manifestation of God first experienced in Eden and awaiting the elect in the new creation.*

THE PRESENCE OF GOD: MANIFEST AND RELATIONAL

Let us think through the individual elements of our definition above. Fundamental to both aspects of divine presence is the reality that God has made himself known. Even though our fallen nature as culpable sinners restrains our knowledge, God's free decision to reveal himself in word and mighty acts has nevertheless blessed us with an understand-

---

[43] In the next chapter (chap. 3) we will trace out how the presence of God is central to the covenant/redemptive promises that drive the advancement of salvation history to the completion of these blessings. For his people's pleasure and his glory, God promises a genealogy and a geography or, to put it another way, a people and a place among which his perfect, unmediated eschatological presence will dwell.

[44] To see how the redemptive presence of God is the means to the eternally relational presence of God, we will survey the redemptive work of the presence of God in both the Old and New Testaments, highlighting the manifest work of the Lord in the exodus, his promises in the Prophets, the fulfillment of these promises in Christ our Immanuel, the glorious indwelling presence of God in the Holy Spirit, and the divine presence in the new temple of the church.

ing of his presence. In a particular aspect of his revelation, the Lord chose to manifest himself and enter human history in order to disclose himself to humanity progressively over time in a logical and comprehensible way. As Frame summarizes, "God's presence is temporal; he is present 'now'" and "he is also 'here.' God is present in space as well as in time."[45] The Lord of heaven is also the Lord of earth, and he is manifest *in* his creation.

From Genesis 3:8, where the Lord is said to "walk" among his people in the garden, to the culminating reality of Revelation 21:1–5, where believers finally enter into the dwelling place of God for all eternity, the biblical authors centrally concern themselves with the special revelation of God in time and space. In harmony with the opening and closing books of the Canon, the rest of Scripture also underscores the manifest presence of the Lord within space and time.[46] God is said to "come" and "go" (e.g., Gen. 17:22; 20:3; 31:24; 35:14; Num. 20:9; 2 Sam. 7:23; cf. Mark 1:14, Acts 1:9–10). He is described as being in the midst of his people and near to creation. We see him come down to evaluate the evil plots of the Tower of Babel (Gen. 11:5–7) and Sodom and Gomorrah (Gen. 18:2). We hear that he inhabits Sinai to covenant with Moses and Israel (Exodus 19; 33). We know that he "tabernacles" in flesh in the coming of Christ (John 1:14).[47]

The Lord manifests his presence in physical and/or audible appearances (e.g., Gen. 32:23; Ex. 3:1–15; 33:18–23; Isa. 49:3). This is evident in the theophanic and prophetic revelations of God detailed in the Old Testament (e.g., Gen. 18:1–15; Josh. 5:13–15; Dan. 3:19–26). More perfectly, it is expressed in the New Testament's disclosure of divine presence in the person of Christ (John 1:1–17; 14:9; Col. 1:15; cf. 1 Thess. 5:16). We also see that God is manifest spiritually, which is most explicitly communicated in the person of the Holy Spirit and his indwelling believers (e.g. John 14:17).

The biblical expressions of God's presence revealed in time and space are diverse and, at times, abstract. Even in its physical expres-

---

[45] Frame, *Doctrine of God*, 97.

[46] There are, of course, dissimilarities between the pre- and post-lapsarian experiences of God's presence owing to sin, which we will cover later in this section.

[47] The rest of this volume will flesh out the specifics of God's redemptive relational presence as it is revealed across the Canon. To avoid redundancy, I will save the specific description and evaluation of the examples listed here and others for chaps. 3–5.

sion, God's presence is often obscured by the earthly elements of fire[48] and cloud[49] (e.g., Gen. 15:17; Ex. 13:21–22; Deut. 1:33; 4:11–12, 24; 1 Kings 8:10–12; Ezek. 1:27; cf. Heb. 12:29; Rev. 4:5). When God's presence is made visible, whether through fire, cloud, or some other manifestation, it means there has been a human encounter with the transcendent God. The arrival of the Shekinah glory testifies that the Lord has entered his earthly dwelling place to be present with his people (e.g., Ex. 40:34–38; 2 Chron. 7:1–3)—and yet its description is one of nearness and separation. Thus understood, the glorious presence of God is "an image of divine transcendence as it makes itself known to people. It combines awe and terror and simultaneously invites approach and distance."[50] God's glory reveals that the transcendent Lord is near, in a locative sense, to his people and working in history for his redemptive purposes while also declaring his holiness and distinction.

We must remember that "Yahweh is God-with-his people."[51] God becomes present in such ways for the purpose of relationship. As Frame rightfully contends, "[Yahweh] is the one who calls people into fellowship with himself and therefore becomes intimately present to them."[52] This divine-human relationship was foundational to the experience of Eden.[53] From the beginning of creation, God was rela-

---

[48] The symbol of fire to reveal the presence of God is significant for many reasons. This imagery pictures God in a certain way. As "fire purifies and destroys so does God purify the righteous and destroy the wicked ('for our God is a consuming fire,' Heb. 12:29 RSV). Just as fire lights up the blackness of night, so does God overcome the dark powers of evil. Just as fire is mysterious and immaterial, so too is God enigmatic and incorporeal." "Fire," in *Dictionary of Biblical Imagery*, ed. Leland Ryken, James C. Wilhoit, and Tremper Longman III (Downers Grove, IL: InterVarsity, 1998), 287.

[49] The cloud, as seen in the exodus narrative, is a symbol of God's presence mediated to his people. In Exodus 16:10 we see that the cloud in the wilderness is a representation of divine glory amid the chosen nation of Israel. Symbolically, the cloud "represents God's presence but also his hiddenness (see Lam. 2:2). No one can see God and live, so the cloud shields people from actually seeing the form of God. It reveals God but also preserves the mystery that surrounds him." "Cloud," in Ryken, Wilhoit, and Longman, *Dictionary of Biblical Imagery*, 157.

[50] "Glory," in Ryken, Wilhoit, and Longman, *Dictionary of Biblical Imagery*, 330.

[51] Peter Toon, *Our Triune God* (Wheaton, IL: Victor, 1996), 89. Toon notes that God's self-disclosure in the name Yahweh tells that he is a God with and for his people. In his own name God has shown himself to be present and relational.

[52] Frame, *Doctrine of God*, 94.

[53] More specifically, God's presence is covenantally relational. The basis of any redemptive relationship with God is established in covenant. When we assess the Scriptures, the purpose of the covenant is clear: God will be with a people to be their God and to make them his people (e.g., Gen. 17:7; Ex. 6:7; 29:45; Lev. 26:12; Jer. 7:23; 11:4; 24:7; 30:22; Ezek. 11:20; 14:11; 36:28; 37:27; Heb. 11:16; Rev. 21:3). Thus understood, "God is not merely present in the world; he is *covenantally* present. He is *with* his creatures to bless and judge them in accordance with the terms of the covenant." Frame, *Doctrine of God*, 94, emphasis his. This promise reveals the relational basis that undergirds each aspect of the covenant the Lord establishes with man. Building on the relational nature of God's presence, the Lord manifests himself in redemptive history for the purpose of salvation. The presence of God centers on redemption. The Lord does not simply want to relate with the unrighteous; he wants to redeem them

tionally present with Adam. He communed and even "walked" with the first man in the cool of the day (Gen. 3:8). Paradise was paradise because it was where God's presence was; Eden was where his perfect and full relationship with creation and his relational presence with man began.[54]

Such a beginning suggests that God has always intended to be relationally present with his people. Moreover, the rest of Scripture details that the recovery and even expansion of this Edenic experience are central to the Lord's redemptive mission.[55] For this reason, the divine-human experience of Adam in the garden provides a paradigm for what will be the even fuller experience of the eschatological presence of God in the new heaven and new earth. For instance, in the New Jerusalem—where there is no temple and, therefore, no limitation to the dwelling of God as there was following Adam's rebellion—we find that God's presence is freely accessed as it has never been before. It is a relationship where the believer is able to bask in the unending and unquenchable light of the divine presence while simultaneously being fully cognizant of God's grace, his own need for and provision of divine mercy, and his desire to glorify the one in whose presence he shall eternally stand.

THE PRESENCE OF GOD: REDEMPTIVE AND MEDIATED

Though it is true that God is manifest and relational throughout all of redemptive history, there is a distinct change in the experience of his presence following Adam's rebellion. After the fall, God becomes present to restore the relationship lost in sin; God is present to redeem. In a sense, this *is* the storyline of redemption: the Lord time after time extends himself redemptively to a person (e.g., Abraham and the patriarchs) or a people (Israel and the church). He does so in order to redeem this people and reestablish the Edenic-type unmediated, eschatological presence of God found in the new creation. God's presence after Adam's

---

so that the relationship can be made right and he can be glorified in full. So God becomes manifest in time and space to deliver blessings to the faithful or curses to those who reject him.

[54] Though classifying the experience of God's presence in a sinless context is difficult and can lead to conjecture, Scripture does indicate that Adam's relationship with God was free and full. This will be fleshed out in more detail in chap. 3.

[55] See also the more universal reality of God's presence in the Spirit of God dwelling within creation since its origin (Gen. 1:2).

transgression is best understood as an agent of redemption rather than pure relationship.[56]

With this shift in function, there is a shift in the overall experience of God's presence. Sin separates the unrighteous from the righteous, and the relationship that was once free and unrestricted prior to the fall now demands mediation.[57] We see repeatedly in Scripture that the Lord shrouds his presence in symbol, image, and/or physical barriers because of his holiness and for the protection of humanity.[58] Bavinck explains that the mediated presence of God, particularly in the Old Testament,

> does not exhaustively coincide with his being. It does indeed furnish true and reliable knowledge of God, but not a knowledge that exhaustively corresponds to his being. The stone at Bethel, the pillar of cloud and the pillar of fire in the wilderness, the thunder on Mount Sinai, the clouds in the tabernacle, the ark of the covenant (etc.) are signs and pledges of his presence, but do not encompass and confine him. Moses, with whom God spoke as with a friend, only saw God after he had passed by him (Ex. 33:23). One cannot see God and live (Ex. 33:20; Lev. 16:2). He is without form (Deut. 4:12, 15). One cannot make an image of him (Ex. 20:4). He dwells

---

[56] The decision to classify God's manifestation after the fall as his redemptive presence is meant to distinguish this function of the Lord's presence from the relational presence associated with the beginning and end of salvation history. Still, I acknowledge that even as God's presence is an agent of redemption, some form of relationship is implied—a form, however, that is distinct from the relationships known in Eden and the new creation.

[57] As will be shown in detail in the chapters that follow, mediation and God's redemptive presence go hand in hand. The Old Testament is replete with institutions and practices pointing to the mediation of God's presence. For instance, God introduces the temple as his dwelling place among his chosen people. This location is where he has chosen to manifest himself to his people, but at the same time, he has also ensured separation from them through the concentric structure of the building and the partitioning veil of the Most Holy Place. The sacrificial system as a whole was established to address the problem of sin and provide a means by which the Lord could remain in the midst of a sinful people. Sacrifices are offered perennially, and, as with the climactic Day of Atonement, this constant repetition and recurrence reveals that the atonement and forgiveness the faithful remnant seek so diligently will, in all actuality, never be finished in their own power. This requisite distance that stands between God and man is also the basis for the role of mediator evidenced in the persons of Moses, David, and, most importantly, Jesus the Christ. He is the one who rends the veil of the temple from top to bottom and secures the atonement for sin once and for all. Christ's death and resurrection deal sin its death blow (Heb. 10:1–14). He is the final Mediator. Christ stands before the presence of God on behalf of his people, taking their punishment upon himself (Heb. 9:24–28) in order to secure eternal access to the presence of God (Heb. 7:25; 10:18–22; cf. Rev. 21–22).

[58] One of the most famous examples of this mediated divine presence is Moses's encounter with Yahweh on Mount Sinai. In this familiar story, Moses, hoping to know God more intimately, pleads with the Lord to see the fullness of his glory-presence (Ex. 33:17–18). The Lord graciously responds, allowing his presence to be revealed, but only in a restricted way so as not to consume his prophet. Before passing in front of Moses, the Lord hides him in the cleft of the mountain for his own protection, permitting his prophet to see the "back" of Yahweh but not Yahweh's "face" (Ex. 33:18–23). If it were not for the Lord's gracious protection of Moses and humanity from himself, Yahweh's holiness would consume those exposed to his presence (Ex. 33:20). Thus, because of his transcendent holiness, the immanence of God requires mediation.

in darkness: clouds and darkness are the signs of his presence (Ex. 20:21; Deut. 4:11; 5:22; 1 Kings 8:12; 2 Chron. 6:1).[59]

The moral and epistemic deficiencies marking mankind in the fallen state require this type of mediation.

This veiling allows God to be manifest with his people while, at the same time, protecting the people from his holy and consuming presence. Mediation, therefore, is for both the sanctity of God and the security and furtherance of man (e.g., Num. 4:15; 2 Sam. 6:6–7). Even in God's merciful manifestations, fallen humanity is laid bare before a transcendent, holy, and infinite being.[60] There is always the stricture of unrighteousness and finitude that separates God from humanity, even in the Lord's decision to draw near to his people. If not, sinners would be consumed, for the unholy cannot stand in the presence of the holy. As the testimony of Scripture reveals, when Yahweh draws near for redemption, the biblical pattern is that his presence is almost always revealed in a restricted and mediated sense.

Conclusion

God is present because he wants to be; he is present because it brings him glory. There is nothing forcing him to draw near other than his very character. We see that the transcendence of God is the source of his immanent presence with and for creation. His nature—typified by holiness, control, and authority—is free to relate to a broken world in the ways he deems fit and in ways that exalt him. It is only in this understanding of God that we can truly grasp what the presence of God really is. Out of the Lord's transcendence and freedom emerges his decision to draw near—to redeem us and to be our hope. God enters this world to establish a covenant relationship with us, to redeem us, and to usher us into new creation filled with his presence. Understand-

---

[59] Bavinck, *Reformed Dogmatics*, 2:35.
[60] Even the presence of God in Christ, the fullest manifestation of the Lord, is mediated through the incarnation. In agreement with Chalcedonian christology, we correctly affirm that Christ is fully God. However, as the transfiguration clearly disclosed, Christ's divinity was veiled in his humanity. Furthermore, in his second coming we will see a fuller revelation of such attributes as his justice, wrath, and conquering. In the fulfillment of this eschatological promise, the restrictions and limitations of God's presence will no longer be required. The division between the general ontological presence of God and the special particular presence of God will be removed with the coming of the new creation. With Christ's final work there is a "'specializing' of the 'general' as there will be no distinction between God's general presence and special presence as he will be specially present to all in the holy city." Strange, "A Little Dwelling," 229.

ing who God is and what his presence means, then, gives us a vision of its importance for Scripture's own theological message. We know that God's presence is both eschatological—it is our future hope—and redemptive—it is our means of salvation. So with our "location scouting" completed and "storyboards" in place, we turn our attention fully to the divine script. In the next chapter we will begin at the most strategic place to understand a story: the story's end.

Part One

Fade to Light

The Presence of God and the Goal of Redemption

In this section we will survey the eschatological reality of the presence of God. The divine author of the biblical drama wants us to see that all of redemptive history is leading to the eternal experience of his presence. So like a good film critic, we will begin with the end of the story so that we can understand the story's purpose. When we do, we find the presence of God in the midst of a people. What is more, when we return to the beginning of Scripture, we find the same emphasis. Finally, we will investigate how God's eschatological presence informs not only the start and conclusion of Scripture, but all that happens in between Genesis and Revelation as well. Between the two bookends of Scripture, we again find that the rest of the story is centered on the covenants, and in each of these covenants God promises to make a people and a place so that he will be present with them eternally.

3

Beginning at the End

Creating and Redeeming a People and a Place for God's Presence

We all have those books and movies that we return to over and over again. The book's spine is tearing and the pages are yellowing from our touch. The DVD box is cracked, and we always have to wipe the finger-prints off the disc before we put it in the Blu-ray player. These are the stories that shape our lives, language, and relationships. (I am almost convinced that we subconsciously choose friends based on whether or not they recognize *our* movie quotes.) We know these works the way writers know their keyboards, and yet we still come back to take up the adventure again, to reconnect with lost friends, or to hear once more (and recite audibly, much to our loved ones' annoyance) the lines we have consumed a million times over.

Why do we do it? Why do we come back to these works? Well, for one thing, we simply love their stories. They build characters we want to be, ones we already know, ones we love to hate, and ones we hate to love. The authors take us places we would never go on our own and force decisions on us we would otherwise never face. In short, our fa-vorite works construct. They fabricate a world that pulls us in with its Death Star–like tractor beam—a world we want to immerse ourselves in, not just to escape our world but to help us understand our world better. This is what the beautiful stories do. And we were created to want that. We were created to need that.

This love is usually what pushes the door open to our favorite works, but there is more to it when we keep coming back to these stories. We pick up Lewis, Tolkien, Austen, Shakespeare, Percy, Faulkner, O'Conner, and even Rowling because we want something more from them. They know life and humanity in a way we've missed, wanted, or been unable to articulate. But when we read them, we find a missing puzzle piece. Things make sense. And they change us for the better. They provide clarity that our finite eyes could not make out on their own. These stories give us not only knowledge, but wisdom.

This is why so many of us return: we come back to these stories—either consciously or subconsciously—as informed seekers. The first time through we fell in love with the storyline, but we pick up the book or walk in the theater again because we want more. Like traveling the familiar road that takes us back home, we know where we are going because we have been there before. To borrow from Tolkien and Bilbo Baggins—we've "been there and back again," and knowing the end makes the beginning and the middle so much more the next time through. It opens up new thematic vistas and terrain. We begin to see the intricacies, notice the subtleties, and hear the hints more and more each time through. For instance, we notice (spoiler alert) the temperature drop every time Bruce Willis's character walks on screen in *The Sixth Sense*. We hear faint echoes of sacrificial love in Severus Snape's callous condemnations of Harry Potter after we've read *Harry Potter and the Deathly Hallows*. "Rosebud" means more than it ever did after we've seen *Citizen Kane*, and Strider is hard to imagine without his crown once we have followed him to the gates of Mordor in *The Lord of the Rings*.

The Purpose-Driven Bible

As we come back to our favorite works again and again, the purposes and reasons for these stories take focus. As Christians, this is true for the way we mature in Scripture. As we come back to the Bible again and again, reading from cover to cover, a grand narrative—with purpose and objectives—begins to take shape. In this way, Scripture is not unlike a skyscraper. Each narrative component or book builds on another to form a larger story, the way individual floors build on each other to create the high-rise.

The more familiar we become with this overarching story, the more we begin to see that the whole biblical drama has a point. It is working toward something. There are purposes, objectives, and themes running through Scripture just as there is rebar running through the skyscraper to hold it together. This fact is simple enough; yet we often forget it, overlook it, or do not recognize it. We need to be reminded that "the Scriptures . . . constitute a text with a developing story[,] . . . a story that clearly progresses toward the accomplishment of specific goals."[1] Once we realize that Scripture is more than a collection of tedious, obsolete stories with no integrated purposes or application, we can truly begin to understand God's objectives in the world and God's objectives for us.

Beginning at the End: The New Jerusalem and the Goal of Redemption

To find the point toward which the divine story is moving, it is best to begin at the end of that story.[2] We start here because the book of Revelation chronicles God's redemptive work and arguably contains the most comprehensive expression of God's future goals and their fulfillment. In particular, Revelation 21–22 beautifully captures the culmination of God's creative and redemptive activity and is essential if we are going to understand the divine objectives toward which the biblical storyline develops.[3]

---

[1] Richard Lints, *The Fabric of Theology: A Prolegomenon to Evangelical Theology* (Grand Rapids: Eerdmans, 1993; reprint, Eugene, OR: Wipf and Stock, 1999), 262. Methodologically, Michael Horton argues that "eschatology should be a lens and not merely a locus. In other words, [eschatology] affects the way we see everything in scripture rather than only serving as an appendix to the theological system." He also makes a helpful distinction between two types of eschatology: "While eschatology in the narrower sense [as one of the loci of systematics] may be left intact at the conclusion . . . eschatology in the broader sense [is] the form and shape in which redemptive revelation comes." Michael Horton, *Covenant and Eschatology: The Divine Drama* (Louisville: Westminster John Knox, 2002), 5.

[2] Granted, beginning a study of salvation history with an examination of its conclusion is a bit of a unique approach, but there are benefits with starting at the end. Beginning with the consummation of redemptive history accomplishes several things for our current purposes. First and foremost, it highlights the teleological nature of God's presence. When we review this theme from an eschatological perspective, we see that the presence of God actually determines the future goals of redemptive history. God's presence is itself a chief aim and purpose with his redemptive plan. As a consequence, this objective informs numerous aspects of God's redemptive mission because, very simply, the Lord saves in order to dwell in the midst of a people in fullness once again. Second, beginning at the end also helps us know where our final destination lies, which is an indispensible component of any kind of journey, including (and maybe especially) a theological one. In order to understand the *goal* of redemption, we should first know the eschatological "destination" where the Lord will finally realize his salvific aims and, consequently, where his redemptive purposes are most discernible. For examples of other works that have stressed the theological significance of Revelation 21–22, please see William J. Dumbrell, *The End of the Beginning: Revelation 21–22 and the Old Testament* (Eugene, OR: Wipf and Stock, 2001); Dumbrell, *The Search for Order: Biblical Eschatology in Focus* (Grand Rapids: Baker, 1994); T. Desmond Alexander, *From Eden to the New Jerusalem: Exploring God's Plan for Life on Earth* (Nottingham, UK: InterVarsity, 2008).

[3] My approach to eschatology is not only a study of last things, which is the typical usage of this term according to systematic theological categories, but also, to borrow from Gordon Thomas, that eschatology is actually a study of

As you can imagine, Revelation 21–22 carries great theological import.[4] It is the prophetic picture of forthcoming hope and consummation of God's creative and redemptive mission. In a sense, these chapters are the "closing argument" of Scripture; they bring together Scripture's major theological themes and set the stage for the coming realization of the divine promises. This conclusion provides a lens through which we can see the overarching purposes of redemptive history.

It is quite telling, then, that the presence of God lies at the heart of the Bible's conclusion. Here John, describing the fulfillment of God's redemptive purposes, reports:

> Then I saw a new heaven and new earth, for the first heaven and the first earth had passed away, and the sea was no more. And I saw the holy city, new Jerusalem, coming down out of heaven from God, prepared as a bride adorned for her husband. And I heard a loud voice from the throne saying, "Behold, the dwelling place of God is with man. He will dwell with them and they will be his people, and God himself will be with them as their God. He will wipe away every tear from their eyes, and death shall be no more, neither shall there be mourning, nor crying, nor pain anymore, for the former things have passed away." (Rev. 21:1–4)[5]

Graeme Goldsworthy argues that these verses

"ultimate things." Thomas continues: "Biblical scholarship might do better justice to the material in Scripture by defining eschatology as 'the doctrine of ultimate things.' Ultimate reality is not just what will transpire at the end of time, but which has always existed in the heavenlies and which God apparently has always sought to make a present reality." Gordon J. Thomas, "A Holy God among a Holy People in a Holy Place: The Enduring Eschatological Hope," in *Eschatology in Bible and Theology: Evangelical Essays at the Dawn of a New Millennium*, ed. Kent E. Bower and Mark W. Elliott (Downers Grove, IL: InterVarsity, 1997), 55. In sum, eschatology pervades all Scripture from beginning to the end, from Genesis to Revelation, and I will argue that the core of this eschatological purpose is the presence of God. God's eschatological objective from Eden to the new creation was to cover the world and a people with his presence. That is a central strand of the canonical storyline. Thus, Scripture is eschatological throughout, and moreover, this eschatology is concerned with ushering in the presence of God. As Beale maintains, "The apostles understood eschatology not merely as futurology but as a mindset for understanding the present within the climaxing context of redemptive history." G. K. Beale, "The Eschatological Conception of New Testament Theology," in Bower and Elliott, *Eschatology in Bible and Theology*, 17; for other examples of this view on eschatology, see W. D. Davies and D. C. Allison, *The Gospel according to St. Matthew*, vol. 1, ICC (Edinburgh: T&T Clark, 1988), 149–55; D. C. Allison, "Eschatology," in *Dictionary of Jesus and the Gospels*, ed. J. B. Green, S. McKnight, and I. H. Marshall (Downers Grove, IL: InterVarsity, 1992), 206–9; L. J. Krietzer, "Eschatology," in *Dictionary of Paul and His Letters*, eds. G. F. Hawthorne, R. P. Martin, and D. G. Reid (Downers Grove, IL: InterVarsity, 1993), 253–69; G. K. Beale, "Eschatology," in *Dictionary of the Later New Testament and Its Developments*, ed. P. H. Davids and R. P. Martin (Downers Grove, IL: InterVarsity, 1997), 330–45.

[4] I am not trying to argue for levels of importance within God's Word; rather, I am trying to highlight that there is much going on theologically in this text. Moreover, its placement at the end of the Canon should also be understood theologically in that it stands as the last words before our Lord returns.

[5] See also Rev. 7:15; 22:3; and Lev. 26:11–12 for passages articulating this redemptive-historical objective.

sum up and contain the entire message of the Bible. The whole of the history of the covenant and redemption lies behind this glorious affirmation. Every aspect of the hope of Israel—covenant, redemption, promised land, temple, Zion, Davidic prince, new Eden—is woven into this one simple and profound statement: *the dwelling of God is with man.*[6]

These verses are so important to the divine message because they detail the divine objectives God has been revealing to us through his Word.

In particular, John organizes redemption's goals into three main categories: the place (dominion), the people (dynasty), *and* the presence (dwelling) of God.[7] Revelation 21:1–4 tells us that God's redemptive purposes conclude when he is freely and fully manifest in his new creation. Or as Richard Bauckham summarizes, the vision of Revelation 21–22 establishes the "coherent and richly evocative image of a *place* in which the *people* live in the immediate *presence* of God."[8] But we need to go further. These not only are a part of the structure of Revelation 21:1–4 but inform the larger theological purposes of the Lord's overall redemptive mission as well. God works to create a people and a place *for* his presence. That means that all of Scripture is about the Lord's redemptive mission centered on bringing the redeemed to a greater world covered by the presence of God. To understand the significance of the presence of God, we need to follow John's lead and consider the dominion and dynasty of the Lord and, more specifically, how these objectives culminate in the enjoyment and expansion of God's presence.[9]

---

[6] Graeme Goldsworthy, *The Gospel in Revelation: Gospel and Apocalypse* (Carlisle, UK: Paternoster, 1984), 145.

[7] Richard Bauckham, *The Theology of the Book of Revelation* (Cambridge: Cambridge University Press, 1993), 132. The categories of people, place, and presence are simply synonyms for dominion, dynasty, and dwelling, the terms used earlier. Bauckham simply uses the aspect of people, place, and presence to organize his description of the New Jerusalem, but he does not associate them with the eschatological purposes of redemption. And though he stops short of this argument, his thesis would seemingly lead to such conclusions. Concerning the categories themselves, though overlap cannot be avoided, the classification of people, place, and presence greatly benefits our thinking through the structure of Revelation's eschatological objectives and, in a broader sense, the motivation of the redemptive mission as a whole.

[8] Ibid., emphasis added.

[9] I am indebted to Stephen Dempster for his categories of dominion and dynasty, which, he argues, direct and inform the structure of the Hebrew Bible. He maintains that the bracketing books of the Old Testament [Genesis and Chronicles] keep "the main storyline [of the Old Testament] in view with two of its important themes—dynasty and dominion." Stephen G. Dempster, *Dominion and Dynasty: A Theology of the Hebrew Bible*, NSBT 15 (Downers Grove, IL: InterVarsity, 2003), 49. However, the idea of dwelling/presence is not a focus of Dempster, though I hope to show that it too is a central, if not the most necessary, reality for understanding the purposes of God for redemption. This terminology will be used throughout this chapter and will have much bearing on the evaluation of how the presence of God eschatologically informs redemptive history.

The New Creation and the Promise of Dominion

John begins Revelation 21 with a discussion of the eternal location of God's reign, what the prophet terms the "new heaven and new earth." Here, at the end of all things, God promises to remake his world—the old cosmos will pass away, the new earth will come (Rev. 21:1). This new creation will be qualitatively superior to the fallen one we currently occupy. The Lord pledges a radical transformation of the cosmos—a renewal of sorts—that will drastically reform this world into the way it was always supposed to be.[10]

To highlight the distinction between the old creation and the new, John turns to the Old Testament. Like the prophets before him, John describes a coming world so different and so grand that "the former things shall not be remembered or come into mind" (Isa. 65:17). He utilizes ancient symbols to show us that the new heaven and new earth will also be morally superior to this world. For example, when John observes that the sea—a common symbol associated with chaos by the ancients—"was no more" (Rev. 21:1), he is telling us that God will restore his creation not only physically but ethically as well.[11] This image shows us that Yahweh has once and for all conquered the moral and sinful confusion typifying this world.

But John does not stop there. He uses similar allusions and symbols to reveal the masterful work of God that is to come. Physical modifications such as replacing the garden with a city (Rev. 21:2, 9–22) and the

---

[10] Still, the momentous changes resulting from God's redemptive activity do not completely eradicate the first creation. Rather, the Lord makes that which was old and fallen new again (Rev. 21:5). Thus, this new heaven and new earth are best understood as a type of "re-creation," or a "perfection" of the world that once was. A parallel is the resurrection body. There will be great differences in the resurrected body but enough similarities for us to be identified as the people we once were. Similarly, the new world will be radically altered, yet still will be recognizable as the heavens and earth, albeit, a new one. See, in particular, Rev. 21:5 ("I will make all things new"). See A. M. Farrer, *The Revelation of St. John the Divine* (Oxford: Clarendon, 1964), 213; J. P. M. Sweet, *Revelation*, SCM Pelican Commentaries (London: SCM, 1979), 297. See also the use of the Greek term καινός, which usually implies a newness of quality. See Walter Bauer, *A Greek-English Lexicon of the New Testament*, ed. and trans. William F. Arndt, F. Wilber Gingrich, and Fredrick W. Danker, 2nd ed. (Chicago: University of Chicago Press, 1979), s.v. καινός; cf. Gregory K. Beale, *The Book of Revelation: A Commentary on the Greek Text*, New International Greek Testament Commentary (Grand Rapids: Eerdmans, 1999), 1040.

[11] This detail designates that order has been restored to creation. The chaos so often imaged by open waters in the ancient Near Eastern tradition has finally been conquered by Yahweh. Beale is helpful here, again, when he summarizes the apocalyptic symbolism of the sea as follows: "(1) origin of cosmic evil (especially in light of OT background), (2) the unbelieving, rebellious nations who cause tribulation for God's people, (3) the place of the dead, (4) the primary location of the world's idolatrous trade activity, (5) a literal body of water, sometimes mentioned together with 'the earth,' used as a synecdoche in which the sea as a part of the old creation represents the totality of it." Beale then contends that the use of the sea in Rev. 21:1 is not just picking up on one of these ideas but encompasses each of these particular nuances. See Beale, *Book of Revelation*, 1042. For further discussion on this point regarding its ancient Near Eastern and biblical background, please see chap. 2 in Gregory A. Boyd, *God at War: The Bible and Spiritual Conflict* (Downers Grove, IL: InterVarsity, 1997), 73–92.

dissolution of sun, moon (21:23), and night (21:25; 22:5), along with the straightforward declaration that "nothing unclean will ever enter [this city]" (21:27), communicate the surpassing greatness of God's coming new creation over the old.

Each change suggests that the new heaven and earth will be a place purified and prepared for God to dwell with his redeemed people. To make this even more explicit, John uses the imagery of Old Testament sanctuaries of God to detail the new creation. The new heaven and new earth is also the new Eden, the New Jerusalem, and the new temple.[12] By applying these Old Testament realities to the new heaven and new earth, John shows that God's new creation completes and surpasses their former patterns. Thus understood, God's re-creation is more than just a better heaven and earth, or a new setting for the people of God; it is the unmediated and unrestricted dwelling place of God.

NEW CREATION AS PARADISE

Evidence of Genesis 1–3 permeates Revelation 21–22. For example, both reference the waters of life (Gen. 2:10–14; Rev. 22:1–2), the tree of life (Gen. 3:22–24; Rev. 22:2), the precious stones (Gen. 2:11–12; cf. Ezek. 28:13; Rev. 22:18–21), and the presence of God with his people (Rev. 21:3–5, 22–23; 22:4–5). This symmetry signals an important connection between the two locations; namely, the new heaven and new earth completes what the first creation began. John wants us to see that the new creation of Revelation 21–22 is the fully developed Edenic paradise,[13] the garden-city of God encompassing the world.[14] The new creation is "the world in its natural state, rescued from the destroyers of the earth, reconciled with humanity, filled with the presence of God,

---

[12] Though there is great overlap in these classifications, this does not negate their individual emphases evidenced throughout this pericope.

[13] The Latin Vulgate translates the term for "garden of Eden" as *paradises voluptatis*, which roughly translated means a "delightful paradise." Furthering this idea of paradise is its Hebrew homonym meaning "pleasure" and/or "delight" (2 Sam. 1:24; Ps. 36:9; Jer. 51:34; cf. Isa. 51:3; Ezek. 31:9, 16, 18; 36:35). cf. Gordon J. Wenham, *Genesis 1–15*, WBC (Thomas Nelson: Nashville, 1987), 61.

[14] For this reason, I contend that the paradigm for Eden is the New Jerusalem, not vice versa. In other words, the new heaven and new earth was always the end for which Eden was created and for which man was given dominion. The garden of Genesis 1–3 was therefore a testing ground of sorts for the worldwide expansion of God's manifestation. If Adam had lived in continued obedience and worship, the borders and population of Eden would have progressed and developed until it covered the world with the presence of God. But as the familiar story goes, Adam and Eve's transgressions negated any possibility of Edenic cosmological expansion. Instead of enlarging the perimeters of Eden, the boundary lines of the garden were lost forever, ultimately shifting the divine focus from man's rule in creation to God's salvation of man in redemptive history.

and mediating the blessings of eschatological life to humanity."[15] The paradise that was once limited to a small plot of Middle Eastern territory will cover all the earth. With the arrival of the new creation, the Lord will reestablish and restructure a greater paradise where he will freely and fully dwell in the midst of his people once again (Gen. 3:8).

NEW CREATION AS CITY

The new heaven and new earth, however, is not only a new garden paradise, but also a new city. It is the New Jerusalem, the future city of God. By linking this urban image with paradise, John synthesizes the locations of Eden and Jerusalem to demonstrate that this eschatological city fulfills both of their purposes. As people of the garden (Eden) and city of God (Jerusalem), Adam and Israel represent the priests-kings (or kingdom of priests) called to complete the Lord's creative and redemptive purposes. However, the sins of the first man and the nation of God incapacitated the fulfillment of their divinely ordained roles. Because of Adam and Israel's failures, God's presence left both Eden and Jerusalem. Yet, as Revelation 21–22 shows us, God in his covenant faithfulness establishes a better Zion, one that descends from heaven, rests atop the mountain, and will forever be the center of God's relational presence.

NEW CREATION AS TEMPLE

John also tells us that the Jewish tabernacle/temple shares a similar design and structural dimensions with the future heavenly city (Rev. 21:16; cf. 1 Kings 6:20).[16] As with the temple, the measurements and organization of the New Jerusalem[17] are unmistakable indicators of per-

---

[15] Bauckham, *Theology of the Book of Revelation*, 132.

[16] The reason for this correlation is that the New Jerusalem is the model for the temple. As Eden is lost in sin, God graciously provides another option for his presence to be among his chosen, which in this case is the tabernacle/temple institution. Again, just as in the garden, the new format is based on the heavenly Jerusalem, leading to the corresponding realities between John's vision and the other locations of God's presence. All are purposed to be the location of God, the ultimate expression being the new creation and, in particular, the New Jerusalem.

[17] Rev. 21:16 reveals that the New Jerusalem is a perfect square, with dimensions that connect it to the perfect square of the Most Holy Place in the tabernacle and temple. Furthermore, as Fesko makes clear, the connection between the heavenly city and the temple is evident in that the city is "situated on a 'high mountain' (Rev. 21:10), as were the archetypal temple and subsequent worship sites in the Old Testament (Gen. 2:10–14; Ezek. 28:14, 16; Ex. 3:1; Ps. 48:1–2). As the river flowed out to water the garden (Gen. 2:10), so too a pure river of life flows out of the eschatological temple (Rev. 22:1). Likewise the tree of life (Gen. 2:9) reappears in the eschatological temple. . . . The precious stones and metals that adorned the garden-temple, the tabernacle, and Solomon's temple also appear in the eschatological temple (cf. Rev. 21:18–20; Gen. 2:10–14; Ezek. 28:13; Ex. 25:11, 17, 24, 29, 36; 28:7–10)." J. V. Fesko, *Last Things First: Unlocking Genesis 1–3 with the Christ of Eschatology* (Fearn, Ross-shire, UK: Mentor, 2007), 180.

fection and holiness, a feature necessary for any location of God's presence.[18] In addition, the precious stones set in the breastplate of Israel's high priest will also adorn the future city's foundations (Ex. 28:17–20; Ezek. 28:12–13; cf. Isa. 54:11–12).

These parallels are more than happenstance. I believe these connections reveal that the New Jerusalem is the pattern for the earthly tabernacle/temple.[19] Like Eden before it, the temple signified something greater than itself.[20] As the Old Testament temple was "the localized dwelling place of God's presence on earth, the temple's correspondence with the cosmos pointed to an eschatological goal that [Revelation] 21:1–22:5 appears to be developing (see 21:3)."[21] The temple represented the dwelling place of God on earth, but, more importantly, it pointed to a greater fulfillment that is to come. It tells us of a day when the relational presence of God will be unlimited and will pervade not only the Most Holy Place, but the world at large.

The new creation is the true location of God, the place where his presence will dwell eternally with his people. As the better Eden, better Jerusalem, and better temple of the Lord, the new heaven and new earth shows us that God has fulfilled his promise to establish dominion over all creation. Each of these archetypes points forward to a better location of God's presence, a location without moral or physical restrictions. With the establishment of the New Jerusalem, God has finally created the promised place where he will dwell freely and fully in the midst of his people.

The New Creation and the Promise of Dynasty

This new dominion demands a new dynasty. The history of redemption recorded in Scripture concentrates on creating a people of God—or

---

[18] Again, it is important that since the fall, the only way for divinity to be manifest with man is through the divine work of God, which he accomplishes on his own accord. The driving factor for this eschatological provision is again the ushering in of his presence among his people. As Ezek. 48:35 declares, the New Jerusalem is also known by the name "The Lord Is There." The eschatological city is known by his presence and created for his presence. Therefore, the New Jerusalem is the conclusion of the temple, the Most Holy Place—the true and final dwelling place of God.

[19] The New Jerusalem shares a likeness with the temple, which, in my estimation, gains its own architectural makeup from the coming city of God. Therefore, the New Jerusalem is the source of the temple. If this is the case, the new heaven and new earth is and has always been the eschatological goal from the inception of creation. The importance of the temple is found primarily in its earthly representation of what is to come in a fuller sense.

[20] Gordon Wenham contends that "every sanctuary is in some way a replica of the divine heavenly abode," including Eden and the temple as representations of the eschatological sanctuary. Gordon J. Wenham, "Sanctuary Symbolism in the Garden of Eden Story," in *I Studied Inscriptions from before the Flood*, ed. Richard S. Hess and David Toshio Tsumura (Winona Lake, IN: Eisenbrauns, 1994), 401.

[21] G. K. Beale and Sean M. McDonough, "Revelation 21:1–22:5," in *Commentary on the New Testament Use of the Old Testament*, ed. G. K. Beale and D. A. Carson (Grand Rapids: Baker, 2007), 1155.

it might be better to say, a people *for* God.[22] The promise of a holy dynasty guides and shapes much of the divine work in creation and redemption.[23] The Lord acts because he wants a people who will be his own and will worship him; he desires a community of God fearers who rejoice to dwell eternally in his presence (Rev. 22:4).

To fulfill this agenda, God prepares the new heaven and new earth as the residence of a new dynasty filled with the redeemed from every nation. As G. K. Beale observes, "The part of the new creation that John focuses on is the redeemed saints. The vision in 21:2–22:5 is thus dominated by various figurative portrayals of the glorified community of believers."[24] Take, for instance, the names of the Israelite tribes and apostles etched on the gates and foundation of the future holy city (Rev. 21:12–14). This architectural symbol reveals a nationalistic fusion "between tribal 'Israel' and apostolic 'Israel' that builds on the Lord's desire to create for himself a special people."[25] God creates the New Jerusalem to populate it with a holy nation.

The New Creation and the Promise of God's Presence

But why does God establish a place and a people for that place? The short answer is so that God would be present in this place with his people for his glory. In other words, the promises of dominion and dynasty originate from his promise to dwell with them eternally. God creates a place for his presence to reside and a people for his presence to enjoy, all in order that he may receive worship. Remember, the new creation's "location" images—paradise, city, and temple—all symbolize God's being with his people. God creates and redeems a people so that they may reside in his presence forever. This is our highest calling and final hope. So, though God's provisions of a "place" and a "people"

---

[22] The upcoming chapters will demonstrate this genealogical emphasis in more detail.

[23] This eschatological impetus within redemptive history will be covered in more detail in the following sections on Eden, covenants, and Christ. At this point, we can say that the divine pursuit of a people is characteristic of all salvation history and evidenced in the creation narrative in God's forming man in his own image, in the covenant offer to man and the subsequent national fulfillment, in the person and work of Christ, and in the final people of God in the New Jerusalem. Redemption is God's overcoming the alienating effects of sin to provide a new covenant people who enjoy God's presence.

[24] Beale, *Book of Revelation*, 1041. Beale also maintains that the emphasis on the people of God is found throughout Revelation and tied to Old Testament allusions. The connections to Isa. 43:18–19 and 65:17 that are picked up in this chapter are applied in Rev. 21:1, 4–5 and the emphasis on the resurrected and glorified people of God.

[25] G. K. Beale, "Revelation (Book)," in *New Dictionary of Biblical Theology*, ed. T. Desmond Alexander et al. (Downers Grove, IL: InterVarsity, 2000), 359.

are distinct themes of great importance to the future objectives of God, they themselves facilitate a greater purpose: that we may dwell freely and fully in the presence of the Lord.

PRESENCE AND DOMINION

We know this because Revelation 21–22 intimately weds the promise of God's presence with the promise of dominion and dynasty. For instance, John's description of the future "dominion of paradise" emphasizes that the new and better Eden will center on an enhanced experience of God's relational nearness. Eden's sanctuary of divine presence realizes its purpose when the future sanctuary of the new heaven and new earth arrives. Once again the relational presence of God will characterize humanity's experience in the new creation just as it did in the first garden. And though Adam's disobedience and rebellion frustrated the divine purposes initiated in Eden, God, in his rich mercy, responded with the hope of a new location of his presence that John reveals will come to pass in the New Jerusalem.[26]

The dominion of God includes not only Eden but also the city of Jerusalem. John makes it clear that just as the future paradise surpasses the first paradise, so also the New Jerusalem will overshadow the first Jerusalem. At the center of the new city's greatness is the presence of God. This is why John describes the heavenly city's descent upon the mountain (Rev. 21:10; cf. Ps. 48:2; Isa. 2:2–3; 4:1–5; 25:6–26:2; 57:15; Ezek. 20:40; 28:14; 40:2; Micah 4:1–2).[27] Locating the new city of God on the mountaintop echoes the consistent prophetic imagery of the summit range as a meeting place between heaven and earth and between God and man.[28] Remember Sinai? In the desert, God manifested

---

[26] And though this will be detailed more below, it may suffice to say here that the distinguishing characteristic of both the first and the final creations is God's dwelling in the midst of his people (Gen. 3:8; Rev. 21:3–5, 23–24; 22:4; cf. Lev. 26:12; Deut. 23:15; 2 Sam. 7:6–7). For further evaluation, see the forthcoming section "Back to the Beginning: Eden and the Goal of Redemption." Interestingly, 2 Sam. 7:6–7 uses the same verb (הלך) that is used to describe God's walking in the garden, therefore connecting God's presence in the temple with his presence in Eden.

[27] As Greg Beale maintains, "'The angel transported John to a great and high mountain,' probably where the new city-temple was located, since OT prophecy understood the coming Jerusalem as situated on a high mountain." Such prophecy includes Isa. 2:2–3; 4:1–5; 25:6–26:2; 40:9; Ezek. 40:1–2; Mic. 4:1–2; Beale, *Book of Revelation*, 1065.

[28] Bauckham notes that the "cosmic mountain is where heaven and earth meet, where the gods dwell, where sacred cities were built with temples at their heart." Bauckham, *Theology of the Book of Revelation*, 133. This is further indicated in the mountainous inaccessibility that "characterized the abodes of El and Baal in the Ugaritic literature, and we are reminded that the Babylonian temple towers (the ziggurats) embodied the same concept whereby the sanctuary was thought to be the point of contact between the two spheres." William J. Dumbrell, *Covenant and Creation: A Theology of the Old Testament Covenants* (Carlisle, UK: Paternoster, 2002), 102. Significantly, Eden is

himself to his people on the mountaintop.[29] He drew near to Moses to mark out the people of God as his own. So when the prophet details the descent of the heavenly city on the mountain in Revelation 21–22, he reminds us that heaven will once again come down to earth, this time on a much larger scale, so that we may once again rejoice that God is with us.

The presence of God not only is on the top of the mountain but imbues the description of the city of the New Jerusalem as well. For instance, the brilliant light of God's glorious presence illuminates the heavenly city (Rev. 21:11), making the sun and moon superfluous (Rev. 21:23; cf. Isa. 60:1–3, 19–22). John goes further, clarifying that the brightness of God's manifestation consumes the darkness of night in the new eternal city. This day-night motif carries with it moral implications as well. When God completes his redemptive purposes, the pure light of God's presence overcomes the "darkness" of evil, and the "unclean," therefore, has no place in the New Jerusalem (Rev. 21:24–27). Only the holy can reside in the heavenly city; only those clothed in the righteousness of Christ can dwell eternally in the presence of the Almighty.

Even the architecture of the heavenly city highlights the goal of divine nearness. The throne of God and the Lamb, the location of God's presence to govern his kingdom, is the center of the city. Likewise, the river of life—another symbol of divine nearness—flows from the royal throne of God's presence. This imagery reinforces the rule and reign of God while also depicting Yahweh as the everlasting king who draws near to his subjects. Beyond the throne room John describes the city as having no walls, no restraints like the earthly temple's Most Holy Place, no secondary rooms, and no exterior gates. The boundaries once in place in the temple to protect Israel from the consuming presence of God are removed in the New Jerusalem so that God can be present in full to his people. Instead of a temple with its divisions, there is the throne where God and Christ rule without limitations in the midst of their joyful subjects.

---

described in later prophetic writings as a garden mountain (Ezek. 28:13–14), as is the new heaven and new earth (Rev. 21:10).

[29] An argument can be made here that in this image there is a reversal of the tower of Babel account, where man strived to reach the heavens and build his way to divinity (Gen. 11:1–9). With the descent of the New Jerusalem on the mountain the opposite has taken place, namely, God has come down to meet with and manifest himself among the redeemed community.

These vivid descriptions demonstrate, once again, that the New Jerusalem "fulfils the ideal of the ancient city, as the place where heaven and earth meet at the centre of the earth, from which God rules his land and people, to whose attraction the nations are drawn for enlightenment, and in which people live in ideal theocentric community."[30] Again, the descriptions of the heavenly city impress upon us that the promise of dominion serves the larger goal of permanently establishing the eternal setting of the presence of God.

Solomon's temple was the center of the first Jerusalem. Yet even in all its glory the first temple was limited. The presence of God that once resided behind curtains and walls is free to fill the New Jerusalem, making this city the eternal stage of God's unrestricted dwelling with man. For this reason, John makes it clear that there is no temple in the New Jerusalem, but then strangely uses temple imagery to describe the city as a whole. What John wants us to see is that God's presence does not dwell in one place like the temple of old, but fills the whole of the new creation.

To reveal the extension of God's presence, John uses the same term (σκηνή; מִשְׁכָּן) that the Hebrews used to speak of the divine presence in the tabernacle/temple to describe God's place in the New Jerusalem.[31] By applying the temple imagery and vocabulary to the heavenly city, John reveals that the city's temple-like structure completes the pattern of Jerusalem's sanctuary cosmologically. So when John "writes that the tabernacle of God is with us, he is saying that God in his great presence has come to dwell with us . . . and this does not suggest a temporary dwelling [but] . . . from this point on God remains with his people."[32] With the arrival of the new creation, type (temple) gives way to antitype (the New Jerusalem). For this reason, in "John's new Jerusalem, [there is] no symbolic structure [that] can displace the actual visible glory of God dwelling there."[33] Finally, the consummation of this future dominion of God (and as we will see later, the coming incarnation of

---

[30] Bauckham, *Theology of the Book of Revelation*, 132.

[31] As Mounce explains: "The Greek word for tabernacle (σκηνή) is closely related to the Hebrew Shekinah which was used to denote the presence and glory of God. In the wilderness wanderings the tabernacle or tent was a symbol of the abiding presence of God in the midst of his people. In the Fourth Gospel, John writes that the Word became flesh and tabernacled (ἐσκήνωσεν) among people so that they saw his glory, the glory of the One and Only ((John 1:14)." Robert H. Mounce, *Revelation*, NICNT (Grand Rapids: Eerdmans, 1998), 383.

[32] Ibid.

[33] Graeme Goldsworthy, *The Lamb and the Lion: The Gospel in Revelation* (New York: Thomas Nelson, 1994), 145.

Christ) renders the earthly temple's formative expression of the divine presence among God's people obsolete. There is no need for a temple structure because the presence of God fills all the worldwide city of the New Jerusalem

From John's perspective, the temple is not an end in itself but rather a "signpost" that points to its eschatological source.[34] The temple is a limited location of God's presence, one that prefigures the unrestricted presence of God in the New Jerusalem. Bauckham writes, "The radical assimilation of the city to a temple, taken further in Revelation than in its prophetic sources, shows how central to the whole concept of the New Jerusalem in Revelation is the theme of God's immediate presence."[35] And as I will show later in further detail, the temple institution is a microcosm of God's redemptive agenda. While being where the mediated presence of God is, the temple is also a promise pledging the expansion of the Lord's presence throughout the cosmos, a promise complete with the coming arrival of the New Jerusalem. As Beale discerns, "Since the Old Testament temple was the localized dwelling of God's presence on earth, the temple's correspondence with the cosmos pointed to the eschatological goal of God's presence tabernacling throughout the earth, an eschatological goal which Revelation 21:1–22:5 appears to describe."[36] Revelation 21–22, therefore, puts the temple in its proper perspective: it is a small-scale version of what God plans to accomplish cosmologically. And the presence of God, once limited by the curtain of the Most Holy Place, will—just as the end of the Canon depicts—extend to the uttermost parts of the new heaven and new earth.

This is why the heavenly city will have no temple (Rev. 21:22). There will be no need for restrictions or barriers anymore. All of the new heaven and new earth will be the sanctuary of God. All that the earthly location of God's presence signifies, the New Jerusalem will fully realize. The Lord works to provide full access to himself, an ex-

---

[34] From this eschatological perspective, the correlation between the temple and the New Jerusalem exists because the Israelite institution is patterned after the heavenly city. Therefore, I would contend that the new creation, like Eden, informs the structure of the temple rather than vice versa. This is of great consequence because it clarifies that history is progressing toward a new and better world.

[35] Bauckham, *Theology of the Book of Revelation*, 136.

[36] Beale, "Revelation (Book)," 359; cf. G. K. Beale, *The Temple and the Church's Mission: A Biblical Theology of the Dwelling Place of God*, NSBT 17 (Downers Grove, IL: InterVarsity, 2004), 170.

perience once limited to the high priest in the Most Holy Place. In the new creation, however, this experience will be made available to all of us who are graciously granted entrance into the future city of God.[37] The Lord, in his holiness, will no longer be separated from his people as the walls and curtains of the former temple demanded. Redemption will be complete, and God will provide access for us to be present with him in a superior and unrestricted manner (e.g., Rom. 5:2; Eph. 2:18; 3:12; Heb. 10:19–22).

As Revelation 21:3 describes, God will dwell eternally with man. The presence of God floods the New Jerusalem. The purposes of the temple are complete. His radiant glory spreads throughout the new heaven and new earth. His presence fills the future city with unceasing light consuming all darkness (Rev. 21:23). It is here in the New Jerusalem that the Lord finally leads his redeemed back to a better paradise, where God's salvific objectives are complete and the presence of God dwells fully and freely among men. This is the Lord's goal and this is our hope.

PRESENCE AND DYNASTY

As we saw earlier, the promise of place assures the promise of people. The Lord created a kingdom to fill it with citizens marked by his grace and presence. In Revelation 21:3, John portrays God as both king and ruler of a people. As we have already seen, the center of the New Jerusalem is the Lord's throne, the very symbol of his kingly reign (Rev. 22:1, 3).

But why does God establish a people for himself? I think the best answer is that God redeems a people so they may know and draw near to the Lord for their good and for his glory. We must remember that redemption is set within the context of God's presence. From every nation, the Lord chooses a people to receive his gentle and healing governance (Rev. 21:4–5; 22:2). This God-ordained dynasty happily and willingly serves the Creator-Redeemer and rejoices in his eternal and

---

[37] Scripture consistently reveals that the temple institution was never able to contain Yahweh in his fullness (1 Kings 8:27–30; 2 Chron. 2:6; Isa. 66:1; Acts 7:48–49; 17:22ff.). With the "in-breaking" of the new creation, however, all limitations are removed, and God will dwell perfectly and completely with his people. As a result, the New Jerusalem "needs no temple, a special place of God's presence, because the whole city is filled with God's immediate presence." Bauckham, *Theology of the Book of Revelation*, 136. Or as John so aptly puts its, there is no temple in the new creation because "its temple is the Lord God the Almighty and the Lamb" (Rev. 21:22).

glorious reign (Rev. 21:3; 22:5). Part of salvation, therefore, includes the salvation of a people to live in his presence under his rule forever.

Moreover, as manifest ruler of his future kingdom, the Lord will be with his people not simply in proximity but also in relationship. Ruling among his people in the new city of God will afford the redeemed the ability once again to see their divine Creator-king face-to-face and place their identity in him (Rev. 22:3–5). As we have already seen in Revelation 21:3, God declares his purpose for the new creation from his throne, announcing, "Behold, the dwelling place of God is with man. He will dwell with them, and they will be his people, and God himself will be with them as their God." Thus, at the center of God's redemptive purposes is the establishment of a people who will reside permanently in the presence of their Redeemer.[38]

The Presence of God: An Overarching Goal of Redemption

By creating a new place and a new people, God prepares the way for the worldwide expansion of his presence. In other words, the future dominion and future dynasty of God stems largely from the Lord's mission to be relationally present.[39]

The Lord creates a dwelling place and redeems a people so that his relational presence may be enjoyed in a way that we never have experienced before. Thus understood, "it is the presence of God, and the fellowship with him of believers, that constitutes the principal characteristic of the coming age."[40] The promised dominion and dynasty are, therefore, best understood as the *stage* (or scene) and *audience* (or recipients) of God's presence. This is why, I believe, the finale of

---

[38] God does not become present to a people out of need or necessity but rather because it will bring him glory. In Ezekiel 36, God declares that the redemption of Israel is not for the sake of the people (though this is certainly a ramification) but for the sake of his holy name. God will be vindicated so that Israel and the nations will know and worship him as the true and living God (Ezek. 36:22–23; cf. 36:32). Concern for his glory drives the eschatological purposes in creation and, in particular, the covenant response to the curses of sin. Redemptive history is the work of God to make the world his dwelling place, the most beautiful expression of God's glory envisioned. For the sake of his name, Yahweh remains fully committed to the cosmological expansion of his relational presence.

[39] Thus Beale concludes: "The theological point of new creation is to underscore that God's glorious presence will be with his people in a way as never before, when their sin formerly prohibited experience of that presence. The inaugurated new creation in Christ allowed them to begin to experience the intimate presence of God, but only in the consummated new creation will that presence be fully experienced: 'behold, the tabernacle of God is with men, and he will tabernacle with them' (Rev. 21:3), and 'they will see his face, and his name will be on their forehead' (Rev. 22:4)." G. K. Beale, "Eschatological Conception," 28. Beale also argues that the "central biblical ideas of . . . the new temple, new Israel, new Jerusalem, and new creation are metaphorical ideas which refer to the same reality [namely] God's intimate, glorious presence with his people. Beale, "Revelation (Book)," 357–58.

[40] Mounce, *Revelation*, 383.

redemptive history is first and foremost concerned with God's dwelling in our midst.[41]

The presence of God grounds the promises of a dynasty and dominion. This is why the presence of God is the *one* promise fulfilled by divine decree. Whereas Revelation 21:1–2 introduces the new heaven and new earth through observation, verse 3 makes clear that it is God himself who announces the advent of his eternal, unmediated presence. The voice from the throne in verse 3 communicates the purpose of the people and place promised in verses 1 and 2. God creates a people and a place so that he may finally and fully dwell in their midst.

We can conclude, then, that God's desire to be relationally present is a major impetus for his redemptive mission. The whole of God's purposes for the world "reaches its eschatological fulfillment when it becomes the scene of God's immediate presence. This, in the last resort, is what is 'new' about the new creation. It is the old creation filled with God's presence."[42] The dominion of the new heaven and new earth is, therefore, established in order that the presence of God can be in our midst forever.

Back to the Beginning: Eden and the Goal of Redemption

Knowing the end of the biblical storyline brings the rest of the story—especially the beginning—into focus. As our brief reflection on Revelation 21–22 shows, the promises fulfilled in the new creation have far-reaching implications for the biblical drama as a whole, especially its commencement. The connections and similarities between these two creation narratives exist because the same purpose links them: both were designed to bring the presence of God to the world at large.[43]

---

[41] Rev. 21:1–4 also suggests the significance of the presence of God. John's final vision begins with a brief description of the new earth (v. 1) and the new city (v. 2). It quickly shifts however to the throne-room declaration of the presence of God dwelling with his people in the new creation (v. 3). These promises clear the way for the completion of God's eschatological purpose. Simply put, the formation of a new heaven and new earth filled with a nation of redeemed people provides both the location for and the recipients of his relational presence. To enter this pure and holy presence of God demands a pure and holy people and a pure and holy place worthy of such a promise. As a result, both the fallen world and sinful humanity must be re-created and redeemed respectively before God's presence is accessed in full. In the new heaven and new earth, faithful mankind will see the Lord face-to-face (Rev. 22:4) and draw near to the Lord most high (Eph. 2:18; 3:12; Heb. 4:16; 7:19; 7:25; 10:22). Finally, verse 4 continues the emphasis on the presence of God through the record of his requisite blessings. Through the presence of God dwelling amid his people the sadness, death, and the cosmological disorder of the old creation is categorically overcome (Rev. 21:1, 4–8).

[42] Bauckham, *Theology of the Book of Revelation*, 140.

[43] As a result, this eschatological goal is embedded in the overall theological framework of the Canon. Scripture progressively advances toward the purpose of preparing the world to be the divine dwelling place, the location of

Protology (the study of first things) informs eschatology (the study of last things), and vice versa. Or, to put it another way, the beginning of the biblical drama tells us about the biblical drama's end, while the end of the story instructs us on how to read the story's beginning.[44] The end, very simply, is a climactic return to the beginning; it fulfills and surpasses the purposes of Eden. Both paradises share the divine objective of the presence of God, and, what is more, both emphasize the role that the promises of dominion and dynasty play in meeting this divinely directed end.

From a "whole Bible" perspective, the objectives completed in the New Jerusalem find their roots in the fertile ground of Eden.[45] Genesis 1–3 is more than an explanation of the inception of the cosmos; it is the origin of "an extended story that moves from the beginning toward the fulfillment of God's purposes for all creatures and the whole creation."[46] It is clear that Eden "sets the stage for the unfolding of the divine purpose and inaugurates a historical drama within which Israel and, in the fullness of time, the church were destined to play a key role."[47] The first garden of God, rightfully understood, is the starting point for what God consummates in the new creation.[48] It follows then, that—as

God's relational manifestation. This eschatological initiative directs the redemptive mission from commencement to conclusion, and, in a broader context, it is imperative in grasping the theological structure of Scripture itself. Therefore, the redemptive mission is largely concerned with reestablishing the intimate presence of God found in Eden in a fuller and more dynamic sense. The presence of God once lost in the sin of humanity is now found in the new and better Eden, the eschatological conclusion of the Lord's creative and redemptive activity in the fallen world and the new world to come.

[44] Gordon Thomas summarizes: "A fair case can be made for the thesis that eschatology is in good measure, though by no means entirely, a recapitulation of protology. . . . Paradise Regained is . . . a handy way of summarizing how the language and imagery of the final chapters of Revelation clearly owe much to the Eden story in Genesis. The sweep of the biblical narrative begins with God enjoying fellowship with the sinless man He has created in an unsullied environment and ends with the Lord God Almighty and the Lamb living among a holy people in a holy city, from which everyone unclean is excluded." Thomas, "Enduring Eschatological Hope," 56.

[45] Eden is formative for the history of salvation because all the theology of creation influences the progression and advancement of redemptive history. As Dumbrell has argued: "The key to the understanding of the nexus between the theologies of creation and redemption therefore appears to be that in both Testaments redemption presupposes creation theology. Hence the first reflection on the significance of redemption, found in Exodus 15, is presented in terms of standard, ancient Near Eastern creation mythology. Likewise, the redemptive theology of Isaiah 40–55 and the theology of Isaiah 56–66 focus redemptive activity on the goal of the appearance of the new Jerusalem, the new creation. In the NT presentation of redemption, the explicit Christological connection between creation and redemption is clear in passages such as John 1:1–18 and Colossians 1:1–20." William J. Dumbrell, "Genesis 2:1–17: A Foreshadowing of the New Creation," in *Biblical Theology: Retrospect and Prospect*, ed. Scott J. Hafemann (Downers Grove, IL: InterVarsity, 2002), 65.

[46] Bernhard W. Anderson, *Contours of Old Testament Theology* (Minneapolis: Fortress, 1999), 92.

[47] Bernhard W. Anderson, *From Creation to New Creation: Old Testament Perspectives* (Minneapolis: Fortress, 1994), 25.

[48] This is summarized when one scholar writes: "The Garden of Eden is not viewed by the author of Genesis simply as a piece of Mesopotamian farmland but as an archetypal sanctuary, that is a place where God dwells and where man worships him. . . . These parallels suggest that the garden itself is understood as a sort of sanctuary." Wenham, "Sanctuary Symbolism," 399–404. Cf. Wenham, *Genesis 1–15*, 41–91; Alexander, *Eden to the New Jerusalem*, 13–73;

we saw in the new creation—the presence of God is also the defining reality of Eden.

The garden represents the way the world was supposed to be and what the world could have been had it not been for sin. Eden was never to be limited to that small territory at the convergence of the Havilah, Gihon, Cush, Tigris, and Euphrates rivers. Paradise was to follow the waters and extend beyond its initial borders; it was to be "a kind of proto-temple that was to be expanded to cover the whole earth."[49] From beginning to end, the biblical plotline is about the expansion of the garden-sanctuary's boundaries and with it the presence of God to the entire world. This central redemptive purpose drives creation and, as we have already seen, will be complete in the new heaven and new earth. The promise of the presence of God, therefore, is not just a divine response to Adam's fall; it informs the reason and hopes of both creation and redemption from beginning to end.

The Way It Was Supposed to Be: The Future Aim of Creation

As touched on above, Eden is the pattern of the better Eden to come. From an eschatological point of view, the garden of God was to be the seat of the worldwide expansion of God's dwelling place.[50] As Wil-

---

T. Desmond Alexander and Simon Gathercole, eds., *Heaven on Earth: The Temple in Biblical Theology* (Carlisle, UK: Paternoster, 2004); Beale, *The Temple and the Church's Mission.*

[49] Beale and McDonough, "Revelation 21:1–22:5," 1155. For further works that argue for the garden of Eden as temple-sanctuary see Beale, *Temple and the Church's Mission*; Meredith G. Kline, *Kingdom Prologue: Genesis Foundations for a Covenantal Worldview* (Overland Park, KS: Two Age, 2000); Wenham, "Sanctuary Symbolism," and Vern S. Poythress, *The Shadow of Christ in the Law of Moses* (Brentwood, TN: Wolgemuth & Hyatt, 1991).

[50] Many scholars have been infatuated with the symbolic correlations that exist between Eden and the Israelite temple (e.g., M. Weinfeld, "Sabbath, Temple, and Enthronement of the Lord—The Problem of the *Sitz im Leben* of Gen. 1:1–2:3," in *Melanges bibliques et orientaux en l'honneur de M. Henri Cazelles*, ed. A. Caquot and M. Delcor (Kevelaer, Ger.: Butzon and Becker, 1981). Much ink has been spilled on this topic, and biblical theology as a whole is better for it. However, often lost in the emphasis on the Eden-temple correlation is the eschatological focus that ultimately determines the function of both divine spaces. The garden is, in all actuality, more than just the pattern for all the subsequent tabernacle/temples in Israel; it is a microcosm of the new creation that John describes in full. It is important to realize that Eden and the temple are always pointing to something greater and never portrayed biblically as ends in themselves. So, to highlight the eschatological emphasis of both institutions, I would argue that the garden *and the temple* find their source not merely in each other, but rather in the new heaven and new earth. What is important to realize is that both the temple and the garden still share the same objective: the cosmological expansion of God's presence. This eschatological purpose has been in place from the beginning of creation and is not just a provisional response to human disobedience. Instead, the garden and the temple are designed on the basis of the new heaven and new earth. They share the template of the coming future-city of Zion. The design for Eden, therefore, is eschatological, and so is the temple structure. Both of these locations of God's presence are prototypes of the New Jerusalem, the final and perfect dwelling place of God. Eden and the temple represent the earthly centers of expansion by which God's presence will cover all of creation. For further treatment of the correlation between Eden and the temple, please see T. Desmond Alexander, *From Paradise to the Promised Land: An Introduction to the Pentateuch* (Grand Rapids: Baker Academic, 2002), 131–32; Beale, *Temple and the Church's Mission*, 66–80; Dumbrell, "Foreshadowing," 57–61; Paul R. Williamson, *Sealed with an Oath: Covenant in God's Unfolding Purpose*, NSBT 23 (Downers Grove, IL: InterVarsity, 2007), 49–51.

liam Dumbrell writes, "Eden is the representation of what the world is to become."[51] Likewise, Willem VanGemeren concludes: "The garden of Eden is a prototype of the world planned by God."[52] Genesis 1–3 is, in one sense, an ancient microcosm of Revelation 21–22; it is the "signpost" that points forward to the worldwide dispersion of God's relational presence.[53]

As in the new creation, the distinguishing feature of Eden is the presence of God dwelling with his people in a temple-like paradise. The garden, as Genesis describes, "is presented as a divine sanctuary—a place in which the immediacy of God's presence is experienced and enjoyed."[54] Meredith Kline explains:

> God produced in Eden a microcosmic version of his cosmic sanctuary. The garden planted there was holy ground. . . . Eden had the character of a holy tabernacle, a microcosmic house of God. And since it was God himself who, present in his theophanic Glory, constituted the Edenic temple, man in the Garden of God could quite literally confess that Yahweh was his refuge and the Most High was his habitation.[55]

Being a type of sanctuary, the garden is a place where God and man enjoy close fellowship; Adam and Eve are able to relate with God and stand in his presence with no inhibitions. So we clearly see, from the beginning of the Canon on, that Eden is "the centre of world blessing" where the "total blessing focus is thrown upon the experience of the

---

[51] William J. Dumbrell, *The Faith of Israel: A Theological Survey of the Old Testament*, 2nd ed. (Grand Rapids: Baker Academic, 2002), 20.

[52] Willem VanGemeren, *The Progress of Redemption: The Story of Salvation from Creation to the New Jerusalem* (Grand Rapids: Baker, 1988), 64. Along the same lines, Eugene Merrill argues that "we refer to the garden as a microcosm of the universe, a sacred space where man and woman first encountered the Lord according to the record." Eugene H. Merrill, *Everlasting Dominion: A Theology of the Old Testament* (Nashville: Broadman & Holman, 2006), 279–80. Cf. Walther Eichrodt, *Theology of the Old Testament*, vol. 1, trans. J. A. Baker (Philadelphia: Westminster, 1961), 102–7.

[53] Dumbrell appears to support the eschatological import of the garden narrative when he writes, "In Genesis 2 we find a preliminary picture of the end of the age, in which redeemed humanity experiences eternal and indefectible fellowship with the Creator." Dumbrell, "Foreshadowing," 65. See also Merrill, *Everlasting Dominion*, 284–87.

[54] Williamson, *Sealed with an Oath*, 49. Making his case that the garden of Eden is a sanctuary, Williamson cites the historical context, stating that "'gardens' (i.e. botanical gardens or parks rather than the domestic variety) were a common feature of ancient Near Eastern temples, and it is therefore not surprising that many of the features of Eden are echoed in the tabernacle and the temple. The key aspect of Eden is its role as a divine sanctuary" (ibid., 50). J. V. Fesko argues that the correspondence between the garden and the tabernacle/temple implies that Eden is a sanctuary. He writes, "Considering [Eden's] features (location in the east on a mountain, river, tree of life, precious stones and metal, cherubim, God's presence and creation of the garden, man's responsibilities and post-fall vestments), there is significant evidence that confirms the garden's temple status." Fesko, *Last Things First*, 73.

[55] Meredith G. Kline, *Images of the Spirit* (Eugene, OR: Wipf and Stock, 1998), 35–37.

divine presence."[56] From the very outset of the biblical drama, God's presence has been a prominent theme.

This is because our enjoyment of his presence has always been God's objective, even from the outset of creation. The sanctuary of Eden constantly points to something bigger and better than itself. In a broader redemptive context, Eden is never meant to remain a small plot of land in Mesopotamia.[57] Again, God creates the garden so that it will encompass the whole world and, with it, so will the relational presence of God.[58] Thus T. D. Alexander helps us see once again, "The opening chapters of Genesis enable us to reconstruct God's blueprint for the earth. God intends that the world should become his dwelling place."[59] This, I believe, is why John so often draws upon Edenic imagery to detail his account of the end of all things. By doing so he shows us that the arrival of the new heaven and new earth concludes God's agenda started long ago in the first garden. He "intends to show that God's redemption finally returns the new Jerusalem, the New Creation, to the Garden of Eden and to the Creator's intentions for humanity."[60] From an eschatological perspective, then, Eden was always to become the new creation before there was ever a need for a "new" creation.

---

[56] Dumbrell, *Covenant and Creation*, 35–36. Dumbrell contends that the presence of God is the defining and all-satisfying reality of Eden based on the way Genesis 2 turns the material values of this world on its head. He writes, "The objects upon which man in our present world places extreme value (i.e. the gold and precious stones of Gen. 2:12) and towards which his energies are bent in the endeavour to secure them, were to be found outside the garden, but not within it." Accordingly, this would seem to imply that the real value of Eden—and that which was the ultimate blessing of God's teleological ends as well—was and will always be that which defines this location, namely, the presence of God. The rampant materialism that defines the world is a result of the fall and sinful man's inability to recognize the real value of relationship with God. Therefore, lost in the search for earthly treasure is the eschatological blessings of being eternally in the presence of God, which, when fully understood, outshines anything an object could offer.

[57] Dumbrell describes Eden as the "axis mundi, the point from which the primal stream radiates to the four quarters of the world." Dumbrell "Foreshadowing," 58. It would seem then that Eden's great rivers underscore the garden's eschatological mission of cosmological expansion. The waters pouring forth from Eden symbolized the presence of God reaching out into the world around it in influence and rule. Through the flow of the rivers, the presence of God will spread over the face of the earth.

[58] The description of the garden in Genesis 2 reveals that it is separate from the world around it. The Hebrew word for garden (גַּן) most often refers to a bordered location or enclosure that can include a wall, hedge, or some kind of barrier (cf. 2 Kings 25:4; Neh. 3:15; Jer. 39:4; 52:7). By way of implication it would seem that Eden is separate from the world but driven by the divine mandate to subsume the rest of creation under its protection. As Dumbrell writes, "The garden of Genesis 2 is to be viewed as a special, localized place that is spatially separated from its outside world," and this external realm "needs to be brought under the dominion of the divine rule for which Eden is the model." Dumbrell, "Foreshadowing," 56. See also the Hebrew word גָּנַן, which means to cover, protect, enclose, fence, according to *Lexicon in Veteris Testamenti Libros*, ed. L. Köehler and W. Baumgartner (Leiden: E. J. Brill, 1958), 190.

[59] Alexander, *Eden to the New Jerusalem*, 26. Furthering the teleological purpose of Eden, Alexander goes on to connect this primordial vision with the eschatological vision of John when he states, "Remarkably, this blueprint is eventually brought to completion through the New Jerusalem envisaged in Revelation 21–22."

[60] Pilchan Lee, *The New Jerusalem in the Book of Revelation: A Study of Revelation 21–22 in the Light of Its Background in Jewish Tradition* (Tübingen: Mohr Siebeck, 2001), 292.

The Future Purpose of the Divine Mandate

Genesis 1–3, therefore, casts the vision for God's future objectives. The garden was never to be a static reality; instead, it was always meant for progression and growth. Eden was to encompass the whole world. Or as Alexander puts it, "God's original blueprint is for the whole earth to become a temple-city filled with people who have a holy or priestly status."[61] This "temple-city" designation, of course, is an apt description of the New Jerusalem, but it is important to remember that this was Eden's future at one time. The garden was the sanctuary of God. Adam was his priest-king, who was to administer the rule and bring the presence of the Lord to the rest of the world.[62]

To accomplish the cosmological expansion of his presence, Yahweh instituted the "creation mandate." More than just a move to keep Adam busy and engaged, the creation mandate is where God implemented his vision for Adam to accomplish the following: (1) Adam was to exercise dominion and authority in his rule over God's creation (Gen. 1:27–31; 2:15), and (2) Adam was to procreate and produce offspring with Eve to fill the garden and, then, the world (Gen. 1:28). By issuing the command, the Lord called Adam to establish a dominion and dynasty that would cover the earth with his Creator's relational presence.[63]

THE DOMINION OF ADAM

Adam was more than just a farmer; Adam's call to subdue the earth had an eschatological, or future, goal.[64] Adam was God's vice-regent, meaning that the first man was the Lord's representative in creation.[65] Under

---

[61] Alexander, *Eden to the New Jerusalem*, 30.

[62] The priestly status and function of Adam will be addressed in the following section, "The Dominion of Adam."

[63] In the divine prerogative, God's purposes still affected man. So although the completion of the divine promises comes through God himself, man still plays a major role in their fulfillment. Even after the fall, God still graciously calls us to be the instruments of his will and mission. God has always seen fit to incorporate man in his divine purposes. Just as he called believers to be involved in the spread of the gospel, he has also allowed believers to play a part in the spread of his relational presence. This continues from Adam to the church today (e.g., 1 Cor. 3:16–23; 6:12–20; 2 Cor. 6:14–18; Eph. 2:11–22).

[64] In Gen. 1:28, the Hebrew word כבש emphasizes the importance of Adam's call to dominion. Its usage throughout the Old Testament indicates God's continued work through humanity, as well as his commitment to his eschatological purposes. Even though this was adversely affected by the fall, the command to exercise dominion still applied after Eden was lost. The term is also used to describe the call to rule Canaan (Num. 32:22–29; Josh. 18:1), David's dominion over the spoils of his enemies (2 Sam. 8:11), and the Israelites' final subjugation of their enemies (Zech. 9:15). Thus it would appear that a chief aspect of man's dominion is eschatological in nature and, more specifically, points to the future seed (Gen. 3:15) of Abraham who will complete the divine mandate in perfection.

[65] As Williamson summarizes, Adam's "position of power and authority is clearly reflected in the . . . divine mandate: 'subdue' and 'exercise dominion' (Gen. 1:28). Thus it would appear that humankind is created as God's vicegerent: to reign in a manner that demonstrates his lordship over creation." Williamson, *Sealed with an Oath*, 46.

the headship of Yahweh, then, Adam was to rule and reign in Eden as the image bearer and steward of God. He was, in a sense, the king who sat on the throne of creation until the true King would take his place of authority once and for all.

God's mandate for Adam to exercise dominion over creation also shows that the first man was to fill a priestly role as well.[66] As Paul Williamson observes: "Adam is portrayed as a priest in Genesis 2, just as he is portrayed as a king in Genesis 1. Hence Adam and Eve were made kings and priests to serve God, and Eden is the model or prototype for what the world was to become."[67] Thus, the first man "exercised dominion over nature by worship and service in the divine presence."[68] Interestingly, the Hebrew terms to describe Adam's work of dominion in Genesis 2:15 (עבד and שמר) are the same words used to describe the tasks of the Levites and the priests in the tabernacle and temple (e.g., Num. 3:7–8; 8:25–26; 18:5–6; 1 Chron. 23:32; Ezek. 44:14; cf. Isa. 56:6; Rev. 22:4).[69]

So as we think about Adam's role within the context of all Christian Scripture, he quickly goes from mere gardener to a great priest-king. His work to rule the land foreshadows the Israelite ideal of being a kingdom of priests (Ex. 19:6; Deut. 7:6; 1 Pet. 2:5–9; Rev. 1:6; 5:10), for it was Adam who was to stand and administer the presence of God to his world. As Dumbrell explains, the first man was "the priest-king, who exercised dominion over nature by worship and service in the divine presence."[70] So throughout the creation narrative, Adam mediated the presence of God first to Eden and then to the rest of the world.

---

[66] See Beale, *Temple and the Church's Mission*, 66; Fesko, *Last Things First*, 71, 75.

[67] Williamson, *Sealed with an Oath*, 49.

[68] Dumbrell, *Search for Order*, 25.

[69] The same words that describe Adam's work in the garden (*cultivate* and *keep*) are also used to describe the priestly work of the temple. As Beale writes, "The two Hebrew words for 'cultivate and keep' are usually translated 'serve and guard [or keep]' in the rest of the Old Testament. . . . When these two words (verbal ['ābad and šāmar] and nominal forms) occur together in the Old Testament (within an approximate 15-word range) they refer either to Israelites 'serving' God and 'guarding [keeping]' God's word or to priests who 'keep' the 'service' (or charge) of the tabernacle (see Num. 3:7–8; 8:25–26; 18:5–6; 1 Chron. 23:32; Ezek. 44:14)." *Temple and the Church's Mission*, 67. And as Wenham comments: "The verb עבד is a very common verb and is often used of cultivating the soil ([Gen.] 2:5; 3:23; 4:2, 12, etc.) The word is commonly used in a religious sense of serving God (e.g., Deut. 4:19), and in the priestly texts, especially of the tabernacle duties of the Levites. . . . Similarly, (שמר) 'to guard, to keep' has the simple profane sense of 'guard' ([Gen.] 4:9; 30:31), but is even more commonly used in legal texts of observing religious commands and duties (17:9; Lev. 18:5) and particularly of the Levitical responsibility for guarding the tabernacle from intruders (Num. 1:53; 3:7–8). It is striking that here and in the priestly law these two terms are juxtaposed (Num. 3:7–8; 8:26; 18:5–6), another pointer into the interplay of tabernacle and Eden symbolism." Wenham, *Genesis 1–15*, 67. Thus, these later Old Testament uses of the same terms seemingly link Eden with the sanctuary of God, a location where the presence of God is experienced. See also Beale, *Temple and the Church's Mission*, 66–70.

[70] Dumbrell, *Search for Order*, 25.

A large part of the divine mandate, then, consisted of Adam's working to bring the presence of God to the rest of creation.

Adam's "subduing and ruling" work in the garden was about the distribution of God's presence. Adam was to expand the borders of Eden to cover the rest of the world. So Beale writes, "It is plausible to suggest that [Adam and Eve] were to extend the geographical boundaries of the Garden until Eden extended throughout and covered the whole earth."[71] As the borders would go out, so too would the boundary markers of God's presence. The garden-sanctuary was to develop in both size and structure through the creation mandate. Eden was the divine dwelling place *planted* (נטע) by God (Gen. 2:8). It was a living thing. Yahweh intended Eden to grow exponentially.

So, as the creation mandate of Genesis 1:28 insists, Adam was to subdue the *whole* earth—not just the garden. He was called to have dominion over everything—"over the fish of the sea and over the birds of the heavens and over every living thing that moves on the earth" (Gen. 1:28). God made it clear that Adam's reign was to be worldwide when he told his image bearer that "*every* plant yielding seed that is on the face of *all* the earth, and *every* tree with seed in its fruit," "*every* beast of the earth and to *every* bird of the heavens and to *everything* that creeps on the earth, *everything* that has the breath of life" would be under the dominion of Adam (Gen. 1:29–30). The refrain of the words "all," "every," and "everything" tells of Adam's holistic dominion. God emphatically told Adam and tells us that the rule of man covers the entire world, and the origin point of that rule was the first garden. Eden was only the *beginning* of Adam's dominion. Through the first man's obedience and care, this temple-garden was to flourish and, with it, the sanctuary of the Lord's presence would broaden to the ends of the earth.

THE DYNASTY OF ADAM

The dominion of God's presence was also to grow with the proliferation of Adam's dynasty. Simply put, the more priest-kings in Adam's genealogical line, the quicker God's presence would expand to the rest of the world. As Williamson suggests,

---

[71] G. K. Beale, "Final Vision of the Apocalypse and Its Implications for a Biblical Theology of the Temple," in Alexander and Gathercole, *Heaven on Earth*, 201.

The first aspect of the divine instruction recorded here is clearly linked to the second; human procreation (i.e. multiplication of the divine-image bearers) and populating the earth are imperative for the second aspect to be carried out as divinely intended (i.e. God wants his rule—as represented by humanity—to spread throughout the whole earth).[72]

Just as Edenic expansion was to come through Adam's rule, it was also to come through *his descendants.*

In this light, the Lord's command to be fruitful and multiply has an eschatological purpose (Gen. 1:28; cf. 9:1, 7; 16:10; 17:2; 22:17; 26:4, 24; Lev. 26:9; Deut. 6:3; etc.).[73] It is for this end that we were made: to delight in and grow the dominion of the presence of God. If Adam had remained obedient, the population of Eden would have multiplied, and the borders of the garden-city would have needed to increase. In addition, there would have been more people in Eden working similarly to bring God's presence to the rest of the world. In other words, the divine command to multiply "impl[ies] that the boundaries of the garden will be extended to fill the whole earth as human beings are fruitful and increase in number."[74] And, with the growth of Adam's dynasty, the garden of God's relational presence would also have expanded its borders.[75] As Adam's descendants grew, so too would Eden have grown, resulting eventually in the whole world's becoming the dwelling place of God.

Conclusion

Redemptive history has objectives, and one of the chief objectives is the presence of God. Genesis and Revelation both demonstrate this to be true. The story begins with a garden where the Lord is present with

---

[72] Williamson, *Sealed with an Oath*, 46.

[73] The dynastic promise, like that of dominion, will also be reappropriated in the covenant promises. This will be addressed more fully in the following sections, but here it is helpful to note that the call to be fruitful and multiply begins in creation and continues even after the fall. This highlights the fact that the eschatological ends of creation are not undone in the fall. Though there are severe consequences, God remains faithful to his mission to bring his relational presence to bear upon the whole world. But there is also a subtle change to the dynastic promise that takes place between Adam and Abraham. The command once given to Adam to fulfill is now God's to complete ("I am God Almighty; walk before me, and be blameless, *that I may make my covenant between me and you, and may multiply you greatly*" [Gen. 17:1–2]). And though God is the one who completes the promise of dynasty and dominion, he has yet to give up on man and continues to incorporate him in his purposes.

[74] Alexander, *Eden to the New Jerusalem*, 25.

[75] Williamson, *Sealed with an Oath*, 49.

Adam and Eve. The story ends with a new heaven and new earth where the Lord is present among a

> ransomed people for God
> from every tribe and language and nation. (Rev. 5:9)

What Eden was in potential, the New Jerusalem is in full. The promised dominion of God's presence that the Lord established in the garden and commanded Adam to extend to the whole world meets its fulfillment in the new creation. The promised dynasty that the Lord began with Adam will reach completion when we, as part of God's people, stand in the presence of God forever in the new heaven and new earth.

As Genesis and Revelation show us, God creates a people and a place, but this people and place are not ends in themselves. Instead, the promise of a dominion and dynasty is much more. The new heaven and new earth is the location of God's eternal, unrestricted dwelling, and the people of God are those who will revel in his divine presence forever. So when we read about the beginning of God's work in creation and catch a glimpse of God's finished work of redemption, we see time and time again that the presence of God is at the center of it all. The Lord begins and ends the history of redemption with his *presence* because the expansion and enjoyment of his own *presence* for his *glory* is a central mission of God. Not only does the presence of God affect the beginning and end of Scripture; it also influences all of the biblical story, as we will see in the next chapter.

4

Conflict and Covenant

The Story's Turn and the Presence of God

Like mountaintops ascending above the mist, Genesis and Revelation afford us with spectacular views of God's presence. As we saw in the last chapter, God who was relationally present with his people in the garden of Eden will one day be with his people again in the garden-city of the New Jerusalem. This is at the very crux of what the Creator has done and is doing in his world. Genesis and Revelation make this abundantly clear. The biblical bookends spotlight the presence of God, clarifying for us that God's desire to be with his people is no mere fleeting wish or whim; it is a divine objective that inherently structures the beginning and end of Scripture's story.

Yet, just as the biblical plot opens and closes with God's presence, this theme deeply influences the rest of the story as well. This is why the perspective of Genesis and Revelation is so consequential: when we see the presence of God lost at the beginning of Scripture and then restored at Scripture's end, we quickly recognize that this divine goal is formative for the whole drama. From our view atop these two biblical peaks, we have a crucial point of orientation for our journey across the rest of the biblical landscape. The panoramic views of Genesis and Revelation will no doubt help us recognize the landmarks of God's presence dispersed throughout the rest of the Scriptures, leading us from Eden to the new heaven and new earth.

The Curses of Sin: Obstructing the Objectives of Redemptive History

But there was one tiny problem facing Adam. Well, make that a major, monumental disaster that barred him and his descendants from the presence of God seemingly forever. As the familiar story goes, Adam rebelled against his Creator and, in doing so, failed to accomplish his God-given mission of bringing the garden paradise to the world at large. As a consequence, the creation project fell into demise, affecting the future trajectory of the garden-sanctuary from this point forward.

By the end of Genesis 3, Adam is in sin and, consequently, cast from the special place of God's relational presence and fellowship. Such "disobedience led to the alienation from God, as Adam and Eve are exiled from the garden (and hence from God and their source of life); to alienation from each other, as the dynamics of their relationship changed; and to alienation from the created world with its thorns and thistles."[1] In short, everything has changed. Adam's sin has made his Creator and sustainer a stranger. Adam, who once freely approached God, now runs and hides from the Lord. Adam's rebellion denies "humankind the further possibility that Eden held out: that humankind might develop and deepen the relationship by which life in God's presence would be retained."[2] Adam, now separated from God, finds himself separated from his purpose and mission—expelled from the location of God's presence, the very place he was called to expand and enlarge.[3]

It is very telling, then, that when the Lord curses his vice-regent, the penalties of Adam's sin parallel Adam's mission. The curses poured out upon the first couple include (1) pain in childbirth (Gen. 3:16), (2) futility in Adam's work (3:17–19), and (3) removal from Eden and the presence of the Lord (3:22–24). From a redemptive-historical perspective, God responds to Adam and Eve's rebellion by cursing their role in creation. God curses Adam's dominion over the earth; the Lord then turns to Eve and makes childbirth nearly unbearable, thereby cursing the possibility of establishing a dynasty; and finally the Lord concludes

---

[1] Paul R. Williamson, *Sealed with an Oath: Covenant in God's Unfolding Purpose*, NSBT 23 (Downers Grove, IL: InterVarsity, 2007), 50.
[2] William J. Dumbrell, *The Search for Order: Biblical Eschatology in Focus* (Grand Rapids: Baker, 1994), 26.
[3] Please note that these universal purposes of cosmological expansion of the divine presence were from the outset to be completed not by the first Adam, but by Jesus Christ, the second Adam, all in order to glorify God.

his curse by expelling his image bearers from Eden, the dwelling place of his presence. As the curses make quite clear, sin impairs every aspect of Adam, including his relationships, his own identity as God's priest-king, and his function and missional purpose in God's creation.

We see very quickly that the curses are by no means arbitrary; instead they are divinely applied to disrupt and inhibit Adam's ability to experience and expand the dwelling place of God. In a simple act of disobedience, man self-sabotages his rule over the land and his propagation of a people. Once a privilege, man's call to subdue the earth and fill it with many generations turns into a source of hardship and misery. And on top of all this, man faces his self-inflicted punishment of both natural and spiritual death—a sentence that starts with his separation from God and ends in his return to the dust. As God righteously responds to Adam's insurrection, the very objectives God has instilled in creation and the certainty of the worldwide dispersal of his presence are threatened and risk abandonment.

But as we know, God is greater than his creation's apostasy. We recognize this when we assess his reaction to Adam's disobedience. At first look, it seems that God's curses are simply harsh punishments doled out by a stern Deity. Some of us may even think—subconsciously—God was being *too* harsh with the first man. Most of us would never say this out loud—our Sunday school teachers would be very displeased—but it might implicitly twist our understanding of the Lord, ourselves, and, finally, our salvation (e.g., who needs saving when we really weren't that bad to begin with, right?). My hope is that we have a broader understanding of Adam's rebellion and the Lord's response to it. We are culpable. Adam's sin distorted the whole universe, hung up the great curtain in the temple, and dug the hole for the coming cross of Christ. But there is more to the curses than judgment—there is also promise. Grace and hope motivate God's righteous judgment of Adam's transgression. Strange as it may sound, the curses that God issues for our punishment are also for our *good*, and we need to understand both.

The Geography Curse

To do this, let's start with the land. Responding to Adam's sin, God curses the ground, which, of course, obstructs Adam's call to exercise dominion over the earth (Gen. 3:17). The previously fertile soil that produced Eden, strewn with abundant trees and delectable fruit, yields thorns and thistles now irrigated by the sweat of Adam's brow (Gen. 2:8–14, 16; 3:17–19). As a result of the fall, what "characterizes the relationship [between man and the ground] is hardship, pain, toil, and distress ([*toil, pain*] signifies both physical and emotional suffering, i.e., pain and sorrow)."[4] What was once a pleasurable vocation is now agonizing labor.

Without question, God curses Adam's divinely ordained mission of subduing the land and exercising dominion over it. Therefore, the "earth curse" signifies more than just difficult work; it confirms that God will restrain Adam's governance. Like its vice-regent, the earth is now in decay and subjected to futility (see Rom. 8:18–25). By cursing the ground, God thwarts Adam's mission to expand the borders of Eden.[5] Because of the intrusion of sin, Adam must work a land alienated from God and his blessing. Without the grace of God, the first man faces certain death and the eternal distortion of his role and purpose.

The Genealogy Curse

Along with the loss of earthly dominion, the ancestral line of the once-consecrated priest-king of Eden is also in jeopardy. For the Adamic line to spread exponentially as it is supposed to, Eve must now, under the curse of sin, overcome the overwhelming pain of childbirth. As a consequence of her rebellion, God declares, "I will surely multiply your pain in childbearing; in pain you shall bring forth children" (Gen. 3:16a).[6] So from that day forward, Eve and her daughters' labor becomes exactly that: labor.[7] Here again, God curses one of the key functions of

---

[4] Dumbrell, *Search for Order*, 28.

[5] It can be assumed that God's cursing Adam's ability to rule the earth also includes God's desire to prohibit the spread of sin. In his rebellion, Adam shows his propensity to pursue his own wishes and own glory. With the power to rule and reign, and the desire to make much of himself, the final result of Adam's life would be even more catastrophic than it has already become in his rebellion. Through his ability to exercise dominion he would be tempted to usurp God by pursuing his own purposes in creation rather than working to spread the glory of God throughout the world. God's immediate remedy to this is to impede Adam's ability to rule the land, whereas the redemptive remedy is found in the divine promise to provide a second Adam who would overcome the first's rebellion through perfect obedience and regain the eschatological objectives set out in Eden through his death, burial, and resurrection.

[6] In Gen. 3:16b, the woman's role as helper to the vice-regent is also frustrated. Ironically, the man who is called to rule over creation now must rule over his wife—the very one who was made to help him rule over creation. Rather than assisting him as he carries out his stewardship, she begins to challenge and resist him.

[7] The curse of labor ties the punishment of sin to the divine mandates of the garden. To reproduce life is the calling of the woman. This is her role in establishing the dynasty of Adam. Thus the application of this curse to

the couple's cultural mandate. With one bite of forbidden fruit, Adam impairs his ability to generate a population that will bring the Lord's relational presence to the whole world.

The Separation Curse

Genesis 3:23–24 threatens many of the promises laid out in Genesis 1–2. God took paradise and its end-time objective away from his image bearer when he "sent [Adam] from the garden of Eden" and "drove out the man" from his immediate relational presence. Before any of God's worldwide purposes were realized, the Lord exiled Adam from Eden, the sanctuary-like location of God's presence. Adam, the one made to experience and relate to the holy and sovereign Lord, now stands separated from his Creator and his calling. Not only is Adam's dominion and dynasty in jeopardy; so too is his relationship with God. At the end of Genesis, Adam stands in the cold, separated from the presence of the Lord, the one who created and defined Adam's existence and purpose.

As a result of the first couple's sin, the Lord puts up the no vacancy sign in Eden and denies Adam's privileged access to the tree of life (Gen. 3:22). God abolishes all semblance of humanity's rule and expansion of the garden-sanctuary. In one swift act, the Lord replaces Adam with the cherubim,[8] who, in an ironic twist, are charged with keeping Adam, the original guardian and protector of Eden, from reentering

---

childbirth is an "appropriate punishment since procreation was central to her divine commission." Kenneth A. Mathews, *Genesis 1–11:26*, NAC (Nashville: Broadman & Holman, 2002), 249. David J. A. Clines is also helpful here as he seeks to answer the question, "What does Adam need Eve's help to do?" Clines's response is quite simple and informative: Adam needs Eve to fulfill the divine mandate of Gen. 1:28 to be fruitful and multiply in order to fill the earth. Clines rightfully argues: "Only with an Eve can Adam multiply. . . . From this viewpoint, the Lord says that 'it is not good that the man should be alone' not because Adam is lonely or has no lively intellectual conversation when he comes in from the garden at nights but because he will have no chance at all of filling the earth so long as there is only one of him." Furthermore, we see this aspect of Eve's helpfulness in light of her curse. When God punishes Eve, he does not do so "by threatening her with demotion to intellectual inferiority or by rendering her incapable of keeping up interesting conversation with her partner, but he most severely punishes her by promising to make the one thing she has been created to do difficult for her. . . . Just as Adam will find his work as farmer painful, so she will find hers as a mother." David J. A. Clines, *What Does Eve Do to Help? and Other Readerly Questions to the Old Testament*, JSOTSup 94 (Sheffield, UK: JSOT, 1990), 34–35.

[8] The cherubim were winged creatures consistently linked to the presence of God (e.g., Ps. 18:10; Ezekiel 10). Their image was on the ark (Ex. 25:18–22; 37:7–9) and the curtains of the Most Holy Place (Ex. 26:1, 31; 36:8, 35), and they decorated Solomon's temple and its Most Holy Place (1 Kings 6:23–29; 7:29, 36). Picking up on later imagery, the whole account resembles the future reality of the temple. As Mathews writes, this passage "continues to share the imagery of Moses' tabernacle by allusion to the 'cherubim' at the 'east side' of the garden ([Gen. 3:]24). The 'east side' of the garden parallels the easterly direction the tabernacle and temple faced, situated west of the altar. The east-west dichotomy indicates that the garden was located west of their first habitat outside of Eden, and we are told that Cain went eastward 'from the Lord's presence' ([Gen.] 4:16)." Mathews, *Genesis 1–11:26*, 257.

the garden that was once his to keep and to tend (Gen. 3:24).[9] Once expelled from the protected borders of the garden, Adam and Eve are stripped of all privileges. Communion and fellowship with the Lord are all but gone, and their call to rule, subdue, and fill the earth is now made arduous by toil and pain.

As you can imagine, sin wreaked havoc on Adam's role as priest-king. No longer was Adam the one bringing about Eden's expansion. Rather, God's image bearer betrayed his Creator and joined those opposed to the Lord's future objective. This treacherous act could finally be overcome only by the death of God's own Son.

Adam, the one created to be God's priest and king is now without a kingdom and without a temple. The moral obstacles of holiness and law (see, e.g., Rom. 3:19–20; 4:13–15; 5:20; 1 Cor. 15:56; Gal. 3:10–14), along with the physical impediments of the walls and curtains of the tabernacle and temple, now guard and deny full access to God's relational presence. In fact, everything initiated in creation is afflicted or in flux because of Adam's decision; the only certainty is the impending promise of death (Gen. 2:16; 3:19) that awaits humanity for this prideful disobedience. And though the promise of physical death is terrifying enough, the spiritual death accompanying man's separation from God's presence certainly compounds the fear and shame of this lonely, disappointing man shuddering in the dark shadow cast by the paradise of Eden.

Grace amid the Curses

And yet, all is not lost. Even within the bleak message of Genesis 3, Adam has reason to hope. Although through one man's sin, the benefits and objectives of Eden are seemingly lost forever, even in meting out punishment, the Lord displays his mercy. Sown among the curses are seeds of divine blessing, seeds that blossom into the drama of redemption that becomes the story of Scripture and our lives. This is the reason why even with death so imminent,[10] Adam still lives to hear that there is a future for him and for God's purposes.

---

[9] Furthering the connection between the call of Adam and the angelic guardians of Eden, the same verbs used to describe Adam's calling in the garden are now transferred to the cherubim in response to his sin. Like Adam, the cherubim are placed in the garden and charged with guarding/caring for (שמר) the garden against all trespassers.

[10] For this reason, the Lord announces the coming death when he reveals that Adam will "return to the ground, for out of it you were taken; for you are dust, and to dust you shall return" (Gen. 3:19).

Because of God's grace the earth is not completely desolate. Though it may not thrive as it once did, its survival is assumed in such divine guarantees as "you shall eat the plants of the field" and "you shall eat bread" (Gen. 3:18–19). So, even in light of sin, hope remains for both Adam and creation. Not only does the Lord continue to provide sustenance; he also answers the problems associated with the couple's newfound knowledge of good and evil. Sin has made them aware of their nakedness and driven them into hiding.[11] But instead of leaving them to fend for themselves, Yahweh affords them grace once again, this time in the form of animal skins to clothe the man and the woman. Adam is outside the garden and can no longer bring the presence of God to the world, but this does not prohibit God's presence from coming to Adam in a limited sense.

Furthermore, even though the pain of childbirth is immense and overwhelming, childbearing still produces offspring.[12] Adam's helpmeet is named Eve for this very reason: she will be the mother of all living (Gen. 3:20).[13] From her womb, then, comes Adam's dynasty, slow and painful as it may be. What is more, the grace of childbirth hints at a future salvation through the promised seed of the woman, who will finally destroy the Serpent (Gen. 3:15).[14] This promise of offspring guarantees that "the blessing for the human couple will be realized, and ironically the blessing is assured in the divine pronouncement of the penalty."[15] As we stand on this side of the cross, it is clear that Jesus Christ is this promised seed who, through defeating death in

---

[11] Adam's running from fellowship with God is an act that foreshadows the couple's final removal from Eden and his divine presence. Furthermore, hiding from an omniscient, omnipotent, and omnipresent God is not a real option. What this shows is that control belongs to Yahweh and not Adam. Separation is the Lord's decision. Man will always be before the eyes of God, but sin separates him from the relational redemptive presence of the Lord.

[12] The curse of childbearing seems to imply that the establishment of a people, or nation of God, will take much longer than what would have been the case had the sin not been committed. With no pain, the line of Adam would be generated quickly, whereas the toil of childbirth inhibits reproduction. Still, the line of Adam agonizingly increases even after the fall.

[13] As Allen Ross contends: "The name 'Eve' (hawwah, 'living' or 'life-giver') interpreted by the narrator as 'the mother of all living (hay),' signifies that the woman became a pledge in the continuation of the race, in spite of the curse. The name celebrates the survival of the race and the victory over death. By anticipating life the name also commemorates the establishment of a new order." Allen Ross, *Creation and Blessing* (Grand Rapids: Baker, 1996), 148–49.

[14] Often referred to as the *protoevangelium*, this verse has been considered the first indication of the gospel and the coming Messiah who will redeem Adam's line and reign in God's kingdom. Gen. 3:15 is the ultimate reversal of all that has been disrupted in the fall. Williamson contends: "Certainly encompassing the ensuing conflict between humanity and evil, the emphasis in Genesis on a promised line of seed suggests that it is a particular seed (i.e. subsequently identified as the seed of Abraham) who would receive a mortal wound and deliver such. Thus understood, the curse on the serpent indeed foreshadows the ultimate triumph of Christ and his church (cf. Heb. 2:14; Rom. 16:20)." Williamson, *Sealed with an Oath*, 51.

[15] Mathews, *Genesis 1–11:26*, 250.

his substitutionary sacrifice and bodily resurrection, inaugurates the conclusive defeat of the Serpent and the curses (Gal. 3:13). Even in the toil in childbearing, God's grace overwhelms us. We see the hope of redemption and redemptive purposes inaugurated in creation and consummated in Revelation 21–22.

The motive of Genesis 1–3, therefore, is no different from the rest of Scripture. Everything is redemptively focused and eschatologically minded. In the wake of sin and shame, the complex drama of redemptive history emerges. Through it, the Lord graciously chooses to reestablish all that was lost in Adam's sin and bring glory to his name. The seed of redemption planted in Genesis and the rest of the Old Testament blossoms into the gospel. In grace, the Lord continues to further the divine purposes of creation by overcoming Adam's sin and establishing the great work of redemption.[16]

So, though sin clearly impedes the advancement of God's objectives, it is important to see that Adam's rebellion was neither the reason behind God's eschatological objectives (they were goals set in motion at creation, before the fall occurred) nor able to stifle their progress. Instead, sin only *hinders* the end-time goals initiated at creation. God comes to do what Adam failed to do. He extends himself in a covenant relationship, and in his doing so, the history of *redemption* begins and, with it, the slow march toward the new Eden of Revelation 21–22.

Reversing the Curse: God's Presence and His Covenant Response

The Lord is not caught off guard by Adam's sin; rather, the world is under his providence even at this low point—a low point that God will use to highlight the beauty of his character and mercy. This is why the signs of grace run throughout the Edenic narrative. As the Creator becomes Redeemer, God initiates a work that will eventually end with his people living in a place created ultimately for the enjoyment of his presence. Everything in this world will declare his glory.[17] As T. D.

---

[16] Therefore, God's redemptive mission "was, in God's mind, from even before the creation of the universe, the means by which all things would be regenerated or re-created" in order to bring about "the reestablishment of the relationship between God, mankind, and the rest of creation." Graeme Goldsworthy, *The Lamb and the Lion: The Gospel in Revelation* (New York: Thomas Nelson, 1994), 135.

[17] From a Hebrew perspective, blessings overturn curses. As Dumbrell has pointed out: "The verb curse ('ārar) is thus an antonym of bless. To bless means to endow with potential for life, to give the power to succeed, prosper,

Alexander explains, after the fall, the story of Scripture turns to answering the issue of "how the earth once more becomes the dwelling place shared by God and humanity."[18] From a whole-Bible standpoint, then, the redemptive storyline of Scripture is, in a very real sense, the drama of God working to reestablish and extend paradise so that his presence will fill the created order.

To reclaim the promises Adam lost in his rebellion, God institutes the covenant,[19] a divine formula the divine king establishes with his fallen subjects that restores and redetermines the relationship[20] between God and man. It is interesting to see that in each covenant laid out in Scripture, God is graciously responding to Adam's rebellion and its penalties. When we look closely, we see that every covenant speaks to the promise of dominion, dynasty, and divine presence. By committing himself in such a way, the Lord keeps working toward the objectives set out in creation. But now God takes the mandate of Adam and makes it his own.[21] God is the one who gave the promises, and God is the one who will fulfill them.

In this light, the covenant is a divine apparatus that God uses to

---

or reproduce. Even when a human mediator intervenes, a blessing is always the gift of God. To curse means to alienate, to remove from the benign sphere, to subject to deprivation." Dumbrell, *Search for Order*, 28.

[18] T. Desmond Alexander, *From Eden to the New Jerusalem: Exploring God's Plan for Life on Earth* (Nottingham, UK: InterVarsity, 2008), 14.

[19] A helpful and succinct definition of the covenant is as follows: "A covenant is essentially a solemn commitment, guaranteeing promises or obligations undertaken by one or both parties sealed with an oath." Williamson, *Sealed with an Oath*, 11. Moreover as many have seen, the structures of the biblical covenant and the ancient Near Eastern suzerainty treaty correlate. Frame writes that both are built around a similar format, which includes: "(1) The Lord announces his name; (2) He describes his mighty deliverances in the past; (3) He sets forth his law, which the people should obey out of gratefulness for their deliverance; (4) He sets forth the sanctions of that law: blessings for obedience and curses for disobedience; (5) He declares how the covenant is to be kept and enforced in the future." In this covenant structure, the Lord details the moral and ethical requirements for his fellowship and graciously unveils the divine promises available to them by way of obedience that ultimately comes through the alien work of Christ. From this covenant formula, Frame argues that this "shows that the Lord is not an absentee landlord, but continues to be with his people, to both bless them for their faithfulness and to judge them for their disobedience." John M. Frame, *The Doctrine of God* (Phillipsburg, NJ: P&R, 2002), 95–96.

[20] The covenant blessings are conditioned upon man's obedience and his ability to keep the law. The history of man shows that this is quite impossible, and therefore the curses of sin keep mounting. Thus, we should not understand the covenant primarily as giving Adam a second chance to fulfill his eschatological commitments. Instead, the Lord uses the covenant to highlight what *he* is going to do for man. It is principally through the Lord's work in redemptive history that the promises of people, place, and presence find their consummation. Man is a recipient of God's gracious aims and commitment to his own glory. In having redemption offered to us through Christ we are able to be involved in these eschatological objectives once again because we are marked by the obedience of Jesus and the indwelling Spirit. Yet, even this provision demonstrates the necessity of the Lord's work to bring about his purposes in his world.

[21] The promises of the covenant are expressions of God's relational nature. Though apparent in the divine-human fellowship in the garden, his commitment to fallen humanity deepens our understanding of this attribute of Yahweh. God's covenant with man is grounded in his grace, mercy, righteousness, and his relationality. Just as the Lord draws near to Adam in his unfallen state, he continues to extend and disclose himself relationally to those who rebel against him. This is the only way the divine-human communion could continue, and in grace he chooses to make himself redemptively present to his elect through the covenant.

pick up the pieces of his eschatological objectives left in the aftermath of Adam's curse. Each covenant serves as a new beginning, a new marker of the new creation and its impending culmination. Thus, we can agree with Scott Hafemann, who argues that "the covenant blessings indicate that the focus of the covenant relationship is on the future,"[22] and "the fundamental provision of God is the presence of God himself."[23] So, even as he justly punishes sin, the Lord mercifully counters the imposed penalties in order to redeem a land and a people so that his relational presence is eternally with man.

This is why the covenant reengages the purposes of the garden and anticipates the eschatological conclusions of the new heaven and new earth. By his own initiative, God promises to restore his presence through the covenantal provision of land (dominion) and kingdom of priests (dynasty).[24] We first see this in the covenant refrain, "I will be your God, and you will be my people" (Gen. 17:7; Ex. 6:7; 29:45; Lev. 26:12; Jer. 7:23; 11:4; 24:7; 30:22; Ezek. 11:20; 14:11; 36:28; 37:27; Heb. 11:16; Rev. 21:3).[25] This phrase shows us that the presence of God is at the very heart of the covenant's project. As John Frame helps us see, by issuing this covenant promise, "the covenant Lord is one who takes people to be his own. . . . He fights our battles, blesses us, loves us. . . . Most importantly, he is *with* us. He places his name upon us (Num. 6:27), so that he dwells with us and we with him."[26] What the covenants reveal, then, is that God pledges to do what Adam could not: he will create a people and a place in order to be present with them eternally.

---

[22] Scott J. Hafemann, "The Covenant Relationship," in *Central Themes in Biblical Theology: Mapping Unity in Diversity*, ed. Scott J. Hafemann and Paul R. House (Grand Rapids: Baker, 2007), 37.

[23] Ibid., 39.

[24] In his biblical-theological work on the themes of the Pentateuch, Clines sees a similar pattern that unites the first five books of Scripture. He proposes that "the theme of the Pentateuch is the partial fulfillment—which implies also the partial non-fulfillment—of the promise to or blessing of the patriarchs. The promise of blessing is both the divine initiative in a world where human initiatives always lead to disaster and a re-affirmation of the primal divine intentions for man. The promise has three elements: posterity, divine-human relationship, and land. The posterity-element is dominant in Genesis 12–50, the relationship-element in Exodus and Leviticus, and the land-element in Numbers and Deuteronomy." David J. A. Clines, *The Theme of the Pentateuch*, JSOTSup 10 (Sheffield, UK: JSOT, 1978), 29. Here Clines picks up on the three main themes that extend from creation onward (which I believe goes beyond the Pentateuch through the covenant). These patterns he sees are not identical with but certainly correspond to the dominion, dynasty, and relational dwelling of God noted throughout this chapter.

[25] The use of the covenant refrain also ties the covenants together under one purpose. Block writes, "This formula . . . provides a unifying thread through the Abrahamic covenant (Gen. 17:7—8), the Mosaic covenant (Ex. 6:7; Lev. 26:12; Deut. 27:9; 29:11–12 [Eng. 12–13]; cf. Jer. 7:23; 11:4; 13:11), the future covenant with Israel (cf. [Ezek.] 11:20; 14:11; 36:28; 37:23; Zech. 8:8), the Christian covenant (2 Cor. 6:16), and the final eschatological covenant made between God and his people in the context of the new heaven and new earth (Rev. 21:3)." Daniel I. Block, *The Book of Ezekiel: Chapters 25–48*, NICOT (Grand Rapids: Eerdmans, 1998), 419.

[26] John M. Frame, *Salvation Belongs to the Lord* (Phillipsburg, NJ: P&R, 2006), 12.

It is through the work of God in the covenant that we can announce with confidence, even in light of human sinfulness, that "all the earth shall be filled with the glory of the LORD" (Num. 14:21; cf. Ps. 72:19; Isa. 11:9; Hab. 2:14; Zech. 14:9). The Lord's commitment to be present with his people is overwhelming—strong enough to conquer sin and death. Nothing can thwart God's plan to be with his people in a relationship that surpasses the intimacy of Eden. God's goal to be with his people still directs the flow and outcome of salvation history as God providentially brings his redemptive mission to completion, a mission accomplished through the covenants.

The Eschatological Objective and the Noahic Covenant

We see God's commitment to his presence in his first formal covenant ratified after Adam's sin. The cultural mandate is twisted in the first bite of the forbidden fruit; instead of spreading God's presence to the world, humanity can only spread sin and destruction. That single sin in Eden proliferates into worldwide rebellion. As the population grows, so too does the disobedience and transgression stemming from Adam's trespass (Gen. 6:1–8). In Genesis 6–9, where Scripture first employs the formal term for covenant (ברית),[27] we see God's beautiful response to the escalating sin problem. God's gracious promises, though, begin with his righteous judgment, "I have determined to make an end of all flesh, for the earth is filled with violence through them. Behold, I will destroy them with the earth" (Gen. 6:13). As you can imagine, divine punishment of man's sin is inevitable; wicked humanity stands in the crosshairs of God's impending wrath.

Yet, even in the midst of rampant sin, God graciously secures his future objectives for humanity and the world. Instead of wiping all

---

[27] The first explicit reference to covenant (ברית) in the Old Testament is used in relation to Noah. However, some scholars find that there is a covenant implicit in creation. Dumbrell concludes that Gen. 6:18 "refers to a divine relationship established by the fact of creation itself." William J. Dumbrell, *Covenant and Creation: A Theology of the Old Testament Covenants* (Carlisle, UK: Paternoster, 2002), 32. For this reason, the Noahic covenant is based upon the creation covenant and as such it picks up on the dominion mandate, making promises that God will fulfill. For further interaction with this debate, see Henri Blocher, *In the Beginning: The Opening Chapters of Genesis*, trans. David G. Preston (Downers Grove, IL: InterVarsity, 1984), 111–34; Dumbrell, *Covenant and Creation*, 11–44; Dumbrell, *Search for Order*, 30–32. J. V. Fesko, *Last Things First: Unlocking Genesis 1–3 with the Christ of Eschatology* (Fearn, Ross-shire, UK: Mentor, 2007), 82–103 Meredith G. Kline, *Kingdom Prologue: Genesis Foundations for a Covenantal Worldview* (Overland Park, KS: Two Age, 2000); O. Palmer Robertson, *The Christ of the Covenants* (Phillipsburg, NJ: P&R, 1980), 67–107. Others disagree and see the initiation of the covenant as occurring with Noah. For a presentation of one who opposes the "covenant at creation position," see Williamson, *Sealed with an Oath*, 17–76.

men from the face of the earth, he covenants with the one righteous man in that sinful generation. Through the salvation of this man, Noah, God assures the survival of all of his promises to and through the line of Adam. Therefore, when we hear the covenant promises of Noah, we should also hear the promises offered once before, in Eden. God continues to save a people and prepare a place for his presence even in the midst of this sinful generation. Not much has changed in God's promises and purposes. As Paul Williamson contends, even with Noah "the primary obligation imposed on humanity was that of fulfilling the role appointed by God in the beginning."[28] In his covenant with Noah, the Lord restates his commitment to establishing a genealogical line and geographical location so that he may be present with his people eternally.

NOAH AND DOMINION

From this perspective, the flood is not only a punishment for sin but a worldwide purification. For instance, the Lord works through the chaos of the storm to restore an Edenic quality to the world. Yes, the waters bring justice, but they also bring a type of regeneration. Again Williamson helps us: "The climax of the Flood narrative is best understood in terms of 'recreation'—a restoration of the divine order and God's visible kingship that had been established at creation."[29] While clearly a testimony of God's righteous hatred of sin, the flood also underscores God's commitment to his eschatological objectives established in Eden. The Creator moves human history from potential chaos toward a new age in which the relations between human beings . . . and their environment will be reordered."[30] Through the chaos of the flood, God

---

[28] Williamson, *Sealed with an Oath*, 63. See also Dumbrell, *Covenant and Creation*, 33; Herman Gunkel, *Genesis*, trans. Mark E. Biddle (Macon, GA: Mercer University Press, 1997), 148; Derek Kidner, *Genesis*, TOTC (Downers Grove, IL: InterVarsity, 1967), 100; Nahum M. Sarna, *Genesis*, JPS Torah Commentary (Philadelphia: JPS, 1989), 60; Gerhard Von Rad, *Genesis*, Old Testament Library (Philadelphia: Westminster, 1972), 131; John Walton, *Genesis*, NIVAC (Grand Rapids: Zondervan, 2001), 341; Gordon J. Wenham, *Genesis 1–15*, WBC (Thomas Nelson: Nashville, 1987), 192; Claus Westermann, *Genesis 1–11*, trans. John J. Scullion (Minneapolis: Fortress, 1994), 462.

[29] Williamson, *Sealed with an Oath*, 61. The similarities between the flood and creation narratives are numerous. As Williamson has shown the two are certainly correlated: "The earth is made inhabitable by the separation of the land from the water (Gen. 8:1–3; cf. Gen. 1:9–10); living creatures are brought out to repopulate the earth (Gen. 8:17–19; cf. Gen. 1:20–22, 24–25). Days and seasons are re-established (Gen. 8:22; cf. Gen. 1:14–18). Humans are blessed by God (Gen. 9:1; cf. Gen. 1:28a); commanded to 'Be fruitful and multiply and fill the earth' (Gen. 9:1b, 7: cf. Gen. 1:28b), and given dominion over the animal kingdom (Gen. 9:2; cf. Gen. 1:28c); God provides humanity—made in his image (Gen. 9:6; cf. Gen. 1:26–27)—with food (Gen. 9:3; cf. Gen. 1:29–30)."

[30] Bernhard W. Anderson, *Contours of Old Testament Theology* (Minneapolis: Fortress, 1999), 95–96.

metes out justice for the outbreak of sin, while simultaneously extending his mercy quietly to one man in the covenantal form of his relational presence. The drama of the flood, then, is one of new creation, or re-creation. Through his covenant, God places Noah in an Adam-like role with an Adam-like mandate (Gen. 1:28).[31] The promise of a people and place now continues with Noah.

To ensure the completion of his future objectives, God promises to withhold flood-like punishment from this point forward. In response to his own judgment of creation, God vows, "This is the sign of the covenant that I make between me and you and every living creature that is with you, for all future generations: I have set my bow in the cloud, and it shall be a sign of the covenant between me and the earth" (Gen. 9:12–13). This promise makes clear Yahweh's commitment to protect creation from the future consequences of humanity's sin. His promise to "never again curse the ground because of man" (Gen. 8:21) demonstrates his commitment to creation and, moreover, points to the fulfillment of his eschatological purposes that will finally come to fruition in the new heaven and new earth.

Not only does Yahweh commit to purifying creation; he also reinstitutes the creation mandate through Noah. God commands this righteous one and his offspring to rule and subjugate the earth. There is a new beginning in the flood, which means the land still needs to be maintained and ordered. God's act of judgment, then, restores both the world and man's role as creation's governor and attendant. This is why Noah is placed in charge of the animals whose very names came from the creativity of the first vice-regent, Adam (Gen. 9:2–3). God casts Noah as the new ruler of dominion by charging this covenant partner with the safety and regeneration of "every living thing" (Gen. 6:17–22; quoting 6:19).

NOAH AND DYNASTY

The Lord commands Noah not only to subdue the earth, but also to be fruitful, multiply, and continue God's dynasty. Noah is the righteous one[32] (Gen. 6:9; cf. 2 Pet. 2:5) who stands out against the backdrop of

---

[31] Dumbrell, *Covenant and Creation*, 59.

[32] It is important to note that Noah is a type of the second Adam as he, like the first Adam, walks with God (Gen. 6:9). As Fesko summarizes, "The parallels between the initial creation and post-deluge creation mean that God started over with Noah as a new Adam, of sorts, giving to Noah the same covenantal tasks as the first." Yet he

universal rebellion. By obedience, he not only ensures the promise of dominion; he also makes way for a reconstituted people of God. This is why the Lord God saves not only Noah from the judgmental waters of the flood but his wife, sons, and daughters-in-law too. The ark is built to save Noah and his family—and in the process, God is saving a people for his presence.

To ensure a God-centered genealogy, Noah receives the same mandate given to Adam: "Be fruitful and multiply, teem the earth and multiply in it" (Gen. 9:7). The flood restarts a dynasty, one that will be cleansed from sin. For Noah, this is one command he can get behind! He and his descendants are *very* obedient to this directive. As the next chapter of Genesis reveals, the line of Noah flourishes (Gen. 10:1–32; cf. 11:10–32).[33] By simply placing his covenant partner's feet back on dry land, the Lord reaffirms his commitment to making a people for the enjoyment of his presence.

NOAH AND THE PRESENCE OF GOD

This commitment to a genealogy and geography with Noah discloses God's ultimate reason to establish the covenant: God is jealous to be present with his people. In Genesis 6:18, God separates righteous Noah from the rest of the wicked world by drawing near to his new covenant partner. The covenant is built upon this divine-human relationship; it takes for granted God's becoming present in a mediated way to be with a people. In other words, Noah's covenant "serves to reaffirm God's original intent for creation which was 'disrupted' by the Flood."[34] It does this through the reestablishment of God's presence for both relationship and redemption. Yahweh is now with Noah, his covenant partner. God is present with him in the midst of the flood (Gen. 8:1) and after the waters relent (8:16); and once the flood has passed, God

---

too falls into sin, revealing the need for a better Adam. Fesko sees this as well when he writes: "This subsequent Adam, however, could not fulfill the requirements set before him in the covenant. Shortly after the beginning of the new creation, that is, the post-flood world, Noah sinned in circumstances reminiscent of the fall." Fesko, *Last Things First*, 118.

[33] Unfortunately, the line of Noah duplicates the line of Adam's regression into sin, as is evidenced in the tower of Babel account of Genesis 11. The reversion of Noah's progeny back into sin foreshadows the Lord's work in the subsequent covenants (Abrahamic, Davidic, and new covenants, in particular) to establish a true and righteous dynasty that will ultimately come through the covenant provision of Christ.

[34] Paul R. Williamson, "Covenant," in *New Dictionary of Biblical Theology*, ed. T. Desmond Alexander et al. (Downers Grove, IL: InterVarsity, 2000), 421.

is with Noah to offer his presence through the formal offer of the covenant (Gen. 8:20–9:17).[35]

The Eschatological Objective and the Abrahamic Covenant

As with Noah, God shines the light of his covenant presence into the darkness of the world's accelerated rebellion (Genesis 3–11).[36] But with Abraham, there is an escalation in the Lord's promises. What had only been hinted at in the preceding covenant(s) is now with Abraham more overtly disclosed.[37] This is critical for our understanding the story of Christian Scripture. It means that the Abrahamic covenant is not one covenant among many, but is formative for the rest of the covenants to come. It is crucial to our understanding of the rest of Christian Scripture. God's covenant with Abraham provides "the basis for all of God's covenant dealings: the Mosaic, Davidic, and New Covenant in Christ."[38] So to understand God's dealings with the world, we need a clear grasp of God's relationship with Abraham. When we do, we discover "a synopsis of the divine agenda in which God's rescue plan for humanity is revealed."[39] The Abrahamic covenant, then, is one of the clearest expressions of God's eschatological purposes in redemption and one that permeates and often influences the rest of God's covenant dealings in Scripture.

---

[35] However, his presence is not only tied to protection and provision. In blessing Shem, Noah announces, "Blessed be the LORD, the God of Shem; / and let Canaan be his servant. / May God enlarge Japheth, / and *let him dwell in the tents of Shem*, and let Canaan be his servant" (Gen. 9:26–27). The Hebrew word for "dwell" or "live" is a term associated with the Lord's presence in the camp of Israel (e.g., Ex. 25:8; Lev. 16:16) and is semantically related to the Hebrew term for "tabernacle" (משכן). Note also the relational title applied to the Lord when he is called the "God of Shem." He has identified himself with his people. Though not conclusive, the text does lend itself to the option that the Lord's relational presence will be experienced again. As VanGemeren has argued, this text quite possibly reveals that the covenant with Noah ends with the promise of God "to deal kindly with his creation and to dwell again on earth (in the tents of Shem), to bless and protect the people among whom he dwells in a special manner." Willem VanGemeren, *The Progress of Redemption: The Story of Salvation from Creation to the New Jerusalem* (Grand Rapids: Baker, 1988), 96. This implies that the divine covenant offered to Noah and his offspring not only prepares the way for a people and a place of God but also prepares a way for the Lord once again to dwell in the midst of his people and be their God, a promise finalized in the arrival of the New Jerusalem. VanGemeren goes on to argue that "whereas the NIV reads 'May Japheth live in the tents of Shem,' the preferable understanding of 'he' is 'the LORD.' . . . The goal of redemptive history remains the presence of God on earth" (ibid., 484). See also Walter Kaiser, *Toward an Old Testament Theology* (Grand Rapids: Zondervan, 1978), 82ff.; Gordon J. Wenham, "The Coherence of the Flood Narrative," *VT* 28 (1978): 336–48.

[36] Dumbrell sees the similarities between Gen. 12:1 and Gen. 1:3 as indicative of the beginning of a "new creation" in the call and covenant of Abraham. He writes: "As in Gen. 1:3 the form of 12:1 is that of a divine speech which includes the virtual imperative, calling a new phase of history into being, just as the words of Gen. 1:3 had called existence into being." Furthermore, "the call of Abram in Gen. 12:1–3 contains in it an allusive reference to Genesis 1, and that therefore the redemptive purposes which are being expressed through the call of Abram are virtually couched in the language of a 'New Creation.'" Dumbrell, *Covenant and Creation*, 58, 61. The significance of this lies in the fact that in Abraham, God has again revealed his commitment to the purposes of creation.

[37] Williamson, *Sealed with an Oath*, 77.

[38] VanGemeren, *Progress of Redemption*, 129.

[39] Williamson, *Sealed with an Oath*, 77.

Like the rest of God's covenant dealings, the Abrahamic covenant takes us back to Eden. In establishing his covenant with Abraham, the Lord pledges certain promises that will, in fact, repeal the curses warranted by Adam's rebellion. Or to put it another way, God's covenant with the patriarch transforms the divine mandate once given to Adam into the promises God will accomplish for Abraham.[40] The Abrahamic covenant is, as William Dumbrell puts it, God's "redemptive response to the human dilemma which the spread of sin narratives of Genesis 3–11 have posed."[41] Against the backdrop of the rest of Genesis, God's promises to Abraham are not promises offered "out of thin air"; they are the divine restoration of the cultural mandate first initiated in Genesis 1:28. This is what the Lord accomplishes through his covenant with Abraham: God fulfills his own divine mandate to establish a people and a place for the enjoyment of his presence. In short, once the cultural mandate is given to Abraham, it becomes the divine mandate in that Yahweh must accomplish it for us.

To complete these objectives, the Lord institutes the following three promises in his covenant with Abraham: (1) the promise of seed, descendants, or offspring that will one day include the rest of the nations (Gen. 12:2a; 13:6; 15:5; 17:5–6; 18:18; 22:17; 26:4; 28:3, 14; 35:11; 48:4), (2) the promise of dominion and land (Gen. 12:7; 13:15, 17; 15:18–21; 17:8; 22:17; 26:3; 28:4, 13; 35:12; 48:4), and (3) the promise of "blessing to the patriarchs, specifically, the presence of God" (12:2b; 15:1; 17:7ff.; 22:17; 26:3; 28:3, 15; 35:11; 48:3).[42] These promises fulfill Genesis 1:28; they also reverse the curses of Genesis 3. The blessing of God's covenant with Abraham therefore goes backward and forward: God works backward to overcome what Adam did while also working forward to do what Adam could no longer do.

ABRAHAM AND DOMINION

This covenant work begins when we first meet Abraham—known as Abram at this time—whom the Lord has called out from Ur of the Chal-

---

[40] N. T. Wright picks up on this when he explains that the Abrahamic "narrative quietly insists that Abraham and his progeny inherit the role of Adam and Eve. There are, interestingly, two differences which emerge in the shape of this role. The command (be fruitful . . .) has turned into a promise ('I will make you fruitful . . .') and possession of the land of Canaan, together with supremacy over enemies, has taken the place of Adam's dominion over nature." N. T. Wright, *The New Testament and the People of God* (Philadelphia: Fortress, 1992), 263.

[41] Dumbrell, *Covenant and Creation*, 47.

[42] VanGemeren, *Progress of Redemption*, 104.

deans. God begins with the promise of dominion: he will give Abraham a better land (Gen. 15:7). Yahweh even prophesies that though Abraham's offspring will be separated from the land in Egyptian captivity for four generations, the land will be theirs upon their return (Gen. 15:8–21). Later, in Genesis 17:8, God reaffirms his dominion promise when he announces, "I will give to you [Abraham] and to your offspring after you the land of your sojournings, all the land of Canaan, for an everlasting possession." So in calling Abraham to leave his birthright and enter an unfamiliar land simply on faith to serve Yahweh, the Lord designates him and his line to be those through whom God will establish the new location for the divine presence and its universal expansion (Gen. 12:1).

What is more, the land that God will give Abraham will be an "everlasting possession." Implied in this blessing is a future fulfillment— one that the book of Hebrews associates with the New Jerusalem. The author of Hebrews, reflecting on this specific aspect of the Abrahamic covenant, explains that Abraham went to possess the promised territory by faith, a faith that looked beyond the physical land of Canaan to the eschatological city built by the Lord himself (Heb. 11:8–10). The text explains that Abraham and his descendants "desire[d] a better country, that is, a heavenly one. Therefore God is not ashamed to be called their God, for he has prepared for them a city" (Heb. 11:16). So from a whole-Bible perspective, the dominion promise given to Abraham is physical and eschatological. Through this covenant promise, Abraham, and those who are counted as Abraham's sons and daughters will one day rest in this eschatological city marked by God's presence.

ABRAHAM AND DYNASTY

Not only does God promise his covenant partner a new territory; he also pledges him a new dynasty. Through the covenant, Yahweh boldly declares that barren Abraham will father a great nation (Gen. 12:2) and through Abraham all the families of the earth will finally receive their blessing. The Lord proclaims:

> Behold, my covenant is with you, and you shall be the father of a
> multitude of nations. I will make you exceedingly fruitful, and I

will make you into nations, and kings shall come from you. And I
will establish my covenant between me and you and your offspring
after you throughout their generations for an everlasting covenant,
to be God to you and to your offspring after you. (Gen. 17:4–7)

Deepening his commitment to his covenant partner, God changes the
patriarch's name from Abram to Abraham, meaning "father of a mul-
titude," thereby reidentifying him as the "fount" from which all of
God's people will spring (Gen. 17:5–6). It follows, then, that through
Abraham the "blessings of this covenant are eventually supposed to
spread to the ends of the earth. Global expansion is the import of the
phrase: In you all the families of the earth shall be blessed (Gen. 12:3)."[43]
The descendants of Abraham will eventually fill the world, just as the
blessings of Eden were supposed to long ago.

Hindering the promise, however, is the constant reminder that
Abraham and his wife, Sarah, are infertile. This depressing reality
hanging over God's elect forces everyone, even us as onlookers, to
see that the onus of the divine mandate to be fruitful and multiply
falls directly upon the Lord. The hope of Abraham's line, just as his
hope for a land of his own, clings to the God of the covenant, for it
is his power alone that can bring life to Sarah's barren womb. The
consequences of Adam's sin are still felt here with Abraham. Since
the exile from Eden all the way until Abraham follows the Lord into
the wilderness, God alone is the only one who can and will complete
his covenant promises (Gen. 17:2, 20; 22:17; 26:4, 24; 28:3; etc.). This
is one of the reasons for the failure of the Ishmael experiment (Gen.
17:18–27). The rejection of Ishmael is, in one sense, a result of Abraham's decision to take the fulfillment of the covenant promises into
his own hands. Yet we quickly learn that the covenant promises are
not Abraham's to fulfill through his own man-made attempts but are
God's promises to be completed his way for his glory. God works to
establish a new dynasty through his chosen heir (Gen. 15:1–6). It is
through Isaac that the Lord once again reassures his people that nothing can impede the fulfillment of his covenant pledge.[44] If sin and

---

[43] Fesko, *Last Things First*, 119–20.
[44] Much of the patriarchal narrative is concerned with this dynastic promise as it is the only pledge that sees
fruition in Abraham's lifetime. What should be emphasized is that the fulfillment of this promise, and the com-

death cannot impede the Lord's future goals, the infertility of Sarah cannot either.

So just as it was with the promise of a place, Abraham secures his great genealogical line through faith. It is through Abraham's belief in the covenant Lord that a people and a nation (one day extending to all nations) that number as many as the stars in the heavens and the sands on the seashore find their origin in an infertile womb. The writer of Hebrews helps us see that

> by faith Sarah herself received power to conceive, even when she was past the age, since she considered him faithful who had promised. Therefore from one man, and him as good as dead, were born descendants as many as the stars of heaven and as many as the innumerable grains of sand by the seashore. (Heb. 11:11–12)

God gives Abraham Isaac and, in doing so, ensures that Abraham will have a line and that line will spread to all the earth.

ABRAHAM AND THE PRESENCE OF GOD

In the Land of Promise and the baby boy Isaac we have the "the good news to Israel that, in spite of Adam and Eve's rebellion in the garden and their subsequent expulsion from Eden, God has renewed a people to himself and has prepared Canaan, a new 'garden' for them."[45] But as we have seen before, these seeds of the covenant promises serve a greater purpose than just establishing a land and people. Rather, both point forward to the reality that God will be with his people. The pledges of dominion and dynasty, in other words, are "indicative of Abraham's positive relationship with the Lord and anticipate the divine presence in the midst of the nation of Israel."[46] In short, the Abrahamic covenant evidences God's commitment to his eschatological agenda. Through the covenant, the Lord makes a way to dwell in this place and among this people.

---

mencement of the teleological objective in the spread of Abraham's line, is a divine act. God opens up Sarah's womb. The Lord gives them Isaac, whose name clearly indicates the sheer hilarity and improbability of their son's birth. This realization clearly indicates that God is now the means for redemption and its fulfillment of the teleological objectives.

[45] VanGemeren, *Progress of Redemption*, 81.

[46] T. Desmond Alexander, *From Paradise to the Promised Land: An Introduction to the Pentateuch* (Grand Rapids: Baker Academic, 2002), 129.

It follows, then, that the rest of redemptive history works toward a future where the Lord dwells in the midst of Abraham's descendants. The covenant refrain in Genesis 17:7–8 captures God's promises, "I will . . . be God to you [Abraham] and to your offspring after you. . . . and I will be their [Abraham's offspring's] God" (Gen. 17:7–8). Such texts show us that the covenant is based in a relationship—one completed in the Lord's drawing near to be present with his people (the impetus for the tabernacle, temple, Immanuel, indwelling Spirit, and new creation). The constant refrain "I will be your God and you will be my people" is just as much a part of the covenant as the promise of a people and place. What is more, this promise of relational presence is *why* God establishes a nation and a land.

In the broader context of the forthcoming covenants, this covenant phrase keeps the promise of God's relational presence ever before the eyes of God's people.[47] Based on the Lord's promise to be their God, Hafemann contends, "The covenant formula itself reveals that the primary provision and promise of the covenant relationship is knowing God himself. Knowing God is not a means to something else, but all of God's other gifts are intended to bring his people into an ever-growing relationship with God himself."[48] God's promise to be relationally present with his people is the goal that drives his covenant engagement, as we see so clearly in his promises to Abraham. To maximize his glory and our good, God prepares a people and a place to experience and enjoy the all-satisfying reality of his relational presence. So in this eschatological framework, Abraham's calling and covenant should be understood as the divine act meant to reestablish the promises of Eden and prepare the way for the universal expansion of God's presence with his people.

The Eschatological Objective and the Mosaic Covenant

The Sinai covenant, like its predecessors, is marked by the Lord's commitment to produce a people and a place for his presence. It too is a restoration of the Edenic purposes, for "through the Exodus the cre-

---

[47] See the following sections on the Mosaic, Davidic, and new covenants for explicit examples on how this is fleshed out biblically. The relationship that God establishes covenantally with his people consists of God's drawing near to the elect and, more specifically, preparing a dwelling place among them.

[48] Hafemann, "The Covenant Relationship," 36.

ation intention for the world is being furthered."[49] In other words, the Mosaic covenant is rooted in Abraham's promises; therefore, this covenant relationship carries with it many of the same functions as the Abrahamic. In fact, as Williamson summarizes, "God's intervention [in the exodus] was clearly motivated by the promises made in Genesis 15, to which there are several clear allusions (cf. Ex. 2:23–24; 3:7–8, 16–22; 6:4–6; 13:5, 11)."[50] The Sinai covenant, then, in a way picks up where the Abrahamic covenant left off. As a result, the commitment to a genealogy and geography established in the garden, extended to Noah, and promised to Abraham continues to direct the Mosaic covenant and its outcome.

MOSES AND DYNASTY

To help uncover the eschatological design informing the Mosaic covenant, let us begin with the promise of dynasty. Up to this point, the *tôlēdôt* (תולדות) structure of Genesis has demonstrated that Abraham's descendants have slowly increased to form the loosely organized nation of Israel. The Lord is fulfilling his covenant promise to the patriarch. "The Exodus event," as Williamson observes, "constitutes the fulfillment of the preliminary stage of the prospect held out in the covenant of Genesis 15—the prospect of nationhood. The 'great nation' promised by God to Abraham (Gen. 12:2) is about to emerge on to the world stage."[51] The exodus narrative reveals that Yahweh is faithful not only to create a people but to redeem them as well. God calls the Abrahamic dynasty out of Egypt, he protects them from the plagues of judgment, he institutes the Passover, and he offers the provision of manna from heaven and water from the rock in order to sustain a people for his presence.

However, the dynastic promise is not something that the Lord completes unilaterally. Rather, there are moral obligations required, and obedience is demanded. Disobedience rightly affects the promise. Instead of full enjoyment of God's blessings, Israel receives discipline and even death as its immediate outcome (e.g., Num. 21:1–9). As with

---

[49] In Exodus 15, allusions to a new beginning are clear as the redemption that the exodus achieves is presented in terms of a "new creation." Dumbrell, *Covenant and Creation*, 101.
[50] Williamson, "Covenant," 424.
[51] Williamson, *Sealed with an Oath*, 96.

Abraham, Noah, and even Adam earlier, the nation of Israel is unable to fulfill God's eschatological purposes on its own. The Mosaic covenant, like those prior to it, demands divine intervention as well.[52]

MOSES AND DOMINION

While the "national" aspect of God's covenant progresses, the promise of dominion remains uncertain until it takes center stage in the exodus narrative. On the heels of the patriarchs' deaths, the Abrahamic line is neither living in Canaan nor fully experiencing the presence of God. Instead the offspring of God's covenant partner are in a foreign land under foreign rule and foreign affliction. The hope long ago associated with Egypt (Genesis 41–50) has been quickly replaced with the oppression of new leadership (Ex. 1:8).

As Israel's dynasty grows, so does Egypt's distrust. Burgeoning within Pharaoh's own empire is another nation. This is a people called by God to multiply and exercise a dominion that will one day include not only Egypt, but the entire cosmos. And though Pharaoh is not cognizant of the divine promises given to this exiled people, his pagan response to their growing population is a natural one. The Israelites, once the reason for Egypt's survival, are now seen as a constant threat to Pharaoh's rule and territory. What Pharaoh—and even Israel for that matter—does not realize is that God has a better land and better promises set aside for his people, including the powerful land of Egypt. Ironically, the foreign king's pride will be instrumental in the realization of these divine promises. What the book of Exodus wants us to see is that nothing and no one, not even the great sovereign Pharaoh of Egypt, can stop the universal expansion of the Lord's relational presence. He alone is God, and only his purposes will stand.

The historical background of the exodus makes this very obvious. Genesis ends with Joseph's declaration to the fledgling tribes of Israel, "God will visit you and bring you up out of this land [Egypt] to the land that he swore to Abraham, to Isaac, and to Jacob" (Gen. 50:24). However, between the time of Joseph's passing and the beginning of

---

[52] This divine intervention will come through the one true Israel, Jesus Christ, the only one who can meet the holy requirements of the Lord and therefore restore a true and faithful dynasty to the Lord. I will develop this idea more in the next chapter.

Exodus, it appears that this prophecy died along with the patriarch. But when God reveals himself to Moses in the burning bush, he also resuscitates the promise of a place for his people. With the plagues, the Passover, and Pharaoh's army in the rearview mirror, Israel stands on the precipice of the dominion promise. Israel now has the opportunity to go from exile to the Promised Land—a land of paradise, reminiscent of the glory days of Eden, and one that could be the center of the universal dispersion of God's presence.

With its emphasis on land, the exodus act is a type of reversal of the exile that took place in Eden, yet with an even greater eschatological purpose in mind. As we saw earlier in our discussion of Genesis 1–3, God removed his people from the place of his presence. From the perspective of the whole Hebrew Bible, Exodus is a tale of the return to an Edenic reality. God brings Israel to the Promised Land to be their God and to establish his presence with them once and for all. It is a land that flows with milk and honey, a place that is lush and perfect for his people to dwell with him. This is the land God has "chosen for his own abode, and his sanctuary shall be established in [Israel's] midst."[53] Through the exodus (see Ex. 15:17), "Israel, now newly constituted, is invited to realise in the promised land . . . , as in Eden, the direct presence of God will be encountered in a way which would parallel the condition of man in Eden."[54] Hence, God's covenant results in a growing nation of promised people being led by God's presence, to a new and glorious land which itself points back to the glorious reality of the garden.[55]

---

[53] Dumbrell, *Covenant and Creation*, 102.

[54] Ibid., 101.

[55] It is important to see that the fertility of the land (Deut. 26:9ff.) reveals Canaan to be a newly restored Eden. As Beale describes, "Israel's land is explicitly compared to the Garden of Eden (see Gen. 13:10; Isa. 51:3; Ezek. 36:35; 47:12; Joel 2:3) and is portrayed as very fruitful in order to heighten its correspondence to Eden (cf. Deut. 8:7–10; 11:8–17; Ezek. 47:1–12)." G. K. Beale, "Garden Temple," *Kerux* 18 (2003): 44. The land is idealized to the point of hyperbole. As Dumbrell summarizes, the Promised Land is described as the "very quintessence of fertility and fruitfulness. . . . Not only will it give forth heavenly fare (milk and honey were traditionally the food offered to a deity [cf. Isa. 7:15]) but it is actually watered from heaven (Deut. 11:11)." Dumbrell, *Covenant and Creation*, 120. This kind of imagery makes it clear that Canaan is a type of paradise symbolizing God's work in history to restore what was lost in the first Eden. Dumbrell also makes the connection and highlights the sanctuary implications for Canaan when he states, "Since Eden is considered a divine space, Canaan is not only paralleled to Eden (Isa. 51:3; Ezek. 36:35) but also fulsomely presented as an Israelite correspondence to Eden (cf. Deut. 8:7–10; 11:8–17), inasmuch as it too in its totality is a divine space (cf. Ex. 15:17; Ps. 78:54)." William J. Dumbrell, "Genesis 2:1–17: A Foreshadowing of the New Creation," in *Biblical Theology: Retrospect and Prospect*, ed. Scott J. Hafemann (Downers Grove, IL: InterVarsity, 2002), 58. Through Canaan, God opens up a new way for the nation of Israel to experience his presence. Unfortunately, because of sin, Israel is expelled from the new Eden, just as Adam was.

MOSES AND THE PRESENCE OF GOD

Behind God's work in the Mosaic covenant to return Israel to a new type of Eden is the divine desire to bring his people back to the place of his presence. Commentator John Durham notes that the centerpiece of the book of Exodus "is the theology of Yahweh present with and in the midst of his people Israel."[56] As Stephen Dempster puts it, "The goal of Exodus is thus the building of the Edenic sanctuary so that the Lord can dwell with his people, just as he once was Yahweh Elohim to the first human beings."[57] Exodus 19:4 and 29:45–46 (cf. Lev. 26:11–13) both suggest that God cuts his covenant with Israel for such purposes. By bringing Israel out of Egypt to himself, the Lord announces to the world that this nation will be the nation of his presence. The bilateral nature of the covenant is supposed to ensure Israel's role as a holy people—a righteous nation that will disclose God to the world and usher in his redemptive purposes. In giving the law, God calls Israel to be like him and to be his representative in the world ("Be holy as I am holy"; cf. Lev. 11:45; 19:2; 20:26).[58] If they could keep the law perfectly, the people of the nation would finally complete the mandate first given to Adam and be the purveyors of God's universal blessings.

From this standpoint, the covenant reveals that the promises of God are the divine solution to the curses facing mankind.[59] We find this in Exodus 29:45–46.[60] On the heels of commissioning the building of the

[56] John I. Durham, *Exodus*, WBC (Waco, TX: Word, 1987), 21.

[57] Stephen Dempster, *Dominion and Dynasty: A Theology of the Hebrew Bible*, NSBT 15 (Downers Grove, IL: InterVarsity, 2003), 100.

[58] The law is revelatory in nature. The covenant regulations revealed at Sinai disclose something of the nature and character of Yahweh. Israel's consistent sin reveals that man can never complete the law on his own. It requires the work of God. More specifically, it demands the new covenant promise of the Spirit who indwells believers and leads them to righteousness as well as Christ, the one who completes the requirements of the law.

[59] In Ex. 19:4–6, God reminds Moses of his role in redemption, declaring in his own words: "You [the people of Israel] yourselves have seen what I did to the Egyptians, and how I bore you on eagles' wings and brought you to myself. Now therefore, if you will indeed obey my voice and keep my covenant, you shall be my treasured possession among all peoples, for all the earth is mine; and you shall be to me a kingdom of priests and a holy nation." Here it is unmistakable that God destroys the enemies of Israel and saves his people in his strength and power to be present with them once again. In declaring this reason for the exodus, Yahweh unites redemption with his own presence. God saves people so that they can know him, love him, serve him, and draw near to him as a "kingdom of priests and a holy nation." Through obedience and covenant keeping, Israel will return to an Eden-like reality, and the Lord will be honored by his people and all the nations. As Gorman proposes, "The holy God dwelling in the midst of the holy community is a constitutive image of Israel's identity." Frank J. Gorman, *Leviticus: Divine Presence and Community* (Grand Rapids: Eerdmans, 1997), 10.

[60] A similar message is found in Exodus 6. Here God reveals himself to Moses and identifies himself as the one who covenanted with the patriarchs to promise a line and a land that would be their own (vv. 2–4). Because of these earlier promises, Yahweh comes to his people to redeem them and replace their suffering with the joy of divine-human relationship (vv. 5–6). In short, he draws near to Moses in order to fulfill the patriarchal promises. From this point of view, the covenant with Israel is cut for the same reason the Lord covenanted with Abraham, namely, to bring his presence to a location and be among a people he himself has covenantally formed and established. The

tabernacle, God proclaims, "I will dwell among the people of Israel and will be their God. And they shall know that I am the LORD their God, who brought them out of the land of Egypt that *I might dwell among them*. I am the LORD their God." The purpose of this covenant with Israel is to prepare a way for God to dwell with his people. All that God does with and through Moses is done to draw near to Israel and the rest of the world. In this passage we hear echoes of the Abrahamic covenant's relational refrain, "I will be your God and you will be my people." God now ties this particular pledge of divine-human relationship with Moses and the Israelites to his larger agenda of dwelling in the midst of all of his creation for all eternity.

Leviticus 26:11–13 develops this promise further.[61] Here, God declares, "*I will make my dwelling among you, and my soul shall not abhor you. And I will walk among you and will be your God, and you shall be my people*." This passage shows us that the divine-human relationship that sits at the heart of the covenant intrinsically includes the promise of God's presence (Ex. 25:8; 29:45–46).[62] God acts through the covenant so that one day he will again walk with his people as he once did in Eden (Gen. 3:8; 5:22; 6:9; cf. Deut. 23:14). For this reason, God reminds Moses atop Sinai, "I [Yahweh] bore you [Israel] on eagles' wings and brought you to myself" (Ex. 19:4). The Lord delivers Israel so that this nation can draw near to him. This is the relational aspect of the covenant. As David Peterson notes:

Abrahamic promise of geography and genealogy for his presence is confirmed in the repetition of the covenant language "I will take you to be my people, and I will be your God, and you shall know that I am the LORD your God, who has brought you out from under the burdens of the Egyptians" (Ex. 6:7). Here we see that God acts in history on behalf of the Israelites in order to relate to them and bring about the eschatological renewal of creation's aims.

[61] Gorman rightfully concludes that Leviticus looks back to four specific moments in redemptive history for its theological content, all of which, I would argue, underscore the eschatological movement in time to bring about the cosmological expansion of God's relational presence. He indicates first that the instructions of the book "are located within the context of creation theology (especially Gen. 1:1–2:4a)." Gorman, *Leviticus*, 4. He goes on to say that "the instructions of Leviticus are provided as a means of . . . restoring the very good order of creation." Next, Leviticus also "draw(s) on the promise and covenant that God made with the ancestors (especially Gen. 17). . . . Leviticus provides instructions for how the people are to live in the context of the divine promises" (ibid.). Third, Leviticus also recalls "the Exodus from Egypt, God's act of redemption on behalf of Israel" in which 'the Exodus becomes a part of God's enactment of the covenant promises—I will be their God and they will be my people—as well as one way in which Yahweh makes a claim on the people." Building on this is the final context for Leviticus, which is the Sinai covenant itself. From here, "these instructions provide one means for manifesting the life of the covenant community in the presence of Yahweh, a means for enacting the covenant relationship" (ibid., 5).

[62] Ibid. Gorman's thesis is that the book of Leviticus picks up on the covenant at Sinai and "constitutes a significant effort to address the question of Israelite identity. He maintains that the book seeks to address the following in particular: 'What does it mean to be the people of God, redeemed from slavery, called to be holy, with Yahweh in the midst of the community?'" (ibid., 1). To answer this question, Gorman argues that Leviticus is a "book of and about community, and what it means to be a community confronted daily with the promise and warning of divine presence" (ibid.). This assessment once again reinforces the place of presence as an overarching theme or purpose that drives redemptive history toward its teleological ends.

The covenant relationship graciously established by the Lord contained at its heart the assurance that he would be their God and they would be his people (e.g., Gen. 17:7–8; Ex. 6:7). Consequently, he would be uniquely with them, to fulfil his purposes and bring blessings to them (e.g., Gen. 28:13–15; Ex. 3:7–8).[63]

Therefore, for him to be their God and for them to be his people means that Yahweh has come to assure that the future objectives introduced in the garden will in fact come to pass.

Finally, we cannot speak about the emphasis on the presence of God in the Mosaic covenant without mentioning the tabernacle. This institution symbolizes God's end-time pursuits. In Exodus 25–31, God establishes the tabernacle and its worship to reopen his presence in a restricted sense to sinful humanity. This tent represents God's dwelling place in the midst of his people, a reality portrayed in the glory cloud's descent upon the tent, filling the tabernacle with the Lord's presence (Ex. 40:34). The tabernacle is, in itself, a model of Eden and the heavenly temple-city, charged with the opportunity of expansion through obedience and holiness.[64] The tabernacle and its later expression in the temple are both archetypal representations of what will finally be fulfilled in the new city-temple that is the new heaven and new earth.[65] The tabernacle is "a partial but concrete actualization of the ancestral promise, and as the divine dwelling place it is the manifestation of the promise actualized and redemption realized."[66] It foretells the covenant fulfillment of God's eschatological purposes. Through the tabernacle and the promise of dominion and dynasty

---

[63] David G. Peterson, "Worship," in Alexander et al., *New Dictionary of Biblical Theology*, 857.

[64] The Edenic temple and the tabernacle have many parallels. As Fesko summarizes, they are marked by the following similarities: "the seven days of creation and the seven speeches surrounding the construction of the tabernacle; the presence of ornamental trees, precious stones and metal; the menorah as a copy of the tree of life; the veil of the holy of holies with the embroidered cherubim; God walking in the garden and walking about in the tabernacle; God served by Adam the archetypal Levite, as he was served by the Levites; and meeting with God atop a mountain, Mount Sinai (Ex. 19:2)." Fesko, *Last Things First*, 125.

[65] Williamson, *Sealed with an Oath*, 103. Lest we forget, there are also numerous precautions taken in the temple so that God's holiness is not transgressed and sin does not bring about God's wrath. For example, God dwells within the temple, but more specifically, he dwells in the Most Holy Place to which access is granted only to the high priest once a year, and this after numerous preparations. The walls and curtain of the temple also declare that the covenant is concerned with "maintaining the unique divine-human relationship between Yahweh and Israel and thus some means of sustaining communion between a holy God and sinful people was required." Williamson, "Covenant," 424. Thus, the organization of the temple allows God to dwell in the midst of Israel while, at the same time, providing necessary distance. Furthermore, these limits suggest that the tabernacle is by no means the conclusion of God's eschatological objective as it simultaneously provides a hope that there is a better realization of this promise coming by the hands of God himself.

[66] Gorman, *Leviticus*, 12.

reconvened in the Mosaic covenant, the Lord reveals his commitment to be present with his people and his intention to expand this reality throughout all of creation.

The Eschatological Objective and the Davidic Covenant

The divine goal to create a people and a place for his presence is fundamental to the Davidic covenant as well. This covenant, like the one with Moses before it, is built upon the Abrahamic promises of dominion, dynasty, and the dwelling of God. The truth is that "in David, the promise to [Abraham] is fulfilled and renewed."[67] As Williamson argues, 2 Samuel 7 is "full of allusions to the divine assurances given to Abraham," which include "a special divine-human relationship (Gen. 17:7–8; 2 Sam. 7:14; cf. Ps. 89:26), and a special line of 'seed' through which their name will be perpetuated (Gen. 21:12; 2 Sam. 7:12–16)."[68] Thus, the numerous similarities between these covenants reveal that the same eschatological emphases that inform the Abrahamic covenant are paradigmatic for God's commitment with David as well.

DAVID AND DYNASTY

With that said the Davidic covenant does more than simply rehash the promises offered to the patriarchs; it expands them, ironically by narrowing the national and universal promises of God to David and his line. The promise of a people subtly shifts from the nationalistic focus of the covenant with Abraham to a more specific royal dynasty stemming from the root of Jesse (Isaiah 11). In the covenant with David, "attention shifts from Abraham's national descendants to his royal descendants, the 'kings' to whom attention was drawn in Genesis 17:6, 16."[69] So in his covenant with David, God will make David's name great over all the earth (2 Sam. 7:9) and do so by building a house for him (2 Sam. 7:11). In using this "house" image, the Lord is telling Israel's king that he will provide him with a dynasty (see, e.g., 1 Chron. 17:10–14). And as 2 Samuel 7 continues, God tells David how he is going to

---

[67] Bruce K. Waltke, *Genesis: A Commentary* (Grand Rapids: Zondervan, 2001), 53. I would contend that Waltke's use of "fulfilled" may be too strong in this particular instance. Instead, I would use the term *continued*.
[68] Williamson, "Covenant," 425.
[69] Ibid., 426.

do it. Instead of extending his line quantitatively, God will raise up one of David's descendants and place him on his forefather's throne to establish his kingdom forever (7:13).

Here God narrows the promise of dynasty and ties it to the fulfillment of his eschatological purpose. The earlier covenants to this point have been recommitments to objectives introduced in Eden; this new pledge to David, though, hints at *how* God's people will finally be in the land of God's presence *eternally*. God's covenant with David is not simply about the continuation of the Abrahamic blessings but also about how these blessings will finally be fulfilled. In the covenant with David, the Lord reveals how he will gather a people to the place of his presence: there is one who is coming out of David's royal line who will bring these promises to fruition.

But who is this descendant? We see very quickly that it is not David or his immediate sons. If we keep reading we see that the sin problem running rampant through the story is also in David and his offspring. It is the increase of sin and disobedience that ultimately characterizes David's line, not the fulfillment of God's eschatological objectives.[70] In fact, the immediate offspring of David moves the nation away from the presence of God instead of toward it.

This downward spiral forces us to take a closer look at who the promised descendant really is. When we do, we see that there is much more to the promised seed of David than a simple ancestry. God describes him as the true Son of God (2 Sam. 7:14), the king who rules forever (2 Sam. 7:16).[71] He is simultaneously the pinnacle of God's dynastic promise and the one who will complete this promise. In other words, he is the consummation of the promised "seed" first mentioned in Genesis 3:15 and continued in the children of Adam, Noah, Abraham, and David. But even more, this Davidic son is the one who will now overcome the curses of the garden and create a people for the Lord

---

[70] The post-Davidic history of Israel is characterized not by a fulfillment of this promise but rather by degradation into wickedness, save a few righteous kings scattered throughout an otherwise evil generation. As Williamson argues, "None of the Davidic dynasty, even David himself, fully complied with the crucial criterion for divine-human relationship: irreproachable behaviour." Williamson, "Covenant," 426. Once again the sinfulness of man underscores the need for God to work personally in redemptive history to assure that his teleological purposes will reach their ends, an idea that will be addressed in the following chapters.

[71] Block argues that the covenant refrain is actually applied through Father-son terminology in the Lord's covenant with David. The covenant "formula is replaced in the Davidic covenant with the adoption formula, 'I shall be his father, and he will be my son'" (2 Sam. 7:14; cf. Ps. 89:27–28 [Eng. 26–27]). Block, *Book of Ezekiel*, 419.

who can dwell in the Lord's presence. Through him, people from every nation will receive the rich Abrahamic blessings and be invited to reside in God's kingdom.[72] From an eschatological perspective, David's promised ancestor will be the better Adam, the better Israel, and even the better David. He will once and for all restore the Edenic reality to the world at large, complete the Abrahamic promises, and accomplish God's eschatological goals.[73] The Davidic covenant, therefore, inaugurates a better fulfillment of the dynastic promise while also paving the way for the arrival of the greater David and the creation of a people for God's presence.

DAVID AND DOMINION

But as we have seen with the preceding covenants, the Davidic covenant includes more than just the promise of a people; it includes the promise of a place as well. In his own words, God assures David that he, God himself, will procure a land specifically for his people. He announces, "I will appoint a place for my people Israel and will plant them, so that they may dwell in their own place and be disturbed no more" (2 Sam. 7:10; cf. 2 Chron. 17:9). It will be a land of peace free of affliction (2 Sam. 7:10) and enemies, characterized by joy and rest (2 Sam. 7:11). This, of course, evokes Edenic imagery and looks forward to the new creation's fulfillment of these promises (Rev. 21:4ff.). In this sense, the covenant with David "restarts" creation. Through the dominion promise, the Lord reveals his unwavering devotion to the purposes established in Eden.

God will give the people a new paradise, and he will do so through the dynasty of David. So here in the Davidic covenant the promises of dominion and dynasty merge. One of David's descendants will exercise the dominion forfeited by Adam in such a way that all that was meant to take place in Eden will now be brought to fruition. Through this One who comes to exercise perfect dominion, God will finally accomplish his eschatological purposes of the dynasty of David.

---

[72] In Christ, "the dynastic promise has ramifications beyond Israel's borders; it is tied in somehow with God's universal purpose in creation and the prospect of international blessing promised through Abraham (Gen. 12:3) and his royal seed (Gen. 22:18)." Williamson, *Sealed with an Oath*, 129.

[73] Dempster, *Dominion and Dynasty*, 198. This, of course, is ultimately fulfilled in the Davidic descendant Jesus Christ (e.g., Psalm 2; Matt. 1:1).

DAVID AND THE PRESENCE OF GOD

As with all the covenants, the whole Davidic narrative is replete with references to the divine-human relationship. David and his offspring enjoy a bond with Yahweh likened best to a father-son relationship (2 Sam. 7:14). The king will always have the steadfast love of the Lord with him (2 Sam. 7:15), and it is God, present with Israel's king, that establishes the throne of David forever (2 Sam. 7:16). The eschatological goal of God being with his people seems to be within reach now, so much so that David's son Solomon, expressing his hope in God's promises, asks that "the whole earth be filled with his glory!" (Ps. 72:19).

With David and Solomon, we finally have a people of God in the land of God, and at the center of both is the presence of God. Remember how the covenant begins: David aspires to build a dwelling place fit for Yahweh. In a time of relative peace,[74] David finds it unimaginable that he would live in a majestic estate while the ark of the covenant—the distinguished symbol of Yahweh's presence—languished in a tattered tent (2 Sam. 7:2).[75] Yet when David proposes to build a new dwelling place for the Lord, God responds by instituting his own plan—a plan that turns David's righteous desire on its head. Instead of allowing David to build a house for him, the Lord covenants to make David a house of his own (2 Sam. 7:11).

There is more to God's commitment here than just offspring. God vows to use the son of David to finally institute God's temple and bring his presence to dwell with his people (2 Sam. 7:13–14; cf. John 1:14).[76] This promise finds its initial fulfillment in David's son Solomon. He builds the Jerusalem temple where God is to be *permanently* located in the midst of his people for the first time. This is a climactic event for the Israelites. Here in the monarchy of David and Solomon we get closer to

---

[74] The theme of rest should not be overlooked. Along with the divine presence, rest is clearly associated with the fulfillment of God's eschatological purposes. As Williamson helpfully summarizes, "The thematic emphasis on rest signals a salvation-historical watershed. This is suggested not only by how such rest is anticipated in Deuteronomy (cf. Deut. 12:10)—where it is also associated with the establishment of Yahweh's sanctuary (Deut. 12:11)—but also by the reintroduction of the rest motif just prior to the articulation of the dynastic promise itself (2 Sam. 7:11). The 'rest' spoken of in these verses signifies the realization (or, at least, a very significant fulfillment) of God's promises under the national covenant, and the introduction of the next key stage in the outworking of God's universal purpose: the establishment of a royal line from which the anticipated royal seed of Abraham will eventually come." Williamson, *Sealed with an Oath*, 124.

[75] The fact that the ark is with David also expresses God's commitment to his presence. For just in the "coming of the Ark to Jerusalem, Yahweh's self-imposed exile is finally coming to an end (cf. 1 Sam. 4–5). Yahweh is once again enthroned in the midst of his people" (ibid., 122).

[76] For examples of the future fulfillment of this promise in Christ, see Matt. 1:23 and John 1:14.

the way the world is supposed to be—the way the world was in Eden—than ever before. Accordingly, the temple is more than a building; it is the new paradise where the Lord's presence is poised once again to expand from this site in Jerusalem to the rest of the world.

Conclusion

With Israel set to become the new Eden, let us take a brief moment to remember where we have been. We who were once in sin received our just curses, but also received, out of God's sheer grace, a covenant relationship with our Creator and Redeemer that ensures the eschatological goal of becoming a people in the place of his presence. In light of this, may our hearts revel in the God of our salvation, who covenants with us to secure his glory and our hope and happiness. And what is more, God is not done. Our look back upon God's work before David should draw our eyes forward to what God will do next. What we see when we look ahead is our Lord pulling the common threads of all of the previous covenants together to create the beautiful fabric of the new covenant. It is here where we see how God will bring his objectives to completion, and it is to the new covenant that we now turn our attention in the next chapter.

5

The Promise of a Hero

The New Covenant, the New Adam, and the Presence of God

Like an old movie constantly rerun on basic cable, Israel's story after David is one we have seen before. In particular, it is the same as Israel's story *before* David, a story of sin and desperation. God's beautiful promises to David have not reached fulfillment; instead, they lie in shambles at the feet of the Assyrians and Babylonians. The promised son of David, it turns out, is not Solomon or any of the reprobates who followed him. And instead of God's eschatological objectives going out from Jerusalem to the rest of the world, the rest of the world's ideals inundate Jerusalem. So as disobedience replaces obedience in the nation, war and judgment replace peace and deliverance. Only a generation or so after David's covenant there comes the great reversal: God disassembles the nation, drives them from his Land of Promise, and, in one final agonizing blow, uses the sword of Babylon to level the temple of his presence. Once again, God's purposes in creation and redemption appear to be unreachable—well, at least unreachable by any other than God himself.

Yet out of the rubble of David's genealogy and the nation's faithlessness, God responds. He gives us the next great act in his cosmic screenplay, centering on two major movements: a new covenant and a new covenant hero.

God's Eschatological Objective and the New Covenant

As we have seen time and time again, nothing and no one will stop the Lord from reaching his redemptive goals, not even those whom he wishes to bless. This is why the Lord establishes a new covenant; in it comes a climactic fulfillment by which the Old Testament covenant promises—promises of a people, a place, and divine presence—are unified and even surpassed.[1] Similar to its predecessors, the new covenant continues to emphasize the Lord's eschatological goals but, in a distinct way, demonstrates that there will be a comprehensive removal of transgression (Jer. 31:34; Ezek. 36:29, 33), a wholehearted internal transformation (Jer. 31:33; Ezek. 36:26), and a deeper relational intimacy between God and his people (Jer. 31:34; Ezek. 36:27).[2] By way of the new covenant, God secures his future purposes and lights the fuse for redemptive history's glorious resolution.

A People for the New Covenant

The transcendent nature[3] of the new covenant influences the way we conceptualize God's promises from its inception forward. For instance, the new covenant makes it clear that while God remains committed to a people, the promises of this covenant go beyond those simply identified ethnically with Israel. Instead of limiting his blessings or just removing them all together, the Lord institutes the new covenant to *expand* the line of Abraham to include a new kind of descendant, one that is in Abraham through *faith* (Rom. 4:1–25;

---

[1] Paul R. Williamson, "Covenant," in *New Dictionary of Biblical Theology*, ed. T. Desmond Alexander et al. (Downers Grove, IL: InterVarsity, 2000), 427.

[2] Ibid.

[3] Jeremiah 31 is probably the most apparent and succinct representation of the new covenant as it is the only place where the specific phrase "new covenant" (ברית חדשה) occurs in the Old Testament. A significant discontinuity is described in this text. Jeremiah announces that "days are coming" in which God will bring about a new covenant with his people, one distinct in certain respects from the earlier expressions of the covenant. In particular, the new covenant will be accomplished (Jer. 31:31–32) by God himself. Bruce Ware contends: "It is . . . clear from this text [Jer. 31:31–34] that the expressed obligation is unilateral or asymmetrical in its direction. That is, it is directed from God to his people with no corresponding obligation expressed in the people's part of God." Ware continues, clarifying that "to say that the obligation is on God's side alone does not mean that Israel is excluded from any role in the covenant. In fact, the opposite is the case. Israel has a crucial role to play, but it is the role of a recipient and beneficiary, not that of an initiator or benefactor. In the new covenant, God will act on behalf of his people, and they will be benefited by his powerful and gracious work." Bruce A. Ware, "The New Covenant and the People(s) of God," in *Dispensationalism, Israel, and the Church: The Search for Definition*, ed. Craig A. Blaising and Darrell L. Bock (Grand Rapids: Zondervan, 1992), 74. In sum, the Lord promises to be the one who will bring about the requirements of the covenant. He will write the law on the people's hearts (Jer. 31:32), instill the knowledge of God in their minds, and forgive their sins and forget their iniquities forever (Jer. 31:34). The Lord ensures that the requirements of the covenant will be met and the eschatological goals of creation will be accomplished (Jer. 24:7; 32:39) by becoming the one who fulfills the covenant demands. Thus, Yahweh is the provider of the new covenant.

Gal. 3:8).[4] This true and full covenant goes beyond simple national-istic boundaries to bring the hope of God's dynastic promises to the ends of the earth and all the peoples therein (e.g., Isa. 42:6; 49:6; 55:3–5; 56:4–8; 66:18–24).

This is all accomplished by God's hand. We have seen repeatedly the Israelites' response to God's merciful commitment to his own cov-enants. They continue in their idolatrous ways. In the exodus long ago, we noted, "The Israelites had nothing to commend them for divine election when he rescued them from the bondage of Egypt, and they certainly have no merit now (cf. [Ezek.] 36:21)"[5] as they await a new exodus. The nations grafted into the people of God are the same way. To make a people for himself the Lord has to do just that: *make* a people for himself. God promises through his grace-based new covenant to cleanse those he will make his own (Ezek. 36:25) and replace their hearts of stone with hearts of flesh (36:26). God pledges to put his Spirit in them (36:27) and bring them to a saving relationship with him.

When we get to the New Testament, this new covenant comes alive. The Spirit works not only among the nation of Israel but also among the Gentiles. In doing so, God fulfills his mandate to be fruitful and multiply and his promise that he would create a great people. In other words, the new covenant completes the dynastic promise (John 3:6–8; 6:63; Acts 10:44; Rom. 2:29; 8:1–17; 1 Cor. 2:14; 2 Cor. 3:6; 2 Thess. 2:17; Titus 3:5–6; 1 Pet. 1:1–2; 1 John 3:24; 4:13). As Daniel Block com-ments, Ezekiel 37:26–27 discloses that "Yahweh will *multiply* the na-

---

[4] Though the new covenant is often promised to Israel alone in the Old Testament, there are examples of the inclusion of the Gentiles. As Ware notes, "One new-covenant text that seems to suggest that whereas the new covenant is given particularly to Israel, it nonetheless extends beyond Israel to the nations, is Isaiah 55:3–5." Ware, "The New Covenant," 72. In engaging this text, Ware concludes: "The everlasting covenant spoken of here [in Isa. 55:3–5] is specifically said to be an expression of God's love promised to David. Israel will have its leader and commander, as promised long ago to David. But there is an additional element in this text, for this new David, who rules under a new everlasting covenant, will also summon nations and peoples Israel does not know. So while the new covenant is uniformly (here and elsewhere in the Old Testament) directed to the nation of Israel, we see from this text that the new covenant made with Israel includes a host of Gentile participants, not directly addressed as God's covenant partners" (ibid., 73). Cf. Robert L. Saucy, *The Case for Progressive Dispensationalism: The Interface Between Dispensational and Non-Dispensational Theology* (Grand Rapids: Zondervan, 1993), 127–34; William J. Dumbrell, *Covenant and Creation: A Theology of the Old Testament Covenants* (Carlisle, UK: Paternoster, 1984), 165–200. This makes sense in light of Isaiah's prophecy of the Servant of God, fulfilled in Jesus Christ, who is to be a "covenant for the people" through whom the nations will be reached. God's servant is to be a "light for the nations" (Isa. 42:6; 49:6; cf. John 8:12). As Isaiah announces the word of the Lord: "It is too light a thing that you should be my servant / to raise up the tribes of Jacob / and to bring back the preserved of Israel; / I will make you as a light for the nations, / that my salvation may reach to the ends of the earth" (Isa. 49:6). Here, God makes clear that his redemptive work through the new covenant extends beyond the borders of Israel to include the salvation of many peoples, therefore growing and expanding the dynastic promise of in the everlasting covenant through Christ, the servant of the Lord.

[5] Daniel I. Block, *The Book of Ezekiel: Chapters 25–48*, NICOT (Grand Rapids: Eerdmans, 1998), 422.

tion, an expression that alludes to the promises of Abraham to multiply his descendants as the stars of the sky, the grains of the sand on the seashore, and the dust of the earth."[6] In the new covenant, the promise of a new people begins to take shape in ways never thought possible. In an unimaginable move, the new covenant unifies the dynastic promise given to Abraham and the promise that Israel will be a light to the nations. The purpose for this is to establish a people for God that expands beyond national borders, filling the world with the promises begun in Eden. For God works through the new covenant to bring the "light to the nations" so that his "salvation may reach to the ends of the earth" (Isa. 49:6; cf. 42:6).

A Place for the New Covenant

Creating a new covenant people requires that a place be made for them as well. Isaiah hints that the Lord has cosmological intentions with the new covenant just as he set out in the garden. Take Isaiah 65:17 for example. In the words of the prophet, Yahweh will

> . . . create new heavens
>   and a new earth,
> and the former things shall not be remembered
>   or come into mind.

This reminds us of the eschatological design of the Lord. In the verses that follow, we see that there is a "qualitative contrast between the 'former' earth, where the 'first affliction' of captivity occurred, and 'a new heaven and new earth,' where there will be only enduring 'joy and exultation.'"[7] The subsequent description of the new heaven and new earth reads like a reversal of Adam's curse: there will be no more weeping (65:19); there will be no more death of young or old (65:20); they will domesticate the land and rule over it, building homes and eating their harvest (65:21); their dominion will be restored (65:25; cf. v. 22); and their dynasty will be established (65:23–24). This picturesque world captures both the past beauty of Eden and the expanded

---

[6] Ibid., 419–20, emphasis original.

[7] G. K. Beale and Sean M. McDonough, "Revelation 21:1–22:5," in *Commentary on the New Testament Use of the Old Testament*, ed. G. K. Beale and D. A. Carson (Grand Rapids: Baker, 2007), 1150.

future reality of the new heaven and new earth. And again, in Isaiah 66:22, the new creation promises a future world that will "remain" forever. This "Edenization" will cover the whole earth, showing us that the new covenant is an eternal and expanding covenant and revealing that God's redemption is a worldwide mission.

But again we are stuck. How will sinners like us enter this new heaven and new earth according to the new covenant? It's the same problem we have run into with the other covenants. What each moral collapse to this point has shown us is that Adam and Israel could not even receive the covenant promises, much less accomplish God's eschatological purposes on their own merits (Isa. 26:16–18). Instead of the land being a place of blessing, Israel has made it "a permanent place of death, thoroughly defiling it by means of bloodshed and idolatry, making it a place unfit for divine habitation by the living God (Ezek. 36:18)."[8] As a result, the Lord removes the Israelites from the Land of Promise, much as he banished Adam from Eden. Despite their disobedience, however, the Lord does not give up on his people. Instead, he makes it clear that he himself will fulfill the demands of the covenant in order to complete his covenant pledge. As we see in Ezekiel 36:24 (cf. Ezek. 11:17; 37:21–22), Yahweh reassures the people of his promise to bring them out of exile into a land of their own, a land that recalls the imagery of Eden and forecasts the details of the new heaven and new earth (34:23–31; 36:35; chaps. 40–48).

This is also the case in Ezekiel 47. In verse 12, Ezekiel describes the new creation in Edenic imagery, stating that "on both sides of the river, there will grow all kinds of trees for food. Their leaves will not wither, nor their fruit fail, but they will bear fresh fruit every month, because the water for them flows from the sanctuary. Their fruit will be for food, and their leaves for healing." Greg Beale and Sean McDonough note, "The scene in Ezekiel itself is modeled partly on the primal garden and its adjacent river of Gen. 2:9–10, so that Ezekiel and Revelation (cf. Rev. 22:2) envision an escalated reestablishment of the garden of the first creation in which God's presence openly dwelt."[9] Here we see the eschatological dominion promise crop up again. The Lord offers the

---

[8] Iain M. Duguid, *Ezekiel*, NIVAC (Grand Rapids: Zondervan, 1999), 414.
[9] Beale and McDonough, "Revelation 21:1–22:5," 1154.

new covenant not only to tell us how to be people of the promise but also how to enter into this prospective Eden-like reality (Isa. 11:9–10; Hab. 2:14). Even in the middle of Israel's judgment and exile, God holds fast to his eschatological vision. In the wasteland of post-Babylonian Israel, God promises a new land that transcends the original garden and teems with covenant elect (e.g., Ezek. 36:37). The primary point here is that the new covenant, and the eschatological objective behind it, portrays the dominion promise as a new Eden, one that will finalize and surpass the divine purpose first introduced in Genesis 1–3, thus making the whole world the Lord's dwelling place. The new covenant is God's commitment to restore the now cursed land, so much so that the people of promise will one day say, "This land that was desolate has become like the garden of Eden, and the waste and desolate and ruined cities are now fortified and inhabited" (Ezek. 36:35).

The Presence of God and the New Covenant

Let us not forget that the reason God creates a people and a place is so that he can be relationally present. This is the emphasis of the new covenant as well. Regarding the future arrival of the Lord, Isaiah commands:

> In the wilderness prepare the way of the LORD;
>   make straight in the desert a highway for our God.[10]
> Every valley shall be lifted up,
>   and every mountain and hill be made low;
> the uneven ground shall become level,
>   and the rough places a plain.
> And the glory of the LORD shall be revealed.
>   and all flesh shall see it together,
>   for the mouth of the LORD has spoken. (Isa. 40:3–5)

Through the prophet the Lord tells an exiled people—a people facing a future without a temple—that he is once again coming to dwell with them. He will reveal his glory—a term used to describe divine

---

[10] In the New Testament, this quote is applied to John the Baptist, who prepares the way for the coming Christ, himself Immanuel, God with us (Matt. 3:3; Mark 1:3; Luke 3:4; John 1:23). He is the one coming out of the wilderness that Isaiah and John proclaim, for salvation comes only through God's breaking into history, a theme that will be covered in greater detail in the following chapters.

presence[11]—and in his appearance all the future objectives established in creation and continued in the covenants will find their conclusion. As the beginning of the biblical story spotlights, God always intended to draw near to his creation, and it is finally through the promises of the new covenant that this will come to pass. This is why Isaiah paints an eschatological picture of the new heaven and new earth as an eternal dominion created for an eternal dynasty that will reside eternally in the presence of their covenant Lord. For this reason, Isaiah declares:

> For as the new heavens and the new earth
> > that I make
> shall remain before me, says the LORD,
> > so shall your offspring and your name remain.
> From new moon to new moon,
> > and from Sabbath to Sabbath,
> all flesh shall come to worship before me,
> declares the LORD. (Isa. 66:22–23; cf. Rev. 7:15–17)

Here, dominion is no longer the earth of old; it is now the new creation, the whole cosmos. Furthermore, the promise of dynasty is no longer limited to the nation of Israel but is chosen from "all flesh," meaning that believers from all nations are now privy to God's covenant promises, and they will stand in the presence of God (e.g., Isa. 11:10; 35:2; 40:5; 58:8; 59:19; 60:1–2; 66:18). Similarly, in Isaiah 12:6, the prophet declares that the Holy One of Israel is great in the midst of the inhabitants of Zion (the redeemed remnant of God's people).

We also find the presence of God in Jeremiah 31, where we once again hear the familiar covenant refrain, "I will be their God, and they shall be my people." Though this should fill our minds with earlier covenant passages, we should also hear the hints that there is something new in this promise now. In the context of the new covenant, God pledges both to restore access to his presence and to regenerate his

---

[11] *Glory* and *divine presence* are often synonymous in Isaiah and Scripture as a whole (Ex. 16:7, 10; 25:8; 29:43; 40:34; Pss. 26:8; 63:2; Isa. 57:15; Zech. 2:10–11). In particular we see that *glory* is used to describe the manifestation of the Lord in the temple and tabernacle (Ex. 40:34–35; 1 Kings 8:11). In Isaiah in particular its connection is seen throughout (cf. Isa. 35:2; 40:5; 58:8; 59:19; 60:1–2; 66:18). Take, for example, Isa. 6:3. Here the *glory of the Lord* is a term used for the relational and manifest presence of God for which the seraphim cry out in expectancy of its global fulfillment, making the world his dwelling place forever.

elect in order to enter his presence. The new covenant finally answers how sinners, disobedient and separated from their Creator, can enter his holy presence. God will do it. God will come to cleanse them. God's commitment to be their God is ultimately achieved through the "complete removal of sin (Jer. 31:34), inner transformation of the heart (Jer. 31:33), and an *intimate relationship with God* (Jer. 31: 34a)."[12] Through this final covenantal expression, the Lord commits personally to draw near to the people, to relate to them eternally, and finally to dwell among them.

We find the same refrain, along with the same commitment to God's eschatological objectives, in Ezekiel 37:15–28. In this beautiful passage God promises himself. He covenants to provide land (37:21), nationhood (37:22a), Davidic kingship (37:22b, 27), salvation (37:23–24), an eternal relationship with God (37:23), an everlasting covenant of peace (37:26), and, ultimately, *his permanent presence in the midst of his people* (37:26). Verses 26–28 reveal that God's faithfulness to his eschatological aims centers on the forthcoming reality of the Lord's coming to be with man (e.g., Isa. 12:6; 60:19–21; Joel 2:27; 3:17). In this text, the Lord announces,

> I will make a covenant of peace with them. It shall be an everlasting covenant with them. And I will set them in their land and multiply them, and will set my sanctuary in their midst forevermore. My dwelling place shall be with them, and I will be their God, and they shall be my people. Then the nations will know that I am the LORD who sanctifies Israel, when my sanctuary is in their midst forevermore.

Here we gain insight into the eschatological hope of God's new dynasty: the holy God will soon dwell in the midst of a new, redeemed people in a new, redeemed land. This passage shows us that the reason for the dominion and dynasty promises is so that the presence of God may be accessible to the ones he saves. The future goal of the Lord in redemption is to dwell in a new place among a new people for his glory and our good. God has given up on nothing. The purposes of Eden and the promises of Abraham are still

---

[12] Williamson, "Covenant," 427, emphasis added.

alive in the new covenant.[13] As the covenant promises, he will be their God, and they will be his people, in order that he may dwell freely, fully, and eternally with his redeemed.[14] The presence of God is a sure promise not only because the Lord offers the people his presence, but also because in the new covenant, he shows us how he will secure it.[15]

Similarly, the book of Zechariah casts the new covenant in an eschatological framework and, like so many other texts, reveals the pinnacle of the covenant to be God's dwelling with his people. Speaking of the Lord's return, Zechariah the prophet writes, "Thus says the Lord: I have returned to Zion and will dwell in the midst of Jerusalem, and Jerusalem shall be called the faithful city, and the mountain of the Lord of hosts, the holy mountain" (Zech. 8:3; cf. Ex. 25:8). A few lines later, the word of the Lord declares: "Behold, I will save my people from the east country and from the west country, and I will bring them to dwell in the midst of Jerusalem. And they shall be my people, and I will be their God, in faithfulness and in righteousness" (Zech. 8:7–8).[16] Here we see the covenant refrain connected with the divine promise to be present with his people. More emphatic, though, is that even in the Lord's righteously judging the rebellious city (Ezekiel 10), he graciously promises to dwell in Jerusalem once again—a prophecy inaugurated when God's presence entered the city on the back of a colt (Zech. 9:9; Matt. 21:1–11;

---

[13] Dumbrell, *Covenant and Creation*, 188.

[14] In his commentary on Leviticus, Wenham shows the connection between Ezekiel and the previous covenantal expression of Leviticus 26. He writes: "It is Ezekiel who makes most use of Leviticus as a direct inspiration for his prophecies. He looks forward to a new age when God would send a faithful shepherd, like David, to save the people from wild beasts (Ezek. 34:25; cf. Lev. 26:6). In the new covenant there will be abundant rain and harvests (Ezek. 34:26–27; cf. Lev. 26:4–5, 13). The people will not be oppressed by the nations (Ezek. 34:28; cf. Lev. 26:7–8). *They will be multiplied and fruitful (Ezek. 36:10–11; cf. Lev. 26:9). They shall become God's people and his dwelling shall be with them (Ezek. 36:28; 37:24–27; cf. Lev. 26:2; 11–12).*" Gordon J. Wenham, *The Book of Leviticus*, NICOT (Grand Rapids: Eerdmans, 1979), 330, emphasis added.

[15] God's same commitment to be eternally present with his people characterizes Ezekiel 43. Speaking to his prophet, God declares, "Son of man, this is the place of my throne and the place of the soles of my feet, where I will dwell in the midst of the people of Israel forever" (Ezek. 43:7). Here the Lord reveals that he will fill the temple with his glory and points us to the fulfillment of God's future purposes, showing us that "the end-time temple would be 'where' God 'will dwell [*kataskēnōsei*] among the sons of Israel forever." Beale and McDonough, "Revelation 21:1–22:5," 1151. So we see the connection between the new covenant and the presence of God: through the prophets the Lord makes it clear that the intent of his redemption is to once again be present with his people, a promise that will be complete in the new heaven and new earth. Such texts reveal that, from its inception, the world was to be the sanctuary-temple where God was relationally manifest.

[16] Zechariah also takes up the covenant refrain again to reassure his audience that the relational presence of God will return to the people of promise. As Boda writes concerning the refrain, "This statement is a familiar formula drawn from the covenant tradition of Israel, emphasizing the relational purpose behind God's redemptive activity." Therefore, Zechariah, like the rest of the history of salvation, is concerned "with God and his people reunited in the city of his presence." Mark J. Boda, *Zechariah*, NIVAC (Grand Rapids: Zondervan, 2004), 382.

Mark 11:1–11; Luke 19:28–40; John 12:12–19) and to be consummated when God's presence fills the New Jerusalem.

The new covenant promises that God's presence will be for all peoples, Jew and Gentile alike. According to Zechariah, God will redeem the nations, and his presence will be the mark of their salvation.

> Sing and rejoice, O daughter of Zion, for behold, I come and I will dwell in your midst, declares the LORD. And many nations shall join themselves to the LORD in that day, and shall be my people. And I will dwell in your midst, and you shall know that the LORD of hosts has sent me to you. And the LORD will inherit Judah as his portion in the holy land, and will again choose Jerusalem. (Zech. 2:10–12)

The New Covenant and the New Adam: Christ and the Eschatological Objective of Redemptive History

The new covenant points to a new movement in God's redemptive drama, and that is exactly what God brings about. To complete his promises, God introduces us to the story's great action hero: the new Adam, the true son of David, the true Son of God, Jesus Christ. To this point, God's people have failed. They cannot obey; they continue to break God's covenant. God's purposes in creation and redemption seemingly hang by a thread, a thread made up solely of God's gracious commitment to his own ends. But this is why the new covenant carries with it a new type of promise. It is a covenant that instructs all of God's people to look to God, not themselves—something they should have been doing all along. In Isaiah's plea, the future hope lies solely in the God who

> would rend the heavens and come down,
>   that the mountains might quake at [his] presence. (Isa. 64:1)

In the new covenant, God comes down in Christ. God becomes present to complete the very reason for creation. Thus Paul argues in Colossians 1, "All things were created through [Jesus Christ] and *for* [Jesus Christ]" (1:16). Jesus not only creates; he is also the *purpose* for creation. Christ is the one who completes the objectives informing the world. The God-man comes to "reconcile to himself all things, whether on earth or in heaven, making peace by the blood of his cross" (Col. 1:20). The God-man comes to pick up the pieces left by Adam's curse.

This is why Paul casts Jesus as the new Adam. He comes to do what the first Adam could not: complete God's purposes for creation (Rom. 5:12–21; 1 Cor. 15:22, 44–49). He is from the line of Adam, Noah, Abraham, and David because he is the one who finally establishes a people and a place for the presence of God (Matt. 1:1–17; Luke 3:23–38). As this new divine representative of humanity, Christ conclusively removes the curses of the garden and inaugurates the fulfillment of God's future intentions. Thus, Christ is Adam in true eschatological fullness. He typifies what the first man was supposed to be and joyfully completes the divine mandate broken in the fall (Rom. 5:14; 1 Cor. 15:44–49). Jesus reverses the disobedience of the first man and, through his cruel death on the cross, unites those in Adam to himself, their perfect representative. In bringing the covenant promise of dominion and dynasty to fruition, the last Adam provides final access to the new Eden, where God dwells in the midst of his people. Thus it is only through the new covenant work of Christ, our better Adam, that God accomplishes his purpose of spreading his presence to all creation.

The Eschatological Focus of the New Adam

Christ's active obedience and sacrifice for sin are both aspects of the Adam-Christ typological relationship applied in Scripture.[17] In these acts, Jesus overcomes the sin of the first Adam and prepares the way of redemption and reconciliation. But it must be noted that Christ's saving work as the new representative of man includes an oft-forgotten eschatological dimension. At the same time that Jesus's mission negatively confronts Adam's rebellion, he positively reclaims God's end-time directives frustrated in the fall. We can agree with Beale that

---

[17] As Davidson develops the relationship: "Adam (like the new Adam, Christ) is the 'head' and inclusive representative of the human race. There is a 'solidarity' between Adam and the rest of humanity. What is true of Adam, the representative man, says Paul, is true of Christ the (new) Representative Man." Davidson shifts then to highlight the negative realities of the Adam-Christ typology. He writes: "Christ's act of righteousness has not merely counterbalanced Adam's act of sin; he has counter-acted and annulled, overcome, surpassed, defeated, and done away with them. . . . If it is certain that 'the many' died through Adam's trespass . . . it is 'much more' certain that God's grace in Christ has overflowed to 'the many.'" Richard M. Davidson, *Typology in Scripture: A Study of the Hermeneutical* τύπος *Structures* (Berrien Springs, MI: Andrews University Press, 1981), 300–304.

the doctrine of Christ as the Last Adam . . . [is] to be understood as references to Christ re-establishing a new creation as God's new, reigning vicegerent, since the first creation was commenced with a human also called Adam, who was in the image of God and called God's son. As such, Christ is the Son of Adam, or the "Son of Man," who has begun to do what the first Adam should have done and to inherit what the first Adam should have.[18]

Christ reinstitutes the new creation, which I have argued involves the re-creation of a new dominion and new dynasty for the experience of God's presence. Christ's passive and active obedience respectively overcome separation from God in death and provide access to God's presence eternally (Heb. 10:19–25). So in the coming of the second Adam, the "eschatology, forfeited for humanity in Adam by his disobedience, has been secured for the new humanity in Christ, the last Adam, by his obedience."[19]

Thus we see that, as with Adam, Christ's mission and purpose are closely tied to his future objectives. Adam's call always included God's eschatological imperatives and, in particular, the cosmological dissemination of his presence. This eschatological focus is one of the greatest continuities between the pre-fall Adam and Christ: both are driven to bring about the culmination of God's creation purposes. What Adam starts, Jesus finishes.

As we have seen, the Lord called Adam to pursue his eschatological ends; yet, in his transgression, the first man's sinful desires quickly and surreptitiously usurped Yahweh's creative purposes. Because of this, Adam's "order is first and has become subject to corruption and death through human sin (Rom. 5:12ff.; 1 Cor. 15:21–22)."[20] Owing to sin, the end-time orientation of Adam was distorted and demands a full-bore reclamation project if it is to continue.

In response, God provides Jesus Christ, the new and better Adam

---

[18] G. K. Beale, "The Eschatological Conception of New Testament Theology," in *Eschatology in Bible and Theology: Evangelical Essays at the Dawn of a New Millennium*, ed. Kent E. Bower and Mark W. Elliott (Downers Grove, IL: InterVarsity), 25.

[19] Richard B. Gaffin, "Last Adam, the Life-Giving Spirit," in *The Forgotten Christ: Exploring the Majesty and Mystery of God Incarnate*, ed. Stephen Clark (Nottingham, UK: Apollos, 2007), 208. Gaffin makes this claim, based on Paul's argument in 1 Cor. 15:44–49, that the apostle's reflection on Adam in this passage includes his role and function prior to the fall. Christ's coming therefore includes taking up the eschatological purposes of Adam and bringing them to their rightful conclusions.

[20] Ibid.

who tears down the man-made barriers to God's end-time promises. Whereas Adam's order was sinful and short-lived, "the order of Christ is second and last; it is incorruptible and eschatological."[21] In this light, Christ's goals are, in one sense, the goals originally appropriated to the first man. So J. V. Fesko concludes, "God's intended goal for the creation has not changed"; rather, "the mandate remained the same throughout redemptive history and awaited the arrival of the second Adam, who would take up the abandoned work of the first Adam."[22] From this perspective, Christ's work is more than moral and remedial; it is eschatological. Part of Christ's mission as the new representative of man is to salvage Adam's mission and bring it to completion.

This means that his death and resurrection have an eschatological purpose. Christ is not only saving people from their sin, though he is doing that; he is saving them to be *a people*, to create a paradise for them, and to give them access to God's presence forever. Christ restores what was lost with Adam. As the better Adam, "Christ is the means de facto by which the eschatology in view for the creation since the beginning is now being realized."[23] Thus Christ comes to fix what Adam's sin destroyed: he reestablishes and expands the promises of dominion and dynasty in order to bring about the global expansion of God's presence. In short, through the second Adam, the purposes begun in Eden finally find their conclusion.

THE NEW ADAM AND THE PROMISE OF A PEOPLE

The first words of the New Testament are written so that you and I clearly understand that the new Adam is here to redeem an eschatological people for God.[24] In Matthew 1:1, the apostle unveils Christ as "the

---

[21] Ibid.

[22] J. V. Fesko, *Last Things First: Unlocking Genesis 1–3 with the Christ of Eschatology* (Fearn, Ross-shire, UK: Mentor, 2007), 164.

[23] Gaffin, "Last Adam," 206.

[24] In Luke 1, the prophecy of Zechariah (John the Baptist's father) also depicts Christ as the procurer of God's redemptive purposes. Through the advent of Jesus, the Lord God of Israel "has visited and redeemed his people / and has raised up a horn of salvation for us / in the house of his servant David, / as he spoke by the mouth of his holy prophets from of old, / that we should be saved from our enemies / and from the hand of all who hate us; / to show the mercy promised to our fathers / and to remember his holy covenant, the oath that he swore to our father Abraham, to grant us / that we, being delivered from the hand of our enemies, / might serve him without fear, / in holiness and righteousness before him all our days" (Luke 1:68–75). Out of the house of David, comes Christ, the one who promised, the one who came to restore the cosmos to its original order and deliver the people of God from their enemies into the presence of God forever. Christ is God's covenant fulfiller, and thus the Savior who inaugurates the completion of the eschatological objectives of redemptive history.

son of David, the son of Abraham." Describing Christ this way reminds us immediately of Yahweh's promise to provide Abraham with a seed who would bring forth a nation and a kingdom. Christ's being the "'son of Abraham' traces Jesus' lineage back to the founding father of the nation of Israel, ensuring . . . the echoes of God's promises to Abraham that his offspring would bless all the peoples of the earth (Gen. 12:1–3)."[25] In a similar way, Matthew also reveals that Christ descends from the royal line of David. Matthew is telling us that the promises of 2 Samuel 7 are being fulfilled before our very eyes. This seemingly ordinary Nazarene is the "son of David" who will sit on his forefather's throne forever. Not only that, Jesus completes the dynastic promise given to Israel's great king;[26] as the seed of Abraham and seed of David, Christ is the one true way to be a part of the eschatological people of God.

More specifically, if we are united to Christ in faith, it places *us* in the Abrahamic and Davidic line. If one focuses on the Abrahamic "announcement that 'all the nations will be blessed through you' (Gen. 12:3; 18:18) it is clear that Paul argues that Christ 'redeemed us in order that the blessing given to Abraham might come to the Gentiles through Christ Jesus, so that by faith we might receive the promise of the Spirit' (Gal. 3:14)."[27] Later in Galatians, the apostle contends that "the promises were spoken to Abraham and to his seed. The Scripture does not say 'and to seeds,' meaning many people, but 'and to your seed,' meaning one person, who is Christ" (Gal. 3:16). Consequently, "according to Paul's reading of history, Christ is the true Heir of the promise, of the universal inheritance, and He determines the fellowheirs."[28] It is through Christ, then, that we are made Abraham's sons and a part of God's dynasty. Those united by faith to Christ become the people of God, partakers of Abraham's promises and the joys of the Lord's eschatological objectives. Moreover, Christ's work as the new Adam casts him as the new Israel. According to the Old Testament,

---

[25] Craig L. Blomberg, *Matthew*, NAC (Nashville: Broadman & Holman, 1992), 52.

[26] As the fulfillment of the promised Davidic king who would sit on the throne forever, Christ the sacrificial Lamb exercises the righteous authority in his kingly reign, completing the creation mandate of dominion (2 Sam. 7:12–16; cf. Rev. 5:13; 7:9–17; 11:15; 22:1–3). Dempster concludes, in Christ "humanity has been restored to its original position, and this has been brought about by a Davidic king—a new Adam. The scion of David has conquered the serpent of Genesis 3." Stephen G. Dempster, *Dominion and Dynasty: A Theology of the Hebrew Bible*, NSBT 15 (Downers Grove, IL: InterVarsity, 2003), 176.

[27] T. Desmond Alexander, "Seed," in Alexander et al., *New Dictionary of Biblical Theology*, 769.

[28] Ronald K. Fung, *The Epistle to the Galatians*, NICNT (Grand Rapids: Eerdmans, 1988), 156.

the Hebrew nation is basically an extension of the Adamic reality on a nationalistic scale. Like Adam before, Israel, the free recipient of God's eschatological promises, sinned and was cursed for its disobedience (e.g., Isa. 42:1–9; 49:1–3; 50:4–9; 52:13–53:12). So as Christ does for Adam, he also does for God's nation. As this new Israel himself, "Jesus appears not just as the Savior of Israel in fulfillment of prophetic expectation, but also as an embodiment of Israel as they should be." The Gospel of Matthew shows us that Jesus's work reenacts the history of God's people in order to accomplish what was lost in their rebellion. He lives out "the Exodus from Egypt (Matt. 2:19–20), the crossing of the Red Sea (Matt. 3:13–17), the temptations in the desert (Matt. 4:1–11), even the arrival at Mt. Sinai to receive the law (Matt. 5:1–2)."[29] In doing this, Christ does both what Adam could not do and what God's chosen nation could not accomplish; namely, he restores God's eschatological objectives. Even though "Israel fell under the curse of the covenant (Gal. 3:10; quoting Deut. 27:26) . . . the promises of blessing are not made void, because Jesus stepped into the position of those born under the law to redeem them (Gal. 4:4–5), and so the promises are realized in him."[30] Christ, therefore, saves a dynasty through his life, death, and resurrection to ensure access into God's everlasting presence.

THE NEW ADAM AND THE PROMISE OF A PLACE

As God brings forth a dynasty through Christ, through Christ he also fulfills the promise of dominion. "Christ's work," Beale asserts, "reveals that the end of the world and the coming new creation have begun in his death and resurrection."[31] Christ, therefore, is the "firstfruit" of the experience of the New Jerusalem. In Adam's place (and Israel's too), the Lord "raises up another individual Adamic figure, Jesus Christ, who . . . inaugurates a new creation which will not be corrupted but find its culmination in a new heavens and new earth."[32] Through his death and resurrection, Christ throws open the doors to a new and better dominion filled with the presence of God. From this perspective, Scripture's story is about the "movement 'from creation to new creation by

---

[29] Stephen Motyer, "Israel (nation)," in Alexander et al., *New Dictionary of Biblical Theology*, 584.
[30] Ibid., 585.
[31] Beale, "Eschatological Conception," 19.
[32] Ibid., 26.

means of divine redemptive interventions,' climaxing in Christ's death, resurrection and second coming which concludes all things."[33] Those who are in Christ are new creations themselves (2 Cor. 5:15–17)—with the old curses, sins, and disobedience having passed away and the new dominion of a better Eden having come now through the reconciling work of the new Adam.

So even though there is little emphasis placed on a physical land promise in the New Testament, that does not mean the theme is absent. Instead, the promise of land is best understood as inaugurated in Christ and awaiting final consummation. The fulfillment of the dominion promise, therefore, will be the eschatological "re-creation" of all that was lost in Eden. God's land pledge points back to the garden-sanctuary before corruption and sin interfered and picks up on the similar but limited expression of God's presence found in the institution of the tabernacle/temple as well.

We see the inaugural work of Christ's creating a new dominion in Colossians 1:20, where Paul declares that Christ has come to "reconcile to himself all things," which includes things "on earth or in heaven." Though this verse has more often than not been applied to the salvation of believers, it also has serious ramifications for the way we are to understand the effects of Christ's atoning death on the earth as a whole, especially with respect to the coming new creation. In commenting on Colossians 1:20, New Testament scholar Douglas Moo asserts, "Fallen human beings are the primary objects of this reconciliation. . . . But it would be a serious mistake to limit this 'reconciling' work to human beings."[34] Instead, this verse reveals that Christ's work on the cross also brings about "cosmic restoration/renewal."[35] So "through the work of

---

[33] Ibid., 21. See also William J. Dumbrell, *The End of the Beginning: Revelation 21–22 and the Old Testament* (Eugene, OR: Wipf and Stock, 2001), 166, 196.

[34] Douglas J. Moo, *The Letters to the Colossians and to Philemon*, PNTC (Grand Rapids: Eerdmans, 2008), 137.

[35] As Moo maintains: "In speaking of the reconciliation of all things to Christ, the 'hymn' presupposes that the Lordship of Christ over all things (vv. 15–18) has somehow been disrupted. Though created through him and for him, 'all things' no longer bear relationship to their creator that they were intended to have" (ibid., 134). Part of this "intention" is to be the dwelling place of God's presence, which is lost in the fall. Moo continues, stating that all these aspects of humanity and creation are in need of reconciliation, which raises the question, "What is the nature of this reconciliation?" He answers that the New Testament use of this word reveals that "reconcile/reconciliation refers to the restoration of fellowship between God and sinners" (ibid.). Again I would argue that this itself ties in with Christ's work to bring about the presence of God and reestablish the Edenic reality of the divine-human relationship. Furthermore, Moo makes it clear that "the 'all things' of v. 20 occurs five other times in the context, and in each case the referent is the created universe. And, and of course, in this context [that of Colossians 1:20], Paul goes on to specify that the scope of 'all things' includes *things on earth or things in heaven*" (ibid., 134–35).

Christ on the cross, God has brought his entire rebellious creation back under the rule of his sovereign power."[36]

Christ's work on the cross remakes not only sinners but the world at large. Paul reveals that the blood of Christ reconciles *all things on earth and in heaven*. This is the cosmic scope of Christ's atoning sacrifice. His blood removes the curses of Genesis 3 and sets the stage for the new and better creation promised in the New Jerusalem. In this sense, the work of the Son of Man "not only enables a person to be justified, by taking away their moral guilt, but also leads to the eventual transformation of nature back into the perfect state of the original creation."[37] Christ has come finally to bring about a true dominion in order to set it right for the culmination of the eschatological promises in the new and better garden (cf. Rom. 8:18–25). As the new Adam and new Israel, Jesus restores and transcends the first paradise and offers the Land of Promise: the temple-city of the New Jerusalem.

Christ comes not only to offer a better land, but also to restore rule and reign over creation. He is the fulfillment of Balaam's oracle that "one from Jacob shall exercise dominion," one who overcomes the treachery of the world's conflicting kingdoms. The coming of the Messiah "is the reinstatement of the originally intended divine order for earth, with man properly situated as God's vicegerents."[38] This restoration of control is why Paul announces in Romans 8:18–25 that creation[39] awaits the redemption of God's people. As the elect are saved, so too is the earth. The world will no longer be subjected to futility and will be freed to fulfill its eschatological objectives (Rom. 8:18–25).[40] Redemp-

---

[36] Ibid., 137.

[37] Andrew S. Kulikovsky, *Creation, Fall, Restoration: A Biblical Theology of Creation* (Fearn, Ross-shire, UK: Mentor, 2009), 284.

[38] Dan G. McCartney, "*Ecce Homo*: The Coming Kingdom as the Restoration of Human Vicegerency," *Westminster Theological Journal* 56 (1994): 2.

[39] This reference to creation (κτίσις) here in Romans 8, as Thomas Schreiner contends, does not likely refer to people, whether believers or unbelievers, "for the creation is distinguished from [believers] in verses 19, 21, and 23" and "it is hard to see why [unbelievers] would long for the future age"; therefore this term most appropriately "refers to non-human creation and that creation is personified in these verses (cf. Wis 2:6; 5:17; 16:24; 19:6)." Thomas Schreiner, *Romans*, BECNT (Grand Rapids: Baker, 1998), 435.

[40] C. E. B. Cranfield writes that it is best to take the Greek term for "futility" (ματαιότης) in the "word's basic sense as denoting the ineffectiveness of that which does not attain its goal . . . and to understand Paul's meaning to be that the sub-human creation has been subjected to the frustration of not being able to fulfill the purpose of its existence, God having appointed that without man it should not be made perfect." C. E. B Cranfield, *Romans 1–8*, vol. 1, ICC (Edinburgh: T&T Clark, 1975), 413. This is also demonstrated by the use of the two verbs "groan" (συστενάζω) and "suffer" (συνωδίνω). Schreiner states that the application of these two verbs shows that the "created order has not fulfilled its purpose; the futility, decay, and frustration of the present world signal its incompleteness and failure to reach its full potential. In Jewish literature the fulfillment of creation's purpose is

tion removes the curses of Genesis 3, the curse relating to earth's barrenness (Gen. 3:17–19).[41] So it is the atoning work of the new Adam that finally removes the obstacles inhibiting God's eschatological promise of dominion. Futility no longer defines Adam's line, and it no longer defines the earth.

Still we are consistently reminded that Christ's work to fulfill the covenant promise awaits consummation, especially with regard to the promises of place. As Paul Williamson confirms, "While the new covenant has certainly been inaugurated in the New Testament era, the ultimate eschatological reality awaits the 'new heavens and new earth, where righteousness is at home' (2 Pet. 3:13, NRSV)."[42] So, along with creation, we await the day when what has been inaugurated will be consummated, and with it God's eschatological outcomes will be eternally established.

THE NEW ADAM AND THE PROMISE OF GOD'S PRESENCE

Finally, Christ's coming as the second Adam signals the arrival of God's relational presence. This commencement begins in Matthew 1:23, which announces Jesus to be Immanuel, God with us. The Gospel of John goes on to show that the better Adam is also typologically the new and better temple. In other words, Christ is the presence of God who "tabernacles" (σκηνόω) among us (John 1:14). In Christ's coming, the Christian has full access to God and stands in the presence of the Lord (Eph. 2:18). He has torn the veil separating God's presence from the rest of the temple from top to bottom (Matt. 27:51), and by his blood believers boldly approach the throne of grace (Heb. 4:16; 1 John 2:1–2). In Christ,

> men and women may know the presence of God as never before. Not only did he live for a while among us (John 1:14), he also is with us

---

promised when the new heavens and earth become a reality (Isa. 65:17; 66:12; 1 Enoch 45:4–5; 2 Bar 31:5–32:6; 2 Esdr [4 Ezra] 7:11, 30–32, 75)." Schreiner, *Romans*, 437.

[41] It is important that we heed the warning of Schreiner: "We should note that creation, even though it is the subject of these verses, does not constitute the center stage of Paul's vision. What creation longs for and waits for is the eschatological unveiling of the children of God. The focus is not finally on the transformation of the created world, although that is included, but the future redemption that awaits God's children" (ibid., 437). This connection between the salvation of man and the cosmos is still very telling. Salvation removes the curse of Adam, which was ultimately the curse of the ground, and restores humanity to its role of vice-regent, the one who practices dominion over the earth, now a new earth. Both man and earth are now fulfilling their potential and purpose because both are now in the presence of God.

[42] Williamson, "Covenant," 429.

always (Matt. 28:20). He maintains his continual presence through the Holy Spirit, who has descended upon the church (Acts 2) and now dwells within the hearts of believers in Christ (John 14:17).[43]

But Christ's work as Immanuel not only brings about a temporary experience of God's presence as seen in his life, death, resurrection, and ascension; it also affords an eternal and eschatological conclusion to the promise. One Old Testament scholar puts it this way: "Even the magnificent fulfillment of 'God with us' is not the final one, for one day all of God's people will dwell with him and he with them for all eternity."[44] It is in the work of the new Adam in this world—a concept we will cover in detail in the chapters to come—that the dwelling place of God is eternally established with man. Through Christ's recapitulation of Adam's responsibilities, the presence of God, seen first in Eden and subsequently in the tabernacle and temple, will reach its goal in the New Jerusalem (Rev. 21:1–5). Consequently, "a new heaven and new earth surfaces, for the first heaven and earth, the domain of the first Adam, have been superseded by the domain of the eschatological Adam."[45] By way of the cross, Christ offers the redeemed direct access to the holy God, a reality that extends throughout eternity.

In summary, "Jesus' public career is to be understood as the completion of the original creation, with the resurrection as the start of the new."[46] It is apparent then that Christ is the center of redemptive history, through which the eschatological objectives of Adam and the subsequent covenantal promises of the patriarchs and Israel find their fulfillment. So, in his first coming, Christ inaugurates creation's original intentions by taking upon himself the curses of Adam's sin and satisfying the consequent covenant promises. Williamson summarizes:

> It is only after Jesus has put "all his enemies under his feet" (1 Cor. 15:25) and "the kingdom of the world has become the kingdom of our Lord and of his Messiah" (Rev. 11:15), that the blessings of the new covenant—and thus, the eternal blessings foreshadowed in all previous covenants—will come to ultimate fulfilment, and God's

---

[43] Willem VanGemeren, *The Progress of Redemption: The Story of Salvation from Creation to the New Jerusalem* (Grand Rapids: Baker, 1988), 125.

[44] Ibid.

[45] Fesko, *Last Things First*, 178.

[46] N. T. Wright, *The Resurrection of the Son of God* (Minneapolis: Fortress, 2003), 440.

universal purpose will at last be realized. Then and only then—in the eschatological reality, the New Jerusalem—will the hope expressed in the age-old covenant formula be most fully experienced: "God's dwelling place is now among the people, and he will dwell with them. They will be his people, and God himself will be with them and be their God" (Rev. 21:3).[47]

In the provision of Christ, God displays his commitment to create a people and place for the enjoyment of his presence eternally. For it is only through the new Adam that all covenant blessings will be brought to fruition, and the possibilities of Eden restored.

Back to the Future: The Consummation of God's Eschatological Objectives

So we have come full circle.[48] From Eden to the new heaven and new earth, God's desire to make the world his dwelling place—the location of his relational presence—influences the outcome of all of creation and redemptive history. Here at the end, we see that what was initiated in Eden, impeded by the fall, reinstated in the covenants, and inaugurated in Christ is finally to be consummated in the new heaven and new earth. In short,

> the eschatological vision of Revelation 21–22 presents the Holy City, the new Jerusalem, as the eschatological fulfillment of the Garden of Eden. The garden of peace, beauty, and tranquility, where God and man walked in harmonious fellowship, now takes the shape of a beautiful, glowing, walled city.[49]

As we have seen, it is for this reason that the new creation narrative is pregnant with images and allusions portraying redemptive history as

---

[47] Paul R. Williamson, *Sealed with an Oath: Covenant in God's Unfolding Purpose*, NSBT 23 (Downers Grove, IL: InterVarsity, 2007), 210.

[48] As shown thus far, all of redemptive history moves toward the consummation of God's eschatological objective. Goldsworthy is right when he states, "Hope without a time of fulfillment is a delusion." Graeme Goldsworthy, *The Lamb and the Lion: The Gospel in Revelation* (New York: Thomas Nelson, 1994), 133. Yet, God does not leave humanity without a foundation for hope. Rather, God provides an end to which redemption is moving. Once again we return to Revelation 21:1–4 to find the description of God's future objectives: "Then I saw a new heaven and new earth, for the first heaven and the first earth had passed away and the sea was no more. And I saw the holy city, New Jerusalem, coming down out of heaven from God, prepared as a bride adorned for her husband. And I heard a loud voice from the throne saying, 'Behold, the dwelling place of God is with man. He will dwell with them, and they will be his people, and God himself will be with them as their God. He will wipe away every tear from their eyes, and death shall be no more, neither shall there be mourning, nor crying, nor pain anymore, for the former things have passed away'" (Rev. 21:1–4).

[49] Kulikovsky, *Creation, Fall, Restoration*, 280.

finally meeting the Lord's eschatological directives. Most specifically, the emphases on a people, place, and presence of God found in Revelation are obviously tied to the purposes established in creation and the culminating expressions of the Lord's covenantal response to Adam's rebellion. The end of salvation history completes the Lord's divinely directed purposes by bringing about his glory through the universal expansion of his relational presence.

A second look at the new creation informed by this broader canonical perspective illustrates the great influence the eternal purposes of God have on the overall flow and outcome of the divine drama. To begin, the promise of *dominion* clearly finds its consummation in the new heaven and new earth. Here in Revelation 21–22, "Eden is back with its fullness of blessing multiplied many times."[50] To make this connection, the new creation, as we have seen, is replete with Edenic symbolism (i.e., river of life and tree of life symbolism in Rev. 22:1–2, 14, 19), and the new covenant promise of a new heaven and new earth is settled in the heavenly city (cf. Isa. 65:17–25; 66:22). So what began in the garden is finally consummated in the New Jerusalem, where dominion is restored to those who belong to the new Adam (e.g., Eph. 2:6; Rev. 20:6).

But the new creation entails much more. As Gaffin aptly summarizes, "The end is not simply 'Paradise Regained' but 'Paradise Plus.'"[51] In this new world, the wilderness will blossom with beauty (Isaiah 35), filling the earth with grain and fruit (Isa. 4:2; Amos 9:13), making Israel a land flowing with milk and honey, oil, and wine (cf. Isa. 27:2–6; Hos. 2:22; Joel 3:18; Amos 9:13).[52] The "new creation is better than the first [creation] because it will be perfect, holy, and characterized by the presence of God the Father and the Lord Jesus Christ (Rev. 21:22)."[53] Revelation 21–22 invites us to see that "God will make the end like the beginning, though the consummated garden will exist on an escalated scale in comparison to the first."[54] Or to put it another way, the new earth is superior to the garden because it is a fulfillment of what the garden was meant to be.

---

[50] Vern S. Poythress, *The Returning King: A Guide to the Book of Revelation* (Phillipsburg, NJ: P&R, 2000), 193.

[51] Gaffin, "Last Adam," 205.

[52] Warren Austin Gage, *The Gospel of Genesis: Studies in Protology and Eschatology* (Winona Lake, IN: Carpenter, 1984), 52–53.

[53] VanGemeren, *Progress of Redemption*, 64.

[54] Beale and McDonough, "Revelation 21:1–22:5," 1154.

Likewise, when John speaks of the people of God, he also empha-sizes the fulfillment of his *dynastic* promise. In the New Jerusalem, there is a new nation of God—one that consists of all people groups and ethnicities. It is a dynasty made up of all who come to faith in the second Adam, the son of Abraham, the son of David. Through his work, Christ brings about a people made for the explicit purpose of resting in God's presence. To do this, the second Adam removes the curse brought on by the first Adam. As Revelation 22:3 declares, "No longer will there be anything accursed" (cf. Rev. 7:15).[55] Those once separated from the people of God are now given the opportunity to become sons of Abraham and sons of God through faith in Christ. The Lord will fully remove the curse and "will wipe away every tear from their eyes, and death shall be no more, neither shall there be mourning, nor crying, nor pain anymore, for the former things have passed away" (Rev. 21:4). In the end, the curses of the fall are gone, death is defeated, and the advancement of God's people is complete.

The final realization of the promise of place and people paves the way for the eschatological reality that God has become relationally present. Supporting the centrality of this theme is the reissue of the covenant refrain. In Revelation 21:3, God announces once again and finally that he will be their God and they shall be his people. That God will draw near is the climactic victory cry of the *eschaton*, when God's glory is supremely manifest in the joy and pleasure of those dwelling in the midst of the Lord. The divine announcement, "They shall be my people," signals the fulfillment of God's covenant purposes by the new and better Adam.[56]

At the culmination of redemptive history, God's covenantal response to the curse will be complete.[57] God's purposes cannot be stopped. He

---

[55] The vision of John echoes the promise of Zechariah 14:11, which states, "And they will live in [Jerusalem], and there will no longer be a curse, for Jerusalem will dwell secure." Grant R. Osborne, *Revelation*, BECNT (Grand Rapids: Baker, 2002), 772.

[56] G. B. Caird, *The Revelation of St. John the Divine*, Black's New Testament Commentaries, 2nd ed. (London: A&C Black, 1984), 264. Caird writes that the "promise first made in the covenant with Israel at Sinai (Lev. xxvi.12; Jer. vii.23; xi.4; cf. Hos. i.9), renewed in the promises of the prophets (Hos. i.23; Jer. xxx.22; Ezek. xxxvi.28; xxxvii. 23, 27; Zech. viii.8), and realized in the new covenant with Christ (Rom. ix.25; 1 Pet. ii. 10)" are finally completed here in the covenant refrain of Rev. 21–22. "'God himself will be with them' is the assurance given to Moses at the burning bush (Exod. iii.12), enshrined in the prophetic name Immanuel (Isa. vii.14), echoed in the missionary hope of the restored nation (Zech. viii.23), and ratified by him who made the title Immanuel his own (Matt. i.23)" (ibid., 265).

[57] As Poythress writes, "The theme of returning to Eden continues with the reversal of the curse . . . , which an-swers Genesis 3:14–19." Poythress, *Returning King*, 193. Also, as Lee argues, "seeing God's face and reigning with

will be glorified. He will have both a people and a place that serve the all-encompassing purpose of bringing about the reality of his dwelling fully and freely among his elect.[58]

Conclusion

As a goal of God's redemptive plan, the presence of God not only is evident in the beginning, middle, and end of the biblical plotline; it also governs the whole outcome of the history of salvation. The divine presence typifies the experience of the garden, the covenants, Jesus Christ, and the new creation because it is a central theme running through each of these redemptive-historical epochs. From this canonical perspective, we see that the presence of God is central to the Lord's redemptive mission and the theological structure of Scripture. It directs his covenantal purposes and conditions the objectives to meet their divinely ordained ends. So, just as the throne of God's presence is at the center of the New Jerusalem, the presence of God is at the center of all redemptive history. The question that still remains is, How do we, sinners that we are, enter into this unmediated, eternal presence of God? To this we now turn.

God can be considered in terms of the reversal of the curse in the first Paradise." Pilchan Lee, *The New Jerusalem in the Book of Revelation: A Study of Revelation 21–22 in the Light of Its Background in Jewish Tradition* (Tübingen: Mohr Siebeck, 2001), 292.

[58] The Greek term used for God's "dwelling" (σκηνή) with those in the New Jerusalem is a transliteration of the Hebrew word that describes God's presence in the tabernacle and the temple. This insight implicitly reveals that the "whole of the new Jerusalem is now the real holy of holies for God's immediate presence fills it." Richard Bauckham, *The Theology of the Book of Revelation* (Cambridge: Cambridge University Press, 1993), 140.

Part Two

Enter Stage Left

The Presence of God and
the Means of Redemption
in the Old Testament

Not only does the divine scriptwriter compose the story, informing it with his gracious themes and eschatological purposes; he also enters the drama and becomes the main protagonist. As Richard Lints puts it, "God is integrally involved in human history serving not only as the author of the 'story' of redemptive history but also as a genuine character in the story."[1] In other words, Yahweh is no bystander; he gets "dirty," jumping headlong into his own creation and history. God becomes present to pick up the pieces of the fallen world and restore it to what it was supposed to be, the place of his glorious, eschatological presence. This is what we will call the functional reality of the redemptive presence of God: to attain his eschatological goals, the Lord enters time and space to ensure, through his own gracious power, a *place* for his *people* filled with his unrestricted *presence*. Divine presence, then, is more than the *goal* of salvation; it is also the *means* by which God secures everything he set out to accomplish. God becomes present to make a way to his presence.

---

[1] Richard Lints, *The Fabric of Theology: A Prolegomenon to Evangelical Theology* (Grand Rapids: Eerdmans, 1993; repr., Eugene, OR: Wipf and Stock, 1999), 263.

Scripture reveals that the Lord appropriates his purposes primarily through the means of this functional, redemptive presence. God becomes present not solely as a promise awaiting us in the glories of the new heaven and new earth; he becomes present also as the limited, mediated reality revealed within history to accomplish his own eschatological agenda. In sum, God's presence is manifest *in* salvation history *for* the consummation of salvation history.

6

The Curtain Rises

Paradise to Patriarchs

Most people familiar with the power of story cringe when they hear the phrase *deus ex machina* (god from the machine). Generally, writers introduce this dramatic device when they have painted themselves into a corner in their work and cannot find a way out. Enter the new character or the unforeseen plot element—or as it was in the ancient Greek dramas, a god—to bring resolution to a seemingly irresolvable conflict. It's the reason for those "Oh, come on!" moments. Some of us utter these words when we read of the giant eagles swooping in to rescue Bilbo, Gandalf, and Thorin Oakenshield's warring party from wolves, goblins, and the fiery woods in *The Hobbit*; or the very unsubtle arrival of the sword of Godric Gryffindor via Fawkes the Phoenix just when Harry Potter needs it to defeat the basilisk in the Chamber of Secrets. In stories like these—stories we are invested in—we often let the issue slide, but can we blame the reader or observer who feels cheated at such an anticlimactic resolution?

All other stories aside, what if the god who enters the story is the God who wrote the story? Even more, what if this God has been telling you from the beginning of the drama that the only way to overcome the great conflict is by his breaking into the storyline? This is exactly the point of the Christian narrative. What have we seen time and time again in part 1 of this book? Man is done; the purposes of creation and the opportunity of redemption are lost without the God who becomes present to make everything good, acceptable, and perfect again. God has to enter the story because it is only as God the just becomes God the justifier that there still is a story and a hope for a "happily ever after" finale (Rom. 3:26).

The Lord draws near, then, not only to continue his eschatological agenda; he draws near to complete it. This is evident from the very beginning of the story. In the Torah, or the Pentateuch—the first five books of the Hebrew and Christian Bible—God works *in* creation to save a people for himself, prepare for them the Land of Promise, and offer them the experience of his glorious, unmediated, eschatological presence. So it is through the instrument, or function, of his *redemptive* presence that God removes the barriers of sin and death so that his *eschatological* presence will one day encompass all the cosmos for his glory and his people's joy.

We will explore what God's entering into his own story means for the story, specifically as it plays out in the Old Testament. Granted, a comprehensive exegetical study of each instance of God's presence in the Old Testament is beyond our current scope; so we will direct our attention toward a number of key Old Testament passages detailing how God's redemptive presence secures his eschatological presence.[1] We will first see the presence of God in the Torah as it establishes the Old Testament's redemptive model.

To organize our discussion, I will utilize the Hebrew Old Testament,[2] an arrangement of the Old Testament built around a theological framework informed greatly by the presence-of-God theme (an argument

---

[1] Space limitations preclude my addressing some books and sections of the Old Testament in detail, such as the Wisdom Literature and Ruth and Esther. This is not to say that these books do not speak to the redemptive presence of God; in fact, I would contend that they do. However, other texts deserve deeper analysis, and so we must bypass particular Scriptures in order to focus on the redemptive means of God's presence in other, more central texts. For scholarship that speaks to the presence of God in these texts, see Samuel Terrien, *The Elusive Presence: Toward a New Biblical Theology* (New York: Harper & Row, 1978), 350–89; and James M. Hamilton Jr., "Divine Presence," in *Dictionary of the Old Testament: Wisdom, Poetry, and Writings*, ed. Tremper Longman et al. (Downers Grove, IL: InterVarsity, 2008), 116–20.

[2] The organization of the Hebrew Old Testament, also known as the Tanakh, accentuates the importance of the presence of God in the history of Israel and the Old Testament as a whole. Through the Tanakh's composition of historical narrative, then poetic commentary, then historical narrative, stress is consistently placed on God's manifestation in history to judge and redeem so as ultimately to bring about the teleological purposes once encumbered by Adam's transgression. In order to demonstrate the centrality of the divine presence and its purpose within the Old Testament, the following will, therefore, be organized around the theological layout of the Tanakh, which I believe to be based, in part, on the presence of God and its function for the consummating purposes of the divine mission. For a helpful example of another author applying the Tanakh's organizational framework of narrative-commentary-narrative in order to portray the nature and character of God in the Old Testament, see Jack Miles, *God: A Biography* (New York: Vintage, 1996).

we will take up in the next section). My hope is to show that from the beginning of salvation history, the presence of the Lord has been instrumental in the fulfillment of his own eschatological purposes. The following chapters, therefore, will outline, in chapter 6, how the Torah grounds our understanding of the relational-redemptive presence and tells us how his presence works to reach his redemptive objectives; in chapter 7, how the Prophets show the repercussions of Israel's sin, the perpetual jeopardy of Yahweh's presence, and the Lord's gracious manifestation for his redemptive and eschatological purposes, all the while looking forward to a future work of God's presence to overcome sin and reconcile humanity to his end-time presence; and, finally, in chapter 8, how the Writings expose the existential realities and future messianic promises that pave the way for the New Testament fulfillment of the redemptive purposes of the incarnational revelation of God's presence.

Divine Presence and the Theological Structure of the Hebrew Bible

Before we jump into our broader discussion, a brief assessment of the Hebrew Bible's—or the Tanakh's—theological structure is in order. This is necessary because I believe the Tanakh's structure and God's redemptive presence are closely connected. In other words, because God's presence plays such a dynamic role in redemptive history (the chief argument of part 2) it plays a pivotal role in the theological organization of the Hebrew Bible.

To begin, the defining characteristic of the Tanakh is its organization around the three major literary structures. They include:

the Torah, consisting of Genesis, Exodus, Leviticus, Numbers and Deuteronomy; the Nevi'im (the Prophets), comprising Joshua, Judges, Samuel, Kings, Jeremiah, Ezekiel, Isaiah and the Twelve; and the Ketuvim (the Writings), composed of Ruth, Psalms, Job, Proverbs, Ecclesiastes, Song of Songs, Lamentations, Daniel, Esther, Ezra-Nehemiah and Chronicles.[3]

---

[3] Stephen G. Dempster, *Dominion and Dynasty: A Theology of the Hebrew Bible*, NSBT 15 (Downers Grove, IL: InterVarsity, 2003), 36.

According to this structure, the Hebrew Bible starts with a narrative that

> begins with creation [and] moves to the exile of Judah in Babylon, from Genesis to 2 Kings; then the narrative is interrupted by poetic texts—largely prophecy, psalms, and wisdom literature—before being resumed with Israel back in Babylon in the book of Daniel, moving on to the return of the exiles to Judah and concluding with a narrative summation of the entire history of Israel from creation to exile in the books of Chronicles.[4]

This organization is in no way haphazard; rather, it is intentional and represents a unity constructed around a *theological* understanding.[5] Simply put, the Hebrew Bible is a theological work—one that both teaches theology and finds its organization in theology.[6] Or as Stephen Dempster summarizes, "The overall design of the Tanakh provides a hermeneutical lens through which its content can be viewed."[7] Dempster continues:

> Canonization provides a literary context for all the texts, creating one Text from many. The fact that the Hebrew canon is structured in terms of a narrative sequence with commentary means that canonization does not "flatten" the text into a one-dimensional uniformity; rather, it provides for evolution, diversity and growth within an overarching framework in which the various parts can be related to the literary whole.[8]

---

[4] Ibid., 22.

[5] As Dempster maintains: "There is no question that the Hebrew Bible, or Tanakh, as it has come down to believing communities was viewed as a unity. The diverse literary collection was viewed as a whole for theological reasons. While having many authors, it was also believed to have one. But the question remains: is this a unity in any literary sense or is it artificially imposed? Is the result simply a hodgepodge of old religious traditions (at worst) or an anthology of ancient literature (at best)? The facts indicate conceptual unity. . . . Despite the literary heterogeneity, there is at the same time a remarkable structural homogeneity, for this vast variety of genres is set within books which are placed within an extraordinary narrative outline commencing with creation and ending with the exile and return of the Jewish people" (ibid.).

[6] Rolf Rendtorff, *The Canonical Hebrew Bible: A Theology of the Old Testament*, trans. David E. Orton (Leiden: Deo, 2005), 1. Later in Rendtorff's introduction he goes as far as to argue that the theological nature of the Tanakh is so apparent that "an account of the 'Theology of the Old Testament' therefore scarcely requires special justification" (ibid.).

[7] Dempster, *Dominion and Dynasty*, 42.

[8] Ibid., 43. See also Stephen G. Dempster, "Geography and Genealogy, Dominion and Dynasty," in *Biblical Theology: Retrospect and Prospect*, ed. Scott J. Hafemann (Downers Grove, IL: InterVarsity, 2002), 68. Dempster also brings to our attention the insightful remarks of Harry Gamble who writes: "In the nature of the case, canonization entails recontextualization of the documents incorporated into the canon. They are abstracted from both their generative and traditional settings and redeployed as parts of a new literary whole; henceforth they are read in terms of this collection. In this way their historically secondary context becomes their hermeneutically primary context." Harry Gamble, *The New Testament Canon: Its Making and Meaning* (Philadelphia: Fortress, 1985), 75.

This means that the Hebrew Old Testament is not a collection of individual writings lacking congruity and synthesis but, rather, a larger text structured around its own theological message driven by a purpose and plot—a purpose and a plot that I would argue has the presence of God at center stage of its redemptive story.[9]

The Place of Divine Presence in the Old Testament

The functional aspect of God's presence stands out within the Tanakh because it is part and parcel of the Tanakh's conceptual unity (e.g., Num. 35:34; Deut. 6:15; 7:21; Isa. 12:6; Hos. 11:9; Joel 2:27; 3:17, 21; Zeph. 3:15, 17; Hag. 2:5; Zech. 2:10–11; 8:3). The whole story is about the God who wants to create a people and a place for his presence, and because no one else can do this, God himself comes to save the day. Dempster writes,

> Is it any surprise that [the Tanakh] was understood to be a unity, from Genesis to Chronicles? It begins with a creation story of humanity in the garden of Eden, continues with their exile from this place of God's presence because of disobedience, and ends with a nation in exile as a result of disobedience yet called back to the province of Judah to engage in the task of temple reconstruction— the supreme symbol of God's presence.[10]

Hinted at in Dempster's argument, and woven through almost every page of the Old Testament, is God's redemptive presence.

The Tanakh declares that God comes to punish and save for his glory.[11] For the purposes of redemption and redemption's objectives, Yahweh comes to Eden, Egypt, Sinai, and Jerusalem to redeem his people from the dark and lonely wilderness of the ancient Near East and

---

[9] This theological cohesiveness that ties together this particular organization of the Hebrew Scriptures is, in fact, key to determining the theological message of the Tanakh. From beginning to end, the biblical plotline brings the overall theological significance of the Old Testament to bear on the individual texts and passages that make up the Old Testament. In other words, the many (specific passages) are to be read in light of the one (the Tanakh as a whole), and vice versa. This hermeneutic allows the broader context of the theological message of the Scriptures to provide a conceptual unity that incorporates and informs the numerous texts of the Old Testament, while the individual words and passages form the content of the whole.

[10] Dempster, *Dominion and Dynasty*, 33.

[11] The purpose of this volume is to address the presence of God and its place and work within redemption. Thus, as mentioned before, addressing God's presence in judgment and damnation—a theme worthy of much work on its own—beyond these cursory explorations will regretfully not be an emphasis of this particular project.

open the doors to the unquenchable light of the new heaven and new earth.[12] As the Hebrew Bible tells us, the resuscitation of the Edenic purposes is firmly rooted in the fertile reality of the Lord's coming *to save*. In sum, the Lord guides redemptive history *by* his presence *to* his presence.

The Unique Identity of Israel's God: Present with His People

The reference point for Israel is the presence of God in the midst of the nation (e.g., Jer. 14:9).[13] That God comes to relate to and redeem the Hebrews defines them as the people of God and distinguishes them from the surrounding pagan nations.

One of the clearest examples of this is found in Exodus 33.[14] In this chapter, the Lord calls the nation to leave Sinai and enter the Land of Promise. But, owing to the people's sin, Yahweh threatens to abandon Israel in the wilderness. The Lord declares, "Go up to a land flowing with milk and honey; but I will not go up among you, lest I consume you on the way, for you are a stiff-necked people" (Ex. 33:3). In response, Moses boldly demands that the Lord manifest himself, asking, "For how shall it be known that I have found favor in your sight, I and your people? Is it not in your going with us, *so that we are distinct*, I and your people,

---

[12] As Scott Hafemann argues: "God's great acts of provision and deliverance, from the creation to the new creation, together with God's rule over the lives of his people, are not isolated acts of divine power and love. God's promises never stand alone. Every act of God's provision in the *past* brings with it promise for the *future*. In fact, the history of redemption demonstrates that the promises of God for the future are extensions of what he has done in the past." Scott Hafemann, "The Covenant Relationship," in *Central Themes in Biblical Theology: Mapping Unity in Diversity*, ed. Scott J. Hafemann and Paul R. House (Grand Rapids: Baker, 2007), 36. Hafemann sees that the Lord's work in history grounds what he will accomplish eschatologically. When applied to our current thesis, the redemptive work of the Lord's manifest presence in time and space establishes his future promises, which, as I have argued, center on the presence of God dwelling with a new people in a new Eden eternally.

[13] Even though God identifies himself with the Israelites, this does not mean that these are the only people over whom Yahweh, in his authority and kingship, presides. The Lord "is no mere tribal deity with sovereignty over a particular territory, 'for to Yahweh is the Kingship, and he rules among the nations' (Ps. 22:28)." Hamilton, "Divine Presence," 116.

[14] Yet this is just one example among many (see also Ex. 14:24ff.; Lev. 20:26; Num. 2:2; 14:13–14; 1 Sam. 5:1ff.; 2 Sam. 7:23–26; 1 Kings 8:53). God's presence defines his people time and time again. The Lord associates himself with a people (e.g., "I am the God of Abraham, Isaac, and Jacob"), and he does, in fact, manifest himself to them. The presence of God sets God's people apart from the larger and more powerful nations looming at their borders (e.g., Ex. 34:12–16; Lev. 20:22–26). God's redemption of the Hebraic nation is meant all along for the whole world; for it is through this nation that, in his providence, he has purposed to usher in salvation and therefore his teleological objectives to the ends of the earth. The surrounding nations also understand that Yahweh is identified with Israel. Even pagan onlookers see that the Lord is relationally present with Abraham and his offspring. For instance, the foreign king Abimelech, in seeking a treaty with the patriarch, declares, "God is with you [Abraham] in all that you do" (Gen. 21:22), and similar words are spoken to Isaac when the king announces, "We see plainly that the LORD has been with you" (Gen. 26:28). In light of this defining quality, it is perfectly clear to Israel and even the pagan outsider that the Lord is manifest with his people. See also Exodus 14:4, where God reveals his lordship to Egypt through his righteous wrath.

from every other people on the face of the earth?" (Ex. 33:15–16). In this audacious request, Moses clarifies that both his individual identity and Israel's corporate identity find their origin in the Lord's presence with the nation. The potential loss of his presence jeopardizes the nation's identity, their election, and the eschatological hope held out to them in the covenant. The presence of God defines who Israel is and the nation's function in redemptive history (e.g., Deut. 4:7–8; 33:29).[15]

From this perspective, the presence of God is a distinguishing mark of Israel and essential to understanding the theology of the Old Testament. Israel "could thrive without the hope of a Messiah but never without the hope of God's dwelling with his people."[16] I will argue that the presence of God fills the pages of the Old Testament because the Lord's presence is the means by which he accomplishes his future blessings for this small, insignificant nation and all who enter into it. Thus, at the center of the Tanakh (and all Christian Scripture, for that matter) is the presence of God because he is the one who draws near not only at the end of salvation history, but also throughout history to redeem, reconcile, and usher us into his presence eternally.

---

[15] The divine commitment to redeem the whole world actually undergirds God's election of Israel. Thus Robin Routledge contends, "Israel's call and redemption need to be set in the context of God's purposes for all creation: his commitment to the redemption of the world precedes his commitment to the redemption of Israel." Making the connection between Israel and the world, Routledge continues, "Israel's life in relation to God may be seen as a microcosm of what God intends for the whole earth." Robin Routledge, *Old Testament Theology: A Thematic Approach* (Downers Grove, IL: InterVarsity, 2008), 322. Cf. John Goldingay, *Old Testament Theology: Israel's Faith* (Downers Grove, IL: InterVarsity, 2006), 517. Old Testament scholar Christopher Wright concludes, "The Old Testament itself quite clearly intends us to see Israel's history, not as an end in itself or for the sake of Israel alone, but rather for the sake of the rest of the nations of humanity." Christopher J. H. Wright, *Knowing Jesus through the Old Testament* (Downers Grove, IL: InterVarsity, 1992), 36. Arguing that the very structure of the Canon reveals the centrality of Israel's mission to the world, Wright continues: "The uniqueness of Israel's historical experience, however, was because of the special role and function in the world. They were to facilitate God's promise of blessing to the nations" (ibid., 41). For other examples of works dealing with Israel's mission to the nations, please see Richard Bauckham, *The Bible and Mission: Christian Witness in a Postmodern World* (Carlisle, UK: Paternoster, 2003); Arthur Glasser, *Announcing the Kingdom: The Story of God's Mission in the Bible* (Grand Rapids: Baker, 2003); Walter C. Kaiser Jr., *Mission in the Old Testament: Israel as a Light to the Nations* (Grand Rapids: Baker, 2000); Andreas Köstenberger and Peter O'Brien, *Salvation to the Ends of the Earth: A Biblical Theology of Mission*, NSBT 11 (Downers Grove, IL: InterVarsity, 2001); R. Martin-Achard, *A Light to the Nations: A Study of the Old Testament Conception of Israel's Mission to the World* (Edinburgh: Oliver & Boyd, 1962); H. H. Rowley, *Israel's Mission to the World* (London: SPCK, 1939); F. L. McDaniel, "Mission in the Old Testament," in *Mission in the New Testament: An Evangelical Approach*, ed. W. J. Larkin and J. F. Williams (Maryknoll, NY: Orbis, 1998), 11–20. Charles H. H. Scobie, "Israel and the Nations: An Essay in Biblical Theology," *TynBul* 43 (1992): 282–305; Christopher J. H. Wright, *Mission of God: Unlocking the Bible's Grand Narrative* (Downers Grove, IL: InterVarsity, 2006).

[16] R. J. McKelvey, "Temple," in *New Dictionary of Biblical Theology*, ed. T. Desmond Alexander et al. (Downers Grove, IL: InterVarsity, 2000), 810. Though McKelvey makes a powerful claim, there is no need to separate the messianic promise from the pledge of divine presence. As the Canon will show, the Messiah *is God dwelling with his people*, for he is the one through whom salvation comes and the one who concludes the eschatological blessing. So while McKelvey's point is helpful, I would argue here and in the following chapter that the Messiah and the presence of God are not at odds, as they may have been in the Hebrew mind, but are one and the same. The Messiah comes as Immanuel, God with us, the Son of God incarnate, to open the doors to the new creation and bring his people back to their future hope rooted in the presence of God.

A God Present to Save: The Beginning of the Torah Narrative

The Torah is vital to our understanding of the presence of God.[17] New Testament scholar Roy E. Ciampa writes:

> Much of the theology of the Pentateuch has to do with the issue of the presence of God. God is present with Adam and Eve in the Garden. He appears from time to time in the patriarchal narratives, but one never knows when or where he will appear next. The material regarding the tabernacle and sacrificial system and the return to or entry into the promised land in Exodus, Leviticus, and Numbers all relates to the establishment and maintenance of the conditions in which God's presence will be with his people, whether on the way back to the Promised Land or once they have been reestablished within the land.[18]

As Ciampa recognizes, the first narrative section of the Tanakh stresses the functional role of the redemptive presence of God. God does more than establish covenants for his eschatological purposes; he comes to complete them. So from the garden on, the biblical narrative of the Torah is about the Lord drawing near—to the first couple, the chosen patriarchs, and his elect nation.

Promises and Curse: Edenic Judgment and the Presence of God

From the creation account, it is apparent that divine-human relationship is assumed. It is the only context Adam and Eve know prior to the fall. From the beginning, God creates man to experience his relational presence and calls on the first couple to spread this Eden temple over all the face of the earth (Gen. 1:28).

But with the intrusion of sin everything changes. Two truths arise from the fall: (1) sin demands separation from God,[19] and (2) God, in his

---

[17] For a helpful summary of the Torah's common expressions and consistent emphasis on divine presence, please see James M. Hamilton Jr., "God with Men in the Torah," *WTJ* 65 (2003): 113–33. See also Terrien, *Elusive Presence*, 63–226.

[18] Roy E. Ciampa, "The History of Redemption," in Hafemann and House, *Central Themes in Biblical Theology*, 267–68.

[19] In their newly acquired experiential knowledge of good and evil, Adam and Eve clearly understand now that they are evil and unable to stand before God in his goodness. So instead of running to the Lord in repentance, the couple recoil from their Maker, exchanging presence for distance. Not only are Adam and Eve's eyes opened to their nakedness and shame; they also recognize the sheer magnitude of God's communion with them and, conversely, what a curse it is to be cast from his presence. The couple's response makes it clear that they understand

grace, makes himself present in a new way to restore his relationship with his fallen image bearers.[20] In short, the response to Adam's sin produces judgment (distance) and redemption (presence). This is why God, even with his full knowledge of humanity's sinful action,[21] is still in the garden—a response that hints at the mercy to come.[22] Remember, the only one trying to hide in Genesis 3 is Adam. God remains present. God still comes to question and curse; yet, in grace, he is also near to counter Adam and Eve's punishment. And why does he do this? Because it is only through his immanence that Adam, Eve, the world, or any of us can be reconciled to the joys of God's future blessings. God does not give his people over to their own demise; instead, he comes to judge, *and* through that judgment bring redemption.

After Adam's fall, we have nowhere else to turn. The only means to accomplish God's purposes for creation is God himself.[23] From the

they can no longer stand before God, much less fellowship with him like they once did. The repercussions of Adam's transgression include the loss of the free and unhindered reality of the presence of God.

[20] Mathews explains, "The means and extent of access to God's presence was altered because of sin, but divine mercy overtook the wayward man and woman." Kenneth Mathews, *Genesis 1–11:26*, NAC (Nashville: Broadman & Holman, 2002), 258. In the context of such an exile, redemptive history begins. In this act of sin, we see that "Adam and Eve are in need of a salvation that comes from without. God needs to do for them what they are unable to do for themselves." Victor P. Hamilton, *The Book of Genesis: Chapters 1–17*, NICOT (Grand Rapids: Eerdmans, 1990), 207. The drama of redemption shows us that he does just that.

[21] I take the Lord's questions to Adam, "Where are you?," "Who told you that you were naked?," and "Have you eaten of the tree of which I commanded you not to eat?," and to the woman, "What have you done?" all to be rhetorical questions to bring Adam and Eve to conviction of sin and their need for grace. Thus understood, the Lord's questions in this passage do not reflect ignorance on the Lord's part but are rather used to stimulate the couple's confession. Mathews agrees: "God is depicted as a gentle father seeking out his own. The means of uncovering their deeds (like the serpent's means of entrapment) is interrogation rather than charge and denunciation. The effect is pedagogical and permits the guilty to witness against themselves by their own admissions." Mathews, *Genesis 1–11:26*, 240.

[22] For further development of this biblical theme, see James M. Hamilton Jr., *God's Glory in Salvation through Judgment: A Biblical Theology* (Wheaton, IL: Crossway, 2010). As Hamilton contends here and in his earlier articles leading up to his book, "Yahweh's word of promise that he will save the righteous and judge the wicked also communicates his nearness to his people (see esp. Ps. 73:17–18, 23–28; cf. Deut. 32:35)." Hamilton, "Divine Presence," 117. Thus, part of his judgment includes, ironically, his drawing near to separate the lost from his relational presence forever, whereas to fulfill the promise of salvation Yahweh comes to bring his people back to his relational presence for all eternity (e.g., Ex. 33:3; Deut. 4:7, 37–39; 7:7–8; 2 Kings 13:23; 17:20; 24:20; Pss. 10:11; 27:9; 44:24–25; 50:11; 73:27–28; 102:2; 145:18; Isa. 45:15; Jer. 7:15; 15:1; Lam. 3:57–59; 4:16; Hos. 5:15). Interestingly, there is a connection between salvation and judgment, namely, that salvation comes *through* judgment. Hamilton adds that this theme of salvation through judgment for God's glory is the central motif of biblical theology: "Throughout the Bible those who experience God's deliverance experience it through his judgment. Judgment falls on the enemies of God so that God's people are delivered, but the saved themselves experience judgment before they enjoy the blessings of redemption." James M. Hamilton Jr., "The Center of Biblical Theology: The Glory of God in Salvation through Judgment?," *TynBul* 57 (2006): 62. In other words, all are judged—the righteous and the unrighteous—which makes it clear that gracious redemption is simultaneously coupled with God's holy judgment. For his specific position and its further development, see Hamilton, "The Center of Biblical Theology," 57–84.

[23] Granted, Adam is still the "seed provider" through whom the better Adam will come. For this reason, the Lord continues his commitment to man and the cultural mandate. This, however, is only accomplished because God has become redemptively present to him to offer this hope. Furthermore, the whole act of salvation is no longer in the hands of Adam and his line but in the hands of the Lord, who graciously provides a new Adam in Christ— one who is fully God and fully man, thereby combining the promise of Gen. 3:15 with his promise to be present with his people. So, in one sense, the Lord continues to work with and through sinful man to accomplish his

throes of judgment, the Lord provides a new hope, a hope evidenced in his gracious decision to be present, rather than simply destroy from afar. Not only does he spare their immediate lives; he also commits to being present with them to restore his image to his fallen image bearers. So although Adam deserves death, the Lord stays his punishment temporarily to spotlight his grace in salvation.

Mediating the Promises: Cain, Abel, and the Presence of God

The rest of Scripture is a response to Genesis 3:1–7. It is no mere coincidence, then, that directly on the heels of humanity's removal from the Edenic sanctuary, the biblical account of Cain and Abel takes up the subject of the presence of God.[24] This passage is our first encounter with the Lord since the first couple's judgment, and, as such, the narrative of Cain and Abel is critical to the way we understand the purpose and role of the presence of God in a post-fall context.

One of the great disparities between the experience of Eden and that of Adam's descendants is the new requirement of mediation.[25] Specifically, the whole account of Cain and Abel stems from the Lord's evaluation of the two brothers' sacrificial offerings and their motivations

---

eschatological objectives. However, in the end, the Lord's purposes are ultimately accomplished through himself and, in particular, through his presence in the world.

[24] It should be noted that Cain and Abel are themselves expressions of the Lord's commitment to his redemptive purposes. Gen. 4:1 is clearly a declaration that the objectives of the Lord will not be thwarted by sin. Even after the fall, "Adam knew Eve his wife, and she conceived and bore Cain . . . and again she bore his brother Abel." Here, the seed of dynasty is sown along with the seed through whom salvation will come (Gen. 3:15). In Eve's procreation of sons (Seth included) the Lord fulfills his promise of expanding the people of God and, with it, his presence throughout the world, though in a different way than is laid out in Eden. Now the cultural mandate, along with its role in spreading the dwelling place of God, comes primarily through God's power and grace (i.e., the provision of Seth, through whose line comes the future covenant promises, Gen. 4:25–26).

[25] Gen. 3:21 seems to support the connection between sin and death, as well as the origin for sacrifice. Here, the Lord is said to cover the sin-marred couple with the skins of animals. R. T. Beckwith asserts, "By clothing them in this remarkable manner, God instituted sacrifice indirectly rather than directly." R. T. Beckwith, "Sacrifice," in Alexander et al., *New Dictionary of Biblical Theology*, 754. This being the first possible expression of sacrifice, it would seem to imply that Yahweh initiates the act of sacrifice and that it is mediatory in purpose. Still, Merrill's warning is appropriate when he cautions, "One must be careful not to infer too much of the notion of substitutionary atonement from this rather cryptic account, though it will be clear at a later point that atonement for sin did indeed call for animal sacrifice which involved, among other things, a covering or a 'smearing' (Heb. *kpr*) of a victim's blood on an altar." Eugene H. Merrill, *Everlasting Dominion: A Theology of the Old Testament* (Nashville: Broadman & Holman, 2006), 228. Taking into consideration the original context and audience of this passage helps shed light on the meaning of these offerings. In this particular case, Moses was writing to an audience that had been exposed to the tabernacle and the institution of the sacrificial system. It would seem then that this background would influence the reading and hearing of this text so that Cain and Abel's "offerings" would be seen and understood in light of the Israelite cultus. For further development of this approach to Old Testament historiography hermeneutics, see Richard L. Pratt Jr., *He Gave Us Stories: The Bible Student's Guide to Interpreting Old Testament Narratives* (1990; repr., Phillipsburg, NJ: P&R, 1993). For further argument supporting a hint of the sacrificial system in Cain and Abel's offerings, please see John S. Feinberg, "Salvation in the Old Testament," in *Tradition and Testament: Essays in Honor of Charles Lee Feinberg*, ed. John S. Feinberg and Paul D. Feinberg (Chicago: Moody, 1981), 59.

behind them (Gen. 4:1–16).[26] Sometime between Genesis 3 and Genesis 4, Adam and his household have learned the importance of sacrifice and why it is necessary for their relationship with their Creator.[27] David Peterson, seeing the mediatorial implications in the brothers' sacrificial actions, explains, "Even in their fallen state, both Cain and Abel are moved to bring their respective offerings to God and to express some sense of gratitude or debt for the blessing of creation (Gen. 4:1–7)."[28]

It seems, then, that to revive the divine-human relationship marred by Adam's sin, the Lord introduces the idea of sacrificial offerings so that he may again draw near to his people—this time to redeem. The sacrifices of Cain and Abel demonstrate the Lord's commitment to his people. He does not abandon them. He graciously grants provisions to draw near to Adam's sin-stained sons without compromising his holiness.

But as we know, the effects of sin are far-reaching. Cain and Abel's transgressions are even able to tarnish and corrupt sacrifices supposedly given in the Lord's honor. This is clearly the case for Adam's eldest son, Cain. The Lord rejects his sacrifice because his offering pales in comparison to that of his younger brother, Abel.[29] Instead of repen-

---

[26] Though a point given little explanation in this particular passage, it bears mentioning that it is only after Adam's sons offer sacrifice that the Lord is shown to be present with his creation once again.

[27] Several scholars argue that Genesis 4, which records the first appearance of sacrifice, does not account for Yahweh's provision of sacrificial offerings. As a result, they contend that Cain and his brother must have learned their actions from other peoples' religious performance, not from God himself. In response, I would argue that this assessment of the pagan source of sacrifice is based on assumption as much as, or more than, any assumption that grounds the argument that the brothers' work flowed from the commands of God. I would also cite the response of the Lord to the sacrifices of Cain and Abel as proof that the act is meant to be pleasing in his eyes, in that critique and discipline are necessary when Cain's sacrifice is not administered correctly. The acceptance and institution of sacrifice are expressed later in the Old Testament, so much so that sacrifice is a defining aspect of Israelite worship and identity. If this were a foreign act contrary to the character of God, the Lord would have shut it down rather than accept its role in the divine-human relationship. For further treatment on the various theories concerning the origins and purposes of the Hebrew sacrificial system, see R. E. Averbeck, "Offerings and Sacrifices," in *NIDOTTE*, ed. Willem A. VanGemeren (Grand Rapids: Zondervan, 1997), 4:996–1022.

[28] David Peterson, "Atonement in the Old Testament," in *Where Wrath and Mercy Meet: Proclaiming the Atonement Today*, ed. David Peterson (Carlisle, UK: Paternoster, 2008), 2.

[29] God denies Cain's sacrifice because of Cain's attitude in submitting his offering. Mathews argues: "God's response toward Cain and Abel, therefore, was not due to the nature of the gifts per se, whether it was grain or animal, but the integrity of the giver. The narrative ties together the worshiper and his offering as God considers the merit of their individual worship: 'the Lord looked with favor on Abel and his offering, but on Cain and his offering he did not look with favor' (vv. 4–5)." Mathews, *Genesis 1–11:26*, 268. Hence, the major issue is Cain's heart and motive disclosed in his decision to hold back gifts from the Lord and to save the best produce for himself. At the other end of the spectrum, Abel gives the Lord the best portions (Gen. 4:4: "Abel brought the firstborn of his flock and of their fat portions") while also making a sacrifice in faith (Heb. 11:4). As a consequence, only Abel's gift is accepted by the Lord. Cain's disdainful response to God's judgment only reinforces his depraved attitude and distinguishes him from his righteous brother (Gen. 4:5, 8ff.). For further development of this position on God's rejection of Cain's sacrifice, see Bruce K. Waltke, "Cain and His Offering," *WTJ* 48 (1986): 363–72; F. Spina, "The 'Ground' for Cain's Rejection (Gen. 4): 'dāmāh in the Context of Gen. 1–11," *Zeitschrift für die alttestamentliche Wissenschaft* 104 (1992): 319–32. For other positions, see H. Gunkel, *Genesis* (Macon, GA: Mercer University Press, 1997); J. Skinner, *A Critical and Exegetical Commentary on Genesis*, ICC (Edinburgh: Clark, 1930); B. Vawter, *On*

tance, though, Cain responds to God's judgment in anger. Genesis 4:6 describes Cain's face as "fallen"—a reflection of the fallen condition of his heart suggesting that the real reason for God's rejection of his sacrifice is his iniquity (see similar expressions in Job 29:24; Jer. 3:12).

In response to Cain's wicked reaction, the Lord becomes present to confront and encourage him to righteousness. God's inquiry into Cain's predicament is one of the first expressions of God's drawing near to reconcile fallen man to himself. The Lord graciously approaches Cain to question him and warn him that if his anger persists, it will consume him and condemn his rebellious heart (Gen. 4:7). To help Cain, God poses two simple questions: (1) Why are you angry? and (2) If you act righteously, will not you and your sacrifice be accepted?

Sadly, God's intercession does not slow Cain's swift descent into besetting sin. Instead, the son of Adam ignores the Lord's counsel. Cain hated that God favored Abel and his offering. So Cain's sin escalates, first into anger and resentment toward his brother, then to the rejection of God's merciful plea, then to the horrible act of fratricide (Gen. 4:8), and finally to his expulsion from the presence of God altogether (Gen. 4:16). Cain's actions are devastating. Not only does he take the life of his younger brother; he also impedes the redemptive promises of God foreshadowed in Genesis 3:15. God promised that through Eve a Redeemer would come to reconcile humanity to God and bring about the Lord's purposes.[30] But with Abel's blood covering Cain's hands, redemption and God's mission are, again, up in the air.

And how does God respond to Cain's murderous act? God draws near. He comes to judge Cain. As with his father,[31] Yahweh questions

---

Genesis: A New Reading (Garden City, NY: Doubleday, 1977); John Calvin, *A Commentary on the Book of Genesis 1–11*, trans. I. Abrahams (Jerusalem: Magnes, 1964); S. R. Driver, *The Book of Genesis*, Westminster Commentary (London: Methuen, 1904).

[30] As we have been arguing, the Lord's presence is the *one* instrument through which he accomplishes his redemptive objectives. Yet, God is gracious to include his creation in his salvific agenda. As Gen. 3:15 makes clear, mankind still has a role to play in the salvific drama, for it is through the line of Adam and the womb of Eve that there will be one who will come to consummate the promises of God. The function of humanity in redemption in no way contradicts the agency of divine presence. Instead, the two meet in the person of Jesus Christ. He is both from the line of Adam and likewise God with us. He is the Son of Man and the Son of God. This idea will be accented further in this chapter, as well as in the chapter on the New Testament means of the presence of God.

[31] In a very real sense, the whole account of Cain's judgment is a reenactment of what took place in the Edenic judgment. As Old Testament scholar Gordon Wenham explains: "The divine interrogation of Cain and the subsequent pronouncement of curses resemble the similar treatment of Adam. Many of the key words of chap. 3 reappear here too: ידע 'know,' שמר 'guard,' ארור 'cursed,' אדמה 'land,' גרש 'drive.'" Gordon J. Wenham, *Genesis 1–15*, WBC (Thomas Nelson: Nashville, 1987), 106. The Lord is manifest to judge (Gen. 3:8–24; 4:9ff.); the questions asked are similar (Gen. 3:9, 13; 4:9–10); Cain's response reveals a lack of repentance (Gen. 3:12–13; 4:9); Yahweh curses the ground (Gen. 3:17–19; 4:11); and, again, the sinner is driven from the presence of the Lord (Gen. 3:22–24; 4:14,

Cain. He asks, "Where is Abel your brother?" and "What have you done? The voice of your brother's blood is crying to me from the ground" (Gen. 4:9, 10; cf. Gen. 3:9, 13). In the curses that follow, the Lord declares, as he did with Adam, that the earth he once governed will no longer respond to Cain's rule (Gen. 4:11; cf. v. 2). The curse of the ground first pronounced in Eden is now Cain's too. This act undermines Cain's identity, vocation, and dominion. But God goes further. As it was with his father, the Lord drives Cain from family and from his presence. Cain, now isolated from Adam's dynasty, sets out in futility to start another genealogical line, which will eventually find its end in the torrential waters of the flood. Echoing the punishment of Eden, the Lord's separation of Cain from the bounty of the land removes him from the promise of dynasty and exiles him from the divine presence.

Feeling the heavy hand of the Lord's justice, Cain considers all he has forsaken through his bloody offense. We see this in Cain's blind protests of his judgment when he declares, "My punishment is greater than I can bear. Behold, you have driven me today away from the ground, and from your face I shall be hidden" (Gen. 4:13–14). In his dissent, Cain acknowledges that he will no longer be allowed to see the *panim*, or *paneh* (פנים or פנה), the face of God. In other words, Cain's sin has finally driven him from the privilege of God's reconciling presence.[32] No more will he reside in the redemptive and merciful presence of Yahweh; now, because of sin, Cain is forever banished to the land of Nod, a location far removed from Eden.[33]

---

16). Again, as Wenham argues: "God's opening question, 'Where is Abel your brother?' like 3:9, is essentially rhetorical, for God knows where Abel is (v. 10). It invites Cain to acknowledge his responsibility for his 'brother'" (ibid.). So just as God approached Adam and Eve in the garden after their sin, he comes to Cain with similar questions, to which he already knew the answers. God's questions to both Adam and his son do not reveal limitations in his knowledge but the expanse of his grace. The fact that he comes to interact with sinners is one of the greatest expressions of mercy. But his inquiries extend his grace further. Yahweh's questions are merciful in that they provide sinners an opportunity to confess, repent, and receive the care of God once again. Adam and Eve ultimately come to this conclusion, whereas Cain does not. For further discussion, see A. J. Hauser, "Linguistic and Thematic Links between Gen. 4:1–16 and Gen. 2–3," *JETS* 12 (1980): 297–305.

[32] English translations of the Old Testament typically translate the face (פנים) of God with the English term *presence*. This helps us understand the anthropomorphic basis needed for conceptualizing God's divine presence. Thus Jim Hamilton argues that in the Old Testament, "Yahweh is characterized as possessing a face, as seeing and hearing, as having a nose and breath, as having strong arms and hands. All these physical characteristics communicate the reality of his noncorporeal presence." Hamilton, "Divine Presence," 117. The anthropomorphic aspect of God and its connection to God's presence emphasizes Yahweh's commitment to communion, revelation, and redemption. He has revealed himself in such a way that fallen humanity can understand. He has stooped to communicate himself not only in word but also in his presence to relate and redeem.

[33] The continued application of exile as the punishment for sin highlights the importance of the presence of God as the *telos* of redemptive history. Instead of promoting closeness to God, the sins of man widen the expanse that stands between God and his creation. This is seen in Adam's exile from Eden, Cain's exile to the land of Nod, Israel's exile in Egypt, and Israel and Judah's exile from the Land of Promise. As we have noted in the preceding

His response to his judgment is quite telling: in full candor, the one thing the murderer regrets the most is his permanent separation from God.[34] For Cain, it is a wicked irony. It is only through the Lord's presence to judge Cain's personal rebellion that the rebel finally recognizes and esteems the Lord's presence to redeem. By becoming "a fugitive and a wanderer on the earth" (Gen. 4:12), Adam's eldest realizes that access to his Creator and reconciler is no longer available—not even through sacrifice. Hopelessness marks the rest of Cain's existence, as it does for all who spurn the Lord's redemptive presence.[35]

In the wake of Cain's departure, the Lord turns his attention to the uncertainty of salvation and his eschatological promises. In the last part of Genesis 4, God shines light in the darkness of sin's advancement and the growing disdain for his glory. We find our hope once again in the womb of Eve. As pronounced in Genesis 3:15, redemption comes from the line of Adam. The expectant Eve's announcement that God has appointed another offspring instead of Abel tells us that God is at work in history to restore the seed promised in the garden. Through Adam's line, redemption will come, and with it the eschatological goal of creation will reach its appropriate ends.

This is why Eve gives birth to Seth. As Kenneth Mathews concludes, "By bearing 'again,' the hope of 'another seed' (literally) born to Eve meant a righteous lineage is possible through Adam's son Seth (cf. 3:15)."[36] With Seth and his progeny,[37] the promises of Eden are kept

---

chapter, exile is more than just removal from a particular place; it also involves a distancing and separation from the presence of God.

[34] Cain's persistent sins reverse the purpose of his sacrificial offerings. Instead of preparing a way for a redemptive relationship, Cain's actions culminate in the removal of Yahweh's presence from him. His actions throughout the narrative disclose the depravity of his heart and the limited value he initially places on the presence of God.

[35] Faced with the separation from dominion, dynasty, and dwelling, Cain realizes that his being removed from the redemptive presence of God also means that he has lost the one who cares for and protects him from the dark world bearing down upon him. Cain despairs, claiming that without the provision of God's presence he will surely die at the hands of his avengers (Gen. 4:14). But, in response, the Lord graciously answers his objections, offering the transgressor protection from and vengeance against any potential threats that would arise against him (Gen. 4:15). Still, even with this expression of mercy, the Lord does not reinstate Cain to his redemptive presence. God's judgments are final, and in the end, the Lord drives Cain and his descendants from the line and land of his presence forever—and, as such, from the opportunity of redemption as well (Gen. 4:16). So although safe from the wrath of the world, Cain must forever suffer from his separation from the Lord.

[36] Mathews, *Genesis 1–11:26*, 290.

[37] After Seth, Enosh, Seth's son, continues the line of Adam and his promised seed (Gen. 3:15). What is interesting about Enosh is the meaning of his name. In Hebrew, Enosh can be a proper name or can be used as a common noun to refer to man (e.g., Job 5:17; 36:25; Ps. 8:4; cf. Pss. 10:17–18; 90:3; 103:15–16; Isa. 13:7) much like the use of Adam (e.g., Gen. 4:26; 5:6, 7, 9–11; 1 Chron. 1:1). It would seem, then, in the provision of Enosh, there is now another "Adam/man" through whom the dynasty of promise will flourish again and the redemptive objectives of the Lord will ultimately be met. Or as Mathews puts it, "'Enosh' then is the new 'Adam' who heads a new line that will receive the blessing and survive the Flood (5:1–11:29)" (ibid., 290).

from premature termination. The Lord provides a new line, one that replaces righteous Abel (Heb. 11:4) and fills the void left by the fallen Cain. So even in the death of Abel and the banishment of Cain, Eve remains the mother of all living (cf. Gen. 3:20) through Seth, whose birth provides reassurance that the Lord's end-time mission will reach completion. In Seth, there is a glimmer of hope amid the disaster and judgments of Eden and Nod. There is new seed of Adam, a people who, unlike Cain and his descendants, are near unto the Lord, identified by the Lord's presence, and redeemed by his presence from the rising waters of the coming flood (Gen. 6:9–9:28).

Preserving a People and a Place: The Flood and the Presence of God

As quickly as we can turn the pages of the biblical script, humanity goes from "call[ing] upon the name of the Lord" (Gen. 4:26) to covering the earth with the sinful and rebellious nature that marked Cain (Gen. 6:5–7). On a much larger scale, the whole world and its inhabitants, like Adam and Cain earlier, face divine wrath in the form of the flood. The flood narrative "extols the God who actually came into history and brought judgment with him. . . . The same glorious presence that fashioned Creation also fashioned the Flood."[38] As Genesis 6 reveals, Yahweh "saw that the wickedness of man was great in the earth, and that every intention of the thoughts of his heart was only evil continually. . . . So the Lord said, 'I will blot out man whom I have created from the face of the land'" (6:5, 7). This is the same as God's response to Adam's and Cain's sin but with one key difference—the punishment once applied to individuals is now applied on a worldwide scale. All creation (save Noah) is rightfully indicted for its universal wickedness.[39] All that humanity can do is cling precariously to the promises that God would intervene.

---

[38] Jeffrey J. Niehaus, *God at Sinai: Covenant and Theophany in the Bible and Ancient Near East* (Grand Rapids: Zondervan, 1995), 170–71.

[39] The fact that this judgment comes upon "many peoples" displays that the cultural mandate "to be fruitful and multiply" has been advancing. Yet, part of the reason for such a widespread punishment is to regain the proper outworking of the mandate. In other words, not only are there to be many people; the people are also to be righteous and ready to enter God's presence. From this perspective, the flood comes as a demonstration of the Lord's persistence to have a people who will dwell with him eternally, not a people characterized by sin. To do this, Yahweh demonstrates in Genesis 6–9 that he comes to bring destruction to the rebellious world and to institute a new covenant people.

Enter the redemptive presence of God. Just as in his dealings with Cain and Abel, we learn that the Lord's presence comes to Noah not only to judge, but to bring redemption for his glory and our good in the furtherance of his eschatological mission. For this reason, the judgment Genesis 6:5–7 details is tempered by the merciful declaration of verse 8, "Noah found favor in the eyes of the Lord." This simple phrase demonstrates that the Lord extends his promises and purposes to his world through this one man of righteousness (Gen. 6:9). In Noah, Adam's line continues (Gen. 3:15ff.) and, along with it, the cultural mandate and the promise of a seed (see Gen. 8:17; 9:1, 7, 19; cf. 6:18–22; 10:1–32).

To redeem by means of this watery judgment, the Lord draws near to Noah. First, Yahweh becomes redemptively present to save Noah *physically* from the impending waters of judgment. The Lord commands Noah to build an ark, protect his family and God's creation, and prepare for worship (Gen. 6:11–17). Through each imperative, the Lord ensures the physical salvation of Noah and his line and thereby secures the continuance of God's redemptive agenda. The ark of gopher wood—filled with Noah, his family, and the animals of the earth—is a physical sign that the promises of dynasty, dominion, and divine dwelling remain secure, even in the stinging rain and treacherous waters of the flood.

Second, the Lord provides a spiritual redemption (Gen. 6:18–22). As we have seen, God becomes present to Noah to covenant with him and establish a relationship of redemption and promise (Gen. 8:20–9:17). Through the covenant, the holy God establishes a way to be in the midst of an unholy people for the purposes of redemption and, ultimately, to fulfill his covenant blessings. By drawing near to Noah, the Lord connects the means and ends of redemptive history. The covenant assimilates both the functional and future aspects of the presence of God. The covenant details and restates the eschatological objectives of God *for* redemptive history and is a result of the work of God manifest *in* redemptive history. In cutting the covenant, the Lord sets the stage for his drawing near to bring forth salvation and open access to his future, relational presence. The covenant, therefore, carries both an eschatological dimension and a functional one.

Even with the covenant and the cleansing waters of the flood, the effects of sin remain. It is interesting that Noah's first act after setting foot on dry land again is to build an altar and sacrifice to the Lord (Gen. 8:20).[40] This particular response to God's gracious deliverance reveals that the relationship between these covenant partners is not one of equality. There is need for mediation because even though Yahweh has stooped low to be redemptively present, the unrighteous cannot relate directly to the righteous. Still, the covenant remains—a covenant predicated on God's gracious decision to be present with and for his elect. In this light, Noah's offerings, like those of righteous Abel, reemphasize the salvific function of the divine presence: sacrifice is made so that the Lord may be present with sinful man and thereby procure his redemptive ends.

The flood clarifies that God draws near to redeem. He pours out his wrath on a dissident earth while simultaneously pouring out his merciful love on Noah. This is the one man (with his family) whom God delivers from the waters and the one with whom he covenants. But as we have seen, God's presence with man remains greatly changed, even with righteous Noah. No longer does the Lord freely fellowship with humanity as he once did in Eden; God's presence is now a mediated reality. Still, in the flood narrative, God comes and continues to complete his eschatological agenda.

Clarifying the Means: The Tower of Babel and Divine Presence

As seen before, the Torah is a story of the Lord's redemptive response to humanity's compounding failures. This is certainly the case for those on the plain of Shinar. Not only has the world already forgotten the judgment of the flood, but people once again arrogantly pursue their own glory by attempting to pierce the heavens with their own architectural ingenuity.[41] Sinful man plans to build a city that can reach the very dwelling place of God (Gen. 11:3–4). This evil takes the positive and innate desire to be present with God—a desire grounded in creation and covenant—and twists it to feed human arrogance and disobedience.[42]

---

[40] By implication, the divine command to put a certain number of animals on board for sacrificial purposes indicates the need and approval of this act for maintaining the presence of the Lord.

[41] The structure being built in Babel is probably a ziggurat, an ancient Near Eastern building that often has a temple at its pinnacle. If this is the case the tower has some religious significance, in particular, one that will apparently be contrary to the worship of Yahweh at this time.

[42] Ironically, this wicked society recognizes the importance and purposes of divine presence, but pursue it through their own sinful means. The building of a city-tower by human hands, to reach God's presence, circumvents

This act is a clear perversion of God's command to advance the dwelling place of God worldwide. Tainted by rebellion and wickedness, the people of the earth distort the creation mandate for their own prideful purposes and try to make their own way into God's presence.[43]

In an unexpected twist, the Lord "comes down" to deal with the people's arrogance. The Lord deems it pertinent to "go down and there confuse their language, so that they may not understand one another's speech'" (Gen. 11:7). The unrighteous cannot stand before the righteous, and no usurpers or insurgents can stand in Yahweh's presence on their own status.[44] The only entrance into the relational presence of God is through the redemptive work of God in the midst of his people.

Even at the Tower of Babel, though, the Lord's presence to judge reveals his presence to save. An uninvited and unholy people cannot enter the presence of a holy God without Yahweh's reconciliatory work. If the people could, in fact, reach the heavens on their own standing, it would only end in their destruction. The Lord punishes this people, but in doing so, he also protects them from the consequences of their own wickedness. As with the exiles from Eden, whom God kept from eating the tree of life and living forever in their sinful state, the Lord scatters this rebellious humanity across the earth and alters the peoples' language to mitigate the repercussions of their transgressions. God's judgment, then, is also his mercy.

The Tower of Babel narrative shows us that sin must be dealt with before sinners may access the presence of the Lord. This is why the Lord becomes present after the fall. For the lost to draw near, God must first draw near to reconcile the lost—an act accomplished only through God's redemptive presence. Sinners cannot enter heaven on

the agency of the Lord's presence. Instead of *overcoming* sin, humanity tries to enter the dwelling place of God *through* their sin for their prideful aspirations. The redemptive means of the presence of God is moved aside in order that the teleological presence of God may be accomplished through human creativity and pride as people seek to exalt themselves and undercut the rightful glory of God. Though the rebellious people pursue the right thing (the presence of Yahweh), they do it for the wrong reason (a name for *themselves*) and through the wrong means (building *themselves* a city).

[43] In light of the audience of Genesis, this text would seemingly conjure up images of the tabernacle that was with Moses and the people in the wilderness. More than likely, the tower would be seen as a sinful contradiction to the provision of the tabernacle: the location of the Lord's presence with his people in his place, mediated and honored appropriately.

[44] Though it will be taken up in the next chapter in more detail, Pentecost, described in Acts 2, is a reversal of the judgment of the Tower of Babel. With the outpouring of the Spirit, the presence of the Lord comes to indwell believers, overcome language barriers, and pour out redemption on those who hear and believe the gospel of Jesus Christ.

their own accord, either through metaphorical ways or through the very real Tower of Babel. We enter God's presence only if the ruler of heaven becomes present to redeem us first.

Establishing His Promises: The Patriarchs and the Presence of God

God's manifestation to the patriarchs marks a significant shift in the role his presence plays in the story of Scripture. In his covenant with Abraham, God ties his work in time and space to this patriarch forever. So, as the Torah narrative narrows from a worldwide perspective to a nationalistic one, the occurrences of God's presence increase, and so too do his reasons for entering history. Genesis 3–11 emphasizes the Lord's presence to judge, while his "seed" promise of Genesis 3:15 gradually fades to the background. But with Abraham, God flips the script. In Genesis 12, the Lord's gracious and redemptive presence receives full attention, and so much of what follows in the Torah is a comprehensive description and advancement of his functional presence.[45]

THE REDEMPTIVE PRESENCE OF GOD WITH ABRAHAM

The Lord's gracious presence with Abraham shines brightly against the dark, sinful backdrop of the Tower of Babel narrative. The shift from Genesis 11 to Genesis 12 turns our focus from sin's worldwide expansion to the hope that Abraham and his descendants will one day see God face-to-face and experience his redemptive purposes.[46] God becomes present to "intervene decisively in the story of Abraham in order through him to inaugurate both the revelation and the realization of his economy of grace."[47]

By demanding that Abraham forfeit his land and forsake his family

---

[45] To be sure, there are elements of judgment laced throughout the rest of Genesis. I am not arguing that sin and punishment are not evident in the Torah. Instead, I contend that in this context of rebellion and judgment, the patriarchal narratives give prominence to the Lord's presence as the means to redeem (e.g., Gen. 6:5–7; 11:1–10; 12:17–20; 19:23–29). In short, because there is sin, God draws near to save, which is the ultimate focus of Genesis 12 and beyond.

[46] It has always been the Lord's intention to use this particular nation—an insignificant and feeble one at that—to redeem the rest of the world (e.g., Gen. 12:3; 18:18–19; Isa. 4:1–2; Jer. 2:3, 4:2; Ps. 65:5). The act of electing Israel as his people, therefore, does in fact have cosmological implications. This nation was to be a light to the nations (Isa. 42:6; 49:6; 60:3; cf. Matt. 5:14). Though the people fall short of this calling themselves, the Lord provides his Son, Jesus Christ, to accomplish this purpose and open up access to eternity and his presence through his death (e.g., Eph. 2:11–22; Acts 2:37; Heb. 10:19–22).

[47] Yves Congar, *The Mystery of the Temple*, trans. Reginald F. Trevett (Westminster, MD: Newman, 1962), 4.

(Gen. 12:1, 7),[48] God calls him to relinquish his personal future. This paves the way for the great covenantal promises of Genesis 12:2–3. Here, the Lord comes to the patriarch to tell him, "I will make of you a great nation, and I will bless you and make your name great, so that you will be a blessing. I will bless those who bless you, and him who dishonors you I will curse, and in you all the families of the earth shall be blessed." As with Adam, God uses Abraham to make a people and establish a place to dwell with the patriarch and his descendants. Yet Abraham carries the same corruption and sinful nature as Adam. To provide Abraham this glorious future, God has to first call him out of his pagan idolatry. And for this reason, the Lord requires the patriarch to give up his self-made identity for his God-wrought election. Yahweh quite literally promises him the world if he will follow the Lord.[49] Through Abraham will come a better line, a better land, and an eternal place in the Lord's presence.[50]

Even more momentous is the unilateral covenant in Genesis 15. Here, the Lord manifests himself through the symbols of the smoking pot and the flaming torch passing between the animal halves (Gen. 15:17–19; cf. Ex. 13:21–22).[51] Such images make it abundantly clear that Yahweh is simultaneously covenant maker and covenant keeper.

---

[48] As with Noah, this instrumental aspect of God's presence is in large part tied to the covenant itself. The presence of God is the means of covenant procurement. Each instance of blessing, each covenant established, is rooted in the Lord's becoming present with his people in order to secure his eschatological purposes. As addressed in the previous chapter, the covenant with Abraham unveils once again the Lord's purposes for creation by promising the patriarchs a people, a place, and his presence. These are the objectives that drive redemptive history and, as I am arguing now, bring the Lord to manifest himself in time and space to guarantee their fulfillment. So in cutting the covenant with his elect, the Lord's presence is yet again highly visible in Abraham's salvation.

[49] Abraham follows the Lord in faith, as we see in Gen. 15:6, where it is declared that Abraham "believed the Lord, and he counted it to him as righteousness" (cf. Rom. 4:3; Gal. 3:6).

[50] Significantly, it is the Lord himself who brings all his covenant promises to fruition and does so by being present with Abraham. For example, in a vision the Lord becomes present to Abraham to convey his covenant blessings of line (Gen. 15:1–6) and land (Gen. 15:7–12). Accordingly, such evidence supports Yahweh's presence as the means to his eschatological ends.

[51] The Torah consistently links fire and smoke with the presence of God as it does here in Genesis 15 with the smoking pot and flaming torch (e.g., Ex. 13:21; 19:18; 20:18). Mathews writes: "The 'smoking firepot with a blazing torch' symbolized the presence of God as it passed between the animals. . . . 'Smoke' (ʿāšān) attends divine theophanies (Isa. 6:4), functioning as a veil, and . . . God's appearance at Sinai (Ex. 19:18) brings together the four elements of 15:17: smoke (ʿāšān), furnace (kibšān), fire (ʾēš), and lightning (lappîd at Ex. 20:18). There is an unmistakable association between the covenant reality of this passage, see G. F. Hasel, "The Meaning of the Animal Rite and eerie presence of God (cf. Ezek. 1:13; Dan. 10:6). . . . The thunderclaps and lightning (lappîd) with the thickly veiled smoke (ʿāšān) at Sinai (Ex. 20:18) created fear in the Israelites, who begged Moses to meet with God in their behalf (20:19)." Kenneth A. Mathews, Genesis 11:27–50:26, NAC (Nashville: Broadman & Holman, 2005), 173–74. For further discussion of the covenant reality of this passage, see G. F. Hasel, "The Meaning of the Animal Rite in Gen. 15," JSOT 19 (1981): 61–78. For further connections between theophany and fire, see Douglas K. Stuart, Exodus: An Exegetical and Theological Exposition of Holy Scripture, NAC (Nashville: B&H, 2006), 113; and "Fire," in Dictionary of Biblical Imagery, ed. Leland Ryken, James C. Wilhoit, and Tremper Longman III (Downers Grove, IL: InterVarsity, 1998), 286–89.

The unilateral nature of this covenant places the conditions of the Abrahamic promises on Yahweh's power and presence[52] rather than anything inherent within Abraham.[53] The Lord's decision to take the full responsibility of the covenant upon himself assures its consummation but, as is often overlooked, also sets the agenda for God's redemptive presence. For the covenant to be completed and salvation accomplished, everything must come through the Lord—not Adam, Noah, Abraham, or any other fallen person, for that matter. Salvation belongs to our God (Rev. 7:9–10; cf. Jonah 2:9). The Lord is the one who redeems and, in his grace, manifests himself to do so. Thus, just as the Lord is present before Abraham to walk through the sacrificial pieces to guarantee the covenant promises, he remains present for redemption and redemption's goals.

The divine manifestation to Abraham at the oaks of Mamre continues to characterize the instrumental nature of God's presence. In this mysterious account,[54] Yahweh specifically explains to a barren Sarah

---

[52] With the presence of God linked to this covenant ceremony it is evident that God himself walks between the sacrifices. Williamson concludes: "The important point to note is that God alone (represented by the theophanic imagery of fire and smoke) passed between the dissected animals, indicating the unilateral nature of the covenant. God alone took on obligations; Abraham remained a passive spectator of the ritual." Paul R. Williamson, "Covenant," in Alexander et al., *New Dictionary of Biblical Theology*, 422–23.

[53] The Lord later puts conditions in the covenant to ensure the responsibility of his covenant partners. As seen in a later installment of the covenant, Abraham is called to walk before the Lord and be blameless in his sight (Gen. 17:1–2; cf. 48:15–16). Implicit in this command is the relational experience of divine presence for the covenant members who are holy and righteous, which again connects the presence of God with the requirement of holiness (cf. Gen. 17:8). Placing such a condition upon Abraham echoes the pre-fall existence of Adam, in the garden, who was blameless in his innocence and enjoyed complete fellowship with the holy God. Thus, from one perspective, the covenant is based on Abraham being a new Adam, which, like the first man, Abraham clearly failed to accomplish due to sin. This demonstrates that the call placed upon Abraham is not a command he can keep on his own. God must bring this holiness about for his people, which, as will be demonstrated later, he will accomplish on his own through the alien righteousness of Jesus Christ, himself the presence of God among man. Therefore, the conditions of the covenant placed upon Abraham, though not achievable on his own, are available through faith in God who fulfills the covenant requirements fully through the means of his presence most clearly evident in the person and work of Christ (Gen. 15:6; Rom. 4:3–9, 22; Gal. 3:6; James 2:23; cf. Genesis 22).

[54] Many evangelicals have taken the three "men" described in Gen. 18:9–15 to be a christophany, or a preincarnate appearance of Christ. They support this position from v. 33, where the text connects one of these men to the Lord himself saying, "the LORD went his way, when he had finished speaking to Abraham, and Abraham returned to his place." Gen. 19:1, the next verse, also conveys that the other two "men" with the Lord were angels sent by Yahweh to Sodom to search out the righteous and judge the fallen. Needless to say there is much ambiguity in this narrative, but I would argue that such ambiguity is purposeful in that it reveals that there is constant mediation between the holy God and unrighteous sinners. There does, however, seem to be some sort of theophany/christophany taking place at the oaks of Mamre. The mystery surrounding this account (and other Old Testament expressions of the Lord's presence for that matter) demonstrates the need for separation in the midst of nearness. The Lord is never fully revealed due to his majesty and perfection. There is always a cloud, a pillar of fire, a cleft in the rock, a Most Holy Place, or in this case, a theophanic representation distancing the righteous and unrighteous while still opening up the possibility of redemption. Thus, before Abraham, the Lord mediates his presence in order to continue his covenantal and redemptive purposes with his elect. So, as Hamilton argues, theophanies and christophanies "capture the whole point of biblical theology in that they show the incomparability of Yahweh as he reveals himself to save his people through the judgment of their enemies. In this he is showing mercy to those who fear him and justice to those who disregard his claim on their allegiance (see Ex. 34:6–7)." Hamilton, "Theophany,"

that when he returns in a year's time, she will be with child (Gen. 18:9–15). True to his word, the Lord[55] "visited Sarah as he had said, and the LORD did to Sarah as he had promised" (Gen. 21:1). Here, God is present to enliven Sarah's womb and assure the fulfillment of his dynastic promise. In other words, God manifests himself to bless the patriarch with a child through whom the covenant promises will continue and, more importantly, through whose line the Messiah will eventually come.[56] In the birth of Isaac, therefore, we see God's commitment to creating a people and, in particular, the promised seed of Genesis 3:15.[57]

THE REDEMPTIVE PRESENCE OF GOD WITH ISAAC

The Lord's presence fills the lives of the rest of the patriarchs as well. Take Isaac for instance. At the time of Abraham's death, the only territory he could claim as his own was the small plot of Canaanite land where he was buried (Gen. 25:8–10). Likewise, to count the covenant descendants of Abraham's dynasty only required one hand (actually one finger), not the grains of sand on the shore or the stars in the sky promised earlier (see Gen. 22:17).

Still, God is with Isaac to continue his eschatological mission. The

---

in Longman et al., *Dictionary of the Old Testament*, 817. See also Hamilton, "Salvation through Judgment," 57–84; Terrien, *Elusive Presence*, 79–81.

[55] As Eugene Merrill contends: "While communicating with his creation, he is totally different and distant from it. Only by intermediation can that chasm be bridged, and that intermediation is what we are describing as revelation in all its forms." Merrill, *Everlasting Dominion*, 83. See also Stuart, *Exodus*, 112–13. Still, I would disagree with Merrill in his conclusion that the angel of the Lord is merely a representative of Yahweh and not the Lord himself. Consider the telltale response of those encountering this divine representative. The people who come face-to-face with the angel of the Lord do more than just revere the angel; they call him Yahweh (e.g., Gen. 16:7–14; 21:17–19; 22:11–12; 31:13; Ex. 3:2; Judg. 6:11–23) and go as far as to worship him—an act that the angel of the Lord does not reject (e.g., Judg. 13:1–22; contra Rev. 22:8–9). Accordingly, I would argue that the angel of the Lord is God's presence mediated before men in a way that the cloud, fire, and temple curtain mediate him in other Old Testament examples. So it is both–and; or as one Old Testament scholar summarizes, the angel of the Lord "is in some cases an expression of God himself." R. North, "Separated Spiritual Substances in the Old Testament," *CBQ* 29 (1967): 419–49. Yahweh, therefore, is both present and distant in this divine revelation; he appears but never in the fullness of his essence. For further insight into the connection of the angel of Yahweh as a prototype of Christ, see Geerhardus Vos, *Biblical Theology: Old and New Testaments* (Grand Rapids: Eerdmans, 1948; repr., Carlisle, PA: Banner of Truth, 2000), 74–77.

[56] Moreover, in Genesis 20, the Lord is also present to protect this dynastic and redemptive promise. To clarify that the child in Sarah's womb is in fact Abraham's—a valid question due to her brief stint as Abimelech's wife—God appears to Abimelech to warn the pagan king to return Sarah to her husband. Isaac, therefore, is Abraham's son and the son of the covenant. In coming to Abimelech, the presence of God reensures redemption and his commitment to his teleological agenda.

[57] Beyond the birth of Isaac, the Lord continues his presence with Abraham to ensure salvation and salvation's teleological outcome. This is evident in the sacrifice-of-Isaac narrative (Gen. 22:1–24). Once Abraham's faith (Gen. 22:8) and fear of God are visibly displayed in his obedience (Gen. 22:12), the Lord comes to stay Abraham's hand as it is poised to sacrifice his only son, the beginning point of the Abrahamic dynasty. In Isaac's stead, Yahweh provides a substitute (a ram caught in a nearby thicket), an offering that highlights the provision and protection of the Lord and simultaneously points to a greater substitute through whom the Lord will ultimately guarantee his teleological objectives.

covenant promises are not lost or forgotten with the death of Abraham; instead, in a seamless manner, the blessings of land, line, and presence are bestowed upon Isaac, the son of promise (Gen. 25:11). To extend his purposes to Isaac,

> the LORD appeared to [Isaac] and said, "Do not go down to Egypt; dwell in the land of which I shall tell you. Sojourn in this land, and I will be with you and will bless you, for to you and to your offspring I will give all these lands, and I will establish the oath that I swore to Abraham your father. I will multiply your offspring as the stars of heaven and will give to your offspring all these lands. And in your offspring all the nations of the earth shall be blessed. (Gen. 26:2–5)

Isaac follows the Lord's direction and reaps the benefits of the redemptive work of Yahweh's presence in his life.

Consequently, at the center of Isaac's identity and hope is that familiar covenantal phrase "I will be with you."[58] This refrain reinforces the fact that Yahweh has already appeared to the patriarch for his purposes. Yahweh's relational presence is, therefore, the way to his eschatological presence, not only with Isaac, but also for those who follow him. God is with Isaac. He knows the Lord *is* with him then and *will* be with him forever. Thus, in delivering this simple promise, Yahweh draws near to continue the advancement of his redemptive purposes. So, as with Abraham and the nation of Israel that follows, the presence of God characterizes and defines Isaac's own existence to the point that the surrounding nations discern God's nearness to the patriarch as Isaac's identifying characteristic (Gen. 26:28ff.; cf. 21:22–24). God is present with Isaac to redeem both him and the divine agenda for the world.

---

[58] Isaac's place in redemptive history is grounded in the fact that "the LORD appeared to him" to assure him that the covenant promises are his, saying, "Fear not, for I am with you and will bless you and multiply your offspring for my servant Abraham's sake" (Gen. 26:24). Here God reveals his intentions to be present with Abraham's son and to continue his covenant promises and redemptive purposes. So as I argued in the previous chapter, the promise "I will be with you" is an eschatological objective providing grounds for the blessing of dominion and dynasty. And though the promise of God's presence is future, he is also present with Isaac at the proclamation of the promise. What this and the rest of the patriarchal narratives unveil is that, not only is the presence of God a goal anticipating a future fulfillment; it is also a contemporary and functional reality—as mediated and mysterious as it may be—given in grace to Abraham, Isaac, and the rest of God's people. The pledge that "God will be with Isaac" is rooted in the fact that he already is with Isaac to make and fulfill such a promise.

THE REDEMPTIVE PRESENCE OF GOD WITH JACOB

This redemptive presence of God distinguishes the rest of the patriarchs as well, including Isaac's son. In fact, the Lord is present with Jacob to an almost greater extent. Yahweh approaches Jacob to transfer the covenant blessings of his fathers and, in doing so, continues the promise of dominion, dynasty, and divine dwelling (Gen. 28:13–14).[59] In Genesis 28:15, Yahweh pledges, "Behold, I am with you and will keep you wherever you go, and will bring you back to this land. For I will not leave you until I have done what I have promised you." As with Isaac, the Lord again connects the covenant blessings to his redemptive presence. Here, God vows to be with Jacob until his eschatological mission is realized.

Jacob rightfully responds to his vision of God's presence with fear and awe. Reveling in his theophanic experience, Jacob proclaims, "Surely the Lord is in this place," a place which "is none other than the house of God . . . the gate of heaven" (Gen. 28:16–17). In turn, Jacob names the land Bethel, meaning house of God, and builds an altar of remembrance to remind himself and others of the promise and the work of the Lord, who is with him (28:19).

As one can imagine, this divine encounter is a defining moment in the young patriarch's life. Jacob's very own calling and place in redemptive history is based on the Lord's becoming present, as is seen when he vows, "If God will be with me and will keep me in this way that I go, and will give me bread to eat and clothing to wear, so that I come again to my father's house in peace, then the Lord shall be my God, and this stone, which I have set up for a pillar, shall be God's house" (28:20–22). Jacob's words express his complete reliance upon the Lord's presence for provision, protection, and promise. His life and his redemption are fully dependent upon the presence of Yahweh.

Another mysterious manifestation of the Lord's presence takes place at the ford of Jabbok, where Jacob is suddenly and unexpectedly wrestled down by an unknown man. In this confrontation, the patriarch

---

[59] While asleep, Jacob envisions "a ladder set up on earth, and the top of it reached to heaven. And behold, the angels of God were ascending and descending on it" (Gen. 28:12). At the top of the ladder is God himself who, in confronting Jacob, reveals himself to be "the Lord, the God of Abraham your father and the God of Isaac" (Gen. 28:13). Thus, this whole narrative centers on God's presence coming to Jacob for his covenant purposes. God approaches the patriarch, and God reestablishes his agenda—all of which he does through his redemptive presence.

quickly recognizes his opponent's preeminence, which leads Jacob to the conclusion that this wrestler is likely God himself in some form or fashion.[60] Upon realizing the supremacy and authority of his challenger, Jacob demands to be blessed (Gen. 32:26) and asks for the name of his adversary (32:27). In reply, the enigmatic figure blesses Jacob; however, instead of announcing his name and thereby allowing Jacob to exercise authority over him, his opponent exercises his own authority over Jacob, renaming him Israel, meaning "he strives with God."[61] This name implicitly confirms the patriarch's suspicions concerning his opponent's divinity. So, as at Bethel, Jacob renames the land of his divine encounter, this time Peniel, meaning "face of God," to acknowledge that he has indeed come face-to-face with Yahweh (Gen. 32:30).[62]

Over time, the Lord leads the patriarch from Peniel to Laban and, finally, back to Bethel.[63] At the location of his first manifestation to Jacob, the Lord appears yet again to ratify his covenant and its blessings. Yahweh reconfirms that Jacob is now Israel. He also calls on Jacob to fulfill the creation mandate to be fruitful and multiply (Gen. 35:10–11a). Through the agency of his presence, God works through Jacob's obedience to advance his eschatological agenda. Out of Israel, nations and kings shall come forth (35:11b), and the land promised to his fore-

---

[60] As was the case with Abraham at the oaks of Mamre in Gen. 18:1–15, we find the presence of God again masked in mystery, but this time taking the form of a man. Though undoubtedly the identity of this wrestler is initially hidden from Jacob, his power and authority clearly reveal his divine nature. Soon Jacob begins to understand who his opponent is, and in response, he demands this man's blessing and his name. In the end, it becomes clear that the Lord himself has confronted Jacob, as is evidenced in the patriarch's response at the conclusion of the narrative and the name he gives the land.

[61] There is a debate over the name *Israel* and its proper definition. Some have argued that it means "he has striven with God." Others have contended that it should be translated "God rules/strives." Taken in context, however, it appears that *Israel* means the former. I would agree with Mathews that "if we follow the typical pattern of theophoric appellatives, 'Israel' means 'God [*El*] struggles' or 'May God [*El*] struggle.' The explanation of the name given by the 'man,' however, reverses this sense by saying that it was Jacob who had 'struggled' successfully 'with God [*Elohim*] and with men' (32:28[29]; cf. Judg. 9:9, 13)." Mathews, *Genesis 11:27–50:26*, 559. For examples of the debate, see W. F. Albright, "The Names 'Israel' and 'Judah' with an Excursus on the Etymology of *Tôdâh* and *Tôrâh*," *JBL* 46 (1927): 154–68; R. Coote, "The Meaning of the Name Israel," *HTR* 65 (1972): 137–46; Victor P. Hamilton, *The Book of Genesis: Chapters 18–50*, NICOT (Grand Rapids: Eerdmans, 1995), 334–35; M. Noth, *Die israelitischen Personennamen im Rahmen der gemeinsemitischen Namengebung* (Hildesheim: Olms, 1966), 207–8.

[62] We know from the rest of Scripture that the true "face" of God cannot be seen. For this reason, when Moses asks to see the glory of Yahweh, the Lord retorts, "You cannot see my face, for man shall not see me and live" (Ex. 33:20). With this understanding, it would appear that Jacob's pronouncement that he has "seen God face to face" (Gen. 32:30) is a way of explaining that he has seen a mediated representation of the Lord in his human opponent. What should not be lost in this is the reality that Jacob has encountered the Lord in a close, intimate, and relational way, though, for the patriarch's protection, the full nature of the Lord has not been revealed (cf. Ex. 33:11).

[63] The presence of God motivates Jacob's obedience. To remain in the Lord's presence and its protection, the patriarch responds to the divine commands, as is evidenced in his fleeing Laban with Rachel and Leah (Gen. 31:3). God promises Jacob that if the patriarch leaves Laban with his wives, then Yahweh himself will be with him throughout his journey. In obedience Jacob follows the Lord's command, and in Yahweh's faithfulness, his presence goes with Jacob, providentially guiding his steps and redemptive history.

fathers will be given to Israel and his descendants (35:12). By reinstating the creation mandate, God shows himself faithful once again to his covenant and his promises—all by becoming redemptively present.

Even at the end of Jacob's days, the presence of God is active in his life. The divine presence commands Jacob to go to Egypt and leads him there to be reunited with Joseph, setting the stage for the great salvific act of the exodus. In particular, the Lord appears to Jacob, declaring, "Do not be afraid to go down to Egypt, for there I will make you into a great nation. I myself will go down with you to Egypt, and I will also bring you up again" (Gen. 46:3). Not only does Yahweh make preparations for the exodus; he again ties his covenant promises of dynasty and dominion to his presence. By drawing near, God will expand Jacob's line, and, moreover, he will be present to bring Israel to the Land of Promise.[64]

Finally, foreseeing his death, Jacob blesses his sons, announcing, "Behold, I am about to die, but God will be with you and will bring you again to the land of your fathers" (Gen. 48:21). Jacob's assurance of the future work of God's presence and its redemptive outcome is grounded in his own personal experience of God's presence to redeem and restore. It is the presence of God confronting and directing Jacob that brings redemptive history to this particular point, and it is the presence of God that will bring about redemptive history's future consummation. For Jacob and his descendants, the presence of Yahweh is a contemporary reality, one of provision and protection, one of guidance and control. Through his repeated encounters with the divine presence, Jacob is set apart to be the Lord's, and so too will it be for the rest of Israel's line. According to Jacob and the rest of the patriarchs, the only true and sure way to redemption is through the Lord who is present to save. And as redemptive history will soon show, it is the presence of God that will bring them to Egypt, and it is the presence of God that will lead them out of Egypt as well.

---

[64] Once in Egypt, Jacob, foreseeing his death, initiates the blessings of his sons, the heads of the twelve tribes of Israel—an act that epitomizes the firstfruits of Jacob's dynastic promise. In his dealings with his sons, Jacob conveys the functional aspect of the Lord's presence and its influence and effects on his own story and the greater story of the forthcoming Israelite nation. For instance, in blessing Joseph, the son marked by the Spirit (Gen. 41:38) and by his own experience of the presence of God (Gen. 39:21–23), Jacob describes Yahweh as the "God before whom my fathers Abraham and Isaac walked" and the "God who has been my shepherd all my life long to this day" (Gen. 48:15). Clearly, Jacob is expressing his understanding and awareness of the divine presence and its work in the lives of his fathers, as well as the Lord's supervision and control over his own existence. He then calls on Yahweh to do the same for Joseph in order that the covenant promises will continue to advance.

Conclusion

With the patriarchs, we see that the Lord's presence brings about the goals of redemption. For this reason, each covenantal expression is accompanied by a flurry of divine manifestations. The Lord comes to Abraham, Isaac, and Jacob to establish his covenant and its redemptive outcomes. From an eschatological vantage point, the promises fulfilled in Revelation 21–22 are made possible because the Lord draws near to the patriarchs and works redemption among them. He comes to Abraham, guides him through the Canaanite sojourn, and visits Sarah for the provision of Isaac. The Lord does the same with Isaac and the same for Jacob at Bethel and Peniel. Throughout the patriarchal experience, then, the redemptive presence of God is the driving force behind the story of salvation and its eschatological promises.

7

On Center Stage

Out of Egypt

The Lord continues to detail the functional role of God's presence for redemption in the drama of the exodus. To this point, one scholar has even argued that the centerpiece of the exodus "is the theology of the Lord present with and in the midst of his people."[1] It is true that God is consistently present throughout the exodus. Indeed, I would argue that this section of the Old Testament is, in a way, representative of the broader redemptive-historical storyline.[2] The Lord's gracious presence to reconcile a people from their bondage captures the essence of all salvation history. So just as we have seen in the earlier sections of the Torah, God is present and the exodus narrative emphasizes this in a new and definitive way.[3]

---

[1] John I. Durham, *Exodus*, WBC (Waco, TX: Word, 1987), 21. Durham expands this position, arguing that "the story of Exodus is the story of God's Presence. Every turn of its ongoing narrative is a part of a cumulative confession of the palpable reality of His Nearness. The covenantal formulary of the book of Exodus is a response to God's Presence. Every general and particular requirement of its life-shaping obligation is a part of a studied response to the astonishing revelation that he has come to be with his people. The liturgical expectation of the book of Exodus is a reminder of God's presence. Every word and every action of its ritual ceremony is a protocol of memory designed to keep Israel aware that he is always and immediately at hand." Durham, *Understanding the Basic Themes of Exodus* (Dallas: Word, 1990), 4–5.

[2] The exodus is the definitive work of salvation and deliverance in the Israelite conscience. This is why, in explaining the place of the exodus in redemptive history, J. G. McConville says: "The Exodus tradition lies at the heart of the faith of the OT. It is the supreme example of Yahweh's saving activity on behalf of his chosen people, and as such it becomes a paradigm for all acts of salvation." J. G. McConville, "Exodus," in *NIDOTTE*, ed. Willem A. VanGemeren (Grand Rapids: Zondervan, 1997), 601.

[3] A helpful definition of redemption within the context of the exodus is as follows: "Redemption is God's act of judgment upon his enemies whereby he retrieves his lost people and makes them his in the place he prepares for them (Ex. 6:6–8). It is thus a supernatural act of salvation worked by God for a people powerless to help themselves (Ex. 3:19–20; 7:3–5; 10:1–2; 14:13–14). Interwoven with these events is a sacrificial offering, the slaying of the Passover lamb, which delivers Israel from judgment so they can go free." Graeme Goldsworthy, *According to Plan: The Unfolding Revelation of God in the Bible* (Downers Grove, IL: InterVarsity, 1991), 136–37.

Leading His People to His Dwelling Place: Divine Presence and the Exodus

The Lord boldly announces, "I will dwell among the people of Israel and be their God. And they shall know that I am the LORD their God, *who brought them out of the land of Egypt that I might dwell among them*" (Ex. 29:45–46; cf. 25:8).[4] Thus summarizes God's reason for Israel's deliverance. Exodus 29:45–46 is one of the clearest expressions of the merger of the functional and eschatological aspects of the Lord's presence in Scripture. In this fundamental act of Old Testament redemption, Yahweh becomes present to lead Israel out of Egypt so that he might dwell with them—a purpose evidenced first in the tabernacle, and ultimately completed in the new creation (Rev. 21–22).[5] God draws near to the Israelites to deliver them ("I am the LORD their God, who brought them out of the land of Egypt") in order that those who embrace God's work will have access to his presence eternally ("that I might dwell among them").

Consequently, there are two central elements to God's redemptive presence in the exodus narrative: removal and placement. The first, and most recognizable, is that the Lord is present in time and space to save Israel from its very immediate and very real oppressors. He comes to the Hebrew nation to release its people from their current circumstances. Still, even with this great act of deliverance, the Lord does not merely lead his people out of Egypt. Undoubtedly, he redeems his people from oppression, *but he redeems them in order that he can place them in a better land, a land imbued with a further and greater dimension of his promised eschatological presence.* Yahweh manifests himself not only to redeem his people from tyranny and suffering but also to guide them back into the fullness of his relational presence—first in the tabernacle/temple and, ultimately, in the unrestricted, worldwide dwelling place of God. The exodus, therefore, begins with Israel's removal from a foreign land marked by the absence of God and ends with Israel on the precipice of the

---

[4] A similar declaration is made in Ex. 3:8 when God tells Moses, "I have come down to deliver [my people] out of the hand of the Egyptians and to bring them up out of that land to a good and broad land, a land flowing with milk and honey." Yahweh "comes down," or draws near to Israel, so that his people can escape their oppressor and live in the Land of Promise, the future dwelling place of God. The Lord is present to save and bring forth salvation's purposes.

[5] On the connection between the tabernacle/temple and the new creation, please see chap. 3.

Promised Land, the divinely designated site of God's dwelling among his people.

To understand this purpose of the exodus, we also need to understand that God himself is the main protagonist of this deliverance story.[6] Moses thoroughly understands that redemption comes specifically from and through the Lord. He knows that it is God, present among the people, who initiates and executes each and every mighty act of the exodus, including Moses's own call.[7] As the prophet declares, the Lord "brought you [Israel] out of Egypt with his own presence, by his great power, driving out before you nations greater and mightier than you, to bring you in, to give you their land for an inheritance" (Deut. 4:37–38). God is the only one who can bring about the exodus. As J. V. Fesko observes, the rest of the Torah explains that

> even though Israel is God's son, placed in a paradise, and given the mandate to be a light unto the nations unto the ends of the earth, just as Adam who was God's son before them, Israel was constantly reminded that it was God who was ultimately at work in them. God was the one who delivered them from bondage (Ex. 20:1); he was the source of their sanctification (Ex. 33:13).[8]

So just as he has manifested himself to Abraham, Isaac, and Jacob, God also draws near to Moses to continue the redemptive agenda he set out in his covenant promises.

Contextual Background for the Exodus

To set the stage for this great act of redemption, we should note that the promises of genealogy, geography, and presence afforded to the

---

[6] Because the exodus is the definitive act of redemption in the Old Testament, Moses rhetorically asks "whether such a great thing as this has ever happened or was ever heard of. Did any people ever hear the voice of a god speaking out of the midst of fire, as you have heard . . . ? Or has any god ever attempted to go and take a nation for himself from the midst of another nation, by trials, by signs, by wonders, . . . I have sent you" (Ex. 3:12). Yahweh is shown in this pericope, and throughout the Old Testament, to be the author of redemption and its outcomes.

[7] Take for example the Lord's work in the call of Moses. The verbs in this narrative almost always have the Lord as their subject: "I will send you to Pharaoh" (Ex. 3:10); "I will be with you, . . . I have sent you" (Ex. 3:12). Yahweh is shown in this pericope, and throughout the Old Testament, to be the author of redemption and its outcomes.

[8] J. V. Fesko, *Last Things First: Unlocking Genesis 1–3 with the Christ of Eschatology* (Fearn, Ross-shire, UK: Mentor, 2007), 140.

patriarchs appear to be forgotten by the time of Moses. The people of God are stranded in Egypt, miles away from the Promised Land, living under a cruel Pharaoh who has forgotten Joseph and his benefits (Ex. 1:8). As time has passed, the Jewish experience in this foreign land has turned from blessing to curse and, eventually, collapsed into slavery. Vanishing from the Hebrews' collective consciousness is Joseph's promise that "God will visit you and bring you up out of this land to the land that he swore to Abraham, to Isaac, and to Jacob" (Gen. 50:24).[9] Under such arduous circumstances, these once hope-filled words begin to ring hollow in the ears of this scorned and defeated people.[10]

In fact, Israel's current experience under Pharaoh is almost the exact opposite of Joseph's promise. To the Hebrews, the Lord is nowhere to be found (Ex. 1:8–21). The only domain they can claim is Abraham's small burial plot (Gen. 49:28–33). Even the promise of dynasty is in jeopardy. Though the Israelites "were fruitful and increased greatly" (Ex. 1:7; 12:38; cf. Deut. 1:10–11; 10:21–22),[11] they are still a fledgling nation suffering in the shadow of the vast and formidable Egyptian empire.[12] The grip of their Egyptian oppressors is tightening around this small and persecuted tribe, a grip too strong for them to overcome by their own strength and one that will ostensibly tighten until the Hebrews are extinct. Such dire circumstances call for a fresh manifestation of God to redeem his people from the hand of their oppressors. After 430

---

[9] For emphasis, hope, and remembrance, Joseph demands that the promises of God be repeated among the people of God. As it is revealed in Gen. 50:25, "Joseph made the sons of Israel swear, saying, 'God will surely visit you, and you shall carry up my bones from here.'" Still, Genesis ends with the simple statement that "Joseph died, being 110 years old. They embalmed him, and he was put in a coffin in Egypt" (Gen. 50:26). The stark reality that Joseph remained buried in Egypt did little to reassure his descendants of the completion of these promises. Therefore, it seemed like God's promises, in a sense, remained buried with Joseph and, with continued persecution, Joseph's declarations were soon to be forgotten.

[10] For a helpful resource on this time prior to the invasion of God's presence to redeem Israel from Egyptian captivity, see Donald E. Gowan, *Theology in Exodus: Biblical Theology in the Form of a Commentary* (Louisville: Westminster John Knox, 1994), 1–24.

[11] The Lord is the source of the Israelites' dynastic multiplication. Ex. 1:20–21 states: "So God dealt well with the midwives. And the people multiplied and grew very strong. And because the midwives feared God, he gave them families." Through Yahweh's work, the number of men at the time of the exodus reached six hundred thousand (Ex. 12:37).

[12] Even with such power and might, the Egyptians see the Israelites as a threat primarily because of the recent fulfillment of the dynastic promise. Their growing into a great nation is, indeed, the reason the Egyptians enslave and persecute God's people (Ex. 1:9–11). However, the bonds of Egypt cannot hold down the promises of the Lord or the advancement of his eschatological objectives. So as a consequence, "the more [the Israelites] were oppressed, the more they multiplied and the more they spread abroad. And the Egyptians were in dread of the people of Israel" (Ex. 1:12). The Egyptians, therefore, rail against the Israelites because the Lord is fulfilling his covenant purposes (Ex. 1:1–7). The foreign persecution impedes the Hebrew's acknowledgment of God's faithfulness. To make it explicit to Israel and the world, Yahweh comes to be redemptively present and take his people from the throes of hopelessness.

years of assumed absence, the Lord responds to their cries for justice (Ex. 2:23–25; 3:7–8) and enters history to deliver Abraham's descendants, establish them as his redeemed nation, lead them into the Land of Promise, and once again dwell in their midst.

Presence and Call

This saving activity of God's presence in the exodus is first highlighted at Horeb, the mountain of God (Ex. 3:1).[13] Here, Yahweh draws near to Moses, in the "flame of fire out of the midst of a bush" (Ex. 3:2), simultaneously an expression of distance and proximity articulating both the necessity for mediation and the nearness of God to confront his chosen servant.[14] From out of the fire, the Lord declares, "I am the God of your father, the God of Abraham, the God of Isaac, and the God of Jacob" (Ex. 3:6). In effect, the Lord is saying, "Just as I was present to accomplish my eschatological goals through your forefathers, so now I am present with you to advance these same purposes through you, and I will do so by delivering you." Overwhelmed by Yahweh's presence, Moses can only hide his face in fear. The God of Abraham, Isaac, and Jacob has decidedly manifested himself to Moses, a man running from his past in the barren wasteland of the ancient Near Eastern wilderness.

For the purpose of his eschatological *and* redemptive agenda, the Lord overcomes Moses's fears and graciously calls him to stand as mediator between the Israelites and himself (e.g., Deut. 5:5; cf. Ex. 20:18–21; 24:2).[15] But Moses doubts his divine appointment—a doubt

---

[13] Mount Horeb is possibly a synonym for Mount Sinai, the mountain of God where God and his people meet in the latter half of Exodus. Others have contended that it classifies the broader region that holds Mount Sinai. Either way the significance of this place is based upon the presence of God with his people. Mountains stand between heaven and earth, and, accordingly, Scripture applies this symbol to incidents where the presence of God comes to be with his people in relationship, redemption, and consummation.

[14] Separation between God and his prophet is still necessary. Accordingly, Yahweh warns Moses not to come too close because the land he is standing on is holy ground. Making this nondescript parcel of earth holy is the Holy One's presence (Ex. 3:8). Hence, this account demonstrates God's nearness and distance; or as Bruce Waltke argues, the presence of God "in the bush exemplifies God's humility (Ex. 3:2) and holiness. The Eternal lowers himself into a bush amid dirt and rocks. . . . Yet, his humility does not compromise his nature, for none, not even Moses, may enter his presence with dirt on their shoes. . . . This paradoxical idea is intensified by the next paradoxical image, a purifying fire (i.e., God) dwells in a bush that is fit for kindling (i.e., Israel) without consuming it. This symbolic theophany also foreshadows God's grace to stay in the midst of his people after they commit adultery with a fertility deity on their wedding night with *I AM* (Ex. 20–34, esp. 32–34)." Bruce K. Waltke, *An Old Testament Theology: An Exegetical, Canonical and Thematic Approach* (Grand Rapids: Zondervan, 2007), 363.

[15] In his mediatory role, Moses will receive instruction from the Lord and then lead the people according to the divine directive. Throughout their relationship, Yahweh commands Moses to do the seemingly impossible. For instance, the Lord commands him to go back to Egypt, the land where he last stood condemned as a murderer, and lead a people who have just rejected his leadership (Ex. 2:14–15). Again, a consistent emphasis throughout Exodus and the Old Testament as a whole is God's work in redemptive history despite his people, their sin, and

to which the Lord tellingly responds not by lauding the gifts and offerings of this sojourning murderer, but by assuring his servant that *God will be present with him*.[16] Yahweh answers Moses with the simple phrase, "I will be with you" (Ex. 3:12), a response that should remind us of the Lord's promises to protect, provide, guide, and bless the patriarchs. God knows that the demands he places on Moses cannot be accomplished by Moses, but can be achieved only by the presence of God *with* Moses.[17] This simple promise of presence is fundamental to the redemptive drama to follow. God's presence with Moses brings the Hebrews out of Egypt and leads them to the Land of Promise. Redemption rests not on Moses's shoulders, but squarely on God and his being present with his people.

Still, even with the promise of the divine nearness, Moses is hesitant. Moses knows that if he does return to Egypt, he will need the name of the Lord to convince Pharaoh to free his people. Moreover, Moses needs the name of Yahweh to persuade the Israelites of his divine calling and leadership. The Hebrews have rejected Moses before, and without the presence of God, the Israelites will surely reject him again. In his grace, Yahweh offers him his divine name, declaring himself to be, "I AM WHO I AM" (Ex. 3:14). Though there has been considerable ink spilt over the meaning of the name we transliterate as *Yahweh*,[18] the

their doubt. God calls Moses, not to honor Moses, but to glorify himself through Moses. He comes to save a broken people through a broken man in order that the fallen world may see the gracious work of the Lord's redemptive presence. It is the Lord who ultimately completes Moses, which once again reminds us of the divine source of Israel's redemption.

[16] Moses is in the perfect place. He understands that what is being asked of him cannot be accomplished in his own power. Only a man in Moses's circumstances can grasp this, and it is one like Moses whom the Lord can use to fulfill his purposes and highlight his glory in doing so.

[17] Moses's role as leader of the Hebrew nation is based upon Yahweh's presence with him. For this reason, Yahweh reminds the Israelites that he sent Moses, and that redemption comes through his presence, not through the mediator alone (Ex. 3:15). The foundation for Moses's calling, therefore, is the Lord's presence with him and the provision of the name Yahweh. Because of Yahweh's presence with the mediator, the Israelites accept Moses and his leadership. With their mediator's arrival, the presence of God has come again to Israel, causing the Hebrew elders to exclaim, "The LORD, the God of the Hebrews, has met with us" (Ex. 3:18).

[18] For a survey on the debate over the name Yahweh, please see W. F. Albright, "Contributions to Biblical Archeology and Philology," *JBL* 43 (1924): 363–93; William R. Arnold, "The Divine Name in Exodus iii. 14," *JBL* 24 (1905): 107–65; G. Beer, *Exodus*, Handbuch zum Alten Testament (Tübingen: Mohr, 1939), 29; F. M. Cross Jr., "Yahweh and the God of the Patriarchs," *HTR* 55 (1962): 229–59; D. N. Freedman, "The Name of the God of Moses," *JBL* 79 (1960): 151–56; W. H. Brownlee, "The Ineffable Name of God," *Bulletin of the American Schools of Oriental Research* 226 (1977): 39–46; R. Abba, "The Divine Name Yahweh," *JBL* 80 (1961): 320–28; S. D. Goitein, "YHWH the Passionate: The Monotheistic Meaning and Origin of the Name YHWH," *VT* 6 (1956): 1–9; Tryggve N. D. Mettinger, *In Search of God: The Meaning and Message of the Everlasting Names*, trans. F. H. Cryer (Philadelphia: Fortress, 1987), 14–49; R. W. L. Moberly, *The Old Testament of the Old Testament* (Minneapolis: Augsburg, 1992), 5–35; Sigmund Olaf Plytt Mowinckel, "The Name of the God of Moses," *Hebrew Union College Annual* 32 (1961): 121–33; E. C. B. MacLaurin, "YHWH: The Origin of the Tetragrammaton," *VT* 12 (1962): 439–63; Julian Obermann, "The Divine Name YHWH in Light of Recent Discoveries," *JBL* 68 (1949): 301–23; Samuel Sandmel, "Haggada within

context in which the Lord provides his name recalls his earlier promise of divine presence. The translation "I AM" (אהיה, 'ehyeh, "I am/will be") can also be rendered, "I will be," connecting the divine name with God's prior pledge that he "will be" with Moses (Ex. 3:12). From this perspective, his name, at minimum, connects the Lord with his earlier self-identification as the God who is present—a title that underscores the functional aspect of his presence in and for redemption. For this reason, the name Yahweh in the context of Moses's call shows us that God is present to save.[19] And this has ramifications for the way we understand the rest of this passage (Ex. 3:11–4:17). As one Old Testament theologian argues, this whole section of Exodus can be translated as follows:

> 3:11–12: Moses asks "Who am I?" God responds, "I am with you."
> 3:13–15: Moses asks, "What is your name?" God answers, "I AM WHO I AM"—that is, "so pure in sublimity that you can count on me."
> 4:1–5: Moses argues, "They will not believe me." God gives him the sign of the rod that turns into a snake as his cachet. 4:10–11: Moses continues to resist: "I am not eloquent." God replies, "I am ('ehyeh) with your mouth." 4:13–17: Moses protests for the last time: "Send someone else." God becomes angry and sends Aaron as his assistant, promising, "I am with your mouth and his mouth."[20]

So what is the point of God's name going with Moses to Egypt? It is that God will be present with his mediator to save his people. God is essentially saying, "You have my name, which, more importantly, means you have me." The reality of God's identity is intimately tied to his presence. And why is he present? He is present to deliver. The name Yahweh, therefore, is more than just a proper name; it is an expression of divine character that centers on his being redemptively present with and for a people.[21]

Knowing God's name ensures everything that the Lord is to Moses.[22]

Scripture," *JBL* 80 (1961): 105–22. Samuel Terrien, *The Elusive Presence: Toward a New Biblical Theology* (New York: Harper & Row, 1978), 119.

[19] Waltke, *Old Testament Theology*, 367.

[20] Ibid.

[21] For further development of this idea of God being with Moses, see Gowan, *Theology in Exodus*, 54–126.

[22] Owing to his particular calling and place in redemptive history, Moses's relationship with the Lord is unique, to say the least. As mediator between God and Israel, Moses meets with the Lord "face to face," as is evidenced in his shining face coming down from Sinai (cf. Ex. 34:29–34). He experiences Yahweh in a way unknown to the rest

His name is his promise of communion, power, hope, and salvation—all because he will be present to accomplish all of these things and more. When God gives Moses his name, he opens the door to a relationship.[23] If a deity in the ancient Near East (the setting for the exodus) offered its name, it "assured the deity's commitment; within the name the deity's character was disclosed."[24] In the provision of his name, then, Yahweh solidifies his promise to be present with Moses and the nation of Israel as God's nation. He assures "Moses and Israel of Yahweh's presence in the nation's developing history."[25] Through this historical and covenantal context, Yahweh's self-disclosure reveals that the "'I am that I am' (Ex. 3:[14]) may well be taken as 'I will be to you as I was with them' (the fathers of Ex. 3:13), or 'I will be there—with you in Egypt—as I am here.'"[26] The name *'ehyeh* and the relationship it signifies guarantee the success of Moses's future work, including his confrontation with the world's most power leader, Pharaoh. But Moses has more power than Pharaoh ever will because God has given Moses his name. And by having the name of God, Moses has Yahweh's promise to be present to deliver and redeem.

With the continued reassurance of God's name and, accordingly, his presence, Moses finally submits to the Lord's call.[27] Not only that,

---

of the people of God (e.g., Ex. 33:11; Deut. 34:10). For, as the Lord declares, only "with [Moses] I speak mouth to mouth, clearly, and not in riddles, and he beholds the form of the Lord" (Num. 12:8). Thus, Moses is the mediator and representative of God and his presence before the nation of Israel, and there is no other like him who is used in this way to inaugurate the Lord's mighty acts among Israel and the nations (e.g., Num. 16:28) and to advance his teleological objectives. It is interesting, though, that later Moses reminds Israel that "the Lord spoke with you [the Hebrew people] face to face at the mountain, out of the midst of the fire" (Deut. 5:4). The "face to face" declaration has been reserved to describe divine interaction with Moses. However, here it appears to be speaking about the presence of God in a more general sense, which the qualification "out of the midst of the fire," a symbol of distance throughout Exodus, would seem to substantiate. There is, therefore, a significant difference in the extent to which Moses and Israel experience the presence of God. Nevertheless, even in his special manifestation to Moses, it is for his redemptive work with and for Israel.

[23] We have seen that having the divine name is essential to the prophet because to "the ancient Near Eastern person the name of a deity opened the possibility of relationship." William J. Dumbrell, *The Faith of Israel: A Theological Survey of the Old Testament*, 2nd ed. (Grand Rapids: Baker Academic, 2002), 33.

[24] Ibid.

[25] Ibid., 35.

[26] Michael D. Williams, *Far as the Curse Is Found: The Covenant Story of Redemption* (Phillipsburg, NJ: P&R, 2005), 29. Williams continues to argue for such a translation when he writes: "In its other occurrences, the name Yahweh appears in covenantal contexts, in the midst of God entering personal relationship with his people. Thus, Yahweh is the divine name associated with the ark of the covenant, the tabernacle, and the temple—primary emblems of God's presence with Israel. Yahweh also tends to be the central name of God when the issue is God's historical action, whether past, present, or future. . . . It is the covenantal and historical reality of God that is fundamentally at issue in the name Yahweh" (ibid., 30).

[27] Even with the presence of the Lord before him in promise and name, Moses continues to doubt. He questions how Israel can be certain that the Lord has sent him. Yahweh acquiesces to Moses's concerns by performing great signs (turning Moses's staff into a serpent, his skin leprous, and the water to blood). Doing so shows both Moses and his Israelite audience that Yahweh is indeed present with his mediator and that he has called him out from among the nation to act on his behalf (Ex. 4:1–9). In other words, the signs demonstrate that "the God of Abraham,

but the Hebrew elders initially accept Moses's divinely established promise of deliverance and follow his leadership. With the arrival of their new "mediator"—one who knows the intimate name of God and whose words and actions are accompanied by signs and promises—it becomes obvious to the Israelites that God is "visiting"[28] his people again, this time to bring forth their salvation and covenant renewal (Ex. 4:31). In store for Israel is both its immediate deliverance from Egyptian persecution and its deliverance back into God's perfect presence. Yahweh promises "not only to be 'with' Moses as he [brings] Israel out of Egypt but also to bring him back [to Horeb/Sinai] to worship God 'on this mountain' (Ex. 3:12) and from there lead them 'to a good and broad land, a land flowing with milk and honey, to the place of the Canaanites'" (Ex. 3:8).[29] God's fellowship with Moses in the burning bush, therefore, is only the beginning of God's redemption— a redemption that we see once again is brought forth *by* his presence *for* his presence.

Presence and Passover

Armed with the name of God and the temporary confidence of Israel, Moses returns to Egypt to plead the case for the Lord's people before the unjust and hardened Pharaoh (Ex. 4:21–22; 5:1–4).[30] Moses is able

---

the God of Isaac, and the God of Jacob, has appeared to [Moses]" (Ex. 4:5). In Moses's next objection, Moses cites his lack of eloquence. Now burning with anger, the Lord quickly admonishes Moses for his lack of faith, and yet he still graciously provides Aaron to be Moses's mouthpiece. In overcoming his skepticism, God demonstrates that his presence is in fact with Moses and that Moses, through Aaron's voice, will proclaim the redemptive agenda to the Hebrew people. Even in utilizing Moses and Aaron, Yahweh makes it undoubtedly clear to the people of God that their redemption is from the Lord, and this chosen mediator only acts on his behalf. We see this when the Lord declares to Moses, "I will be with your mouth and with his mouth and will teach you both what to do" (Ex. 4:15). The ensuing work of redemption, therefore, is not based upon the work of Moses and Aaron but on the One who has manifested himself to them.

[28] It is interesting that the same verb (פקד) used here is the one used when God visited Sarah with the birth of Isaac. As these examples both show, the Lord's "visits" are active relational interactions between creature and Creator. He comes to bring about his purposes. His visits are for the progression of redemptive history and the advancement of his eschatological program. This has been the case since Adam's fall, for it was then that Yahweh's relationship with humanity went from creation and free fellowship to redemption and restitution.

[29] R. E. Averbeck, "Tabernacle," in *Dictionary of the Old Testament: Pentateuch*, ed. T. Desmond Alexander et al. (Downers Grove, IL: InterVarsity, 2003), 822.

[30] Unfortunately, with each of Pharaoh's denials, the power and purposes of Yahweh fade in the eyes of Moses and his Hebrew constituents (Ex. 5:20–23). To this point, the Israelites could only see that the Lord's plan of deliverance has resulted not in their freedom, but in more disdain and punishment being leveled against them (Ex. 5:6ff.). Under such considerable persecution, the faith of Israel begins to wane, the hearts of his people begin to fail, and their spirits begin to break (Ex. 6:9). In a merciful response to their lack of faith, the Lord reassures Moses and his people, not by annihilating the Egyptian nation immediately, but by reissuing the covenant promises to his chosen people. Doing so demonstrates that the God who appeared to their fathers to advance the covenant blessings is the same God who has drawn near to them in order to do so again (Ex. 6:3a). The Lord cuts through the haze of their repression and affliction by declaring his faithfulness to his covenant and redemptive purposes. So in response to

to confront Pharaoh again and again through God's presence with him.[31] The Egyptian king obstinately denies the Lord's commands to free Israel. Pharaoh soon finds out, however, that keeping the Hebrews from their God comes with dreadful consequences. Yahweh comes to Egypt to bring the mighty Pharaoh to his knees and liberate the nation of Israel from his tightening grip (Ex. 7:14–10:29).[32] Not even the armies of this superpower will stop the Lord's redemptive purposes.

The tenth and final curse plays the most significant role in Israel's salvation history, for it is through the Passover that Yahweh finally delivers his people from Egyptian oppression. He does this by becoming present to judge and save. In particular, the Lord establishes the Passover[33] as a ceremony by which the Israelite people are to separate themselves from sinful Egypt and identify fully with the God of their salvation.[34] Through Moses's prophetic word, Yahweh institutes the specific requirements of the Hebrews to avoid the forthcoming judgment on Egypt and enter God's covenantal blessing. Their redemption hinges upon each household sacrificing an unblemished lamb at twilight on the fourteenth night of the month (Ex. 12:3, 5–6).[35] Once the

---

their continued persecution, God proclaims: "I have heard the groaning of the people of Israel whom the Egyptians hold as slaves, and I have remembered my covenant. Say therefore to the people of Israel, 'I am the LORD, and I will bring you out from under the burdens of the Egyptians, and I will deliver you from slavery to them, and I will redeem you with an outstretched arm and with great acts of judgment. I will take you to be my people, and I will be your God, and you shall know that I am the LORD your God, who has brought you out from under the burdens of the Egyptians. I will bring you into the land that I swore to give to Abraham, to Isaac, and to Jacob. I will give it to you for a possession. I am the LORD'" (Ex. 6:5–8). As this passage obviously depicts, Yahweh draws near to make Israel his people, to bring his people into his land, and to be relationally present as their God.

[31] Moreover, the Lord emphasizes the functional and redemptive aspect of his presence with Moses and Israel by reminding them that he has given his name to them, the very name that reveals his presence, the very name that was not afforded to the patriarchs (Ex. 6:3). To emphasize this, the Lord bookends his speech with "I am" and reveals it (three times) throughout this pericope as well. Consequently, the people of Israel have the promises of the covenant as well as the promise of God's name. In these, the Lord's purposes are sure. He is among them to bring them to the Land of Promise. His purposes cannot be thwarted, not even by the most powerful king and kingdom reigning on earth.

[32] In the plagues of blood, water, frogs, gnats, flies, dead livestock, boils, hail, locusts, and darkness, the Lord's presence is evident in his powerful mastery over his universe, and each plague attacks creation and its original intent, symbolizing the effects of the fall in concentrated form. The results of these plagues also form the backdrop of what lies across the Jordan River in the Land of Promise. It is the foil of the Lord's beautiful and wondrous provision for his people. In short, in Egypt they are in chains and surrounded by plagues; in the Promised Land they will be free and surrounded by God's presence.

[33] The Passover is so important that it marks the beginning of the Hebrew calendar. It is a memorial reminding the people of God's grace for all time (Ex. 12:2, 14–20). Thus, the Passover, in a sense, is Israel's point of origin. It commences the nation's redemption and fulfills its election, and thus is to be forever before the Israelites' eyes.

[34] For further development of the Passover and the theories surrounding its origin and meaning, see T. Desmond Alexander, "The Passover Sacrifice," in Sacrifice in the Bible, ed. R. T. Beckwith and M. J. Selman (Grand Rapids: Baker, 1995), 1–24.

[35] The Passover "is the first time that the blood of the sacrifice, symbolizing the life laid down in death, receives special attention and it underlines the atoning significance of the sacrifice (cf. Lev. 17:11)." R. T. Beckwith, "Sacrifice," in New Dictionary of Biblical Theology, ed. T. Desmond Alexander et al. (Downers Grove, IL: InterVarsity,

lamb is slain, the family is then to spread its blood on their door frame to symbolize their need for the Lord's mercy during the Lord's righteous wrath against Egypt (3:7). The Israelites are to ready their garments for immediate departure (belts fastened, sandals on, and staffs in hand), consume the Passover meal, and, leaving nothing behind (3:8–11), be fully prepared to leave their oppressors forever.[36]

With the Israelites primed for deliverance, God enters history to judge the Egyptians for their tyranny and to deliver his covenant people from death and despair. As Moses has promised Pharaoh, the Lord walks in the land of Egypt to bring judgment upon the nation's first-born sons and livestock (Ex. 11:4–5). For Israel, however, the blood of the lamb on the doorposts is a sign to Yahweh, present to judge, that mercy is to be afforded to these households. Instead of feeling the wrath of God, the Israelites are spared by the shed blood of their paschal sacrifice.

In the Passover, God is again present both to judge and to save. Yahweh himself avows:

I will pass through the land of Egypt that night, and I will strike all the firstborn in the land of Egypt, both man and beast; and on all the gods of Egypt I will execute judgments: I am the LORD. The blood shall be a sign for you, on the houses where you are. And when I see the blood, I will pass over you, and no plague will befall you to destroy you, when I strike Egypt. (Ex. 12:12–13)

In this definitive moment of the exodus, it is the Lord who comes to put his enemies in their place—Yahweh is sovereign; Pharaoh is not. Still, in the case of his elect, God is present in mercy and grace. He spares a people to secure their redemption, keep them from destruction, and prepare them for the installation of his covenant blessings

---

2000), 758. Thus, the act of sacrificing the perfect lamb and spreading its blood on the door frame foreshadows the forthcoming sacrificial system as we see in 2 Chron. 35:11, where the blood of the Passover lamb is spread on the altar of the temple courts by the Israelite priests for atonement purposes. In the Passover, then, the unblemished lamb receives the wrath of God in the place of the Hebrew households, whereas the Egyptians not covered with the blood of the sacrificial lamb pay the penalty for their own accounts.

[36] The ceremony is performed not only to save Israel from impending judgment; it also prepares the people for the coming exodus and its redemptive outcome. In short, the requirements of the Passover are practical, in that they ready the people of God for deliverance and freedom. Yahweh fills their stomachs for the difficult journey to the Land of Promise. Through the Passover regulations, the Hebrews are outfitted for a hasty departure and a swift pace. Likewise, nothing of the meal is to be left. Their exodus is permanent; they will never return. Their trust now rests in the Lord, the one who has promised to be with them.

(Ex. 11:4–5; 12:29; cf. Ezek. 20:3ff.). Through the Passover, a covenant people remain because God is present to redeem. Yahweh is faithful to his redemptive promises to create a people for his glory, to give them a land, and to dwell with them in fullness.[37]

Presence in the Wilderness

Though definitely a high-water mark in the biblical drama, the Passover is not the end of the redemptive work of God's presence. God draws near to liberate his people from the grasp of Egypt *and* to lead his people back to the land he first promised to Abraham. In this second act, Yahweh pledges his presence to protect and provide for the Hebrew exiles, and to plan and pilot their journey to Canaan—the land that is to be theirs, a land that is to be the locus of God's dwelling on earth.

To procure this future,[38] God manifests himself to the Hebrew nation in fire and cloud (Ex. 20:21; cf. 14:19, 24; 40:38; Num. 10:34; 14:14; Deut. 1:33; Neh. 9:12, 19; Pss. 63:2; 78:14; 99:7; 105:39).[39] In particular, the Lord uses the cloud of his presence to direct Israel's steps to Canaan during the day and the pillar of fire to light their way at night (Ex. 13:21–22; cf. Num. 9:15–17).[40] These forms of God's pres-

---

[37] Even in escaping Egypt, the Israelites are pursued by their oppressor, a reality that forces their continued reliance upon God. With Israel removed from Egypt's protection and provision—as malicious as it was—the people now stand vulnerable in a barren wasteland facing the fundamental questions concerning their survival. To assuage their fears, Yahweh draws near to meet their needs, providing food and water to sustain them on their journey (Ex. 17:6–7; cf. 16:9–12). Supplying sustenance is more than a work of provision; it is also an advancement of his redemptive agenda. Yahweh is present to keep them alive in the desert because he is faithful to his covenant promise of dominion, dynasty, and dwelling.

[38] The Lord's presence to bring a people out of a foreign land in order to make them his own and the recipients of his blessings is not without historical precedent. In fact, the account of the exodus, in several ways, echoes the work of the Lord's presence in calling Abraham out of Ur of the Chaldeans. As with the patriarch before, the Lord leads the people of Israel away from all they have known into the wilderness. The children of Abraham must do just as their father did: they too must leave the only world they have known for the promises of God. As the rest of the story will show, they will struggle to exercise the same faith Abraham did (e.g., Ex. 14:11–12; 15:24; 16:2; 17:3).

[39] Yahweh so consistently manifests his presence before the Israelites that even the pagan nations surrounding Israel marvel that their Lord is in their midst. The inhabitants of Canaan see that the Lord is "in the midst of this people. . . . Your cloud stands over them and you go before them, in a pillar of cloud by day and in a pillar of fire by night" (Num. 14:14). Therefore, it is apparent to both God's people and pagan nations that Israel's redemption and security are based upon the Lord's presence with his people (Num. 14:15–19). The pillars of cloud and fire are constant reminders that provision, protection, guidance, and deliverance come solely from Yahweh.

[40] Cloud references in the Old Testament are often linked with a manifestation of God's presence (e.g., Ex. 19:16; 24:16, 18; 33:9–10; 34:5; 40:34–38; Lev. 16:2; Num. 9:15–23; 1 Kings 8:10–11; 2 Chron. 5:13–14; cf. Ezek. 10:3–4). As Goldingay explains concerning the Sinaitic emphasis on clouds, "Yhwh also speaks of coming down on the mountain, in/with/on a mass of clouds (Ex. 19:9; 11)—a cloud is both God's means of transport and a means of veiling Yhwh's presence (cf. Ex. 24:15–18)." John Goldingay, *Old Testament Theology: Israel's Gospel* (Downers Grove, IL: InterVarsity, 2003), 387. We see this in Ex. 16:10, where Scripture "associates the cloud in the wilderness with the glory of God. The cloud and the fire represent God's presence with [the Israelites] during their sojourn." "Cloud," in *Dictionary of Biblical Imagery*, ed. Leland Ryken, James C. Wilhoit, and Tremper Longman III (Downers Grove, IL: InterVarsity, 1998), 157.

ence separate Israel from their Egyptian pursuers and bring down the waters of the Red Sea upon the mighty Egyptian army (Ex. 14:19–20, 24). Such mighty acts of God's presence to deliver reinforce the redemptive function of Yahweh's presence.[41] A people are saved and are on the path to the place of promise *because* of God's presence. We must remember that Israel's salvation comes not from Israel itself or even Moses, but explicitly from the power and presence of Yahweh (Ex. 13:22).[42]

Moved by his recognition of the Lord's devotion to deliver and direct, Moses sings,

> You have led in your steadfast love the people whom you have
>   redeemed;
>   you have guided them by your strength to your holy abode.
>   (Ex. 15:13)

Everything the Lord does, including his guidance, provision, and protection for his chosen nation is done to bring his people into his "holy abode." In other words, he enters history to bring his people to himself (cf. Gen. 21:22; Ex. 3:12; Deut. 2:7; Josh. 1:5; Ps. 46:7, 11; Isa. 41:10). Moses recognizes this and declares,

> You will bring them in and plant them on your own mountain,
>   the place, O Lᴏʀᴅ, which you have made for your abode,
>   the sanctuary, O Lord, which your hands have established.
>   (Ex. 15:17)

Moses rejoices in God's becoming present to pluck a people from slavery to bring them to the sanctuary of his eternal presence.

---

[41] Ex. 14:31 would appear to show that the presence of God is the means of salvation and is used by Yahweh to elicit faith among the people of Israel. Thus Brevard Childs concludes that when Israel is confronted by God and his salvation, they "acknowledge and trust his special office (14:31)." Brevard Childs, *Exodus: A Critical and Theological Commentary* (Philadelphia: Westminster, 1974), 368.

[42] Responding to the Israelites' fear of the pursuing Egyptian army, Moses reassures God's people of the power of Yahweh's presence when he declares: "Fear not, stand firm, and see the salvation of the Lᴏʀᴅ, which he will work for us today. For the Egyptians whom you see today, you shall never see again. The Lᴏʀᴅ will fight for you, and you have only to be silent" (Ex. 14:13–14). As Moses, reflecting on these historical events, responds, it is "the Lᴏʀᴅ your God who goes before you [Israel]" and who "will himself fight for you, just as he did for you in Egypt before your eyes, and in the wilderness where you have seen how the Lᴏʀᴅ your God carried you, as a man carries his son, in all the way that you went until you came to this place" (Deut. 1:30–31). It is most significant that to display his power for salvation, Yahweh reveals his presence. In his final action against Egypt, the cloud of the Lord's presence "moved from before [the Israelites] and stood behind them, coming between the host of Egypt and the host of Israel" (Ex. 14:19–20; cf. Isa. 52:12; 58:8).

A Holy God with His Sinful People

However, in order to achieve his redemptive ends, God must first deal with Israel's sin. Just as in Eden, sin continues to threaten God's purposes in the world even as he works salvation in the midst of his people. At the foot of the mountain of God's presence, the Israelites turn from Yahweh and, in his place, worship the man-made image of the golden calf (Ex. 32:1ff.).[43] And this is not an isolated event. Deuteronomy 9:7 recounts, "From the day you came out of the land of Egypt until you came to this place, you have been rebellious against the Lord" (cf. Num. 11:18, 20). Sin characterizes Israel and, regrettably, the nation's

> abject and seemingly incurable spiritual separation from the Lord and God's inexorable movement to "bring every deed into judgment, including every hidden thing, whether it is good or evil" (Eccles. 12:14), are twin truths seen in the unfolding biblical history of redemption.[44]

The rebellion of Israel jeopardizes the people's redemption and, as a consequence, puts their experience of the covenant promises in question.

The Lord, who is present with them, also requires separation from this sinful people. We repeatedly see in the exodus that God commands Moses to keep the rebellious Israelites away from his presence (Ex. 19:21, 24; 24:2; 33:5; cf. Heb. 12:18–24). This shows us that even as God is present, distance is required as well.[45] The fullness of God's glory cannot be on full display because it would consume the unrighteous. In response, Moses commands the Israelite assembly to stay at the foot of the mountain as he reenters the presence of Yahweh for instruction (Ex. 19:12, 21–25). If any Hebrew touches Sinai, contaminating the

---

[43] It is ironic that the Hebrews, in their apostasy, demand that Aaron make gods for them that will go before the people (Ex. 32:1). What they seem to forget in the short amount of time that Moses is atop Sinai is that their desires have already been met by Yahweh. He is ever before his people, caring for them and leading them to his gracious purposes. He is present in an appropriate way, a mediated way. Thus, there is no specific form of God ever manifest before the people of Israel—only a voice or enigmatic representation such as the angel of the Lord, fire, or cloud. The reason for such mystery is to keep Israel's hearts, which are so inclined to idolatry, from turning the *manifestation* of Yahweh into an idol.

[44] R. W. Yarbrough, "Atonement," in Alexander et al., *New Dictionary of Biblical Theology*, 389.

[45] Even with the commands for distance and separation, the Lord comes down "on Mount Sinai in the sight of all the people" (Ex. 19:11), and Moses also "brought the people out of the camp to meet God" (19:17). God's presence, therefore, is revealed to Israel, but in a much different and less direct sense than Moses's experience.

holy space of Yahweh with sin, such rebellion will result in death (Ex. 19:13, 21).

The fire, smoke, and cloud coming down on Sinai emphasize this need for separation (Ex. 19:16, 18). These physical signs of divine presence point us to the fact that, even as the Lord draws near, the sinful and rebellious nature of these people makes it impossible for him to manifest himself completely (e.g., Ex. 33:3, 5). As in the fire and cloud leading them in the wilderness, there is presence as well as distance. Now atop Sinai, the presence of God takes the form of shadow and cloud, fire and smoke, to reinforce this mystery (Deut. 4:12–16). Here there is physical representation but enough separation to keep us from our own sinful demise. God allows only one man a fuller glimpse of his presence, and that is Moses, the divinely appointed mediator. Even here, God protects Moses from his divine holiness.

In response to this frightful display of divine nearness and separation, Israel finally feels the weight of God's glory. The people beg Moses to be their mediator before Yahweh. And for a brief moment, the nation knows its true place. The people understand that if they ever enter his perfect and unmediated presence, they will be destroyed (Ex. 20:18–21). Sinai, in a sense, reinforces the effect of Adam's sin, along with the gracious response of God's redemptive presence and the mediated nature of that presence. What is more, the separation attested to on Sinai deepens Israel's longing for the land of God's presence where mediation will no longer be required.

Presence and Law

Sinai, then, is a testament to God's grace as well as his holiness. For though distance from sin is rightly required, the presence of the Lord comes to Sinai to accomplish his salvific purposes (e.g., Deut. 4:10–11; cf. 10:12). God comes to Sinai to continue his restoration of Eden. And this will be accomplished. Deuteronomy 4:31 vows, "The LORD your God is a merciful God. He will not leave you or destroy you or forget the covenant with your fathers that he swore to them." God will accomplish his redemptive agenda. Yet he must do so in a way that does not contradict his holy character. Sin separates the Lord from sinners, and it is because of sin that God draws near to save. Something must be done. There must be something put in place so that God can be in the midst of sinners for their redemption.[46]

The law is one way that the Lord counters the disparity between God's holiness and man's lack thereof. The law provides the moral requirements that, if followed, would make Israel holy as God is holy (e.g., Ex. 19:6; cf. Lev. 11:44–45; 19:2; 20:7, 26; 21:8; 1 Pet. 1:16). The Ten Commandments and subsequent laws, therefore, not only articulate the rules and regulations for Israel, but actually capture the essence of the Lord's holy character. So the commands of Sinai show us that "the ritual provisions of the law are designed to maintain Israel's covenant status as a holy people living in the presence of a holy God."[47] Simply put, if Israel could be covenantally faithful (e.g., Ex. 19:4–5; 20:1–17, 22–26; 21:1–23:19), the distance between Yahweh and his people would be removed (Lev. 26:3–13, esp. 10–11).[48] If the law were kept, the nation would be holy (e.g., Ex. 18:21; 20:23ff.; cf. Num. 3:5; Deut. 4:13). If the nation were holy, God's redemptive project would be complete, along with his eschatological purposes.

From this perspective, the law's rules, regulations, customs, and observances all point to something bigger than themselves. These mandates and policies are instituted to clear the way for God's presence. In other words, the law of Israel is a divine provision for moving his people from divine distance to divine nearness. Thus the Lord declares, "If you will indeed obey my voice and keep my covenant . . . you shall be to me a kingdom of priests and a holy nation" (Ex. 19:5–6; cf. Lev. 20:26–27;

---

[46] In other words, because the "primary concern of the Mosaic covenant [was] the maintaining of the unique divine-human relationship between Yahweh and Israel, some means of sustaining communion between a holy God and a sinful people was required." Paul R. Williamson, "Covenant," in Alexander et al., *New Dictionary of Biblical Theology*, 424.

[47] David Peterson, "Atonement in the Old Testament," in *Where Wrath and Mercy Meet: Proclaiming the Atonement Today*, ed. David Peterson (Carlisle, UK: Paternoster, 2008), 9.

[48] In the beginning of Leviticus 26, the obedience of man and the eschatological blessing of God's presence come together. After listing the agricultural blessing (vv. 4–5) and peace blessing (vv. 6–10), the text culminates in the completion of the covenant promise (vv. 11–13). At its center is the presence of God. According to Leviticus, when man is obedient to the law of Yahweh, Yahweh will again dwell in the midst of his people (v. 11). Hence, one of the most important points of Leviticus is that obedience brings blessing. Obedience ushers man into the culminating blessing of the divine presence. Or as Gordon Wenham puts it: "The blessings reach a great climax in reassuring the people that if they are faithful, all the promises included in the covenant will be fulfilled. God will walk with his people, as he did in the garden of Eden before the fall (Gen. 3:8; cf. Deut. 25:15 [Eng. 14]). What God has repeatedly promised as the goal of the covenant, 'I shall become your God,' will then be seen to be true (Gen. 17:8; Ex. 6:7; 29:45–46; Lev. 11:45; cf. Ex. 19:5–6)." Gordon Wenham, *The Book of Leviticus*, NICOT (Grand Rapids: Eerdmans, 1979), 330. As the New Testament will show, the blessings and promises of Lev. 26:3–13 do in fact come through obedience; but this obedience is ultimately not Israel's. Instead it points to One who will be the presence of God in redemptive history in a way never known before and in One who would one day fulfill these requirements through his perfect life and sacrificial death.

22:32–33; Num. 25:12–13; Deut. 7:6; 14:21; 26:19; 28:9). As a kingdom of priests, all of Israel would have access to the Lord's presence.[49] Old Testament scholar Christopher Wright maintains that the people of Israel

> were to be [God's] priesthood in the midst of the nations (Ex. 19:6)—representing him to the rest of mankind, and being the means of bringing the nations to saving knowledge of the living God. To fulfil that destiny they were to be a holy nation (different from the rest), characterized by walking in the way of Yahweh in justice and righteousness.[50]

Through conformity to the law of God, Israel would become a holy nation and a kingdom of priests inhabiting a new paradise of God's presence and working to spread this paradise throughout creation.

From this vantage point, the law's regulations "function to restore the 'normative' (created) state when it has been disrupted or violated by sin or impurity."[51] The law reveals the moral requirements that, through perfect obedience, could consummate the covenant promises (cf. Jer. 7:23–24) and prepare Israel for the Promised Land—another Eden-like paradise marked by God's relational presence (cf. Deut. 30:15–16; Isa. 48:16–19).[52] It is for this reason that the Lord describes the Land of Promise as "the land in which [the people of Israel] live, in the midst of which I dwell, for I the LORD dwell in the midst of the people of Israel" (Num. 35:34). The law discloses that Israel's redemption involves more than just moving people from one land to another; it also entails an advancement of the Lord's covenant promises, for through obedience, there is potential for reentry into God's eschatological presence.

---

[49] To ratify the covenant, Moses offers sacrifice and spreads the blood of the offering on the altar of God and the people themselves, an act symbolizing the union of Yahweh with Israel (Ex. 24:3–8). Peterson explains: "The blood of the sacrifices was splashed on both altar and people presumably to represent their consecration to God as a holy nation (Ex. 19:6). In between these applications of blood the people swore an oath of covenant loyalty to the Lord (24:7)." Peterson, "Atonement in the Old Testament," 4. Through this covenant and obedience to the law, Israel will, in fact, become a kingdom of priests and a holy nation. To support this, Peterson also connects the covenant ratification ceremony with the consecration of the priest detailed in Exodus 29. The similarities between these two acts reveal that all of Israel, like their priesthood, is being cast in a priestly role through the nation's full submission to the law and covenant fidelity.

[50] Christopher J. H. Wright, *Knowing Jesus through the Old Testament* (Downers Grove, IL: InterVarsity, 1992), 40.

[51] Frank J. Gorman, *Leviticus: Divine Presence and Community* (Grand Rapids: Eerdmans, 1997), 8. Gorman continues, "The purification sacrifices function, in part, to cleanse the holy place of impurity (Lev. 4), and the ritual for the person recovered from a skin disease functions to restore that person to society (Lev. 14:1–20)" (ibid.).

[52] Thus, "to remain in communion with this Lord of glory and enjoy his bounty, [the people of Israel] simply had to serve him and obey his commands." Allen P. Ross, *Recalling the Hope of Glory: Biblical Worship from the Garden to the New Creation* (Grand Rapids: Kregel, 2006), 108.

Presence and Tabernacle

On the heels of giving the law,[53] Yahweh draws near to Moses again to institute a temporary dwelling place where God can be present with his elect people (Ex. 25:8; Deut. 6:15; 7:21).[54] Through the law and the ratification of the Mosaic covenant, Israel is made to be God's people and, likewise, Yahweh identifies himself as Israel's God. This is why the Lord makes his presence a permanent fixture in the life of the Hebrews. R. W. L. Moberley explains:

> Since, at least in the early period, Yahweh's presence was not so much conceived abstractly as connected with some visible symbol or manifestation (cf. e.g., Num. 5:3, 10:35f., 2 Sam. 7:6), and since Yahweh's relationship with Israel has been set upon a permanent and regular basis, some permanent symbol of Yahweh's presence among Israel was now appropriate. It is the ark and the tabernacle (Ex. 25–27) which fulfill this role.[55]

The tabernacle is one of the final pieces of the puzzle in the Yahweh-Israel relationship. The law requires Israel to be ethically like God; the covenant supports God's commitment to the oft-wayward nation; and now with the tabernacle, God demonstrates through his permanent presence that Israel is his and he is her God. In the tabernacle God is with his people in a new way. Instead of temporary manifestations at pivotal moments in redemptive history, Yahweh commits himself to dwell consistently in the Hebrew camp. This tent symbolizes God's election of Israel, not because of who they are but because of who he is, and that he is in their midst to redeem them.[56]

It is, therefore, in the tabernacle that we have a limited fulfillment

---

[53] It is important to notice that the command for the tabernacle is subsequent to the law and sacrificial mandates. The call to holiness given in the law and atonement rituals paves the way for a more settled, established, and corporate experience of the divine presence inaugurated in the tabernacle (e.g., Ex. 40:34–38; Num. 9:15ff.).

[54] Waltke makes an interesting point when he argues that the temple represents both God's omnipresence and his specific, relational presence. He writes, "The tabernacle concretely expresses the unfathomable mystery of God's omnipresence (i.e., his existing in all places at all times [Ps. 139:7–10; Jer. 23:23–24; Acts 17:24–28]), and his immanence (i.e., his unique presence vis-à-vis special interests on earth where mortals may approach him)." Waltke, *Old Testament Theology*, 458.

[55] R. W. L. Moberley, *At the Mountain of God: Story and Theology in Exodus 32–34*, JSOTSup 22 (Sheffield, UK: JSOT, 1983), 45.

[56] As Anderson concludes, the tabernacle is "located not outside but in the center of the camp" because "if God is to be at the center, in the midst of the people, then God's sanctuary must be in the center . . . of the Israelite encampment" (Num. 2:1–2; 3:1–31; 10:11–33). Bernhard W. Anderson, *Contours of Old Testament Theology* (Minneapolis: Fortress, 1999), 109. Moreover, this location hints at the centrality of God's presence not only to the Israelite camp, but to the world as well. It is through Israel that the presence of the Lord is to spread to the rest of creation.

of God's promise. Remember Exodus 29:45–46: "I will dwell among the people of Israel and will be their God. And they shall know that I am the LORD their God, who brought them out of the land of Egypt that I might dwell among them."[57] This portable tent "was to operate as a means by which God's presence and his rule over [his covenant people] was dramatically expressed."[58] By being present in the camp, God reigns over, provides for, and protects his people in a visible and uniform way—a way exhibiting his covenant faithfulness all the more.[59] The Lord's presence that was once atop the mountain, separated from the people, is now in the camp of Israel. This gracious, yet terrifying decision "assured [the Hebrews] of the future supply of their spiritual and material needs, including the fulfillment of the promise that they would possess the land of Canaan."[60] What we have in the tabernacle is a picture of what is and what could be. This tent is the constant re-

---

[57] From a biblical-theological perspective, the sanctuary is a microcosm of Eden, patterned after the Lord's own heavenly sanctuary (Ex. 25:9; see also chap. 3). It embodies what the world once was before the fall and what the world could one day become through Israel's holy obedience to the law. In connecting the garden and the temple, Allen Ross explains, "The house of the Lord was like the Garden of Eden; it was where the people had access to God, received all the blessings of life, and feasted on the peace offerings and drew from the living water." Ross, *Hope of Glory*, 93. Ross continues, "In time Israel built a sanctuary and then a temple patterned after Paradise, not only to recall the memory of Paradise but also to rekindle the hope of glory in the Paradise to come" (ibid., 108). The template for the temple, then, is Eden, the garden which itself was patterned after the New Jerusalem (Rev. 21–22). So, for example, similar to the way Adam and Eve worshiped God and fellowshiped with him in the original garden-sanctuary, the high priest now enters the Most Holy Place to worship God and experience his presence. Furthermore, just as cherubim were charged with protecting the entrance to the garden when the first couple was expelled, cherubim are also on top of the ark of the covenant and are embroidered on the curtains separating the Most Holy Place (Ex. 26:31–33). Cf. Andrew S. Kulikovsky, *Creation, Fall, Restoration: A Biblical Theology of Creation* (Fearn, Ross-shire, UK: Mentor, 2009), 282. Please see chap. 3 for further support for the connection between Eden and the temple of God. For further support and development, see T. Desmond Alexander, *From Eden to the New Jerusalem: Exploring God's Plan for Life on Earth* (Nottingham, UK: InterVarsity, 2008), 13–73; G. K. Beale, *The Temple and the Church's Mission: A Biblical Theology of the Dwelling Place of God*, NSBT 17 (Downers Grove, IL: InterVarsity, 2004); Beale, "The Final Vision of the Apocalypse and Its Implications for the Biblical Theology of the Temple," in *Heaven on Earth: The Temple in Biblical Theology*, ed. T. Desmond Alexander and Simon Gathercole (Waynesboro, GA: Paternoster, 2004), 191–209; Sandra Richter, *The Epic of Eden: A Christian Entry into the Old Testament* (Downers Grove, IL: InterVarsity, 2008), 92–136.

[58] David Peterson, *Engaging God: A Biblical Theology of Worship* (Downers Grove, IL: InterVarsity, 1992), 36. When the Hebrews look upon the tabernacle, they do not first see a tent or type of the eschatological dwelling place of God; instead, they primarily recognize the tabernacle to be the mobile location of God's redemptive presence—the presence that so far has worked out their deliverance by being manifest to covenant with the fathers, come to Moses in the burning bush, judge Egypt in the Passover, lead them through the desert, and appear to Moses atop Sinai for his salvific purposes.

[59] Scripture makes it quite apparent that the presence of God did, in fact, reside in the tabernacle (Ex. 25:8; 29:45; 36:1–4). "The architectural-implemental symbolism of the book of Exodus is a pictographic representation of God's presence. Every material and each dimension of the Tabernacle, the furnishings within it and the space and the altar before it, are a prompting of sensory perception to the continuing signal, 'He is here, He is here.'" Durham, *Themes of Exodus*, 5. From the exodus on, then, God's presence in time and space is to be associated with the tabernacle/temple, though not limited to it. Ex. 25:8 demonstrates this commitment when Yahweh instructs Moses, "Let them make me a sanctuary, that I may dwell in their midst." Moreover, the Lord commits his presence to this tent, for when "the cloud covered the tent of meeting . . . the glory of the LORD filled the tabernacle. And Moses was not able to enter the tent of meeting because the cloud settled on it, and the glory of the LORD filled the tabernacle" (Ex. 40:34–35).

[60] Samuel J. Schultz, *Leviticus: God among His People* (Chicago: Moody, 1983), 30.

minder that God is with his people to care for, rule, define, and redeem them (Ex. 25:8–9) and, simultaneously, the reminder of the eschatological presence of God that awaits us in the New Jerusalem, that city set up like the tabernacle/temple structure.[61]

The tabernacle's architectural design reveals this ongoing tension. Holiness requires separation. But as the tabernacle shows us, Yahweh pours forth his grace by being redemptively present with his people. This is why the tabernacle is arranged the way it is: God has instituted his temporary dwelling place to express both his nearness to redeem and the distance of his eschatological presence. Think about separation. The sanctuary is divided into the three concentric sections of the outer court, Holy Place, and Most Holy Place. Only in the Most Holy Place do we find God's presence. This is a room set apart from the rest of the tabernacle by a thick veil (Ex. 26:33; 34:29–35), a room never to be entered except once a year on the Day of Atonement, and then only by the high priest after his own purification. Moreover, the numerous commands and requirements placed upon all who entered the tabernacle regulate and remove all sin or uncleanness (e.g., Lev. 15:31). These architectural features and legal arrangements make it clear that access to Yahweh is neither free nor immediate, but mediated by the instruction of God himself. In effect, God says through the layout of the tabernacle, "I am here to save, but I am here to save on my own terms for your good and for my glory."

And yet, even in separation, God is with his people. The whole point of the tabernacle is not the partitions but the redemptive presence of God. And at this stage in salvation history, he locates his spirit above the ark of the covenant in the Holy of Holies. The tabernacle, therefore, provides a way for God to be with sinners for their redemption while simultaneously protecting sinners from God's holiness. Even the mediatory aspects of the tabernacle reveal God's presence to redeem and restore his covenantal commitments. The different rooms and spaces set off from the people ensure the Lord's holiness and protect transgressors from Yahweh's righteousness (Ex. 33:5) while making a way for God to be with Israel to redeem Israel.

---

[61] For a more extensive comparison of the earthly tabernacle to the Lord's heavenly dwelling place, see Goldingay, *Israel's Gospel*, 395–96.

Another feature of the tabernacle is its mobility. In the tabernacle we have the presence of God, but because the Promised Land and the fulfillment of the covenant promises lie ahead of Israel, the tabernacle is portable.[62] We must remember that God is working toward an objective, and this requires even a literal movement toward his redemptive goals. As Exodus 40:36–38 expresses, God's presence in the tabernacle guides Israel, for "whenever the cloud [of God's presence] was taken up from over the tabernacle, the people of Israel would set out. But if the cloud was not taken up, they did not set out till the day that it was taken up." Unlike the forthcoming temple—a permanent structure in the Land of Promise—the tabernacle is designed by God for transportation—to go where his presence leads his children for their redemption.

Presence and the Provision of Sacrifice

The law establishes the grounds for the Lord's presence with his people, and the tabernacle prepares the way for this reality; but what the history of Israel shows us is that the people of God cannot keep the commandments, nor do they deserve the tabernacle. Sinai reveals to us that the relationship between God and man is a tenuous one that demands stipulation and condition.[63] By no means is Israel exempt from the penalty of sin by virtue of its privileged position as God's covenant partners (cf. Ex. 15:1–12; 19:9–25; 32:1–34:9). But instead of bringing his justice to bear directly on the covenant breakers themselves, God, in his mercy, chooses provisionally to make a way to atone for sin through the sacrificial system.

The purpose of atonement[64] is to show "God's work on sinners'

---

[62] As Anderson contends: "God's glory could fill the sanctuary, showing the presence of God, but God's glory is not confined to a holy place (Isa. 6:3), even the great temple of Jerusalem. . . . God's glory could leave the temple and go with the people. . . . This symbolism indicates that God is mobile, on the move." Anderson, *Contours*, 111. Going a step further, God is mobile and on the move for the purpose of redemption. He goes with his people to save his people and bring them into the covenant blessings.

[63] As the Old Testament will show, the sacrificial system fails in a sense and, therefore, awaits a better provision to reaccess God's presence. This, of course, as the New Testament details, is complete in Christ, the final and perfect atoning sacrifice. The gospel is, therefore, the final answer to limitations and failures of Israel's inability to keep the law and properly administer the sacrificial system. Thus Michael Horton argues, the "'Law' creates terror in the hearer because of the awareness of sin it engenders, while 'gospel' actually brings life." Michael S. Horton, *Covenant and Eschatology* (Louisville: Westminster John Knox, 2002), 136.

[64] The atonement focus of the sacrificial system is especially evident in Lev. 16:30: "For on this day shall atonement be made for you to cleanse you. You shall be clean before the Lord from all your sins." Speaking of the consecrated priests, Leviticus goes on to declare, "He shall make atonement for the holy sanctuary, and he shall make atonement for the tent of meeting and for the altar, and he shall make atonement for the priests and for all the people of the assembly" (Lev. 16:33).

behalf to reconcile them to himself" through "the divine activity that confronts and resolves the problem of human sin so that people may enjoy full fellowship with God both now and in the ages to come."[65] Here at Sinai, and throughout the rest of Scripture, we see sinners offering sacrifices to the Lord to pay for their sin through the death of another. But what we often forget is the other side of this provision: not only is sin being dealt with in the sacrifice; the sacrifice is also making it possible for the holy God to be present to remove sin and redeem. Each offering made to the Lord (Lev. 1:5) signals the temporary removal of Israel's guilt and provides the necessary means for God's guiding and redemptive presence with his people.

This atoning work takes place in the day-to-day sin and guilt offerings as well as the burnt offerings[66] decreed in Leviticus and rehearsed throughout the rest of the Old Testament (e.g., Lev. 4:1–6:7; 6:24–7:10). In the sin and guilt offerings, hands are laid on the animal prior to the sacrifice so as to transfer the sins of the congregation to the creature for the forgiveness of the people. This introduces the idea of substitution. The shedding of an unblemished animal's blood (Ex. 12:5; Lev. 22:17–25; Mal. 1:6–14; cf. Gen. 8:20) represents the loss of life on behalf of sinners (Lev. 17:10–12; Deut. 12:23–25). Blood is necessary for one's cleansing (Lev. 17:14), for "without the shedding of blood there is no forgiveness of sins" (Heb. 9:22; cf. Lev. 17:11). The death of the sacrifice *substitutes* for the death of the one offering the sacrifice. In the sin and guilt offerings, the unblemished animal suffers the punishment earned by individual sinners, which in turn frees them from the penalty they deserve.

By means of this substitution, God provides a way for his redemptive presence to remain with sinners. We see this in his instruction to Aaron regarding his sacrificial offering. Moses commands Aaron, "Draw near to the altar and offer your sin offering and your burnt of-

---

[65] Yarbrough, "Atonement," 388.

[66] The burnt offerings were "meant to be an expression of consecration to the Lord but also to be a means of making atonement for sins (Lev. 1:3–17; 14:20; 16:24; cf. Gen. 8:21)" (ibid., 389). Gordon Wenham concludes that, in comparison to the other forms, the burnt offering "makes atonement for sin in a more general sense" (cf. Num. 15:24; 2 Sam. 24:25; 2 Chron. 29:7–8; Job 1:5; 42:8). Wenham, *Leviticus*, 57. All in all, each mode of sacrifice shows that "the making of full atonement normally required sin and/or guilt offerings and a burnt offering (Lev. 5:7; 9:7; 14:18–20)." Peterson, "Atonement in the Old Testament," 6. As hinted at in the Passover and made explicit in the Levitical sacrificial ordinances, "deliverance from divine judgment is associated with the offering of animal blood as a substitute for human life" (ibid., 4).

fering and make atonement for yourself and for the people, and bring the offering of the people and make atonement for them, as the LORD has commanded" (Lev. 9:7; cf. 4:20, 26, 31, 35; 5:13, 18; 6:7). The sacrifices of Aaron are to pay for the sins of Israel, but what is fascinating is the reason Moses gives Aaron for offering the sacrifice in the first place. In Leviticus 9:6, Moses tells him that sacrifice is "the thing that the LORD commanded you to do, that the glory of the LORD may appear to you."[67] God comes to establish the sacrificial system to provisionally wipe away sin *so that* he may be present with his people. This is the great cycle of the sacrificial system and the presence of God: God becomes present to establish the sacrificial system and the people's redemption through the removal of sin, *and then* the sacrificial system removes sin so that God may be present to work out redemption.

The pinnacle of the sacrificial system is, of course, the Day of Atonement. On this annual observance, the high priest enters into the very presence of God, who resides in the Most Holy Place. This is the only occasion that the high priest[68] is allowed to pass behind the veil separating the rest of the tabernacle from the sacred location of the Lord's presence. Upon entering, the high priest makes atonement for the nation by sprinkling the blood of the sacrifice on and before the mercy

---

[67] The term "glory" or כבוד, in Hebrew, is one that denotes divine presence. As Anderson explains, this word "pervades the Old Testament and the New (e.g., Isa. 6:3; 40:5; Greek *doxa*, John 1:14; 15:8)." In Hebrew it carries various meanings but "basically means 'weight' and thus applies to a person of weight or importance. When applied to God, it refers to God's visible manifestation, usually in radiance or resplendent light (later, the Shekinah)." Anderson, *Contours*, 110. Gaffin adds that the phrase "'glory of the LORD' occurs frequently in the OT; it is virtually a technical term (e.g., Ex. 16:7; 1 Kings 8:11; Ps. 63:2). God's glory is his visible and active presence. . . . His glory is his presence in the midst of his covenant people Israel (Ex. 16:7). Used in this sense, the word is clearly associated with God's name (Ex. 33:18–19; Ps. 115:1). Related to his grandeur and power as Creator and Redeemer, it is often associated with the phenomenon of light or fire, sometimes of such overwhelming brilliance and unendurable intensity that it is shrouded in a cloud (Ex. 16:10; 24:17; cf. 33:22–23; 34:29–35)." Richard B. Gaffin Jr., "Glory," in Alexander et al., *New Dictionary of Biblical Theology*, 508.

[68] For the high priest to enter the Most Holy Place on the Day of Atonement requires purification of the sanctuary. Because "pollution and sin affect not only the individual and the nation, but also the tabernacle, the seat of God's presence among his people," the "sanctuary must be regularly purged of its impurities or else God will abandon both sanctuary and people to their doom." Peterson, "Atonement in the Old Testament," 7, 12. This process of purification itself involves sacrifice. Alexander summarizes: "On the Day of Atonement the high priest, wearing his special priestly clothing (Lev. 16:4), passed through the curtain which separated the Holy of Holies from the Holy Place. Inside the Holy of Holies he sprinkled blood on and before the cover of the ark of the covenant, cleansing it and the Holy of Holies from pollution caused by sin. This process was repeated twice. On the first occasion a bull was sacrificed as a purification offering; its blood paid for the sins of the high priest and his family. Afterwards one of the two male goats was sacrificed and its blood brought into the Holy of Holies by the high priest to atone for the sins of the whole community of Israel (Lev. 16:15–16)." T. Desmond Alexander, *From Paradise to the Promised Land: An Introduction to the Pentateuch*, 2nd ed. (Grand Rapids: Baker, 2002), 221. This cleansing continues as the high priest works in similar fashion throughout the Holy Place putting the blood of the sacrifice on the golden altar of incense (Lev. 16:17), the horns of the bronze altar in the courtyard (16:18), and the altar (16:19). All of this activity is to purify the sanctuary and the high priest in order that atonement may be made in the midst of God's holy presence.

seat—the special location of God's immediate presence (Num. 10:35–36; 1 Sam. 4:5–9). Here the presence of God and atonement collide, and the Lord secures his people's salvation. For this reason the Lord declares, "I will meet with you, and from above the mercy seat, from between the two cherubim that are on the ark of the testimony, I will speak with you about all that I will give in commandment for the people of Israel" (Ex. 25:22; cf. Lev. 16:2). On the Day of Atonement, the sacrifice stands between God and the high priest of Israel in order that the sins of the nation might be forgiven.

Yahweh also calls upon the high priest to transfer the sins of Israel both to a goat that is to be sacrificed and to a goat that will remain alive. This latter animal is the scapegoat, the living sacrifice "for which atonement is made, and over which the sins of Israel are confessed, after which it is sent away to carry them into the wilderness (Lev. 16:10, 20–22; cf. 4:6–7)."[69] Both goats are Israel's substitutes. The transmission of Israel's sins and death to these animals and, in particular, the scapegoat's isolation in the wilderness visually represent the Lord's redemptive work in Israel to eradicate the nation's mounting disobedience and guilt.

The sacrificial system, therefore, was designed to restore and reconcile humanity to the presence of God. Yet, as the annual act of the Day of Atonement and the daily repetition of the sacrifices demonstrate, sin is constant. If this reconciliation is to take place, humanity's iniquities must be dealt with in a way that is like the sacrificial system and yet surpasses it. For this reason, Scripture couples the act of sacrifice with the reminder that God's power alone can and does redeem. Sacrifice will not save; only God's work through sacrifice can redeem. As shown in Deuteronomy 32:43, "[God himself] will atone for His land and His people" (NASB). In other words, it is only the Lord who provides Israel's atonement and absolution (Deut. 21:8; 2 Chron. 30:18–19). The only real source for atonement and salvation is the Lord God, for it is only he who can remove their transgressions.[70]

From this perspective, the sacrificial system accomplishes two re-

---

[69] Beckwith, "Sacrifice," 759.
[70] As Peterson concludes, "God is the true or ultimate source of atonement, even if he provides certain rituals as the means by which his people obtain this benefit." Peterson, "Atonement in the Old Testament," 10.

lated purposes: (1) it prepares God's people for his future presence, and (2) to achieve this objective, it offers a provisional way for Yahweh's functional presence to remain among his sinful people. In short, the sacrificial system is in place to assure that God is still present to accomplish his covenantal promises. Through sacrifice, the Lord can "dwell among the people of Israel" (Ex. 29:45–46) both in salvation history and at the end of salvation history, dwelling freely and fully with those whom his functional presence redeems for his eschatological presence. As we will see in the chapters to come, this sacrificial system points us to the greater reality of atonement in Jesus Christ, God present in the flesh to redeem, and opens up eternal access to the presence of God.

At the Foot of Sinai: Reassuring the People of God's Presence for Redemption

From Sinai, the Lord faithfully institutes the law, tabernacle/temple, and sacrificial system in order to be present to save and to ensure his eschatological objectives. In God's gracious provisions, Israel is well on its way to entering the fullness of God's redemptive agenda. The people stand at the edge of a new paradise where the Lord has promised to be present with them in a permanent way. By God's presence and power at Sinai, Israel is closer to the objectives started in Eden than ever before. But like Adam, Israel can neither keep the law nor remain covenantally faithful.

Even as God meets with Moses atop the mountain, Israel grows impatient with the Lord and his chosen mediator. Instead of preparing themselves for God's word through Moses, they prepare for themselves idols of gold in the likeness of foreign gods. The covenant is broken even as it is being ratified! In response to Israel's covenant infidelity, the Lord threatens to remove his presence, the one defining feature of Israel and their only hope for salvation. Thus he announces to Moses that he will neither "go up to [Israel]" nor continue to guide the nation to his promises (Ex. 33:3). This judgment has major implications for Israel's future; the removal of God's presence virtually eliminates the nation's identity and purpose. Without Yahweh's presence, Israel would quickly become just another small, insignificant nation languishing in the wilderness as before.

Seeing the ramifications of this terrible impending judgment, Moses intercedes to abate the wrath of God (Ex. 33:12ff.). He even goes so far as to offer himself as an atonement for Israel's sins (Ex. 32:30ff.). Moses "reminds" Yahweh that Israel is his chosen nation to whom he has covenanted himself. As a consequence, his divine name and glory are to be forever associated with this weak, sinful people (Ex. 33:13). Moses continues, arguing, "If your presence will not go with me, do not bring us up from here" (Ex. 33:14–15). Moses understands that it would be better to remain in the wilderness with God than to be separated from his redemptive presence and its associated blessings. Moses also knows that the Lord's presence with the Hebrews is the only viable means to salvation and the attainment of his future blessings (33:16). If God is absent, then the covenant is null and void, and so too are the covenant promises.

In his grace and for his glory, Yahweh overcomes Israel's infidelity. Instead of separation, the Lord reaffirms his commitment to their redemption and his covenantal objectives by reassuring Moses that he, Yahweh, will be present with him. At the Tent of Meeting, where God speaks face-to-face with Moses (Ex. 33:11), Yahweh recommits to leading and guiding his people to the Land of Promise by his presence. Responding directly to Moses's pleas for divine nearness, the Lord promises his prophet, "My presence will go with you, and I will give you rest" (Ex. 33:14).[71] Here, the Lord vows to be manifest redemptively with Israel, to secure the people's salvation, and to usher in the fulfillment of his eschatological goals (Ex. 33:17).

In light of God's merciful reassurances, Moses boldly requests that the Lord ratify his commitment by personally unveiling his glorious presence to him. In one of the most remarkable and astonishing passages in the Pentateuch, the Lord consents, avowing, "I will make all of my goodness pass before you and will proclaim before you the name 'The LORD'" ("I AM" or 'ehyeh, "I am/will be"—Ex. 33:19). As the story

---

[71] Though there is much more that can be said about the biblical-theological theme of rest, especially with reference to the Sabbath, it is important to realize that there is an eschatological background to this concept. In the context of divine presence, rest is part of the teleological goal. It is what takes place once God's people are in God's place in God's presence. So all the struggles the Israelites and the church face in this world are finally over once every believer enters the new heaven and new earth and its promises (Rev. 21:4). The world returns to its Edenic beginnings, but it has also advanced beyond this to a fuller, cosmological rest of believers living fully and freely in the presence of Yahweh.

goes, even with Moses's privileged position, there are multiple limitations and safeguards regulating the mediator's incomparable experience
of the divine presence. Yahweh tempers the revelation of his glory,
asserting,

> You cannot see my face, for man shall not see me and live. . . .
> Behold, there is a place by me where you shall stand on the rock,
> and while my glory passes by I will put you in the cleft of the rock,
> and I will cover you with my hand until I have passed by. Then I
> will take away my hand, and you shall see my back, but my face
> shall not be seen. (Ex. 33:20–22)[72]

In affirming his commitment to be redemptively present with his people and uphold the promise of his dwelling among them, the Lord gives
Moses a glimpse of what is to come when his redemptive mission will
be complete. However, this unique divine-human encounter is only
a partial experience limited by Moses's sin and the need for a better
sacrifice to open up access to the Lord's presence in its eschatological
fullness. Still, it is a glorious episode pointing to the finalization of the
Lord's redemptive agenda when Yahweh will finally pull his hand back
to reveal his unmediated presence to all the redeemed.

With the covenant renewed[73] and the institutions in place, Moses
returns from Sinai's peak visibly marked by the presence of God.
Coming face-to-face (or "face-to-back" might be better) with God has
caused Moses's own face to shine with a brilliant light, so brilliant that
it strikes fear in the hearts of the Israelite congregation. To appease
their concerns, Moses covers his radiant appearance every time he is
before the people. When he stands before God, he removes the veil and

---

[72] For a similar account centering on God's revealing himself to his prophet, see 1 Kings 19:9–18, where God becomes present to Elijah at the cave on Mount Horeb. Here he speaks to his prophet not in thunder, smoke, and fire
atop a mountain but in a faint whisper. And just as Moses covered his face after being in God's presence, so too
does Elijah—an act that Terrien argues "is the recognition of the *mysterium tremendum* of holiness: the theological assent of Elijah to the Mosaic acceptance of not seeing the glory (Ex. 33:23)." Terrien, *Elusive Presence*, 232.
I would also contend that this glory vision shared by Moses and Elijah is the basis for their inclusion at Jesus
Christ's transfiguration. On the holy mount, Jesus Christ briefly peels back his humanity to expose himself to be
the presence of God to his chosen disciples just as it was with Moses and Elijah, who once again share a vision of
God's glory at the transfiguration of Christ (Matt. 17:1–13; Mark 9:2–8; Luke 9:28–36).

[73] Following this glorious display of divine presence to Moses, Yahweh graciously continues to restore his people by
renewing his covenant (Ex. 34:6–7). Moses boldly requests, "If now I have found favor in your sight, O Lord, please
let the Lord go in the midst of us . . . and pardon our iniquity and our sin, and take us for your inheritance" (Ex.
34:9). The Lord grants his mediator's petition and ratifies his covenant with Israel once again, thereby declaring
himself to be the means of its fulfillment (Ex. 34:10–11).

enters into his presence. This unmistakable privilege afforded to Moses alone sets him apart from the rest of Israel and underscores his place as mediator of Yahweh's covenantal purposes. Moreover, the veiled face of their leader is Israel's constant reminder that their path and their prospect come not from Moses but from the source of Moses's light: the presence of God in their midst for their redemption (cf. 2 Cor. 3:1–18).

Conclusion

As with the rest of the Torah, God is with his people at Sinai. The shared confession of the Torah and the Exodus narrative is that "the God whom Israel worships is the 'Holy one in your midst' (Isa. 12:5–6)."[74] Yet not only is he with his people; he is with them to save and prepare a way for his redemptive purposes. As we have seen,

> the Exodus generation has met with God (Ex. 19:17–20:18; Num. 17:4). Yahweh has gone before them in the pillar of cloud and fire (Ex. 13:21–22; Num. 9:15–22; Deut. 1:33). They conduct their lives in the presence of God (Ex. 22:11; Lev. 5:19; Num. 5:16; Deut. 1:45). There is a remnant whose hearts are circumcised (Rom. 11:2–5). Yahweh has promised to be and is with them (Ex. 33:14–16; Lev. 25:23; Num. 23:21; Deut. 20:2).[75]

Here at the mountain, the Lord does not give up on his people; rather, he comes to save them. He offers his presence to guide them through the wilderness, he speaks face to face with Moses for their instruction, and he comes personally to give Israel the institutions by which his redemptive objectives are to be consummated. It is therefore quite evident that the redemption of Israel is because "the LORD your God has been with you," and, in his drawing near, "[Israel has] lacked nothing" (Deut. 2:7). God brings the nation to the threshold of the Promised Land. Certainly, he uses Moses and Aaron to direct their steps, but ultimately it is God who delivers the people into this new Eden-like land flowing with milk and honey (cf. Deut. 4:32–40; 8:7–10).

---

[74] Anderson, *Contours*, 47.
[75] James M. Hamilton Jr., "God with Men in the Torah," *WTJ* 65 (2003): 125.

8

The Curtain Falls (on Act 1)

Back to the Brink

From the outskirts of Eden to the outskirts of Canaan, God showed himself faithful to his promises. The Lord became present to usher his people to within steps of the Promised Land, and in doing so, he brought Israel closer to the fulfillment of his eschatological aims than ever before (cf. Isa. 1:16–20). Israel's entrance into the land was more than just a people receiving a beautiful and fertile land for their own possession; it meant that they were closing in on the fulfillment of the covenant promises and the future presence of God (cf. Deut. 33:27). At the foot of Sinai the eschatological objectives were gaining momentum. If only the nation could remain covenantally faithful, Canaan could one day become the new Eden[1] and the presence of God located in the tabernacle would be clear to reside with the people freely and fully (Isa. 11:9; Hab. 2:14; cf. Ps. 22:27; Zech. 14:9).[2] If they could keep the law, Israel would be the kingdom of priests that could finally stand in the Lord's presence, once again re-creating Canaan as the location of the divine presence and the center of its cosmological expansion (Ex. 29:45–46; Num. 35:34).

It is with such high expectations that the rest of the Old Tes-

---

[1] Goldsworthy concludes, "Israel's experiences of redemption from Egypt and of the presence and word of the ruling Lord at Sinai, point in one direction only: possession of a new Eden, the Promised Land of Canaan." Graeme Goldsworthy, *According to Plan: The Unfolding Revelation of God in the Bible* (Downers Grove, IL: InterVarsity, 1991), 149.

[2] The Lord himself will bring about Israel's safe journey to and capture of Canaan. It is Yahweh who will lay waste Israel's enemies and provide the people with nourishment and blessings on their way (Ex. 23:20–33).

tament begins. Unfortunately, by the final words of 2 Chronicles, doubt and despair replace this once-hopeful outlook. The Former Prophets—that is the second major section of the Tanakh, or Hebrew Bible—tell the story of Israel's long, serpentine descent into sin and consequent separation from Yahweh. As the Lord himself told Moses before his death, "This people [of Israel] will rise and whore after the foreign gods among them in the land that they are entering, and they will forsake me and break my covenant that I have made with them" (Deut. 31:16).[3] Rebellion and punishment characterize Israel's history. Though they have been called out of bondage to draw near to Yahweh, their disobedience drives them further and further away from him to the point where they are altogether removed from the Land of Promise.[4] In the end, Israel's steps from Sinai are not the first steps of a joyous procession into the eschatological experience of God's presence as they should have been, but rather a long and treacherous march into exile.

This is one of the greatest ironies of the Old Testament: God is present to be covenantally *faithful* to a covenantally *unfaithful* people. Israel's story after the exodus makes it quite clear that no one besides God himself can fulfill the Lord's redemptive objectives. But even though Israel's history grows darker and darker as the drama moves forward, there is always a glimmer of light amid the tragedy—a hope that Yahweh is present in Israel's history to accomplish what Israel cannot. This is what the rest of the Old Testament tells us: that even in exile, the Lord remains faithful to be present with his people and to consummate his eschatological agenda.

---

[3] Because of their forthcoming infidelity, Yahweh reveals, "My anger will be kindled against them in that day, and I will forsake them and hide my face from them, and they will be devoured. And many evils and troubles will come upon them, so that they will say in that day, 'Have not these evils come upon us because our God is not among us?'" (Deut. 31:17; cf. vv. 18–21). Israel's sinful decline reveals that salvation comes from Yahweh alone, and, as a consequence, glory for their redemption is his alone. Only the Lord deserves praise for the consummation of his eschatological objectives. Adam could not bring it about, and as the Former Prophets will show, neither can Israel. Instead, only Yahweh can bring true redemption, and he has chosen to do so by becoming present with his people. For further interaction with this theme of covenant infidelity among God's people, see Ray Ortlund, *God's Unfaithful Wife: A Biblical Theology of Spiritual Adultery*, NSBT 2 (Downers Grove, IL: InterVarsity, 2003).

[4] So in a sense, the Former Prophets explain that "the nation of Israel will live out the cycle of Genesis 1–11. The Deuteronomistic story begins with the creation of the nation and their establishment in the Promised Land (Joshua), which, like the Garden in Genesis, is blessed by the very presence of God. However, in Genesis 3–11, as in Judges and in 1–2 Kings, sin and rebellion destroy the relationship and the blessings (Noah and David are both exceptions, although both end up tainted). Ultimately, Adam and Eve are evicted from the Garden (Gen. 3) and humankind is scattered across the earth (Gen. 10–11). Likewise the children of Israel are driven from the Promised Land (2 Kings 17, 25) and scattered into Assyria (2 Kings 17) and Babylonia (2 Kings 25)." C. Marvin Pate et al. *The Story of Israel: A Biblical Theology* (Downers Grove, IL: InterVarsity, 2004), 51–52.

Joshua: The Guidance and Protection of God's Presence

Much of what we see at the beginning of the Former Prophets is similar in nature and execution to what has gone before. As with Moses, the Lord continues to employ a mediator through whom he pronounces his direction and intention. Replacing the great prophet of the exodus is Joshua.[5] And in the first few verses of the book of Joshua, Yahweh speaks to his new mediator much as he did with Moses. He states, "Just as I [Yahweh] was with Moses, so I will be with you [Joshua]. I will not leave you or forsake you" (Josh. 1:5; cf. 3:7). Like his predecessor, Joshua is set apart by and identified with his personal experience of the presence of God (Deut. 31:3, 8; cf. Ex. 3:12).

Through the covenant refrain "I will be with you" (e.g., Josh 1:5, 9, 17; 3:7; 6:27), Yahweh consistently assures Joshua that he, the Lord, will procure victory, lead the people, and consummate his redemptive purposes. God has indeed always been with Joshua. From his first introduction (Num. 14:1ff.) to his installment as Israel's leader (Num. 27:18; Deut. 34:9) the nearness of the Lord has marked Joshua's life.[6] The divine spirit rests upon Moses's successor, the one who is to stand as the mighty warrior of God and conquer the Land of Promise for God's people and God's presence.

For Joshua and the people of Israel, God's drawing near is the assurance of the Lord's redemptive promises. As in the exodus, God comes to Israel's defense and provides his people with everything they need, including the land before their eyes (Josh. 1:6). What is important to see is that the hope associated with this land is achievable only because God "will be with [Israel]"; for this "he will not leave [Israel] or forsake [Israel]" (Deut. 31:8). Again, Yahweh's presence is the only way to the

---

[5] Though Joshua takes over for Moses—a privilege granted by Yahweh himself—his role is not completely parallel to that of the first mediator. As Deut. 34:10–12 makes clear, "There has not arisen a prophet since in Israel like Moses, whom the LORD knew face to face, none like him for all the signs and the wonders that the LORD sent him to do in the land of Egypt, to Pharaoh and to all his servants and to all his land, and for all the mighty power and all the great deeds of terror that Moses did in the sight of all Israel." Only Moses will have this particular experience of God's presence. However, even in this distinction, the presence of God defines Joshua and his role in Israel's history, though his experience of the divine presence is limited compared with Moses's knowledge.

[6] The presence of God plays a major role in Joshua's leadership. Take, for example, Numbers 13. Here the Hebrew spies in the land soon report the overwhelming odds the nation faces in their quest to conquer the inhabitants of Canaan. Even amid the surging doubts, Joshua and Caleb respond positively and point out to the congregation that their basis for taking over the Promised Land could never be based upon their strength, numbers, or military prowess. Instead, as the nation's short history has consistently expressed, their ability rests upon the presence of God, who works among them, bringing forth his own purposes for his own glory. This is why Joshua and Caleb counter Israelite skepticism not with nationalistic self-assurance, but with the refrain, "the LORD is with us." This will also become the "battle cry" of Joshua's military conquest of Canaan (e.g., Deut. 20:1, 4).

Land of Promise. This is why, in his response to Israel's unjustified fear of the Canaanite inhabitants, he announces, "You shall not be in dread of them, for the LORD your God is in your midst, a great and awesome God. The LORD your God will clear away these nations before you. . . . The LORD your God will give them over to you and throw them into great confusion, until they are destroyed" (Deut. 7:21–23; cf. 9:3–5). In this unbreakable vow, we see that it is the *Lord* who will bring Israel into the Land of Promise, not Israel, not Moses, and not Joshua (e.g., Josh. 1:13; 3:7–17; 11:23; 21:43–45; cf. Ex. 23:20ff.; Num. 14:1–38). It is *Yahweh*, in the midst of his people, who will fight for Israel, and it is Yahweh who will deal appropriately with the foreign enemies his chosen ones seek to conquer (e.g., Ex. 23:23, 27). In short, God's redemptive presence is the instrument by which the growing dynasty of Israel enters Canaan.

To underscore the agency of God's presence, Joshua, while standing on the shore of the Jordan River, instructs the priests carrying the ark of the covenant to proceed before the people and enter the waters first (Josh. 3:8). According to Joshua, this simple act represents the living God among his people and his mission to go before them for the provision of the land (3:10). Yahweh uses this opportunity to remind this new generation in Israel that the Lord is present to accomplish his purposes. Subsequently, when the soles of the priests' feet hit the water, the Jordan divides in two, and the nation passes over with ease into Canaan.

The Lord connects Israel's past and future in this magnificent act. The walls of water certainly remind the Hebrews of the wonders of the Red Sea, while the fertile ground of Canaan should incite their hope in Eden and the possible fulfillment of God's covenant promises. God is present again for the nation, this time to heap up the Jordan's waters and lead the people into the Promised Land (Josh. 3:14–17). Every Israelite step on Canaanite soil is a reminder of God's faithfulness (Josh. 1:2). By bringing the Israelites back to their land, Yahweh is fulfilling his dominion promise to Abraham, Jacob, Moses, Joshua, and the people of God as a whole (Josh. 21:43–45). Through his redemptive presence, God begins to dwell with his people in this land of great potential (cf. Gen. 12:1–3; 26:2–4; 28:13–15).

Yahweh's faithfulness, though, does not stop with Israel's entrance into the Promised Land. Instead, it continues throughout Israel's Canaanite sojourn and conquest. For example, God is present with Joshua to take Jericho. Per his presence and instruction, the "new Moses" takes the foreign city into Israelite possession (Josh. 6:2–5). To highlight the place of his presence, Yahweh commands Joshua to keep the ark of the covenant—the physical symbol of the divine presence—at the center of his military exploits (Josh. 6:5).[7] This commandment is to remind us all that it is God's presence with Joshua and the Israelite army that brings about Canaan's conquest.[8]

What is more, Israel falls when God's presence is forgotten by his people, such as when Israel suffers the military setback at Ai. Instead of obeying the Lord and destroying those things prohibited by the Lord at Jericho (cf. Josh. 6:18–21), some of the Israelites secretly keep possessions for themselves. As a result, the Lord removes his presence and protection from the Hebrew army, and they fall into the hands of their enemies. After Israel's downfall, the Lord confronts Joshua, explaining to him that the reason for the nation's demise is its covenant infidelity (Josh. 7:10). As the Lord has warned, "I will be with you no more, unless you destroy the devoted things from among you" (Josh. 7:12). In this light, when Israel is unfaithful to the covenant, the Lord removes his protective presence, thus guaranteeing their defeat by their enemies' hands (cf. Num. 14:39–45; Deut. 1:24, 42–46).

When Israel returns and repents, Yahweh draws near again to redeem the nation and move closer to his covenant purposes (Josh. 7:18–29). Joshua 21:43–45 tells us:

---

[7] The ark of the covenant is associated with the presence of the Lord. Even Israel's enemies understand this (1 Sam. 4:3–22). In 1 Sam. 4:6–8, the Philistines hear the Hebrews rejoicing when the ark enters the Israelite congregation and respond in fear, saying, "A god has come into the camp," and lament, declaring: "Woe to us! For nothing like this has happened before. . . . Who can deliver us from the power of these mighty gods? These are the gods who struck the Egyptians with every sort of plague in the wilderness." Furthermore, 1 Sam. 4:21–22 shows us that the Israelites know that the presence of God is with the ark. After the Philistines capture the ark of the covenant, the Israelites realize that God's presence is gone with it. For this very reason, Phinehas's wife names her son Ichabod, meaning "the glory has departed from Israel." In doing so, she announces that "the glory has departed from Israel, for the ark of God has been captured" (4:22). With the Philistines' possession of the ark of the covenant comes the Lord's wrath poured out upon them. Ironically, the pagan nation reacts to God's punishment better than his chosen people do. The Philistines, whose gods Israel has begun to worship instead of Yahweh, recognize the power and glory of the Lord, which Israel fails to acknowledge (1 Sam. 6:3–5).

[8] For Canaanite conquest, the book of Joshua shows that the Lord comes as a divine warrior to establish Israel's rule over the Promised Land and, ultimately, locate his dwelling place in the land (e.g., Josh. 10:42; 11:19–20; cf. 5:13–15). Throughout Joshua and the rest of Israel's history as well, Yahweh's presence is consistently linked with Israel's victories and land occupation (cf. 1 Sam. 4:3–4). See also Tremper Longman III and Daniel G. Reid, *God Is a Warrior* (Grand Rapids: Zondervan, 1995).

The LORD gave to Israel all the land that he swore to give to their fathers. And they took possession of it, and they settled there. And the LORD gave them rest on every side just as he had sworn to their fathers. Not one of all their enemies had withstood them, for the LORD had given all their enemies into their hands. Not one word of all the good promises that the LORD had made to the house of Israel had failed; all came to pass.

Each of these promises comes to pass through the agency of God's redemptive presence. The book of Joshua shows that the hope of covenant fulfillment is still closely tied to the presence of God. Yahweh will go before his people and clear a place for his eschatological objectives to take root in the fertile Canaanite earth. With Joshua, God is present to redeem his people and finally lead them to the land he promised their forefathers.

Judges: Cycle of Presence and Separation

Sadly, the rest of Israel's story is primarily one of deterioration. From the time of the judges on, there is a growing emphasis on Israel's immorality and rebellion, or as Old Testament scholar Daniel Block puts it, the "Canaanization"[9] of Israel.[10] In particular, the Israelites exchange God—who, in their own words, "brought us and our fathers up from the land of Egypt, out of the house of slavery, and who did those great signs in our sight and preserved us in all the way that we went" (Josh. 24:17)—for the foreign gods of Canaan and idolatrous practices (Judg. 2:3, 11–13, 17, 19; 3:6–7, 12; 4:1; 6:1, 10; 8:24–27, 33; 10:6; 13:1; 17:6;

---

[9] Block goes as far as to argue that the "theme of [Judges] is the *Canaanization of Israelite society during the period of settlement.*" Daniel I. Block, *Judges, Ruth,* NAC (Nashville: Broadman & Holman, 1999), 58. He adds: "The author's goal in exposing this problem is to wake up his own generation." Therefore, the book is more than just a historical account of Israel's degradation; it is also "an appeal to the covenant people to abandon all forms of paganism and return to Yahweh" (ibid.). Holiness means separation, and in order to be Yahweh's people, the Israelites cannot share or take part in pagan practices or worship (e.g., Ex. 20:33; 34:12–16; Deut. 7:4; 12:30; 20:17–20; cf. 2 Kings 17:15; Ps. 106:34–41). Sadly, however, the Hebrews constantly desire to be like the nations around them and spurn the true and living God in order to do so (e.g., Deut. 17:4; 1 Sam. 8:5). This syncretism runs throughout Israel's story. It is one of Israel's greatest struggles and the context for God's prophetic declaration of a new expression of his presence that will overcome sin.

[10] The book of Judges shows that Israel's faithfulness to the Sinai covenant is short-lived. Directly after the covenant renewal and the Hebrews' resounding commitment to "serve the LORD," Joshua warns his followers, "You are not able to serve the LORD, for he is a holy God. He is a jealous God; he will not forgive your transgressions or your sins. If you forsake the LORD and serve foreign gods, then he will turn and do you harm and consume you, after having done you good" (Josh. 24:19–20). And though Israel initially stands by its vow to serve the Lord, the book of Judges documents the exact opposite: the nation's chronic apostasy. Instead of serving Yahweh as pledged, the Hebrews continue in rebellion and covenant unfaithfulness (Judg. 2:1–3, 20–22) that ultimately lead to the exile, where Yahweh distances himself from this nation of transgressors.

21:5). Instead of following Yahweh as the Hebrews have covenanted to do, Israel revolts: "Everyone did what was right in his own eyes" (Judg. 17:6; 21:25; cf. 18:1; 19:1). Specifically, the Hebrews ignore God's call to drive the Canaanites from the land, letting the foreigners remain among them (Judg. 2:2) and allowing their gods to reign in their hearts (Judg. 2:11–12). In response, Yahweh becomes present to judge, to reveal their errant ways, to call them to repentance, and ultimately to bring about their redemption (e.g., Judg. 2:13–15).

Ironically, God draws near to remove his protection and provision (e.g., Judg. 2:3; 16:20–21). As a result, the Israelites again become susceptible to the wickedness of the surrounding nations, and they soon discover that God's judgment endangers the promises of dominion, dynasty, and his eschatological presence. As nation after nation falls upon Israel, Canaan becomes less and less a Land of Promise and more and more a land of destruction. The book of Judges even foretells of a day when Israel will be taken captive and finally removed from the land of God's presence (Judg. 18:30). Likewise, the constant war, chaos, and intermingling of nationalities jeopardizes the dynastic promise. Because of Israel's sin, Canaan does not become the Eden-like land described in Exodus 25:25–31; rather, it slowly becomes the horrible reminder of God's justice for covenant breakers and of the growing distance from his blessings.

Even in Israel's downward spiral, Yahweh remains faithful to his glory and his ends (Judg. 2:1). This dark and foreboding context sets the stage for his powerful response to the continual decline of Israel and the apparent dissolution of Yahweh's redemptive mission. The book of Judges, therefore, not only tells of the nation's decline; it also "offers a profound commentary on the grace of God."[11] As the book details, it is only through the "repeated gracious intervention of God" that the Hebrew people "emerge from the dark pre-monarchic period as a separate people and nation."[12] Instead of letting the promises of people and place be buried under the consequence of their apostasy, the Lord repeatedly counters Israel's rebellion to deliver them and secure his redemptive ends. So as the book takes a generally downward trajectory,

---

[11] Block, *Judges, Ruth*, 58.
[12] Ibid.

God consistently draws near to respond to their occasional repentance and to restore his people to his covenant purposes.

To do this, God enters history to bring forth leaders within the Israelite tribes who themselves serve "as agents of the divine presence."[13] For example, in a call similar to the calling of Moses (Ex. 3:12–14) and the patriarchs, the Lord manifests himself to Gideon in the form of the angel of the Lord.[14] Through this theophanic vision, the Lord asserts to Gideon, "The Lord is with you, O mighty man of valor," showing us that the basis for this newly appointed judge's call and work is the presence of God with him (Judg. 6:12). Yahweh continues, assuaging Gideon's fears and correcting his misunderstanding that Yahweh has in fact abandoned Israel (Judg. 6:13–14) with the assurance of his presence to guide and direct Gideon's ways. The Lord tells Gideon, "I will be with you, and you shall strike the Midianites as one man" (Judg. 6:16). Throughout the history of the judges, Yahweh's presence is the means for Israel's salvation. God becomes redemptively present to his judges to reconcile Israel to himself. For this reason, "the fearful Gideon is . . . transformed into the deliverer of his people by the powerful presence of God" (e.g., Judg. 11:29; 13:3–25).[15] Yahweh works through his judges to overcome the sins of his people, lead them to holiness, and usher his new dynasty into the dominion of his divine dwelling.

Unfortunately, apostasy succeeds each act of deliverance. Every judge is wrought with moral improprieties and ethical failings even though the Lord manifests his presence and power through him or her (Judg. 8:24–27; 11:30–40; 14–16). So as the Lord graciously works through the judges to restore the Hebrew people to their covenant promises, both the Israelites and the judges themselves contradict his

---

[13] Ibid., 131.

[14] It is noteworthy that the MT and the LXX differ in their wording for *Yahweh* and *angel of Yahweh*. The LXX smooths out the text considerably compared with the MT. The LXX replaces the name *Yahweh* with *angel of Yahweh* in order to bring consistency to Judges 6. Still, this is not the harder reading, a fact that would seem to point to the MT as the preferred text. If this is so, such a reading would greatly impact the theology of this account. By reducing the text's difficulty, the LXX also deters an understanding that the presence of the Lord is with Gideon. Though mediated through the angel of the Lord, Yahweh is still very much present with the judge. Again, the nearness of the divine presence is also evident in Gideon's actions. Once he realizes who his visitor is, Gideon refers to him no longer as Adonai, but as Yahweh and, moreover, offers sacrifice before him. Both the usage of the divine name and worship are acts designated for the Lord alone (Judg. 6:11–27).

[15] Block, *Judges, Ruth*, 261. Block goes on to show the consistent emphasis on the presence of God in this text when he highlights the AB BA AB structure of Judg. 6:12–16: "v. 12 a 'the Lord is with you.' b 'Mighty hero.' v. 14 b 'Go in this your strength.' a 'Surely I have sent you.' v. 16 a 'I am with you.' b 'You shall defeat Midian as if they were one man'" (ibid.). This pattern is built on God's presence and his redemptive work with Gideon and through Gideon.

mercies with persistent and intensifying sin. The historical narrative of Judges demonstrates Israel's faithlessness and inability to live by the law time and time again. As a consequence, Israel's spiritual adultery exhibits the nation's need for further redemption and reconciliation and, in particular, its need for a better judge, a king after God's own heart—one who is obedient to the Lord's covenant and can fulfill the divine law (Deut. 17:14–20).

Samuel and Kings: Presence and Kingdom

By the end of the judges' deliverance cycles, the purposes of the exodus seem to be in shambles, and the hopes of Israel's covenant fulfillment decimated.[16] The Lord's redemptive presence largely disappears during these times because of Israel's consistent sin. As 1 Samuel 3:1 details, "The word of the LORD was rare in those days; there was no frequent vision." Without God's revelation, Israel reverts to what it was before God's deliverance: an insignificant band of tribes residing as aliens in a foreign land among a hostile people.

David: The King in the Presence of God

But as with the rest of the Old Testament, God continues his story of redemption and purpose.[17] In particular, God's redemptive purposes find expression in the installation of David as covenant king. In response to the predicament set forth in the Judges narrative—i.e., Israel's descent into apostasy facilitated by a lack of covenant leadership—Yahweh raises up a new Israelite ruler. David's rule, from a canonical standpoint, however, is the exception and not the norm. For this reason, the Davidic narrative stands as a light shining between Israel's dark history in Judges and the ensuing darkness of Kings and Chronicles.[18]

---

[16] The last words of the book of Judges sum up the despair as follows: "In those days there was no king in Israel. Everyone did what was right in his own eyes" (Judg. 21:25).

[17] In his covenant faithfulness, Yahweh breaks his silence and reveals himself to Samuel, calling him out to be his prophet (1 Sam. 3:20). To reinstitute the means of salvation, Yahweh comes to be with young Samuel (1 Sam. 3:19, 21), informing him, "Behold, I am about to do a thing in Israel at which the two ears of everyone who hears it will tingle" (1 Sam. 3:11). Initially, this plays out in the Lord's presence to judge Eli's deviant sons; yet, it also includes his continued revelation to Samuel and his manifest work in Israel's history. Hence, in his farewell address, Samuel highlights God's work in redemptive history when he declares to his sinful countrymen, "The LORD will not forsake his people, for his great name's sake, because it has pleased the LORD to make you a people for himself" (1 Sam. 12:22). For his glory and by his divine presence, Israel is still set apart for the blessings of the redemptive promise.

[18] Even though David is the paradigmatic king and ideal figure of Israel's history, it must be duly noted that he is not sinless and, in fact, deals with sin throughout his life (e.g., 2 Sam. 11:1–12:14; 1 Chron. 21:1–17; cf. Psalm 51).

With Samuel aging, the Israelites plead with their prophet to appoint a king who will rule over them (1 Sam. 8:5, 19–22; 12:12–22).[19] This is not a holy request; in fact it is more of a demand that discloses the depths of their sinfulness. Not only do they neglect to listen to God or respond righteously to his covenant (e.g., they still have not removed their enemies from the land); they now reject God's supremacy over them so that they can imitate the pagan nations that are ruled by godless kings (1 Sam. 8:7).

Though their motivations are sinful, Yahweh uses this evil for good. He does not deny their desires outright. Instead, the Lord reinforces his covenant promises with the provision of his own king (cf. Gen. 17:6, 16; 35:11; 49:10). In comparison with Saul—the one who initially looks the part of Israel's monarch but is actually the king from whom Yahweh departs (1 Sam. 16:14)—David is a righteous monarch. Appointed by Yahweh himself, marked by the Lord's presence (1 Sam. 16:13; 18:14; 2 Sam. 5:10), and recipient of the Spirit (1 Sam. 13:14; 16:13), David is faithful and obedient to the Lord. To the human eye, Saul would be the better king, but God's work is not driven by man's opinion. Instead, God's work is about redeeming man, which the book of Samuel tells us comes through God's presence with David.

As we discussed earlier, the Lord becomes present to David. God raises up the king and puts him on the throne so that Israel might experience a new type of redemption: rest in the Promised Land (2 Sam. 7:1; cf. Ex. 25:30). Yahweh enters into redemptive history to pluck David out of obscurity and, through him (and, ultimately, through his line), bring rest, redemption, and redemption's ends.

To make good on his promises, God is present to protect (2 Sam. 8–9), provide for (8:9–10), and covenant with Jesse's youngest son. God promises to be with him and to give him a great name, just like that of the patriarch Abraham (Gen. 12:2). As with Abraham also (Gen. 12:2; 17:4–6; 18:18), Yahweh draws near to David to make for him a great house of

---

[19] Like the Judges, the kings of Israel are supposed to represent God's presence in rule and leadership as vice-regents over God's coming kingdom. Terrien contends that "the king became the cultic incarnation of Israel. The recipient of the presence [of God] as an individual, he was the single focus and justification of God's descent upon earth." Samuel Terrien, *The Elusive Presence: Toward a New Biblical Theology* (New York: Harper & Row, 1978), 286. Again, Terrien maintains that the "Judahite monarchs became, at least in the minds of their entourage, the instruments of Yahweh in all spheres of human existence, including the destiny of the people spread over the 'widest earth'" (ibid., 296).

descendants (2 Sam. 11). This Davidic line is very significant for God's salvation project. Through the progressive fulfillment of the covenant, Yahweh makes clear that the redemptive promises once associated with the seed of Adam (Gen. 3:15) and Abraham are now distinctly connected to the seed of David.[20] David's son will be the one through whom God will establish his eternal kingdom (2 Sam. 7:12–13; cf. Gen. 49:10).

Yahweh also draws near to David to make Canaan a place of redemptive rest for his people (e.g., 2 Sam. 5:6–12; 17–24; 7:9–11) and to make the temple his permanent residence in Jerusalem (2 Sam. 6:1–23).[21] From a historical point of view, the "conquest of the land was gradual, and 'rest' was not fully achieved . . . until the establishment of the dynasty of David and the capture of Jerusalem (2 Sam. 7:1, 9–11; 2 Kings 5:3–4; 1 Chron. 22:9–10)[22] which made possible the building of Solomon's temple there."[23] Through David, God gives Israel "rest from all his [David's] surrounding enemies" (2 Sam. 7:1; cf. Josh. 23:1; 1 Kings 5:4). At this one moment, Israel comes face-to-face with the possibilities of God's redemptive objectives. Through the work of David, the ark of the covenant enters the city, the foreign nations are finally conquered, and a righteous king reigns upon the throne. In a sense, David's rule reveals a second Eden close at hand, all because God has been present in history to bring Israel to this point. Jerusalem sits at the center of the new installment of the paradise of God, with a divinely appointed vice-regent once again characterized by the presence of the Lord.

The Temple and the Presence of God

Though Israel dwells securely in the land and experiences a semblance of rest, the location of God's presence is still not settled. The ark of the

---

[20] Adam's son promised in Gen. 3:15 is also Abraham's son. Now he is David's son. From this perspective, Eve's seed is now cast into a royal lineage. He will be king and Redeemer (Gen. 3:15). He shall save the people of God and rule over them in justice. What is more, it is through this seed promise that the covenant pledge of dynasty develops exponentially. This son of David will expand David's house not only to Israel but to the world as well through faith. Through the redemptive work of the Davidic son, the people of God will grow to include all those whom this promised descendant comes to save.

[21] McConville contends that "Jerusalem succeeds Sinai as the symbol of Israel's status as the special location of God." Gordon McConville, "Jerusalem in the Old Testament," in *Jerusalem Past and Present in the Purposes of God*, ed. P. W. L. Walker (Cambridge: Tyndale House, 1992), 25.

[22] This section will cite 1 and 2 Chronicles as references as well, even though I will address these books in further detail later in this chapter. This is because the focus is on the conclusion of this chapter will be on the conclusion of 1 and 2 Chronicles to show the theological import of what is detailed there.

[23] R. T. Beckwith, "Sacrifice," in *New Dictionary of Biblical Theology*, ed. T. Desmond Alexander et al. (Downers Grove, IL: InterVarsity, 2000), 756.

covenant resides in an itinerant tent—a location that contradicts the security and permanence of Israel's newfound rest and rule in the Land of Promise. The fulfillment of God's purposes presupposes a physical seat within Israel's land from which the presence of God can dwell among his people and, ultimately, through Israel's mission, take his presence to the rest of the world.

As king of Israel and vice-regent of God's new Land of Promise, David recognizes this glaring omission, and, to expedite the Lord's redemptive purposes, he sets out to build the covenant maker a temple worthy of his name.[24] Though David's intentions are pure (1 Kings 8:18), Yahweh insists that David, being a man of war and unrest (1 Chron. 18–20), is not to construct the Jerusalem temple (1 Kings 5:3). Instead, Yahweh requires that unstained hands build his sanctuary during a time of peace (1 Kings 4:24; 5:4). The job falls to David's son Solomon, the king's descendant who will reap the benefits of his father's military conquest and gain the privilege of building the dwelling place of God (1 Kings 8:17–21; 1 Chron. 22:17–19).[25]

When Solomon takes the throne, one of his first acts is to construct the temple structure his father has already prepared (1 Chronicles 13; 15–16; 2 Samuel 24). With every new phase of development, the Exodus promise of God's dwelling in the land moves forward (cf. Ex. 29:45–46). Like the tabernacle before it, the temple in Jerusalem signifies Yahweh's dwelling in the midst of Israel. The major difference, however, is that the temple is static. Solomon's temple exchanges the mobility of the tabernacle for the permanence of stone and cedar. This fixed dwelling place is at the heart of Jerusalem, reminding the Israelites, and the world, of the centrality of God's presence to their identity. Not only that, the temple also puts God's gracious work of redemption and covenant fidelity on full display (cf. 1 Kings 8:23–26).

---

[24] The king's palace and the temple are connected semantically. As Beckwith writes, "The tabernacle and temple symbolize the court of a king; indeed the same word in Hebrew (*hêykāl*) is used for a temple and a palace" (ibid., 757). Accordingly, the temple is likened to the form of a residence, a place where God can dwell among his people to rule and reign as the king does, but in a greater sense.

[25] Solomon's calling is distinguished by Yahweh's presence with him. This is why at the end of David's charge to Solomon, the king assures his son that all the promises are accessible because the Lord is with him. He commands his son: "Do not be afraid and do not be dismayed, for the Lᴏʀᴅ God, even my God, is with you. He will not leave you or forsake you, until all the work for the service of the house of the Lᴏʀᴅ is finished" (1 Chron. 28:20). According to David, God's presence with Solomon is the only basis for his kingly reign and role as temple builder. It is the Lord who will be with Solomon—the same Lord who covenanted with David—and it is the Lord who will continue his covenant commitments with Israel's new king.

To mark the temple as God's earthly dwelling place, the priests carry the ark of the covenant into the Most Holy Place during the temple's dedication (1 Kings 8:1–9). Upon their doing so, "fire came down from heaven and consumed the burnt offering and the sacrifices, and the glory of the Lord filled the temple" (2 Chron. 7:1; cf. Pss. 114:2; 132:13–14; 135:21). First Kings 8:10–11 adds, "When the priests came out of the Holy Place, a cloud filled the house of the Lord, so that the priests could not stand to minister because of the cloud, for the glory of the Lord filled the house of the Lord." The witnesses of this beautifully terrifying act seem to understand it as a fulfillment of God's guarantee to redeem his people. God is with them once again in a place of rest where his very presence defines the land. God has delivered them from their garden exile, taken them from Egypt, and protected them in Canaan, all the while overcoming their sins to bring them to this point. So the people do the only appropriate thing: they fall on their faces and exalt God's covenant faithfulness, exclaiming, "For he is good, for his steadfast love endures forever" (2 Chron. 7:3). The same God who was present in Eden, Sinai, and the rest of the story has finally descended upon the temple in fire and cloud in a new, better, and more permanent way.

Solomon responds to this glorious scene by immediately blessing Yahweh. He first explains the cloud to be the marker of divine presence, declaring, "The Lord has said that he would dwell in thick darkness. I have indeed built [the Lord] an exalted house, a place for [him] to dwell forever" (1 Kings 8:12–13). No longer is Yahweh's presence manifested in the wilderness; he has come to Jerusalem just as he guaranteed (1 Kings 8:15–16). With rest and fortune now defining the nation, Israel is poised to take the blessing of God's presence to the rest of the world. It can be argued, then, that in Solomon's reign, Israel is the closest it will ever be to the eschatological promises of God this side of the cross.

Still, even with God's glory descending on the temple, Solomon knows there is something more. He knows that this hand-built residence cannot contain the Almighty. In the middle of the temple's dedication, Solomon asks, "But will God indeed dwell on the earth? Behold, heaven and the highest heaven cannot contain you; how much less this house that I have built!" (1 Kings 8:27). Space does not confine the Lord; however, in his grace, God extends his presence to his people for their redemption and their joy. So, though God will dwell in the temple (1 Kings 8:10, 13) Solomon recognizes that the temple is not the only site of God's presence but rather a special place the Lord has set aside for Israel's identity and salvation (1 Kings 8:29; cf. Isa. 66:1–3; Acts 7:47–50).

Based on Solomon's recognition of the infinitude of God, I think it feasible that the temple in Jerusalem is to be understood not as the end of God's presence in the world, but as its beginning point. The point of Solomon's rhetorical questions is to reveal that the temple is limited but God's presence is not. James Hamilton shows us that the "temple is central to [the Israelites'] well being as a nation, but it is incorrect to assume that the temple guarantees God's presence."[26] So, though Yahweh freely chooses to associate himself with this particular place in Jerusalem, he is not confined to it; rather, he is free to manifest himself as he pleases and, as redemptive history exhibits, he does just that (e.g., Christ as the new temple). So the temple does more than just represent the presence of God with Israel during this time. It foreshadows God's future work to extend his presence beyond this singular location.

With this qualification in mind, Solomon still recognizes that all of Israel's past demonstrated a specific functional presence of God with his people. Israel needs to retain this special redemptive presence for the finalization of the Lord's salvific purposes. For this reason, the king calls upon the Lord to draw near for the nation's redemption, exclaiming:

> Blessed be the LORD who has given rest to his people Israel, according to all that he promised. Not one word has failed of all his good promise, which he spoke by Moses his servant. *The LORD our God be with us, as he was with our fathers.* May he not leave us or forsake us, that he may incline our hearts to him, to walk in all his ways and to keep his commandments, his statutes, and his rules, which he commanded our fathers. (1 Kings 8:56–58)

---

[26] James M. Hamilton Jr., "God with Men in the Prophets and the Writings: An Examination of the Nature of God's Presence," *Scottish Bulletin of Evangelical Theology* 23 (2005): 180.

Solomon understands the need for God's redemptive presence to remain with Israel and complete his "good promise." And, what is more, God graciously responds to Solomon by appearing to him once again (cf. 1 Kings 3:4–15) to announce, "I have heard your prayer and your plea, which you have made before me. I have consecrated this house that you have built, putting my name there forever. My eyes and my heart will be there for all time" (1 Kings 9:3). Yahweh is in Israel's midst. The limited experience of God's presence in the temple separated and mediated by walls and curtains can finally reach its culmination if the Hebrews practice obedience and keep the law. So the Lord pledges, "If you will walk in my statutes and obey my rules and keep all my commandments and walk in them, then I will establish my word with you, which I spoke to David your father. And I will dwell among the children of Israel and will not forsake my people Israel" (1 Kings 6:12–13). Through law and holiness, God will bring Israel's redemption to its appropriate ends: he will be present with this people in a way known only once before, in Eden.

God's people are on the verge of fulfilling their inherent purpose at the beginning of Solomon's reign. This temple dedication "is the apex of Israel's national history. Her wisest king reigns; her territory is expansive; her economy thrives; her enemies are subdued; and her God has been pleased to dwell in her midst."[27] In short, "the world is well on its way to being restored."[28] With God's presence located in the temple, Israel is poised to bring the blessing of God's presence to all the earth (cf. Isa. 19:24).

The Fall of the Kingdom: The Need for a Better King

In what seems to be the dawning of new Eden, Yahweh warns the king of Israel—the royal representative of God's people[29]—that the promises of the covenant are his if he remains righteous and faithful. However,

---

[27] Ibid., 174.

[28] Stephen G. Dempster, *Dominion and Dynasty: A Theology of the Hebrew Bible*, NSBT 15 (Downers Grove, IL: InterVarsity, 2003), 226.

[29] Throughout the Old Testament, the kings of Israel and Judah represented the people, so much so that God often punished the kings' subjects for the kings' rebellion. Take for instance David's census. In his arrogance, David offends God, and as a result Yahweh sets out to punish the people of Israel (1 Chron. 21:13–18; cf. 2 Sam. 20:1; 1 Kings 12:16).

if he and his people do not, the entirety of what the Lord has offered will vanish in an instant. To Solomon, Yahweh promises:

> If you will walk before me, as David your father walked, with integrity of heart and uprightness, doing according to all that I have commanded you, and keeping my statutes and my rules, then I will establish your royal throne over Israel forever, as I promised David your father, saying, "You shall not lack a man on the throne of Israel." But if you turn aside from following me, you and your children, and do not keep my commandments and my statutes that I have set before you, but go and serve other gods and worship them, then I will cut Israel off from the land that I have given them, and the house that I have consecrated for my name I will cast out of my sight. And Israel will become a proverb and a byword among all peoples, and this house will become a heap of ruins. Everyone passing by it will be astonished and will hiss, and they will say, "Why has the Lord done thus to this land and to this house?" Then they will say, "Because they abandoned the Lord their God who brought their fathers out of the land of Egypt and laid hold on other gods and worshiped them and served them. Therefore the Lord has brought all this disaster on them. (1 Kings 9:4–9; cf. 1 Chron. 28:7–8; 2 Chron. 7:17–22)

If the covenant is broken, then Israel should expect punishment. The people will once again experience exile and separation from God. Thus, the Israelites, like their leader Solomon, can go one of two ways: (1) through obedience they can experience the blessings of God's covenant promise, or (2) through apostasy and idolatry the nation will experience God's curse and distance from him.

With few exceptions,[30] the general trend from David forward is disobedience and apostasy. In particular, the kings who survive Solomon—and even Solomon himself (e.g., 1 Kings 11:1–13)—demonstrate that this high point in the nation's history is to be short-lived. Israel is on a slow, steady march back into apostasy. The people will soon face separation from God again. The nation splits into two kingdoms, and

---

[30] To show himself faithful, the Lord provides prophets (such as Elijah and Elisha) as well as righteous kings who point back to King David and forward to God's redemptive purposes (Elijah, 1 Kings 19:9; Hezekiah, 2 Kings 18:5–7; Asa, 2 Chron. 15:2–4; Josiah, 2 Kings 22:18–20; 23:3–5, 25–27; 2 Chron. 34:31–34).

the further moral decline of Judah and Israel warns of the possibility of being removed from God's presence and promises. So while Israel falls deeper and deeper into sin, Yahweh distances himself further and further from Israel and Judah relationally.[31]

Even in the midst of Israel's growing iniquity, Yahweh remains faithful to his covenant. To claim God's promises, Israel needs only to seek him and they will find him; but if Israel forsakes the Lord, Yahweh will ultimately reject Israel (e.g., 1 Chron. 28:8; 2 Chron. 15:2, 14–15). In judgment, Yahweh remains faithful to provide his presence and a way for his redemptive ends to be met. For instance, God gives Jeroboam—Solomon's archenemy and the eventual leader of the northern kingdom—the same covenant options afforded to Solomon. Yahweh tells Jeroboam:

> I will take you, and you shall reign over all that your soul desires, and you shall be king over Israel. And if you will listen to all that I command you, and will walk in my ways, and do what is right in my eyes by keeping my statutes and my commandments, as David my servant did, *I will be with you* and will build you a sure house, as I built for David, and will give Israel to you. (1 Kings 11:37–38)

In offering to be with Jeroboam and to procure a lineage for him, God promises to continue his redemptive agenda if indeed this new king will be faithful. As 1 Kings 11:39 implies, Jeroboam does fail (1 Kings 12:25–33), and so do the majority of the subsequent kings. Instead of coming to spread his redemptive presence universally, God comes to judge.

This constant decline in the monarchy and the requisite punishment of God underscore the need for a better son of David—a just and eternal king who will truly establish the dwelling place of God and create a people who can dwell in Yahweh's relational presence forever (2 Sam. 7:13).[32] This son is the one who will overcome the mounting sin beginning with Adam and escalating throughout Israel (cf. Psalm 72).

---

[31] Hamilton acknowledges: "No mention of the temple is made between 1 Kings 14 and 2 Kings 10. As Israel spirals into the likeness of her neighbours, as the kings induce the people to increase transgression, the place Yahweh has chosen to put his name is not part of the story. Eighteen chapters with no mention of the temple is all the more startling when we recognize that the dedication of the temple, with the glory of God filling the temple just as it had done in the tabernacle, was the apex of Israel's national prowess." Hamilton, "God with Men in the Prophets," 178.

[32] We also see in 1 Kings 11:34–36 that the Lord secures the line of David and prepares the way for the Davidic son who will bring all of his eschatological purposes to fruition.

In the story of 1–2 Kings, however, his promise remains unfulfilled. The monarchs who follow David show themselves to be unworthy of receiving the promise, much less being its fulfillment. Not even Solomon can lay claim to this title.

Even so, the Lord promises that Judah will rule forever. David's son will also rule and reign to bring about the completion of God's redemptive mission (Gen. 49:8–12). So in terms of the kingly promises, there is a shift from immediate fulfillment to long-term expectancy. As the Latter Prophets will develop further, wicked kings will not complete God's redemptive purpose; instead, the hope of redemption lies squarely on the shoulders of a future king who will come to reconcile the evils of Israel, its kings, and the rest of the world too—and as we will find out, this Davidic king will be the presence of God.

Exile and Restoration: The Presence and Absence of God

The people of Israel sin against Yahweh, and their sin culminates in their exile from the Land of Promise and, consequently, from the presence of God (2 Kings 17:6–23; 25:21). The Hebrews fear the Canaanite gods, walk in the customs of pagan nations, build high places to worship idols and false deities, set up pillars and Asherim on their hills and under every tree, make offerings to strange gods, and turn a deaf ear to the warnings of the one true Lord (2 Kings 17:7–13; cf. vv. 34–41).

To deal with their syncretism and idolatry, Yahweh sends his prophets to warn Israel and call his people back to salvation. God makes clear, "I will not cause the feet of Israel to wander anymore out of the land that I gave to their fathers, if only they will be careful to do according to all that I have commanded them, and according to all the Law that my servant Moses commanded them" (2 Kings 21:8). Yet, the Israelites "would not listen, but were stubborn, as their fathers had been, who did not believe in the LORD their God" (2 Kings 17:14; cf. Judg. 2:19; Neh. 9:16–17, 29; Ps. 78:8; Jer. 9:14).

Based upon their continued evil and rejection of the prophets, Yahweh comes to exile Judah from Canaan, removing the people from the land of his presence. Second Kings 24:20 says, "Because of the anger of the LORD it came to the point in Jerusalem and Judah that he cast them out from his presence." The house of David and its covenant promises therefore face extinction in the midst of exile. Judah, like the northern tribes earlier, will be cast from God's chosen city, Jerusalem, with its temple, God's residence on earth (2 Kings 23:27). For the compilation of sins, God declares:

> Behold, I am bringing upon Jerusalem and Judah such disaster that the ears of everyone who hears of it will tingle. . . . And I will forsake the remnant of my heritage and give them into the hand of their enemies, and they shall become a prey and a spoil to all their enemies, because they have done what is evil in my sight and have provoked me to anger, since the day their fathers came out of Egypt, even to this day. (2 Kings 21:12–14)

This promise finds completion in the arrival of Nebuchadnezzar, whose Babylonian Empire bears the sword of Yahweh against his own people. This foreign oppressor breaks into Jerusalem, captures God's people (2 Kings 24:1–17; 25:1ff.), drives them away from the Land of Promise, and destroys the temple of Yahweh, ultimately demonstrating the consequences of Israel's covenant infidelity. In one swift act, the sins of the people force the once tightly knit dynasty to be redistributed throughout a foreign land. Undermined in this judgment is the expansion and fulfillment of God's redemptive activity thus far. With the invasion of Babylon, Judah is no longer a unified people, and is separated from the God of their fathers.

Once again the stark realities of the Hebrew's future show us that all the promises of God rest solely on his redemptive presence. Salvation history is based upon hope in the coming presence of God to finish what he has started. This hope is the basis for Solomon's prayer for the Lord to draw near to rescue his people from their impending exile and reconcile them to his redemptive purposes. Calling upon the Lord, Solomon pleads:

> If [the Israelites] sin against you—for there is no one who does not sin—and you are angry with them and give them to an enemy, so that they are carried away captive to the land of the enemy, far off or near, yet if they turn their heart in the land to which they have been carried captive, and repent and plead with you in the land of their captors, saying, "We have sinned and have acted perversely

and wickedly," if they repent with all their mind and with all their heart in the land of their enemies, who carried them captive, and pray toward their land, which you gave to their fathers, the city you have chosen, and the house that I have built for your name, then hear in heaven your dwelling place their prayer and their plea, and maintain their cause and forgive your people who have sinned against you, and all their transgressions that they have committed against you, and grant them compassion in the sight of those who carried them captive, that they may have compassion on them (for they are your people, and your heritage, which you brought out of Egypt, from the midst of the iron furnace). Let your eyes be open to the plea of your servant and to the plea of your people Israel, giving ear to them whenever they call to you. For you separated them from among all the peoples of the earth to be your heritage, as you declared through Moses your servant, when you brought our fathers out of Egypt, O Lord God. (1 Kings 8:46–53; cf. 9:3)

Solomon, looking to the first exodus, cries out to the Lord for a second exodus in which he will once again be present to deliver them from exile. Here, the Israelite king pleads with the Lord to remain with Israel even in her stubbornness and apostasy. And in Yahweh's covenant faithfulness, he does just that. God has exiled Israel; but God also redeems her. He will come again to remove her captors from ruling over her (2 Kings 19:20–37), and "out of Jerusalem shall go a remnant, and out of Mount Zion a band of survivors" (2 Kings 19:31). Once again it is the Lord who will perform this redemptive act (19:31), and he will be present in redemptive history to do so.

The Redemptive-Historical Means of the Presence of God: The Latter Prophets

Building on historical narrative thus far, the Latter Prophets are unique in that their primary perspective is God's perspective; the Prophets' words provide God's point of view on the historical degradation re-counted in the narrative of 1 and 2 Kings and the like.[33] Still, even

---

[33] The Latter Prophets also help formulate Old Testament eschatology which "anticipates not only a renewed humanity, (cf. Isa. 65:20–24) dwelling in edenic blessedness (v. 25) but also—in a theophanic context—'the new heavens and the new earth that [Yahweh will] make' (Isa. 66:22; cf. 65:17; Rev. 21:1)." Niehaus, *God at Sinai*, 149.

though this section of Scripture takes a different viewpoint from other biblical genres, it does not veer from the theological framework of the Old Testament. Like the rest of the Old Testament, this prophetic section discloses that God still draws near to reconcile and redeem. In summary, the Latter Prophets are distinct in perspective but similar in message. For this reason, the Latter Prophets continue the emphasis on the instrumental role of the presence of God in redemptive history and disclose this reality from a prophetic viewpoint.

The Latter Prophets do more than just recount the Lord's manifest work in the previous historical narrative; they shed new light on the Lord's redemptive presence as it is currently experienced and will be known in the future. The Latter Prophets[34] recast the fulfillment of God's objectives in an apocalyptic and eschatological light.[35] The prophets detail the particulars of God's presence to finalize and secure redemption and its ends.

In particular, the Latter Prophets tell of the redemptive presence of God coming as the Messiah,[36] a Davidic king who is Immanuel, God with us, who will live and die as the suffering servant in order to "extend his kingdom to the ends of the earth (Mic. 4:3–4; Matt. 28:18–20; John 17:2)."[37] As announced, this Promised One will enter human history to turn tragedy into triumph, decline into deliverance. The Latter

---

[34] Terrien argues that the connection with the Latter Prophets and their God is more than just in their calling and ministry. Instead, "the prophet has been invaded and permeated by the presence of Yahweh in such a way that he has become a living monstrance of the divine reality." Terrien, *Elusive Presence*, 246.

[35] As Richard Gaffin contends: "In the prophets, divine glory becomes messianic and eschatological. In the latter part of Isaiah, for example, the prophet foretells the coming activity of the Lord's anointed servant (42:1–4; 49:1–12; 52:13–53:12; the NT explicitly applies such passages to Jesus, as the Christ, e.g., Matt. 12:18–21; Luke 2:32; 2 Cor. 6:2; Acts 3:13). . . . This future revelation of messianically mediated glory will mean not only the full, eschatological restoration of Israel (Isa. 58:8; 60:1–2, 19; 62:2–3), but will be universal (66:18), including salvation of the nations ('From the west and from the rising of the sun, they will revere his glory' 59:19). . . . This prophetic expectation of the final, saving revelation of the divine glory through the messianic servant is expressed most comprehensively in the hope that 'the earth will be filled with the knowledge of the glory of the Lord as the waters cover the sea' (Hab. 2:14)." Richard B. Gaffin Jr., "Glory," in *Dictionary of Biblical Imagery*, ed. Leland Ryken, James C. Wilhoit, and Tremper Longman III (Downers Grove, IL: InterVarsity, 1998), 508–9.

[36] For further development of the Messiah promise, please see J. Becker, *Messianic Expectation in the Old Testament* (Edinburgh: T&T Clark, 1980); Walter Brueggemann, *Theology of the Old Testament: Testimony, Dispute, Advocacy* (Minneapolis: Fortress, 1997), 616–21; Brevard Childs, *Biblical Theology of the Old and New Testaments: Theological Reflection on the Christian Bible* (London: SCM, 1992), 453–56; Ronald E. Clements, "The Messianic Hope in the Old Testament," *JSOT* 43 (1989): 3–19; Joseph A. Fitzmeyer, *The One Who Is to Come* (Grand Rapids: Eerdmans, 2007); Walter C. Kaiser Jr., *The Messiah in the Old Testament* (Grand Rapids: Zondervan, 1995); Stanley E. Porter, ed., *The Messiah in the Old and New Testaments* (Grand Rapids: Eerdmans, 2007); Helmet Ringgren, *The Messiah in the Old Testament* (London: SCM, 1956); Robin Routledge, *Old Testament Theology: A Thematic Approach* (Downers Grove, IL: InterVarsity, 2008), 280–89; Gerard van Groningen, *Messianic Revelation in the Old Testament* (Grand Rapids: Baker, 1990); H. G. M. Williamson, *Variations on a Theme: King, Messiah, and Servant in the Book of Isaiah* (Carlisle, UK: Paternoster, 1998).

[37] Bruce K. Waltke, *An Old Testament Theology: An Exegetical, Canonical, and Thematic Approach* (Grand Rapids: Zondervan, 2007), 888.

Prophets deliver a hopeful response to the desperate circumstances recited from the book of Joshua to the narrative of 1–2 Kings. To the downtrodden, the prophets give reminders that God has been redemptively present throughout salvation history and that he will remain so. He promises over and over again to be present to save; not only that, he also foretells of a time when his redemptive presence will give way to his eschatological presence where his covenant objectives will have reached their appropriate ends.

The Coming Redemptive Presence

The context of sin, rebellion, and exile, compel the prophets to deal predominantly with judgment and redemption. God's righteous wrath is central to the message of the prophets, so much so that it even defines their calling. For instance, in the middle of the Lord's majestic self-revelation to Isaiah, Yahweh calls upon his servant to

> make the hearts of this people dull,
>> and their ears heavy,
>> and blind their eyes;
> lest they see with their eyes,
>> and hear with their ears,
> and understand with their hearts,
>> and turn and be healed. (Isa. 6:10)

Isaiah's prophetic work, at times, is less about repentance and more about building a case against the nation.[38]

Because of the people's blatant disregard for the covenant, the Lord disciplines them by removing himself from their midst. Thus Isaiah discloses,

> Jerusalem has stumbled,
>> and Judah has fallen,

---

[38] It is interesting that, in answering Isaiah's question about the duration of his prophetic work, the Lord couches his response in covenant-blessing terminology. He tells his newly appointed prophet that his work will continue until the discipline of his people and place is complete—or, in his words, "Until cities lie waste / without inhabitant, / and houses without people, / and the land is a desolate waste, / and the Lᴏʀᴅ removes the people far away, / and the forsaken places are many in the midst of the land" (Isa. 6:11–12). This shows that God's judgment concerns the separation of the people from his covenant promises, including their loss of land, the uncertainty of their line, and finally their exile from the presence of God.

because their speech and their deeds are against the Lord,
defying his glorious presence. (Isa. 3:8)

In response, the Lord removes his redemptive presence from those who have disdained him. We see this when Isaiah tells God's people,

Your iniquities have made a separation
between you and your God,
and your sins have hidden his face from you. (Isa. 59:2)

Ironically, the one hope of the nation's salvation becomes the chief source of the nation's indignation.

But the beauty of the Latter Prophets is found in Yahweh's gracious response to his own righteous judgments. Shortly after separation, God follows with the merciful promises in Isaiah 59:16–20. God "saw that there was no man . . . to intercede" for Israel's sin, but instead of leaving the people to their own demise, the Lord himself comes to redeem. As the prophet puts it, Yahweh's

own arm brought him salvation,
and his righteousness upheld him. (Isa. 59:16)

So even in the midst of judgment there is a reminder of God's work and control of all history for his glory and his people's good (cf. Isa. 41:1–20).

The Latter Prophets, however, do more than reinforce the centrality of the Lord for redemption[39] and its objectives.[40] Instead, they show

---

[39] Like the rest of the Old Testament, the Latter Prophets demonstrate that Yahweh is the source of all salvific expectation. For example, the prophet Jeremiah expresses to his listeners that they should find hope in God's redemptive presence, for it is in the Lord's coming to his people that they will finally be redeemed from Babylon (e.g., Jer. 30:11; 42:11; 46:28; cf. Amos 5:14–17). Likewise, as the Lord proclaims, "I am the one who helps you . . . / your Redeemer is the Holy One of Israel" (Isa. 41:14; cf. 43:1–3, 5; 45:17, 21; 57:15; Jer. 1:8, 19; 3:23; 14:9; Ezek. 37:15–28; Hos. 6:1–2; Hab. 3:13; Zech. 8:7–8). Out of the darkness of their exile, the Lord promises hope through his spokesman, who affirms, "Behold, your God / will come with a vengeance, / with the recompense of God. / He will come and save you" (Isa. 35:4; cf. 40:10–31; Jer. 4:2). Through the Latter Prophets, Scripture once again underscores the role of God as Savior. It is only Yahweh who can save sinners, and it is only Yahweh who should receive glory for salvation (Isa. 43:1ff.). Moreover, this point is so associated with the message of Isaiah that Old Testament scholar Gerard van Groningen claims that the whole "theme of Isaiah's prophecy is 'Salvation is of Yahweh.' Isaiah, whose name signified the same, was called to proclaim this theme. He did so by reminding the covenant people of the faithful, sovereign, and holy covenant-keeping Lord." Van Groningen, *Messianic Revelation*, 516.

[40] Given the necessity of the Lord for redemption, it is also true that only God can realize his redemptive outcomes (cf. Isa. 11:9). As the Lord announces through the prophet Ezekiel concerning his eschatological promises, "On the day that I cleanse you from all your iniquities, I will cause the cities to be inhabited, and the waste places shall be rebuilt. And the land that was desolate shall be tilled, instead of being the desolation that it was in the sight of all who passed by. And they will say, 'This land that was desolate has become like the garden of Eden, and the waste and desolate and ruined cities are now fortified and inhabited.' Then the nations that are left all around you

that a Redeemer, coming from Zion, will fulfill God's work of salvation and its eschatological ends (Isa. 59:20; cf. Rom. 11:26–27). As Isaiah makes clear, when Israel turns and repents, Yahweh "will send them a savior and defender, and deliver them" (Isa. 19:20; cf. 43:11).

THE REDEMPTIVE MEANS AND THE FUTURE DAVIDIC KING

The Latter Prophets make clear that this "savior and defender" will come from the line of David (Isa. 7:10–14; 9:1–7; 11:1–5, 10). This Messiah will enter redemptive history as "a shoot from the stump of Jesse" (Isa. 11:1; cf. v. 10). God announces through Jeremiah that "the days are coming . . . when I will fulfill the promise I made to the house of Israel and the house of Judah. In those days and at that time I will cause a righteous Branch to spring up for David, and he shall execute justice and righteousness in the land" (Jer. 33:14–15; cf. 23:5–6). Through this future seed of Jesse, redemption shall come; by his work, "Judah will be saved, and Jerusalem will dwell securely" (Jer. 33:16).

Accordingly, there appears to be a new dimension to the means of salvation. Yes, Yahweh is the source of redemption; however, his plans now include the son of David as the One who will reconcile the world (cf. Jer. 30:9; Ezek. 37:24ff.). This Davidic king will bring forth redemption and redemption's goals. Through Jeremiah, the Lord declares, "As the host of heaven cannot be numbered and the sands of the sea cannot be measured, so I will multiply the offspring of David my servant" (Jer. 33:22). Applying the language of the Abrahamic covenant, Yahweh explains that, through David's forthcoming son, there will be a great fulfillment and expansion of the dynastic promise.

Likewise, the Latter Prophets tell us that the Messiah and the promise of dominion are intimately connected. Through the "expectation of a kingdom of righteousness and peace under the Davidic Messiah (e.g. Isa. 9:6–7; 11:1–9; Jer. 30:9; Ezek. 34:23–24; Amos 9:11)" comes "a return to Eden (e.g. Isa. 51:3), evident in passages that describe the

---

shall know that I am the LORD; I have rebuilt the ruined places and replanted that which was desolate. I am the LORD; I have spoken, and I will do it" (Ezek. 36:33–36; cf. Isa. 11:6–9; 35:1–2; 51:1–3; 65:20–25; Hos. 2:18). This text shows that it is Yahweh who fulfills his own redemptive promises. It is God who brings forth the new Eden, a better paradise which will ultimately outshine and overshadow the first. For this purpose, the Lord promises, "I will set them in their land and multiply them, and will set my sanctuary in their midst forevermore. My dwelling place shall be with them, and I will be their God, and they shall be my people" (Ezek. 37:26–27). Only the Lord brings true salvation, and only the Lord can fulfill his covenant promises.

harmony with nature that will accompany the new age (e.g. Isa. 11:6–9; 65:20–25; Hos. 2:18)," as well as "passages that liken Israel's restoration to a new creation (e.g. Isa. 40:26–31; 41:18–20)."[41] Based on the righteous Branch of David, his just reign, and the resultant salvation (Jer. 23:5–6), God announces in similar fashion:

> The days are coming, declares the Lord, when they shall no longer say, "As the Lord lives who brought up the people of Israel out of the land of Egypt," but "As the Lord lives who brought up and led the offspring of the house of Israel out of the north country and out of all the countries where he had driven them." Then they shall dwell in their own land. (Jer. 23:7–8)

This coming king will restore to God's people the Promised Land once lost in the invasions by Assyria and Babylon.

Through the Messiah, a new dynasty of God will return to this land and experience the blessings of his divine presence (cf. Isa. 11:12).[42] The promised Messiah will be the king who finally completes the Davidic covenant (2 Sam. 7:1–25) and realizes God's redemptive purposes (Isa. 11:1–5, 10; cf. Rev. 21:1–5). Stephen Dempster concludes:

> This king will rule justly and transform the world into an Edenic paradise, so that wild predators will become tame and infants will be placed at the lairs of serpents. The conclusion is obvious: "They will not hurt or destroy throughout my holy mountain, for the earth will be filled with the knowledge of the Lord as the waters cover the sea" (Isa. 11:1–10; 65:17–25). It would be hard to imagine a clearer representation of the original conditions of Edenic paradise. . . . Humanity has been restored to its original position, and this has been brought about by the Davidic king—a new Adam.[43]

From this redemptive perspective, David's seed comes to restore and surpass what was lost in the garden. As the better king, he will provide the means to salvation and its conclusions. What is so beautiful about

---

[41] Routledge, *Old Testament Theology*, 278.

[42] To explain this Davidic king's accessing Yahweh's presence, Zechariah pronounces, "The man whose name is the Branch . . . shall build the temple of the Lord" (Zech. 6:12). This passage finds its fulfillment in the New Testament, which explains that this new temple is actually Jesus Christ, the son of David and Immanuel. In Christ, the agency of the presence of God and the promise of the Davidic king unite to bring salvation and its eschatological purposes to their divinely ordained ends.

[43] Dempster, *Dominion and Dynasty*, 176.

this promise is that the Messiah and the presence of God are not two ways to redemption but one. This Anointed One who is to come will be, at the same time, God present in the flesh to redeem.

REDEMPTIVE MEANS AND THE SERVANT OF YAHWEH[44]

We see this in the union of two prophetic announcements in the Old Testament. The first is the promise that the future Davidic king will be the humble servant of Yahweh. He will be appointed by God "to bring Israel the restoration and renewal that would enable the nation to fulfil her divine calling to reveal God's glory to the nations of the world."[45] As Isaiah and the other latter prophets make clear, the servant is the king and the king is the servant.[46] According to these coterminous designations, the Messiah carries with him the burden of suffering and death during his mission to rule and reign as the conquering king of God's coming kingdom. Thus, throughout Isaiah, and particularly in chapters 52–53, the accent shifts from the servant-king's majestic royalty to his agonizing humiliation and suffering, all for the fulfillment of the redemptive agenda.[47]

---

[44] Much ink has been spilled in efforts to decipher what the title "servant of Yahweh" refers to. Some have argued that it speaks of Israel as a nationalistic whole, and certainly there are passages in Isaiah that connect the servant with collective Israel (e.g., Isa. 41:8; 49:1–6); cf. Rainer Albertz, *Israel in Exile: The History and Literature of the Sixth Century B.C.E.* (Atlanta: Society of Biblical Literature, 2003), 408. However, in the servant songs, in particular, the servant appears to be identified not as a nation but as a person or individual. This section will deal specifically with those texts in Isaiah which recognize the servant of the Lord as an individual and not as Israel as a whole. For further discussion on the identity of the servant, see Routledge, *Old Testament Theology*, 292–95.

[45] Routledge, *Old Testament Theology*, 295.

[46] This anomalous connection of monarchy and servanthood is evident in Isaiah's description of "the coming Davidic king, who would establish universal justice, restoring the world to its Edenic harmony. He 'was described as a shoot springing up from Jesse's stump, a sprout from its roots (*šorāšāyw*). Echoing this thought, the servant of God 'grows up like a tender root (*šōreš*) in the dry ground'" (Isa. 53:2). Dempster, *Dominion and Dynasty*, 178. We also see that "both were chosen by God and characterized by righteousness and justice (Isa. 9:7; 42:1, 6). The Spirit of God would empower both the king and the servant (11:1–4; 42:1), and ultimately the suffering servant would be highly exalted (cf. 52:13; 53:12) and given the status of a king." Herbert M. Wolf, "Servant of the Lord," in *Theological Interpretation of the Bible*, ed. Walter Elwell (Grand Rapids: Baker, 1996), 726. Furthermore, in Isa. 42:6 and 49:8, the prophet casts the servant as the eternal ruler promised in the Davidic covenant (2 Sam. 7:16) and the righteous One who enters history to inaugurate the new covenant. The other latter prophets who make consistent reference to "my servant David" seemingly combine the Davidic kingship and the servant promise (Jer. 33:21–22, 26; Ezek. 34:23–24; 37:24). Finally, the reference to David in Isaiah 55 could perhaps correlate with the servant as well. As Wright argues, "It is possible, though scholars are not agreed on it, that the 'David' referred to in Isaiah 55:3ff. is actually an identity for the servant figure, previously anonymous and mysterious. If that were so, it would certainly link the expectations associated with the coming 'David' with the mission of bringing God's justice to the nations." Christopher J. H. Wright, *Knowing Jesus through the Old Testament* (Downers Grove, IL: InterVarsity, 1992), 100. For further discussion on the servant of God, please see Van Groningen, *Messianic Revelation*, 571–618.

[47] The appearance of the coming servant, as the prophet describes, contradicts the royal splendor typically associated with the kings of Israel. As Isaiah describes, the servant is quite plain: "He had no form or majesty that we should look at him, / and no beauty that we should desire him. / He was despised and rejected by men; / . . . as one from whom men hide their faces, / he was despised, and we esteemed him not" (Isa. 53:2–3). From a New Testament perspective, the true and final king will first come in service and humiliation in order to complete the same thing David himself sought: the redemption of man and the accomplishment of God's eschatological agenda. With this completed, the servant-king will then come in his royal splendor to rule and reign.

The culmination of this servant's work is his death for Israel and the nations. Paradoxical to the Hebrew mind-set of "an eye for an eye and a tooth for a tooth" (e.g., Ex. 21:24; Deut. 19:21; cf. Matt. 5:38ff.), this nondescript servant-king will walk among his critics and persecutors to save them from their sin through the shedding of his own blood (e.g., Isa. 50:6; 52:13–53:12). In fact, as Isaiah makes clear, the servant will bear our grief and sorrows, be wounded for our transgressions, be crushed for our iniquities, have chastisement placed upon him, and take upon himself the stripes that bring our healing (Isa. 53–4–6; cf. vv. 11–12).[48]

The righteous servant not only atones for human sin; he himself *is* the atoning sacrifice.[49] It is his death that conclusively removes guilt and secures the objective basis of God's redemptive plan. Fulfilling the sacrificial system, the servant of the Lord is likened to the paschal lamb being led to the slaughter (Isa. 53:7). He is the man of sorrows whose shed blood will be poured out for the sins of many (Isa. 53:12). Like a human guilt offering (Isa. 53:10; cf. Lev. 5:15–16), he will reconcile sinners to their God by once and for all removing the transgressions that separate the creature from their Creator.[50]

The servant's suffering, therefore, will attain both salvation and salvation's eschatological mission. The servant comes as a

> covenant for the people,
> a light for the nations,
> to open the eyes that are blind (Isa. 42:6–7)

---

[48] The suffering servant "in Isaiah 53:12 is the only *person* in the Old Testament who is said to 'bear' the sins of others." David Peterson, "Atonement in the Old Testament," in *Where Wrath and Mercy Meet: Proclaiming the Atonement Today*, ed. David Peterson (Carlisle, UK: Paternoster, 2008), 15.

[49] Isaiah reports that the servant will be "like a lamb that is led to the slaughter" (Isa. 53:7). Picking up on the imagery of the sacrificial system, the prophet continues to emphasize the substitutionary and atoning elements associated with the affliction of this Promised One. Moreover, the New Testament shows this lamb imagery fulfilled in Jesus Christ, the final sacrifice of the Old Testament sacrificial system. As the early church father Ambrose contends, "It is the price of our freedom, as Peter says, 'You were redeemed with the precious blood,' (1 Pet. 1:19) not of a lamb but of him who came in meekness and humility like a lamb and freed the whole world with the single offering of his body as he himself said, 'I was led like a lamb to be sacrificed,' and John also said, 'Behold the lamb of God, behold the one who takes away the sins of the world'" (John 1:29). Ambrose, "Letter 69," in *A Select Library of the Nicene and Post-Nicene Fathers of the Christian Church*, 2nd ser., vol. 10, *Ambrose: Select Works and Letters*, ed. Philip Schaff et al. (Peabody, MA: Hendrickson 1994), 309.

[50] This sacrificial/substitutionary background is also found in the servant's work to "sprinkle many nations" (Isa. 52:15). Thus Dempster concludes: "This cultic verb [נזה,"sprinkle"] is usually restricted to liturgical contexts in which sacrifice is involved. It echoes in particular the Day of Atonement rite in which the high priest sprinkled the place of atonement on the ark of the covenant with blood to atone for the sins of the entire community (Lev. 16:15). It suggests a sacrificial or priestly role for the servant. But this servant makes atonement for the entire world!" Dempster, *Dominion and Dynasty*, 178. This verb is also applied at the consecration of Israel at the foot of Sinai, as well as their "re-consecration" following the golden-calf incident. All in all, the verb occurs twenty-four times in the Old Testament, mostly within the framework of the sacrificial system and the priestly work.

and

> to establish the land,
>> to apportion the desolate heritages. (Isa. 49:8)

Simply put, his work ensures a better dynasty and a better dominion. He sheds his blood to incorporate the nations at large and the whole of creation into God's promises. So, through the servant of Yahweh, the democratization of the covenant blessings will finally be accomplished (e.g., Eph. 2:11–3:13; Gal. 3:29). In his atoning work, "not only will he restore Israel; he will be a light to the nations in order that God's salvation may reach the ends of the earth ([Isa.] 49:5–6)."[51] As the New Testament shows, the atonement of the servant engineers the cosmological spread of God's eschatological agenda, exponentially spreading the promise of dynasty through the inclusion of the Gentiles and the promise of dominion through the "Edenization" of the world (Isa. 35:1–10; 65:17–25).

Through this payment of death, then, the broken world of sin and shame will be replaced by the world of God's redemptive promises. Thus, David Peterson maintains, the servant of the Lord "is paradoxically *also the means by which* Israel is restored to God and God's salvation is brought to the nations."[52] Or as God announces through Isaiah,

> Behold, the former things have come to pass,
>> and new things I now declare. (Isa. 42:9; cf. 35:8–10; 43:19–21;
>> Rom. 8:20–21)

As the climax of his redemptive agenda, the servant's humiliation and atoning death will finally tear down the barriers to God's presence, for through his work, "the glory of the Lord shall be revealed, and all flesh shall see it together" (Isa. 40:5; cf. Isa. 52:7–10).[53] Through the servant's sufferings, then, redemption comes. The promises of God come true,

---

[51] Ibid., 177. Or as Anderson concludes, "The Servant had been chosen for a unique role in the accomplishment of God's historical purpose. God had an ulterior motive in delivering Israel from Babylonian bondage: that Israel might be a 'light to the nations' (Isa. 42:6; compare 49:6)." Bernhard Anderson, *The Unfolding Drama of the Bible*, 3rd ed. (Philadelphia: Fortress, 1988), 50.

[52] Peterson, "Atonement in the Old Testament," 19, emphasis added.

[53] The New Testament, of course, shows us that the true identity of this suffering servant is Jesus Christ. As Mark 10:45 explains, "The Son of Man came not to be served but to serve, and to give his life as a ransom for many" (cf. Luke 22:37). The description and implications of Christ's fulfillment of this Old Testament prophetic promise will be detailed in the next chapter, concerning the redemptive means of the presence of God in the New Testament.

and fallen sinners are once again able to hope in a new dynasty, dominion, and dwelling with God.

REDEMPTIVE MEANS AND IMMANUEL

Second, the Messiah is not only the promised servant who takes away
the sins of the world; he is also God with us. If he were just another
one of David's descendants sitting on Jerusalem's throne, this servant-
king's kingdom could only go as far as his human hands could take
it. And, as far as that might have been, it would not come close to the
universal kingdom that God has promised. Solomon and his offspring
make quite obvious that David's human sons cannot keep Jerusalem
from exile, much less bring salvation to the nations. No, instead the
world requires a better monarch, one who is a just and perfect king,
and one who comes to be pierced for our transgressions. As we have
seen throughout this storyline, our moral rebellion against God is at
the heart of the dilemma. Because the unholy cannot make themselves
holy, redemption demands a divine and holy Messiah—one who comes
through the line of Jesse. To realize redemption and its eschatological
outcome, the servant who comes to atone for sin must be one without
sin. The Lamb who takes away the sins of the world once and for all
cannot be stained with any blemish. This servant-king is holy as God
is holy because he is God with us. He is Immanuel; he is God with us
for our salvation and salvation's future promises.

We realize this when we see the promise of the servant-king coupled with Isaiah's promise of Immanuel.[54] Isaiah confronts King Ahaz,
a Davidic descendant himself, who has begun to align Judah with the

---

[54] The oracle of Immanuel in Isaiah 7 and 9 connect the promise of the Davidic king with the promise of divine
presence. Isaiah announces that a child will be born in the line of David who will establish the kingdom of God.
Through this coming king's reign, "Of the increase of his government and of peace / there will be no end, / on the
throne of David and over his kingdom, / to establish it and uphold it / with justice and with righteousness / from
this time forth and forevermore" (Isa. 9:7). From this pronouncement of his sitting on the throne of David it is quite
evident that this One to come will consummate all the promises of 2 Samuel 7. Yet the promise that he will come
as a child links the Davidic king to the sign of Immanuel. A child born of a virgin will sit on the throne of David,
and as Isaiah 7 reveals, this king will also be God with us. Thus there is a hint in this passage that the promised
Davidic king will also be Immanuel. Of course, we find this intimation proven true in the New Testament when
Jesus Christ fulfills all aspects of the prophet's redemptive promises by being both in the line of David and the
promised Immanuel (cf. Matthew 1). For further discussion and support of the Davidic Messiah-Immanuel con-
nection, see R. E. Clements, "The Immanuel Prophecy of Isaiah 7:10–17 and Its Messianic Interpretation," in *Old
Testament Prophecy: From Oracles to Canon* (Louisville: Westminster John Knox, 1996), 65–77; E. Hammershaimb,
"The Immanuel Sign," *Studia Theologica* 3 (1949): 124–42; J. Alec Motyer, *The Prophecy of Isaiah: An Introduction
and Commentary* (Downers Grove, IL: InterVarsity, 1993), 84–85. Herbert Martin Wolf, "A Solution to the Immanuel
Prophecy in Isaiah 7:14–8:22," *JBL* 91 (1972): 449–56; Robert L. Reymond, *Jesus Divine Messiah: The New and Old
Testament Witness* (Fearn, Ross-shire, UK: Mentor, 2003), 89–106.

great enemy, Assyria, in order to protect the nation from the impending threat of Syria and Ephraim. Isaiah brings the king a sign: the promise of a male child who will be born of a virgin[55] and will be named Immanuel, meaning "God with us" (Isa. 7:14; 8:8, 10). The sign of Immanuel stands as a testament against Ahaz and his decision to turn from Yahweh to his soon-to-be captors for deliverance. Isaiah's prophetic announcement shows us that Judah's protection, provision, and redemption come not from the hands of apostate foreigners, but rather from Immanuel—the greatest manifestation of God's redemptive presence who is coming to live among them, suffer for them, and pay the penalty for their sin through his death.

This is the pledge of Immanuel: God's being present with his people to redeem and accomplish his eschatological promises. As commentator Barry Webb writes, "For Isaiah and his followers [the Immanuel sign] meant the promise of God's protecting presence and the eventual fulfillment of God's good purposes for his people."[56] To Ahaz, this sign reveals that God will protect Judah from trespassers such as Syria and Ephraim. From a broader viewpoint, however, it underscores what the rest of the Old Testament makes obvious, namely, that the presence of God is the means to salvation. Through Immanuel, God will come again to redeem

---

[55] Many scholars have interacted with the translation of עלמה in v. 14, especially as it pertains to its Septuagint counterpart παρθένος. Some have rejected the "virgin" aspect of the translation and replaced it with the broader term "young woman," thereby sidestepping the messianic implications of Isaiah 7. In response to the debate I find Wolf's comments both helpful and promising. In dealing with the issue, Wolf concludes: "The solution to the problem may lie in the use of virgin ('almâ) in Ugaritic Literature. . . . Like Hebrew, Ugaritic was a Canaanite language that has been helpful in understanding Hebrew words and culture. In Ugaritic literature, there is a passage that says 'a virgin will give birth'. . . . In its context the phrase means that a particular virgin would soon be engaged and that after her marriage she would become the mother of a son. At the time the prediction was made, she was a virgin. This kind of announcement was a blessing on the upcoming marriage." Herbert M. Wolf, *Interpreting Isaiah: The Suffering and Glory of the Messiah* (Grand Rapids: Zondervan, 1985), 91. This has implications for Isaiah 7. Wolf continues, arguing that chaps. 7 and 8 of Isaiah "reveal the same picture. Isaiah was about to be engaged to a prophetess. The first three verses of Isaiah 8 describe the engagement and marriage. After the wedding Isaiah's wife became pregnant and subsequently had a son named Maher-Shalel-Hash-Baz. The boy may have been referred to as Immanuel in 8:8 (cf. v. 10)—though this cannot be conclusively demonstrated—and he was to be a sign for Ahaz and his generation" (ibid.). In this approach, the historical context is taken into consideration while also allowing for the greater reality of the promise to be borne out in the New Testament incarnation of Christ, the ultimate expression of God with us. Therefore, there seems to be a double fulfillment here that does not preclude the factual basis of Christ as the final Immanuel. For further resources on this translation, see C. Feinberg, "The Virgin Birth in the OT and Isaiah 7:14," *BSac* 119 (1962): 251–58; C. Gordon, "Almah in Isaiah 7:14," *Journal of Bible and Religion* 21 (1953): 106; C. Lattey, "The Term 'almah in Isaiah 7:14," *CBQ* 9 (1947): 89–95; W. Muller, "A Virgin Shall Conceive," *Evangelical Quarterly* 32 (1960): 203–7; M. Rehm "Das wort 'almah in Is. 7:14," *Biblische Zeitschrift* 8 (1964): 89–101; J. Steinmueller, "Etymology and Biblical Usage of 'Almah," *CBQ* 2 (1940): 28–43; Van Groningen, *Messianic Revelation*, 516–37; B. Vawter, "The Ugaritic Use of glmt," *CBQ* 14 (1952): 318–22; Paul D. Wegner, *An Examination of Kingship and Messianic Expectation in Isaiah 1–35* (Lewiston, NY: Mellen, 1992): 69–138. For more general interaction with this debate, see Hammershaimb, "The Immanuel Sign," 124–42; J. Lindblom, *A Study of the Immanuel Section in Isaiah* (Lund: Gleerup, 1958); J. Alec Motyer, "Context and Content in the Interpretation of Isa. 7, 14," *TynBul* 21 (1970): 118–25.

[56] Barry G. Webb, *The Message of Isaiah*, The Bible Speaks Today (Downers Grove, IL: InterVarsity, 1996), 63.

and restore a people to the place of his presence (Jer. 31:31–34; Ezek. 11:16–21; 36:26–38).[57] "What is hoped for, and what provides assurance and motivation . . . to trust Yahweh (cf. Isa. 41:10), is the presence of God with his people (cf. Isa. 8:8, 10)."[58] The only way to salvation is through the promise of Immanuel, the promise that God is with us.[59]

And as the New Testament will show, the promises of a Davidic servant and the presence of God come crashing together in the person and work of Jesus Christ.[60] Through the promise of Immanuel, the prophets vocalize a new and better redemption, one that overcomes the gap between God and man by God *becoming* man and being *with* man. In the Gospel of Matthew, we see that divine-human Messiah—Jesus Christ—is both in the line of David (Matt. 1:6) and the final fulfillment of the Immanuel promise. He is the sign given by the Lord himself, the one born unto a virgin, whose name is Immanuel (Isa. 7:14; Matt. 1:23). The New Testament pronounces Jesus to be the very presence of God with us who comes to suffer on behalf of sinners to redeem humanity and creation for God's salvific purposes.[61] As we will see in the upcom-

---

[57] As addressed in more detail in the prior chapter, the Lord sets up a new and everlasting covenant with his people. Through it, the Lord draws near to "give them a heart to know that I am the LORD, and they shall be my people and I will be their God, for they shall return to me with their whole heart" (Jer. 24:7). In the Lord's redemptive acts, therefore, the people can once again enjoy full relationship with him; they will revel in the radiance of his presence. "You will call upon me and come and pray to me, and I will hear you," announces Yahweh (Jer. 29:12). He continues, "You will seek me and find me, when you seek me with all your heart. I will be found by you, declares the LORD, and I will restore your fortunes and gather you from all the nations and all the places where I have driven you, declares the LORD, and I will bring you back to the place from which I sent you into exile" (29:13–14). Yahweh is faithful to his covenant promises.

[58] Hamilton, "God with Men in the Prophets," 181.

[59] Beyond the explicit Immanuel texts, there are further intimations in the Latter Prophets of God's presence to save. The prophet Zephaniah promises those facing exile that "the LORD your God is in your midst, / a mighty one who will save" (Zeph. 3:17). The prophet adds that the exiles' future rests on God's presence to ensure their salvation and restore their blessings and fortune (3:19–20). The prophet Zechariah describes the people's redemptive future in similar fashion. The prophet speaks hope into the mounting frustrations of Judah's return from exile by testifying of the return of Yahweh's redemptive presence. Through Zechariah, the Lord commands, "Sing and rejoice, O daughter of Zion, for behold, I come and I will dwell in your midst. . . . And many nations shall join themselves to the LORD in that day, and shall be my people. And I will dwell in your midst, and you shall know that the LORD of hosts has sent me to you" (Zech. 2:10–11). Though this promise points first to God's return to dwell in the reconstructed temple of the exile, it points to Jesus Christ, who is the better and final dwelling place of God (Matt. 26:61; Mark 14:58; 15:29; John 1:14; 2:19), and ultimately to the new creation.

[60] The Immanuel sign of Isa. 7:14 will eventually give way to the greater realization of the Immanuel of the Gospels. As Van Groningen asserts: "According to the Evangelist Matthew (Matt. 1:23), the fulfillment of Isaiah's prophecy regarding the virgin giving birth to a son occurred when Mary gave birth to Jesus Christ. The virgin, who was a sign to Ahaz, was an initial fulfillment in the sense that she was a predecessor to, more specifically a type of Mary. Mary's giving birth to Jesus Christ gave full realization to what the virgin's giving birth and naming her son did in an incomplete, but nevertheless, in a real manner. Whereas Isaiah prophesied concerning the birth of Christ as the sure and complete fulfillment of Yahweh's promise to David (2 Sam. 7:12–16), the sign to Ahaz concerning the virgin and her child was a necessary stage in the outworking of Yahweh's plan at a time when the Davidic house was under a severe threat of extinction." Van Groningen, *Messianic Revelation*, 536.

[61] Even with Jesus's fulfillment of the prophetic promises, Judaism still rejected Christ. This is because "Messianic anticipation in Judaism took many forms, but there is little evidence that it took the form Jesus gave it in the period before his reshaping of it. His image was not that which we find in the apocalyptic writings. . . . Nor was it that

ing chapters, Jesus Christ is both God with us and the Davidic king who suffers to bear our iniquities.[62]

The Redemptive-Historical Means of the Presence of God: The Writings

In this final section of the Hebrew Bible, the Writings[63] continue the commentary of the Latter Prophets while also resuming Israel's historical narrative.[64] The Writings, like the rest of the Old Testament, show God's presence to be a central means for salvation. To see this functional reality of the presence of God, we will briefly survey the Writings as they pave the way for a new work of God in time and space to fulfill his mission of opening access to his eschatological presence.

Psalms and Divine Presence

References to the Lord's redemptive presence fill the Psalms (e.g., Pss. 16:7–8; 21:5–6; 23:6; 26:8; 27:4–10, 13; 31:20; 42:5; 44:1–3; 63:2; 65:4; 84:1–2; 91:14–16). Here we see the real personal relationships that arise out of God's coming to be with David and the other psalmists. What

of a political Messiah, scion of the line of David. Both of these references are made of Jesus in the New Testament, but they both recede finally before the burning image of the suffering servant which the passion accounts in the Gospels establish as the fullest statement of God's word in creation." James Sanders, *The Old Testament in the Cross* (New York: Harper and Brothers, 1961), 35. Israel, therefore, anticipated a warrior-king who would judge and admonish her enemies, drive them off, and restore Israel to her earlier glory; yet, in Christ, they received something better: Jesus, the presence of God incarnate, taking on human nature so that through it he might suffer and die redemptively on behalf of both Gentile and Jewish sinners (Heb. 2:14–18). However, the Jewish anticipation is not without warrant; instead, Jesus as warrior-king is a promise tied to his second coming.

[62] Chap. 9 of this volume will address Jesus Christ's fulfillment of these prophetic promises in more detail.

[63] The emphasis on the presence of God in the Writings is one of the main reasons why Terrien argues that divine presence is more central to biblical theology than the other centers that are sometimes suggested, including specifically the covenants. He contends: "The motif of the divine presence, . . . unlike that of the covenant, constitutes an element of religious homogeneity which respects historical complexity without ignoring coherence and specificity. It is the peculiar Hebraic theology of presence which explains the importance of the covenant in Israel's religion, not the converse. The motif of presence is primary, and that of covenant secondary." Terrien, *Elusive Presence*, 3. He goes on to argue that the covenant and other centers fall short because they are not taken up in many sections of the Old Testament, especially the Writings. Thus, according to Terrien, only divine presence does justice to all Scripture, whereas other so-called biblical-theological centers fail. He comments: "While there are explicit allusions to covenant in the Hebrew Bible . . . covenant consciousness did not apparently dominate the preoccupations of the religious leaders in Israel, except Joshua in the twelfth century, Josiah in the seventh, and Ezra in the fourth. Outside of Deuteronomy and a few psalms among the many devoted to the Jerusalem cultus and Davidic monarchy—the mention of covenant is quite sporadic in the preexilic literature." Likewise, the prophets "were grasped by the presence of Yahweh" and the "sapiential literature assigned no role whatsoever to the ideology of the covenant" (ibid., 24–25). Though I would not pit the covenant against the biblical-theological theme of the presence of God as Terrien does, I think it is helpful to notice that the presence of God is crucial to each section of the Tanakh and the purposes of the Lord expressed in the historical narrative and the writings.

[64] This organization of the Tanakh as narrative-commentary-narrative is intentional, for it is the exact same as the Former and Latter Prophets. As Dempster puts it, "The Writings, with their sequence of commentary (poetry) and then story (narratives), are a mirror image of the structure of the Prophets, which is story (narrative) and then commentary (poetry)." Dempster, *Dominion and Dynasty*, 191.

the Psalms record is the reality that "the history of redemption, the covenant, and the prophetic word from God are not merely religious ideas or statements about the past but *encounters with the living God*."[65] Accordingly, there is a very real, very experiential understanding of God's presence in the Psalter. These poetic works constantly call upon the Lord to return for the nation's and the king's salvation, provision, and protection (e.g., Pss. 14:6–7; 23:4; 27:1–14; 30:7; 31:20; 46:1, 4–11; 63:7; 71:3; 91:1–2, 9–10; 140:12–13; 142:5–7). The basis for such bold supplication, of course, is Israel's own storied history defined by Yahweh's redemptive presence working out his redemptive goals. In light of God's presence with and for Israel in the past, the psalmists have a deep-rooted hope that his presence can change their current circumstances and future position.

For instance, David, knowing the power of God's redemptive presence expressed in the exodus, calls upon the Lord to manifest himself again for his salvation. The king writes:

> Bow your heavens, O LORD, and come down!
>   Touch the mountains so that they smoke!
> Flash forth the lightning and scatter them;
>   send out your arrows and rout them!
> Stretch out your hand from on high;
>   rescue me and deliver me from the many waters,
>   from the hand of foreigners,
> whose mouths speak lies
>   and whose right hand is a right hand of falsehood. (Ps. 144:5–8;
>   cf. Pss. 68:7–12; 78:14–72; 97:1–5)

Such vivid description of the Lord's glory echoes the imagery of Sinai, describing David's needs in light of what God's powerful and purposeful presence already accomplished in the exodus (e.g., Ex. 15:18; 16:7; 19:9, 16–18).

To be sure, David himself has experienced the presence of God (2 Sam. 21:1; Pss. 16:10–11; 51:11; 73:28). His whole reign, in fact, finds its beginning and end in the manifest work of the Lord (e.g., 1 Sam. 16:13; 18:12, 14). The king understands that it is through the Lord's

---

[65] Goldsworthy, *According to Plan*, 177, emphasis added.

presence with him that his kingdom will be firmly established (Ps. 97:1) and the people's redemption will be accomplished (Ps. 77:11–15).

David also recognizes that his own salvation relies upon God and his manifest work in his life. This is why he consistently calls for the presence of the Lord through these poetic expressions of worship. He cries out to his Savior,

> Rise up; come to our help!
>   Redeem us for the sake of your steadfast love! (Psalm 44:26)

Moreover, even after David's death and the decimation of Jerusalem and the temple, the psalmist still rejoices, declaring,

> God my King is . . .
>   working salvation in the midst of the earth. (Ps. 74:12)

Based on the Psalms, the God of David is the God who comes near in the exodus and in the exile as well.

Running parallel to the Psalter's emphasis on the historical and experiential reality[66] of God's presence is the revelation of God's future work through a new divine manifestation: the Davidic Messiah who will come to bring the presence of God to his people.[67] We find both in Psalm 16.[68] Regarding his personal experience of God's presence, David writes,

> I have set the LORD always before me;
>   because he is at my right hand, I shall not be shaken. (Ps. 16:8)

Here, David acknowledges that the presence of God is with him and is his delight. It is the basis for his security and confidence.

---

[66] This existential/eschatological aspiration to be in God's presence is seen in David's familiar inquiry "O LORD, who shall sojourn in your tent? / Who shall dwell on your holy hill?" (Ps. 15:1; cf. Pss. 27:4–5; 65:4; 84:1–2, 10; 91:1–2). These questions reveal David's current longing as well as his future hope. Not only does the king wish to experience the presence of God in eternity; he wishes to know the intimacy of God now. What is hoped for both currently and eschatologically finds its answer in Psalm 16. Or as Gerard Wilson explains, "What the psalmist of Psalm 15 desired—to dwell in the presence of Yahweh (15:1)—the psalmist of Psalm 16 joyously anticipates as a promised reality." Gerard H. Wilson, *Psalms*, vol. 1, NIVAC (Grand Rapids: Zondervan, 2002), 313.

[67] David and the Messiah are continually linked in the Old Testament. Routledge explains that the promise of the Messiah was "the hope of a future king through whom the glory associated with David's throne would be restored. This was also related to the hope of the protection, deliverance and future expectation of Jerusalem." Routledge, *Old Testament Theology*, 283. Hence, there is a link between this messianic promise and the promise of God's redemptive presence. The New Testament will go to great lengths to show that Jesus Christ fulfills both promises as David's son and God with us (Matt. 1:1ff.).

[68] For an excellent assessment of Psalm 16 and its usage in Acts 2, see I. Howard Marshall, "Acts 2:24–28," in *Commentary on the New Testament Use of the Old Testament*, ed. G. K. Beale and D. A. Carson (Grand Rapids: Baker, 2007), 536–39.

Still, we know that David's current experience of God's presence will, in the end, give way to a better experience of God's presence. This is the point of the psalm's final stanza. Psalm 16 quickly turns from David's current experience of God's presence to a greater experience of God's presence to come (16:10–11). The God whom David knows as personally and redemptively present in his lifetime (16:7–8) is also the God who will become fully present in the messianic fulfillment (16:11).

We see this when David declares,

> You [God] will not abandon my soul to Sheol,
>   or let your holy one see corruption. (Ps. 16:10)

Of course, historically speaking, David lies buried in a tomb, his body deteriorating in the grave (Acts 2:29ff.). Psalm 16, therefore, points to someone greater than David—someone who will not "see corruption," but will conquer death and unlock God's eschatological purposes. In the New Testament, G. W. Grogan observes, Peter and Paul, in Acts 2 and Acts 13 respectively, disclose that "Psalm 16 goes beyond David's experience and is fulfilled in Christ's resurrection."[69] As Peter explains at Pentecost, David "being therefore a prophet, and knowing that God had sworn with an oath to him that he would set one of his descendants on his throne, he foresaw and spoke about the resurrection of the Christ, that he was not abandoned to Hades, nor did his flesh see corruption" (Acts 2:30). According to the New Testament record, David's prophetic song in Psalm 16 points to the coming Messiah,[70] the son of David who is God with us. This is the one who will end death's reign, bring forth salvation, and consummate God's redemptive purposes. From a canonical perspective, then, this promise finds completion in the resurrection of Jesus Christ, who, as the holy and incorruptible one, defeats death and opens up access to the fullness of joy and pleasures of the eschatological presence of God.

---

[69] G. W. Grogan, "Psalms," in Alexander et al., *New Dictionary of Biblical Theology*, 204.

[70] As we will see in chap. 9, it is the presence of God incarnated in the person of Jesus Christ, the son of David, who will accomplish all these purposes, including the completion of Psalm 16's promises (cf. Acts 13:33ff.). So when we read about the experience of David in this psalm, we are also reading about the Davidic heir who works out the psalmist's hopes. It is, therefore, no mistake that Psalm 16 ends on an eschatological note. Christ is coming as the full manifestation of God in the midst of his people. Through his work on the cross and his final defeat of death in his resurrection, the full experience of the divine presence awaits.

We find a similar emphasis in the rest of the Psalter, specifically in the royal psalms,[71] which often "contain ideals that surpass historical reality and give birth to the messianic expectation: the 'anointed' rules to the ends of the earth (Ps. 2:7–8)."[72] Throughout these psalms we see the Davidic ideal and its preparation for understanding Christ and his role in redemptive history.[73] Take Psalm 72 for instance. This psalm shows that David's heir, ultimately fulfilled in Christ, is the one who completes the Davidic and Abrahamic promises.[74] Psalm 72 affirms that a Davidic descendant will rule in righteousness (72:1–2; cf. 101:1–4)

---

[71] This theme of messiahship and redemption through a great king runs not just in the royal psalms, but also through the whole Psalter. As one scholar argues: "The Davidic king is not conspicuous, but there is a sense in which he subtly dominates the book of Psalms. The genre or category of Royal Psalms may reflect relatively few psalms, yet the concept of kingship is significant if we are to understand the Psalter properly." Jamie A. Grant, "The Psalms and the King," in *Interpreting the Psalms: Issues and Approaches*, ed. David Firth and Philip S. Johnston (Downers Grove, IL: InterVarsity, 2005), 102; see also 101–18.

[72] Waltke, *Old Testament Theology*, 889.

[73] Psalm 101 makes such a connection. Once again portraying the Davidic ideal, this royal psalm explains that the son of David brings judgment and salvation (vv. 5–8). For the redeemed, the king announces, "I will look with favor on the faithful in the land, / that they may dwell with me" (v. 6). As for those practicing iniquity, they will receive the opposite as punishment, for "no one who practices deceit / shall dwell in my house" (v. 7). Canonically understood, the promised Davidic descendant works among the people to draw people into God's presence or drive them away. Likewise, in Psalm 110 there is a Promised One to come who is both priest and king. He is greater than the first David (Matt. 22:44; cf. Mark 12:36; Luke 20:42), and becomes present to bring salvation and judgment. Christ, the messianic ruler, marked by his position of authority (Ps. 110:1, 5), will be sent by God to "rule in the midst of [his] enemies" (Ps. 110:2) and bring forth redemption (v. 3). Later, in Psalm 132, the psalmist also links the teleological objectives of God's redemptive mission with the future king. Echoing 2 Sam. 7:11–16, God promises two things: (1) the Lord pledges to keep his covenant with David by placing his descendant on his throne forever, and (2) he promises also to dwell in Zion eternally. As a canonical reading of Scripture will show, these promises build on each other. In the New Testament, it is Christ who is the son of David who works to remake a better and greater Zion in order that the Lord may dwell in the midst of his people forever. Finally, as Psalm 45 depicts, Christ is the also the "mighty one," full of splendor and majesty, working to bring victory for truth, meekness, and righteousness (Ps. 45:3–4). He sits upon the throne forever and rules in uprightness (Ps. 45:6–7), thereby fulfilling the Psalter's promises of a Messiah and redemptive history's teleological ends.

[74] This is also the case in Ps. 2:6–9 (see also the connection between Psalm 2 and Christ made in Acts 13:33). In his analysis of this passage, Dempster underscores the eschatological impetus of the Psalms and the consistent reminder of God's covenant promises driving redemptive history. He rightly argues that according to Psalm 2, "canonically it is impossible to miss the allusion: a Davidic king (genealogy) will rule over the entire earth (geography). The text looks back to David and forward to the universal reign of his descendant." Dempster, *Dominion and Dynasty*, 195. Grogan agrees: "Even those [psalms] written about a contemporary monarch were based on the dynastic promise, and could be appropriately related to the messianic hope which would confirm that promise forever." Grogan, "Psalms," 204. From this perspective, it is the promised monarch who will finally bring God's teleological purposes to fulfillment; he will enlarge the dynastic promise from nation to nations and the dominion promise from land to lands. So, as in Psalm 16, these promises point to the New Testament person of Jesus Christ, the better David, the Messiah (see משׁיח in Ps. 18:50; cf. Ps. 45:7–9; Isa. 9:6) who comes as Immanuel, God with us, in order to bring salvation to his people. Regarding this messianic foreshadowing, Grant explains that the "later pre-exilic reader, who lived when Judah was politically insignificant and whose experience of kingship was much more mixed (if not negative), would experience a strong degree of dissonance in reading this psalm. The theology of Ps. 2 would be far removed from the reality of their situation. This leads to the process of reinterpretation. If Ps. 2 is not fulfilled in the present kingship, its fulfillment must lie elsewhere, perhaps in a future king of Israel. So a degree of eschatological expectation is added to the reading: 'Yahweh reigns, by all means, but surely the king spoken of is not our king. This must be a king who is still to come.' This is true all the more for the post-exilic reader, for whom the king has become a very distant reality. So is it at all surprising that the early Christian community read and understood Ps. 2 in light of Jesus the Messiah (Acts 4:24–28; 13:32–33)?" Grant, "Psalms and the King," 112. See also Peter C. Craigie, *Psalms 1–50*, WBC (Waco, TX: Word, 1983), 65–68. Thus, in Psalm 2, it would appear that the line of David and its future connection with the presence of God in Christ is the instrument Yahweh will use to fulfill his covenant blessings and consummate his teleological mission.

and complete the deliverance of his people (Pss. 72:4, 12–14; 101:6). As in the exodus, this future coming of God will redeem the faithful and restore them to his eschatological presence. Underscoring the messianic reference, Christ's reign, unlike David's, is to be limitless in time and expanse, and his rule will continue as long as the sun and moon endure (72:5). We also see that his kingdom will encompass not only Israel, but the entire world (72:8–11; cf. Ps. 86:9; Isa. 11:1–5; 60–62).[75]

Such escalation from David to David's promised descendant shows us that God's redemptive purposes will be inaugurated in the coming of the Christ. Under the Messiah's rule, then, holiness will flourish, and the covenant blessings of geography and genealogy will reach their full potential. As verse 8 announces, the Davidic heir will

> have dominion from sea to sea,
>   and from the River to the ends of the earth! (Ps. 72:8)[76]

Dynastically, the psalm also promises that, with the arrival of the Davidic king, the Lord's people will

> blossom in the cities
>   like the grass in the field! (72:16)

So Psalm 72 explains that, through this coming messianic presence of God, the

> people [are] blessed in him,
>   all nations call him blessed, (72:17)

and that, in time,

> all kings fall down before him,
>   all nations serve him! (72:11; cf. Pss. 72:9–10; 106:47; 107:2–3)

With the arrival of Immanuel redemption comes, and so do all its promises and objectives (cf. Ps. 144:12–15).

---

[75] Commentator Derek Kidner explains that "though the New Testament nowhere quotes [Psalm 72] as Messianic, [the psalmist's] picture of the king and his realm is so close to prophecies of Isaiah 11:1–5 and Isaiah 60–62 that if those passages are Messianic, so is this." Derek Kidner, *Psalms 1–72*, TOTC (Downers Grove, IL: InterVarsity, 1973), 254.

[76] The river mentioned in this text is the Euphrates. This promise therefore seems to have a creation or Edenic background. From the seedbed of the first paradise located near this river, the spread of God's purposes would come to encompass the whole world through the means of the Davidic son, who is himself the presence of God.

Finally, Psalm 72 closes by emphasizing the redemptive agency of God's presence. It points out that Yahweh is the sole means of his salvation and its outcome. Verse 18 proclaims,

> Blessed be the LORD, the God of Israel,
>   who *alone* does wondrous things. (cf. Ps. 86:8, 10)

The context of Psalm 72 shows that these "wondrous things" include redemption from sin and its eschatological outcome. This would seem to contradict the psalmist's earlier pronouncement that it is the Davidic heir who brings these "wondrous things." However, what could initially be thought of as an incongruity is rather a revelation that these two means of redemption are one and the same. As we saw earlier, the messianic heir of David and the presence of God are not mutually exclusive but, instead, are united in Christ.[77] The psalmist is not just tacking on a reminder that God is sovereignly at work to bring about a royal son. Rather, the psalmist shows us that God is at work *through* this royal heir and, more specifically, *God is this royal heir*. When Christ arrives, he comes as both Immanuel, God with us, and the son of David who has broken into history to accomplish the "wondrous things" of the Lord.

The Redemptive-Historical Means of the Presence of God: Return to the Historical Narrative

The final section of the K'tuvim (Writings), like the rest of Israel's history, describes God's presence in time and space for the redemption of his people. Of great significance to the Tanakh's conclusion, however, is the inversion of the historical time line. Instead of following a chronological progression, the Hebrew Bible follows a theological one, with the presence of God at its center. Ezra and Nehemiah's emphasis on God's return to restore Israel gives way to Chronicles's focus on judgment and the nation's separation from Yahweh.

So, even though Israel has returned to the Promised Land, the Hebrew Bible closes with the people in exile waiting on God to return and make everything right again. The accent falls foremost on the failure of Israel even in its return to the Promised Land. This is why the Hebrew

---

[77] Chap. 9 will develop this christological fulfillment in more detail.

Bible closes with Israel separated from its God, from his temple, and from his presence. The lasting image of the theological outline of the Hebrew Bible is one of Israel back where it started before the redemptive work of the exodus and, before that, in the wilderness outside Eden. Such a negative emphasis forces the Israelites (and the biblical reader, for that matter) to rethink their grounds for redemption. Israel is incapable of fulfilling the requirements of the law through its own obedience and moral fortitude. Instead of the people's own holiness, Yahweh reveals their need for the presence of God to accomplish their redemption once and for all and, in so doing, give them his own holiness.

Divine Presence in Ezra-Nehemiah

By reversing the order of events, the Hebrew Old Testament picks up at the end of the exile rather than its beginning. In Ezra, Yahweh answers Judah's exilic judgment through Cyrus, the foreign liberator foretold by the prophets. Cyrus, through the providence of Yahweh, allows the Hebrews to return to Canaan and rebuild Jerusalem and the temple (Ezra 1:1–2; cf. Isa. 44:24–45:25; Jer. 25:12; 29:10; 32:36–38). God works through a pagan king to reinstate the promises of people, place, and presence (cf. Ezra 6:12ff.; 7:21–28). However, even with Cyrus, we must not forget that it was God's presence among his people that brought about this new deliverance, not simply a decree of a foreign ruler. As Jeremiah foretold, Judah "shall be carried to Babylon and remain there until the day when I visit them, declares the LORD. Then I will bring them back and restore them to this place" (Jer. 27:22; cf. Ezra 1:7–8; 5:13–17). It is Yahweh who delivers. He comes to his people to restore them to his promises and is capable of using anything or anyone—including foreign kings—to bring his story to its rightful end.

After Ezra, the book of Nehemiah details Israel's return to Jerusalem to rebuild the temple. But before setting out, Nehemiah, in a move reminiscent of Moses and the prophets, seeks the presence of the Lord to go with the people and renew his covenant promises. Nehemiah petitions the Almighty, "Remember the word that you commanded your servant Moses, saying, 'If you are unfaithful, I will scatter you among the peoples, but if you return to me and keep my commandments . . . I will gather them and bring them to the place that I have chosen, to make my name dwell there'" (Neh. 1:8–9). Nehemiah clings to God's promises, for he knows that God is faithful to bring them to pass. Israel's history has told this story quite vividly: God scattered Israel for unfaithfulness, and their only hope was that the Lord (Neh. 1:10) would come to redeem them yet again. Nehemiah knows the Scriptures, which means he knows that God must return to secure Israel's future.

Through Nehemiah's leadership the temple is reconstructed. Upon its completion, the priests and Levites lead the people in the praise and celebration of Yahweh. The temple has returned to Israel and God's presence is again with the people. Many rejoice at the sight. But their shouts of delight and worship are eclipsed by the lamentations and weeping of those who remember the glory of the first temple. This new sanctuary pales in comparison with Solomon's temple. Things are different now. Everything is different. Post-exilic Jerusalem is far removed from pre-exilic Jerusalem (Ezra 6:16–22). Yes, the Israelites have returned, but as much as they may try, their experience will never measure up to the nation's former beauty. This goes to show that the truth of redemption is found not in Israel's return to Jerusalem but in God returning to Israel. The present will never be like the past, which forces God's people to look to the future, for if they have eyes to see, it is far greater than anything Israel has ever been or could be on its own.

What is more, the Israelites are no more prepared to be covenantally faithful now than they were before the exile (Ezra 9:1–2, 7–15). Concerning Israel's restoration, Dempster writes, "The reality depicted in Ezra-Nehemiah—compromise, assimilation to pagan culture, unfaithfulness, and devotion to their own pursuits instead of to the kingdom of God—paints a very bleak picture of the restoration and return."[78] Like Ezra, Nehemiah constantly deals with similar instances of dissent and ethical fallout. So although the books begin with promise, the initial hope devolves into yet another example of Israel's failure to acquire the Lord's covenant blessings and purposes.[79]

---

[78] Dempster, *Dominion and Dynasty*, 224.

[79] Along with sin, Israel's continued captivity also tarnishes the ideal of Israel's return to Jerusalem. That is, even while the remnant is back in the Land of Promise, they are still under foreign authority. Thus Nehemiah, speaking to the Lord, declares, "We are slaves this day; in the land that you gave to our fathers to enjoy its fruit and its good gifts, behold, we are slaves. And its rich yield goes to the kings whom you have set over us because of our sin. They rule over our bodies and over our livestock as they please, and we are in great distress" (Neh. 9:36–37). Also highlighting the deficiency of Israel's return to the Land of Promise is the continued opposition Israel's leaders face in their pursuit of the renewal of the covenant and it objectives.

In the historical narrative of Ezra and Nehemiah, there is the strange dichotomy we have become quite familiar with in reading the Old Testament story. There is restoration, but it is only partial at best. Yes, the people are back in Jerusalem, but it just is not the same without God. And, yes, there is a new temple, but it is nothing like the first temple. What Ezra and Nehemiah show us is that there is hope, but a hope tempered by Israel's inconsistency and outright sin. Israel's return to the land, though promising, comes nowhere near the Davidic-Solomonic reality, much less the eschatological vision foretold in the words of the prophets. Instead, the Ezra-Nehemiah narrative demonstrates a need for a better redemption—one, not reliant on the work of sinners, but on the redemptive presence of the Lord.

1 and 2 Chronicles: Presence and the Possibility of Restoration

After the quasi-hope in Ezra-Nehemiah, the Hebrew Bible concludes with subtle reminders of God's redemptive action in the book of Chronicles. In not ending according to chronological sequence, the Tanakh makes a theological point—one that accentuates the role of divine presence.[80] Dempster summarizes, "By not ending with [Ezra-Nehemiah], the Tanakh purposely ends on an eschatological note."[81] What is not complete in the time of Ezra and Nehemiah awaits a greater fulfillment: the return of God's presence in the world to redeem. And this is what Chronicles delivers. Among the darkness of Israel's ever-expanding sin, there are moments—brief as they may be—of covenant renewal that break through to shine light upon the wonderful possibilities of God's redemptive actions finally succeeding. So while focus remains on the disheartening tale of Israel's sinful descent, Chronicles alludes to God's return to the world to overcome humanity's rebellious inclinations.

The redemptive resurgence of this book is evident from its beginning. The first nine chapters of 1 Chronicles are a genealogical record

---

[80] Others have argued that the reason for the rearrangement of the chronological time line in the Tanakh was to highlight the optimistic ending of Chronicles. See J. Porter "Old Testament Historiography," in *Tradition and Interpretation*, ed. G. W. Anderson (Oxford: Clarendon, 1979), 153. However as Dempster argues, "The reason for the reversal of chronological order . . . is probably more significant"; namely, this arrangement reveals that though the people are back in the land, "the real exile will not be over until the Messiah comes. Thus Chronicles concludes with urging an exiled Judah to return home and build the temple, this temple that will one day stand at the centre of world geography and be located on the highest mountain, this temple that is inextricably tied to the dynasty of David." Dempster, *Dominion and Dynasty*, 225.

[81] Ibid., 224.

comparable only to the *tôlēdôt* lists of Genesis. As does the first book of the Hebrew Bible, the last book highlights the expansion of Israel's people. This catalog of births shows us that God has become present to grow Abraham's seed beyond the patriarch's wildest imagination. These genealogies also remind the Hebrews—themselves caught in the midst of exile and persecution—of their privileged place in God's plan. The first nine chapters, therefore, signify the continuation of God's redemptive presence for his people's future; each name in the genealogical lists is there because of God's commitment to be present in order to create, elect, and deliver a people for himself. When read in light of God's redemptive agenda initiated in Eden, the beginning of 1 Chronicles details Israel's dynastic development and represents the Lord's faithfulness to his redemptive pursuits.

Beyond the genealogies, the author goes on to link the dynastic promise with the forthcoming Davidic son who will reign eternally (1 Chron. 17:1–15) and build God's final dwelling place. As seen before in Samuel and Kings (and the Psalms), the Lord becomes present to protect David, give him victory over his enemies, and achieve, through him, the purposes of redemption (e.g., 1 Chron. 17:8). King David's promised son, the coming messianic servant-king, will accomplish the covenant promises through his death, resurrection, and second coming. Reflecting on his and Israel's privileged place in God's redemptive plans, David prays:

> There is none like you, O Lord, and there is no God besides you. . . .
> And who is like your people Israel, the one nation on earth whom
> *God went to redeem to be his people*, making for yourself a name for
> great and awesome things, in driving out nations before your peo-
> ple whom you redeemed from Egypt? And you made your people
> Israel to be your people forever, and you, O Lord, became their God.
> (1 Chron. 17:20–22)

David understands that Israel's election is based on the Lord graciously coming to redeem his people. Yahweh discloses himself to a people, covenants with them, and becomes present *in order to* redeem them. This is why David declares with great certainty that "the Lord, the God of Israel, has given rest to his people, and he dwells in Jerusalem forever" (1 Chron. 23:25). With David on the throne, the nation is on the verge of experiencing God's covenant promises in a new way. But, as the rest of Chronicles records, the nation's rebellion and apostasy stand in the way.

Even in the midst of Israel's post-Davidic descent into sin, Chronicles tells of the continued presence of God to secure his redemptive agenda.[82] For example, there is a refrain throughout this historical narrative regarding the righteous kings. Take Asa, the righteous reformer of Judah, marked by the Spirit of God. Yahweh warns the king:

> *The LORD is with you while you are with him.* If you seek him, he will be found by you, but if you forsake him, he will forsake you. For a long time Israel was without the true God, and without a teaching priest and without law, but when in their distress they turned to the LORD, the God of Israel, and sought him, he was found by them. (2 Chron. 15:2–4)

In short, if Asa seeks redemption, Yahweh will be present to work in power and strength. Asa does just that and the Lord responds in faithfulness. In the reign of Asa, God draws near to restore his Edenic promises partially, to allow the repentant to find him, and to give the nation rest again from their enemies (2 Chron. 15:15).

The Lord's presence is also with Jehoshaphat, Asa's son (2 Chron. 17:3). In the face of foreign invaders, Jehoshaphat calls upon the Lord for protection and provision. The Lord answers:

> Do not be afraid and do not be dismayed at this great horde, for the battle is not yours but God's. . . . You will not need to fight in this battle. Stand firm, hold your position, and *see the salvation of the LORD on your behalf*, O Judah and Jerusalem. Do not be afraid and do not be dismayed. Tomorrow go out against them, and *the LORD will be with you.* (2 Chron. 20:15–17)

Just as we have seen throughout all of Scripture, Yahweh is faithful to his promises and becomes present in history to ensure their fulfillment.

---

[82] The centrality of his presence is seen in the organization of 2 Chronicles and the emphasis placed on the temple at the narrative's beginning and end. Notes Mark Dever, "An order to build the temple had begun the book (2:4). And now an order to rebuild the temple ends the book." Mark Dever, *The Message of the Old Testament* (Wheaton, IL: Crossway, 2006), 382.

With Judah's covenant renewal, Yahweh draws near again to protect his people and his place and to give them victory and deliverance (2 Chron. 20:29–30).

Like Asa and Jehoshaphat before him, Hezekiah also covenants with the Lord in order that Yahweh's burning anger might turn from his people. Articulating Judah's problem, Hezekiah declares, "For our fathers have been unfaithful and have done what was evil in the sight of the LORD our God. They have forsaken him and have turned away their faces from the habitation of the LORD and turned their backs" (2 Chron. 29:6). According to the king, the Lord's chosen people have been persecuted and taken captive (2 Chron. 29:8) because they have neglected him and denied the importance of his presence in the temple.

To correct this, Hezekiah restores the temple worship, calling on the people to return to the Lord's sanctuary so that they can again hear the word of the law, celebrate Israel's festivals, and offer sacrifice for their sins. Instead of continuing Israel's superficial traditions, which merely paid "lip-service" to their God, the king genuinely calls his people back to the God of their salvation. In reinstituting Passover—the ceremony memorializing God's redemption of Israel from its first exile—Hezekiah commands:

> Return to the LORD, the God of Abraham, Isaac, and Israel, that he may turn again to the remnant of you who have escaped from the hand of the kings of Assyria. . . . Do not now be stiff-necked as your fathers were, but yield yourselves to the LORD and come to his sanctuary, which he has consecrated forever, and serve the LORD your God. (2 Chron. 30:6, 8)

Hezekiah's call to the temple is a call to redemption and a call to see the significance of God's presence. He commands the people to draw near to Yahweh in order that the Lord's salvific purposes will not be lost. If the people do repent, Yahweh promises to once again work among them for their redemption.

As Hezekiah explains, through obedience, they will gain "compassion with their captors and return to this land [of promise]. For the LORD your God is gracious and merciful and will not turn away his face from you, if you return to him" (2 Chron. 30:9). For a fleeting moment, the people respond in contrition, and so the Lord does as he has promised. As the chronicler summarizes Hezekiah's rule, "There was great joy in Jerusalem, for since the time of Solomon the son of David king of Israel there had been nothing like this in Jerusalem" (2 Chron. 30:26). So it is with Hezekiah as it was with Asa and Jehoshaphat. When the people return to the covenant, the Lord becomes present to restore his people to his promises.[83]

Ending with Exile: Waiting for God's Presence and a Promise of Hope

Regrettably, these interludes of restitution are short-lived; eventually, the revival associated with these faithful kings buckles under the weight of Israel's increasing rebellion. The virtuous kings are soon replaced by faithless rulers, and as the kings go, so goes the kingdom.[84] Consequently, the people of Judah return to their idolatry and apostasy, plummeting deeper into sin and paving the way for judgment. As disobedience advances, righteousness retreats. Through the might of foreign armies God drives Israel from the land and the rest of his covenant promises.[85]

In swift justice, the promises of place, people, and presence, like Jerusalem and the temple, appear to be left in shambles. Rather than being the seedbed for the dissemination of the Lord's eschatological purposes, Zion becomes a Babylonian territory, and her people the servants of a foreign emperor (2 Chron. 36:17–18; cf. Jeremiah 52). The land, once flowing with milk and honey, becomes a desolate wasteland defined by neglect and turmoil rather than Edenic fulfillment. Jerusalem—the potential launching pad of God's covenantal agenda—lies in ruins. The city is burned. Nothing is spared, not even the temple of God. The centerpiece of Israel's identity and worship falls at the hands

---

[83] Even in their rebellion, Yahweh calls his people to return. Yet because of their rebellion, his call goes unheeded and his prophets scorned (2 Chron. 36:15–16).

[84] It is true that Jehoiakim, Jehoiachin, and Zedekiah each represent the downfall of Judah and each feels the repercussions of actions in the nation's subjection to Babylonian captivity. Yet, the transgressions are not the kings' alone; rather, sin defines the people as well; so it is written, "All the officers of the priests and the people likewise were exceedingly unfaithful, following all the abominations of the nations. And they polluted the house of the Lord that he had made holy in Jerusalem" (2 Chron. 36:14).

[85] As in the tower of Babel narrative, this wrathful expulsion has a redemptive aspect to it. For if sinful Israel were to stand in the holy presence of God much longer, the only result would be her demise. In the exile, there is hope for salvation. The exile calls the people to repentance and ultimately prepares the way for God to come in Christ to accomplish all that his creation could not.

of her captors, who pillage the Lord's sanctuary and steal what is right-fully the Lord's (2 Chron. 36:16–19).

The temple's destruction represents the departure of the presence of God from the land and makes clear to his people that they are once again separated from their only source of redemption (Lam. 2:7).[86] In the Babylonian captivity "the Israelites had so desecrated and defiled the temple that the glory-cloud presence of the Lord actually departed from there, discontinuing his previously manifest presence there, aban-doning it to destruction (Ezek. 8:4; 10:3–4, 18–19; 11:22–25)."[87] Thus, not only are the city and temple gone, but also the presence of God dwelling in the temple is no longer with his people (e.g., Ezek. 10:4, 18–19; 11:23; cf. Jer. 12:7). Once again, the Hebrews find themselves exiled from God's place and separated from his presence. As before, the people can only hope that God is faithful to his promises and will become present once again to redeem them in spite of their continued rebellion.

The promise of dynasty, too, feels the repercussions of the exilic judgment. Their merciless conquerors kill the Hebrew warriors and many of Jerusalem's inhabitants (2 Chron. 36:17). Those who do not die by the sword are taken into exile to become slaves of the Babylonian Empire (2 Chron. 36:20). With swift violence, the people of God come face-to-face with the consequence of their apostasy. Their covenant in-fidelity challenges their place in God's redemptive plan. By the end of

---

[86] In Ezek. 5:11, God reveals that mounting sin and rebellion ultimately lead to the departure of his presence from the temple. Ezekiel reports, "As I live, declares the Lord God, surely, because you have defiled my sanctuary with all your detestable things and with all your abominations, therefore I will withdraw" (cf. Ezek. 7:22; 8:1–18; 9:3; 10:4–5, 9–22; 11:23). Out of their depravity comes the judgment of separation. The presence of God—the identity of Israel and her salvation—is now gone. But the prophets also tell of a restoration of the divine presence, as, for example, in Hag. 2:3–9. Responding in obedience to the Lord's commands, the Babylonian exiles have returned to Jerusalem and now take up the daunting task of rebuilding the temple. The words of the prophet in this context are quite telling. They emphasize both the diminished nature of the reconstructed temple and the glorious promise that the glory of the Lord's future temple would one day even surpass the grandeur of the first one. Haggai asks, "Who is left among you who saw this house in its former glory? How do you see it now? Is it not as nothing in your eyes?" (Hag. 2:3). Even so, the Lord reaffirms his covenant to be present with his people. He commands them: "Be strong. . . . Work, for I am with you . . . according to the covenant that I made with you when you came out of Egypt. My Spirit remains in your midst. . . . Yet once more, in a little while, I will shake the heavens and the earth and the sea and the dry land. And I will shake all nations, so that the treasures of all nations shall come in, and I will fill this house with glory, says the Lord of hosts. . . . The latter glory of this house shall be greater than the former, says the Lord of hosts. And in this place I will give peace." (Hag. 2:4–9). This text, along with others such as Ezekiel 40–48, shows that God's presence is still working within Israel to rebuild the temple and accomplish the eschatological realities to which the temple points. Moreover, it also discloses God's purpose to restore his pres-ence with his people in an even more glorious location than the temple constructed by Solomon. Ultimately, this glorified temple is shown to be the person of Jesus Christ, the new and better temple. The restoration of the temple will mediate God's presence once again, but as the New Testament discloses, the dwelling place of the Lord will no longer be constructed with cedar and gold but with flesh and blood, which is poured out for the sins of many.

[87] R. E. Averbeck, "Tabernacle," in *Dictionary of the Old Testament: Pentateuch*, ed. T. Desmond Alexander et al. (Downers Grove, IL: InterVarsity, 2003), 825.

the Tanakh, the kingdom of Israel is far from the idyllic times of David and Solomon. The people of God are no longer in the place of promise, nor in the presence of God. Lying under the wreckage of Jerusalem are God's people and, with them, the future of the dynastic promise.

Or so it seems. Amid the exilic judgment there is still a glimmer of hope, a hope proclaimed not by a Hebrew king, but by Cyrus, the foreign king of Persia. The last words of the Tanakh declare: "The LORD, the God of heaven, has given me all the kingdoms of the earth, and he has charged me to build him a house at Jerusalem, which is in Judah. Whoever is among you of all his people, may the LORD his God be with him. Let him go up" (2 Chron. 36:23). Through God, restoration is possible. God enters the story again.

The last lines of Chronicles demonstrate that the end of the story is not exile. Rather, these words cast the covenant promises in an expectant light and clarify, once and for all through Israel's failure, that the only means to these promises is God's presence at work in redemptive history.

Conclusion

In summary, the Tanakh ends where redemptive history begins: like Adam and Eve on the outskirts of the garden, the people of God remain exiled from his presence. God's covenant partners have been expelled from the Promised Land, separated from the divine presence, and they can only hope in a fresh work of God to restore his promises. Instead of concluding with the details of Israel's reception of God's covenant blessings, the Old Testament sputters to an end characterized by frustration and disillusionment.

But just as it was in Eden, God provides a better hope. He promises to become manifest in an even fuller sense to overcome the sins of man and bring his eschatological promises to completion. In this light, the Old Testament prepares the way for the New. In the next act of the biblical story, we receive the final answer to this exile, for it is here that the Lord draws near again to restore his redemptive agenda through the promised Immanuel, Jesus Christ. As the first chapter of Matthew persuasively announces, the redemptive presence of God has entered salvation history in Christ, the God-man, to deliver his people and open full access to God's eschatological presence.

Part Three

Standing in the Spotlight

The Presence of God and the Means of Redemption in the New Testament

When the curtain closes, all hope seems lost. The final vision of the Hebrew Bible is of a scattered and dispirited people, exiled from the temple and God's presence. The people have reaped the consequences of their actions; they stand separated from the Lord and his provisions. Like Adam exiled from the garden, Israel stands outside of God's presence hoping that he will soon draw near in mercy to redeem his people once again and reconcile them to himself. The faithful remnant, still holding out hope in God's redemptive presence, will not find that presence in Jerusalem. All they will find there are the ruins of lost dreams. Instead, the people of God must set their eyes on the future promised by the prophets and evidenced in so many of God's mighty acts up to this point. As the ruins of their city, their lives, and their place in God's mission push in upon them, all that the Israelites can do is look to the horizon for a hero who will pick up these pieces and make everything right again. The believing remnant watches expectantly for the promised Messiah to come and to rectify their bleak situation and, most importantly, reconcile them to their God.

In grace, God's people's experience of him does not end where the Hebrew Bible does—with his people in exile, separated by their sin from the redemptive presence of God.[1] Nor does the theology of God-with-his-people conclude with empty promises from the prophets that their Lord will come again. Instead, Scripture reveals that there is expectancy amid this desperate reality, and there is fulfillment for the longstanding prophetic promises. Behind the curtain, a glimmer of hope begins to break through the darkness. This hope is the testimony of the New Testament—a record of God's gracious return to complete redemption and to consummate his gracious purposes in the world. It is in the New Testament that the bright hope of the redemptive work of God's presence breaks through the desolate circumstances surrounding his people. And it is here that the Lord provides his most evident and most glorious expression of his acts for the purposes of salvation to bring his people, once and for all, into the place of his presence.

Defining this new era of salvation history, then, is the better redemption spoken of by the prophets of old, which comes through the new manifestation of God's redemptive presence in Jesus Christ. In his person, Christ is the presence of God with man, and in his work Christ is the one who opens the gates of paradise once again.

---

[1] We must remember that the presence of God among the Israelites defines their existence, experience, and hope. As Samuel Terrien summarizes, the Old Testament shows us time and time again that "for more than a thousand years, the religion of Israel was dominated by the experience, the memory, or the hope of divine presence. . . . [Israel's] national epic was structured on the stories of epiphanic visitations to the patriarchs and of the Mosaic theophanies. Yahweh was portrayed as descending from the heavens (Ps. 18:10; 2 Sam. 22:10), going forth from Seir (Judges 5:4), marching in the desert (Ps. 68:8ff.), coming from Sinai, shining forth from Mount Paran (Deut. 33:2). The cultus of the early sanctuary and of the Jerusalem temples represented attempts to perpetuate the theophanic moments. It was a theology of cultic presence which informed the thinking of the prophets and of the apocalyptists." Samuel Terrien, *The Elusive Presence: Toward a New Biblical Theology* (New York: Harper & Row, 1978), 405.

9

A Hero Emerges from the Ruins

God Present to Redeem in the Person of Christ

The presence of God in the Old Testament was a preparation for a greater manifestation of God's presence, one that would finally consummate the goals initiated at creation and continued throughout his redemptive plan. So what remained a mystery in the Old Testament, in a sense, becomes uncovered in the New (Rom. 16:25–27; Eph. 1:9–14; 3:1–13; Col. 1:25–27; 2:2). The redemptive presence of God, once mediated by fire, cloud, and smoke, now stands face-to-face with his people in its clearest expression in the person of Jesus Christ. For it is in Christ that the presence of God is most fully manifest in history for redemption.

So with the arrival of Christ, the "new prophet," we enter a new period in salvation history. All that was formerly promised finds its completion in the person and work of Jesus Christ, the one who, as Paul explains, sums up all things (Eph. 1:9–11). This is why, from the very beginning of the New Testament, the Gospel writers proclaim him to be the seed of the woman, the son of Adam, the seed of Abraham, the son of David, the suffering servant, and the Anointed One. And yet Jesus Christ is so much more than a human completion of God's promises; the New Testament also proclaims him to be the divine Immanuel and the Son of God. In Jesus we have the presence of God incarnated to accomplish all that Adam's race was incapable of accomplishing on their own (Rom. 5:12–21). I want us to see God present in Christ, the long-awaited Messiah who is Immanuel, the glory of God, the better temple, and the Son of God. When we understand Christ as the fulfillment of these promises, we understand him as the greatest expression of the redemptive presence of God. It is in Christ that God draws near to complete redemption and consummate his redemptive agenda.

Outside Looking In: Exile and the Need for God's Presence

Now under the control of the mighty Roman Empire, Israel is again a small and insignificant tribal community intermixed with a pagan people and oppressed by a foreign ruler. Once the center of God's redemptive and eschatological agenda, Israel now languishes as an outcast on the world's stage. Yet this all changes with the coming of Christ—though in a way that the Israelites do not expect. Their Messiah does not come as a political warrior who will judge Israel's oppressors and return Israel to her "rightful" place of militaristic and political prominence. Instead, as hinted at in the Latter Prophets, the Messiah comes as the suffering-servant and Immanuel promises combined. He is the presence of God in redemptive history to deal with sin and provide access to the Lord's eschatological promises. He does so not by overthrowing Rome or clawing his way upon another's throne, but by bearing our grief, carrying our sorrows, and being crushed for our iniquities (Isa. 53:4–5). Through Jesus's blood God establishes the true kingdom. In Christ, God provides the means to the ends of redemptive history. Wherever Jesus stands becomes the epicenter of God's mission. With the arrival of this true servant-king, God walks through the dusty streets of Israel so that "cool waters" of salvation will spring forth from the dry well of Israel once again.

God's redemptive efforts recorded in the New Testament diagnose and treat the root cause of Israel's dilemma, the nation's covenant infidelity and sinful nature. As the Old Testament consistently tells us, the depravity of the people leads to their rejection of salvation and the painful consequences of judgment. So even though God has drawn near to set up the law, the sacrificial system, and the temple, clearing a path to his eschatological presence by way of Israel's covenant faithfulness, his chosen people do just the opposite. Instead of abiding by the law, they turn to lawlessness; instead of entering God's presence, their sins push them into exile. And as a consequence, these provisions become tools of condemnation rather than instruments of commendation in light of Israel's propensity for wickedness.

In particular, as the Old Testament drama demonstrates repeatedly, the law does not reveal that Israel can be holy as God is holy. In actuality, it shows us the exact opposite: Israel is not holy and is incapable of being holy on her own account.[1] Israel's covenant unfaithfulness and lawlessness display themselves in the nation's consistent decline into apostasy, idolatry, and wickedness, which leads to their exile from the Lord's presence and promises. God scatters his people and drives them from the Land of Promise. Yet more than just the loss of land and line, the Israelites' sinfulness leads to the temple's destruction and their severance from the very presence of God.

The Old Testament, therefore, ends in what seems to be the demise of God's purposes and promises. But the New Testament shows that Yahweh is not done. "Out of the ruins of human effort," the biblical account makes it evident "that God's purposes can never fail and that all He purposes to do will be accomplished" (cf. Isa. 9:7).[2] God provides a better way, a way reliant not on man but on God and his power to redeem. This new way, as the New Testament proclaims, is the manifest presence of God in Jesus Christ—"the promised Messiah, the Son of David, the Son of God, the Son of Man, Immanuel, the one to whom the Old Testament points."[3] The law, sacrificial system, and even the tabernacle/temple are in a sense "failures" in the hands of man because they do not bring forth the promises of God. Yet their purpose is always to point us to what God is going to do and fulfill in Christ. They accomplish their God-ordained intention by preparing the way for Jesus Christ, the one who comes and who will culminate and complete each aspect of these institutions (Gal. 3:24).

---

[1] Thomas Schreiner writes: "The Qumran community and the Pharisees believed that if the Torah were kept more faithfully, God would fulfill his promises. Israel had been unfaithful to the Lord because it repeatedly sinned and violated his law. Hence they urged rigorous and meticulous observation of the ways of the Lord. By way of contrast, Jesus called on the people to repent and to recognize that God had sent him. The focus is not on the Torah but on Jesus himself and a right relation with him. What Jesus called for was, in one sense, stunningly simple, but it was also remarkably different from the views of his contemporaries, and so opposition developed." Thomas R. Schreiner, *New Testament Theology: Magnifying God in Christ* (Grand Rapids: Baker, 2008), 52.

[2] John Sailhamer, *First and Second Chronicles* (Chicago: Moody, 1983), 115.

[3] D. A. Carson, Douglas Moo, and Leon Morris, *An Introduction to the New Testament* (Grand Rapids: Zondervan, 1992), 81.

As the fulfiller of the law, the once-for-all sacrifice, and the true and final temple, Christ provides the final way for the people of God to be holy. Salvation is of the Lord, and therefore redemption is based not upon our own account but on the righteousness of Christ. In short, believers can be holy *because* God is holy; the Lord draws near to us to be holy *for us*. So, through the restoration of his presence in Jesus Christ, God brings forth redemption and inaugurates its eschatological outcome for our joy.

Who Is This One? Christ as the Presence of God

We must know Christ as the presence of God before we make any claims that the presence of God in Christ is the means to the ends of redemptive history. Therefore, understanding the person of Christ precedes our understanding of his redemptive work. So, to begin, we ask a question similar to Christ's question to his disciples: "Who do you say that I am?" (Matt. 16:15; Mark 8:29; Luke 9:20). When we allow Scripture to answer Christ's question, it becomes clear that the biblical authors recognize Christ to be the very presence of God incarnated for the purposes of redemption.

From a New Testament perspective, then, Jesus fulfills the prophetic promises of God's presence to save. He is the sign of Immanuel. He is the new and better temple. The biblical authors characterize Jesus as the very glory of God incarnate, the Son of God. In the New Testament's development of these ideas, we see that there is more to the promise of presence than was initially sensed in the Old Testament. With the incarnation of God's presence in Christ, we can now see that the promises, which once seemed to run parallel in the Old Testament, intersect in the New. In particular, the salvation promised through the human line of Adam's seed (Gen. 3:15; cf., e.g., Luke 3:38), the Abrahamic descendant, and the son of David collide with the presence of God in Jesus Christ.

Coupled in the incarnation of Christ are the two Old Testament promises of a Savior coming from Eve's womb (Gen. 3:15) and the pledge of God's presence and power for salvation. Jesus, as both Son of God and Son of Man, "embodies all of the promises of the Old Testament; indeed, he is the goal of all of Scripture, as all of the law and prophets are fulfilled in him (Matt. 5:17)."[4] By uniting divinity and humanity in Jesus Christ, all of God's redemptive promises find their "Yes in him" (2 Cor. 1:20).

Immanuel

From the outset, the New Testament links Jesus Christ with the coming of God's redemptive presence. In Matthew 1:17–25, Scripture confronts us with the reality that Jesus is the culmination of the Isaiah references to the virgin-born child, Immanuel.[5] As addressed in the last chapter, when we read Isaiah, we see that there is one to come, one to be named Immanuel, who will represent God and usher in the goals of redemption (Isa. 7:10–23; cf. 8:8–10). Here, Isaiah foretells God's coming to be with his people. Interestingly, Matthew 1 clarifies that the ultimate fulfillment of the Immanuel promise takes place in Jesus Christ. The sign of Immanuel is not only for Isaiah's own historical context, but also for the eschatological objective of God's salvific mission which Christ inaugurates and consummates.

Matthew's link between Christ and the Immanuel sign of Isaiah 7 would surely have flooded the Jewish mind with further testimony of Christ and his fulfillment of Old Testament promises. Not only would this gospel declaration prompt his prophetically minded audience to hear the echoes of Isaiah 7; it would also have reminded his readers of the fuller Immanuel promise detailed in Isaiah 9. When Matthew declares Jesus to be Immanuel, then, he also proclaims that Jesus is the "Wonderful Counselor," "Everlasting Father," "Prince of Peace," and, perhaps most significantly, "Mighty God" (Isa. 9:6). Undergirding the promise of divine presence in Jesus Christ is the

---

[4] Craig L. Blomberg, *Matthew*, NAC (Nashville: Broadman, 1992), 27.

[5] The whole Gospel of Matthew highlights the importance of the divine presence for redemptive history and how that helps organize the Gospel itself. In fact, a "de facto consensus exists: current students of Matthew generally agree that the Emmanuel prophecy and Jesus' promise of presence form a redactional and christological theme of secondary significance in Matthew." David D. Kupp, *Matthew's Emmanuel: Divine Presence and God's People in the First Gospel*, Society for New Testament Studies Monograph Series 90 (Cambridge: Cambridge University Press, 1996), 19. Many see that "allusions to God's being-with-us are drawn throughout the whole Gospel (17:17; 18:20; 26:29). Above all, however, Matthew has created an inclusion throughout the last verse of his Gospel (28:20), which marks a fundamental theme: The presence of the exalted Lord with his community proves to be Immanuel, God with us." Ulrich Luz, *Matthew 1–7: A Commentary*, trans. W. C. Linss (Minneapolis: Augsburg, 1989), 105. R. T. France contends, "This highest level of Matthew's Christology is effectively summed up in two verses (1:23; 28:20) which are often regarded as a 'framework around the Gospel.'" R. T. France, *The Gospel according to Matthew: An Introduction and Commentary* (Downers Grove, IL: InterVarsity, 1985), 48. Taking the significance of divine presence and its role in the Matthean Gospel even further is Kupp, who works to show that the presence motif helps establish the Gospel's "inherent dramatic structure." Kupp, *Matthew's Emmanuel*, 26.

explicit announcement that this coming Immanuel is God Almighty.[6] This is why Christ's birth narrative is so important. It shows him to be the fulfillment of the Immanuel sign, meaning that Christ is also mighty God who comes to be manifest in this world for the finalization of God's redemptive purposes. It is unmistakable, then, that in Christ, God comes to dwell among his people, walk among them as their God, redeem them as only God can, and set them apart for God (Lev. 26:11–12).[7]

Christ's being Immanuel is a gateway to the promises of God and his redemptive purposes. The presence of God once enjoyed in a measure by the patriarchs and by Moses and Israel at Sinai is now manifest in the person of Jesus Christ. And like the presence of Yahweh in the Old Testament, Christ comes to his people to work salvation and restore to them the covenant blessings.[8] Moreover, Jesus as God-with-us unpacks the promises revealed in the divine name Yahweh. His coming shows that God, as he assured Moses through his name, commits to being the "I am/will be" with his people again in the person of Christ for their

[6] See Robert L. Reymond, *Jesus Divine Messiah: The New and Old Testament Witness* (Fearn, Ross-shire, UK: Mentor, 2003), 97. Reymond also cites "numerous New Testament applications to Jesus of other descriptions of the Child found in Isaiah 7–12, the so called 'Volume of Immanuel'" (ibid.). To support this he reveals the following examples of Immanuel's deity as shown in the New Testament: "(1) the 'Lord of hosts' of 8:13 is the 'Lord Christ,' according to 1 Peter 3:14–15; (2) this same 'Lord of hosts' of 8:14 who is 'a stone that causes men to stumble and a rock that makes them fall' is the Christ whom the Jews rejected, according to Romans 9:33; (3) and yet he is to be distinguished from the Lord in some sense for, according to the Author of Hebrews, it is the Christ who says in 8:17: 'I will put my trust in him' (Heb. 2:13); (4) the geographic locale specified in 9:1–2 is applied to the locale of Jesus' ministry in Matthew 4:13–16; (5) the nature of the Child's reign described in 9:7 is the background to Gabriel's statement in Luke 1:32–33; (6) the statement that only a remnant in Israel rely upon the Lord and return to the mighty God in 10:20–23 (see 'mighty God' in 9:6), Paul in Romans 9:27–28 applies to the then-current wide-scale rejection of Jesus Christ; and (7) the root of Jesse to whom the natives will rally in 11:10 is the Christ, according to Paul in Romans 15:12" (ibid.).

[7] Hamilton concludes, "Also adding to the idea that God is present where Jesus is are the prophetic indications that one day Yahweh Himself would tabernacle among his people." James M. Hamilton Jr., *God's Indwelling Presence: The Holy Spirit in the Old and New Testaments* (Nashville: Broadman & Holman, 2006), 148. Hamilton goes on to cite Craig Koester, who maintains that the verb *dwell/tabernacle* as it is applies to Christ in John 1:14 "may also echo passages from the prophets, where God promises, 'Sing and rejoice, O daughter of Zion, for behold, I will tabernacle (κατασκηνώσω) in your midst' (Zech. 2:14 [10]); 'So you shall know that I am the LORD your God who tabernacles (κατασκηνῶν) in Zion' (Joel 3:17); and 'My tabernacling-place (κατασκήνωσίς) shall be among you' (Ezek. 37:27; cf. Lev. 26:11 MT). The promise of God's tabernacling presence was realized when the Word became flesh." Craig R. Koester, *Dwelling of God: The Tabernacle in the Old Testament, Intertestamental Jewish Literature and the New Testament,* Catholic Biblical Quarterly Monograph Series 22 (Washington, DC: Catholic Biblical Association of America, 1989), 104.

[8] Robert Reymond makes an interesting point in his evaluation of the Immanuel title and its application to Jesus. He picks up especially on the preposition "with," arguing that this simple word indicates the gracious and salvific nature of Christ's presence. Reymond writes: "When one reflects on the two parties on either side of the preposition: on the one hand, God, infinitely holy, in whom there is no darkness at all (1 John 1:5), who is of purer eyes than to behold evil with any degree of approbation (Hab. 1:13); and on the other hand, men, of whom none is righteous (Rom. 3:10) and who are all children deserving God's wrath (Eph. 2:3); one could hardly blame God had he sent his Son as 'God against us' or 'God opposed to us.' When, however, he reveals his Son as 'God with us,' the messianic task, full of grace and the promise of salvation, is suggested." Robert L. Reymond, "Immanuel," in *Evangelical Dictionary of Theology,* ed. Walter A. Elwell (Grand Rapids: Baker, 1999), 550.

redemption and their future.[9] This christological connection between Jesus and Yahweh is also evident throughout the Gospel of John, as well as in the "I am" sayings of Christ (John 6:35, 41, 48, 51; 8:12; 9:5; 10:7, 9, 11, 14; 11:25; 14:6; 15:1, 5).[10] Thus, as the New Testament depicts, Christ is the Lord (κύριος, יהוה) and "he is" and "will be" present with his people.

Being the fulfillment of the Immanuel sign and all its implications reveals that Christ is the completion of God's Old Testament promise to be with his people for their redemption, while simultaneously working to consummate God's promise to reopen access to God's eschatological presence. The New Testament announces that Jesus is the perfect manifestation of God's redemptive presence among man (e.g., John 1:14; Heb. 1:1–3). In the Messiah's arrival, "what has come near is not simply the transcendent rule of God that has governed all of God's dealings with Israel but, specifically, the eschatological rule of God that brings fulfillment of all God's promises."[11] Through Christ and Christ alone, God will save humanity from the curse of the fall, thereby reconciling his people to Yahweh and restoring them to God's eschatological presence. So, just as the "loss of the garden or the land [in the Old Testament] was understood to imply the loss of the presence of God . . . the promise of restoration [declared in the New Testament] includes at its

---

[9] As Christopher Seitz contends, "The sentence I am the Lord your God,' is a dense confession, combining two things: the personal and the sovereign." Furthermore, "the phrase 'say to them, "I will be has sent you"'(Ex. 3:14) harks back to the response of God to Moses at verse 12 about his own adequacy ('I will be with you') before the formal explanation is given at verse 14." Thus the "name is presence and testimony to a specific shared history that will continue with this people. . . . God's name is himself; God's name expresses his promise and faithfulness to that promise, to his elected people." Christopher Seitz, "Handing Over the Name," in *Trinity, Time, and Church*, ed. Colin Gunton (Grand Rapids: Eerdmans, 2000), 33–35. When this name is given to Christ, it transfers the same meaning and character to him. Thus, one aspect of the shared title reveals that Christ is the presence of God working to save his people, just as was the case when the title Yahweh was first announced.

[10] Through the "I Am" statements of Jesus in the Gospel of John, we see that Christ associates himself with Yahweh in yet another revelation of his being the presence of God. In Christ's entering human history, he has come to unveil the Father to the world. In Christ's being the Lord, or in Christ's being the I Am, Jesus's divinity is once again in the spotlight of John's Gospel. For it is in his use of the "I Am" that Christ "is publicly applying the divine name of God—and God's authoritative presence—to himself. No prophet or priest in Israelite history would ever have done this. For Judaism it is the most severe christological affirmation of all, leading audiences in the Gospel either to believe in Jesus or accuse him of blasphemy." G. M. Burge, "'I Am' Sayings," in *Dictionary of Jesus and the Gospels*, ed. J. B. Green, S. McKnight, and I. H. Marshall (Downers Grove, IL: InterVarsity, 1992), 356. This union of the Son and Father "is the remarkable step taken by the Fourth Gospel. Jesus is Lord incarnate, and thus, he himself bears the divine name. . . . In fact, it is the Father himself who is present in Jesus." From this reality of deity expressed in Christ's words, we see that "the principle theological contribution of the 'I Am' sayings is therefore christological. It buttresses Jesus' divine status by showing that he can work, speak, and act in the Father's stead. He is no mere human. He is the Word of God dwelling in human flesh. . . . The 'I Am' title he bears is simply one more of his many credentials" (ibid.). For other texts identifying Jesus with Yahweh, see Acts 2:21, 34–35; Rom. 10:13; Phil. 2:9–11; 1 Pet. 3:15–16; Rev. 19:16.

[11] Mark Allen Powell, *God with Us: A Pastoral Theology of Matthew's Gospel* (Minneapolis: Fortress, 1995), 9.

most fundamental level the promise of the restoration of God's presence in the midst of his people."[12] What is incomprehensible about this restoration is that, in order to bring people back to the divine presence lost in the fall, Jesus Christ, God manifest in the world, comes to suffer the curse for that fall on our behalf.

The Glory of Christ

Alongside the Immanuel sign is the announcement that Jesus is the glory of God, the manifest presence of Yahweh in creation for the purposes of salvation. We see this in John 1:1–14. Contending for Jesus's deity—specifically his being very God of very God (John 1:1)—John explains that Jesus is the Word made flesh, the new location of God's redemptive presence among his people. Reading this passage,

> Hellenistic Jews with at least a smattering of Hebrew would be quick to see another connection between John's words and the Old Testament. The corresponding Hebrew verb for "to dwell," šākan, sometimes used of God "dwelling" with Israel (e.g. Ex. 25:8; 29:46; Zech. 2:3) and the noun for "tabernacle," miškān, are cognate with the post-biblical term šekînā. This word, strictly speaking, means "residence," but most commonly refers to the glory of God who made himself present in the tabernacle and the temple. The bright cloud of the presence of God settled (šākan) on the tabernacle, and the glory of the Lord filled it (Ex. 24:16; 40:34–35; similarly the temple 1 Kings 8:10–11). . . . The šekînā-glory was nothing less than the visible manifestation of God. By alluding to such themes, John may be telling his readers that God manifested himself most clearly when the Word became flesh.[13]

Simply put, Jesus is the "en-fleshing" of the Old Testament promise of the redemptive presence of God. As such, all that was promised in the Old Testament concerning the redemptive objectives to be consummated by the divine presence finds its ultimate expression here in Jesus Christ, the "glory as of the only Son from the Father, full of grace and truth" (John 1:14).

---

[12] Roy E. Ciampa, "The History of Redemption," in *Central Themes in Biblical Theology: Mapping Unity in Diversity*, ed. Scott J. Hafemann and Paul R. House (Grand Rapids: Baker, 2007), 267–68.
[13] D. A. Carson, *The Gospel according to John*, PNTC (Grand Rapids: Eerdmans, 1991), 127.

In yet another way, the Gospels announce the arrival of the presence of God through the pronouncements of John the Baptist, the herald of the glory of God in Jesus Christ (Matt. 3:3; Mark 1:2–3; Luke 1:76; John 1:23).[14] To signal the coming of Christ and his kingdom, John, in a telling move, cites Isaiah 40:3, which promises,

> A voice cries:
> "In the wilderness prepare the way of the LORD;
>   make straight in the desert a highway for our God."

John the Baptist casts himself as the current fulfillment of the "voice crying in the wilderness" who prepares the way for God's coming to be with his people. In applying to Jesus these promises in Isaiah, such as "the way of the LORD" and the "highway for our God," the Gospel authors conclusively demonstrate "that the Baptizer is not simply the herald of the Messiah but of God himself, appearing in Jesus of Nazareth."[15] And if we continue to read in Isaiah 40:5, we see that in Jesus's coming to his people, God's glory is revealed and all people can see God's presence. When John prepares the way for the Messiah, he prepares the way for the very glory of God manifest in history for salvation.

Along with John 1 and the Baptist's testimony, the Gospel accounts of the transfiguration communicate the manifestation of divine glory in Jesus Christ as well (Matt. 17:1–13; Mark 9:2–8; Luke 9:28–36). There are numerous correspondences between the transfiguration and other Old Testament revelations of divine presence. For instance, Christ escapes to the top of a mountain where he and his selected company hear the voice of the Lord[16] just as Moses did atop Sinai (Exodus 32–34).[17] At the transfiguration, Moses is once again on the peak of the mountain

---

[14] Another example in the Gospels that declares Christ to be the very presence and glory of God includes the birth of Jesus, in which "'the glory of the Lord' appears as dazzling light (Luke 2:9), evoking praise from the heavenly host, 'Glory to God in the highest' (2:14). Accordingly, the infant Jesus is himself 'a light for the revelation to the Gentiles and for glory to your people Israel' (Luke 2:32; cf. Isa. 49:6; 46:13)." Richard B. Gaffin Jr., "Glory," in *New Dictionary of Biblical Theology*, ed. T. Desmond Alexander et al. (Downers Grove, IL: InterVarsity, 2000), 509.

[15] James R. Edwards, *Mark*, PNTC (Grand Rapids: Eerdmans, 2002), 28.

[16] Christ's deity is also proclaimed by the voice of the Lord, who—in responding to Peter's christological error to build three tabernacles to Jesus, Moses, and Elijah—declares Jesus to be his Son and the one to whom the disciples should listen and obey. This declaration, says Stein, "was God's seal of approval, the heavenly ratification, of Jesus' teaching concerning his messianic calling. Jesus was indeed the Christ, the son of God." Robert H. Stein, *Jesus the Messiah: A Survey of the Life of Christ* (Downers Grove, IL: InterVarsity, 1996), 174.

[17] What is different, however, is that, "whereas Moses in his encounter with God on Mount Sinai radiated God's glory (Ex. 34:29, 30, 35), Jesus on this occasion radiated a foretaste of his own future glory" (ibid., 169).

basking in the glorious presence of God, this time manifest in Christ's transformation. The same is the case for Elijah, who, like Moses, is linked closely with the presence of God in the Old Testament, owing to his unique and personal experience of it as God's prophet. Like the earlier descriptions of the Lord's presence, the Gospels too portray Christ's manifestation of divine glory in terms of brightness (garments are dazzling white in Mark 9:3) and pure light (seen in the face of Christ in Matt. 17:3), both of which remind us of Old Testament revelations of God's presence in creation.[18]

The transfiguration quite visibly depicts the glorious presence of God incarnate in Christ.[19] As one of the disciples chosen to accompany Christ to the mountaintop, Peter later reveals, "We were eyewitnesses of [Christ's] majesty" (2 Pet. 1:16), a description that links Jesus to God himself (Deut. 33:26; Job 31:23; 37:22; Pss. 68:34; 104:1; Isa. 35:2; Mic. 5:4). The account of this temporary glorification of Christ demonstrates to the disciples, and the New Testament audience as a whole, that "God's very presence is associated with Jesus, through whom they have access to full communion and presence with God."[20] Most importantly, "at the transfiguration Moses and Elijah discussed with Jesus the forthcoming 'exodus' in Jerusalem (Luke 9:31–33). The new exodus promised in Isaiah and the new creation anticipated therein will become a reality only through Jesus' exodus at the cross."[21] Christ, the glory of the Lord, the divine presence manifest, stands atop this mountain not only to unveil his glory, but also to show that God is manifest to be hung on the cross for the purpose of reconciling humanity.

---

[18] This connection between Jesus and the presence of God goes beyond the Pentateuch revelations. As Hamilton argues: "The Gospels present Jesus in theophanic glory at the transfiguration (Mark 9:2–8 par.), and the mountain setting, the radiant glory and the human response—a desire to worship—provide points of contact with the theophanies of Psalms" and, I would argue, the rest of the Old Testament. James M. Hamilton, "Theophany," in *Dictionary of the Old Testament: Wisdom, Poetry, and Writings*, ed. Tremper Longman III et al. (Downers Grove, IL: InterVarsity, 2008), 820.

[19] The transfiguration, however, is merely a hint of what is to come, and thus the full-on revelation awaits the resurrection and Christ's triumphal return as king and judge (e.g., 2 Pet. 1:16–18). Stein concludes that "the transfiguration is seen as foreshadowing the glory Jesus will possess at the parousia (the second coming). . . . Matthew 16:28 ties the transfiguration even more closely to the parousia by saying that they would not taste death 'before they [saw] the Son of Man coming in his kingdom.' It would appear, therefore, that both 2 Peter and the Gospel writers understood the transfiguration as a glimpse into the future splendor of the Son of Man at his glorious return." Stein, *Jesus the Messiah*, 171. Furthermore, as Gaffin concludes, "Previewed in the transfiguration (Luke 9:31–32), this [messianic] glory is attained in his resurrection (Luke 24:26), and will be displayed in the future 'when he comes in his glory and in the glory of the Father and of the holy angels' (Luke 9:26 par.), in a cloud with power and great glory (Luke 21:27 par.)." Gaffin, "Glory," 509.

[20] Darrell L. Bock, *Luke 1:1–9:50*, BECNT (Grand Rapids: Baker, 1994), 873.

[21] Thomas R. Schreiner, *New Testament Theology: Magnifying God in Christ* (Grand Rapids: Baker, 2008), 270.

Beyond the transfiguration and the Gospels themselves, Paul applies similar "glory-presence" language to Jesus when he speaks of the "glory of God in the face of Christ." In 2 Corinthians 4, the apostle, responding to those who reject the gospel, reminds his audience that "the god of this world has blinded the minds of the unbelievers, to keep them from seeing the light of the gospel of the glory of Christ, who is the image of God" (4:4). He continues in verse 6, "For God, who said, 'Let light shine out of darkness,' has shone in our hearts to give the light of the knowledge of the glory of God in the face of Christ." In these statements, Paul places the divine presence of God now incarnated in Christ on center stage of the history of redemption. From the beginning,

> Adam was created in the glorious image of God, but fell from it. God consequently barred Adam and Eve from his presence. Israel encountered the glory of God on Mount Sinai, but fell from it. Moses consequently veiled his face. Christ did not fall, but is the revelation of the glory of God to his people. . . . As a result, [Christ] mediates the glory of God in Christ, unveiled, in order to reverse the effects of the Fall as manifested in Israel's history of hard-heartedness.[22]

Echoing the Old Testament background of creation and the glory of God in the exodus, Paul clarifies that Christ's work begins both a new creation and a new exodus. It is the God of creation, the one who commands light to come out of darkness, who ultimately "un-blinds" the eyes of unbelievers to see the new light of glory shining in the face of Christ. Likewise, the testimony of God's presence seen in the shining face of Moses is now evident to believers in a greater way in the face of Christ (2 Cor. 3:16–18).

As the New Testament exhibits, in Christ, we come face-to-face with the presence of God. For this reason, Donald Macleod concludes:

> [Jesus] is the glory of God, the very Shekinah itself, tabernacling among men. The tangible physicalness of this form of the divine presence should not be overlooked. During those years men could see his glory (John 1:14). They could witness with amazement His

---

[22] Scott J. Hafemann, *2 Corinthians*, NIVAC (Grand Rapids: Zondervan, 2000), 179.

mighty acts. They could literally hear Him expound the ethics of His Kingdom. God was on earth, experiencing the human condition at first hand and engaging the Enemy at close quarters. He was present in our poverty, our suffering and our temptation until the last moments of supreme paradox when He dwelt in the anathema.[23]

In short, Christ is the very presence of God who has worked redemption for his people. To see the glory of God in Christ (2 Cor. 4:4, 6) "with an unveiled face ([2 Cor.] 3:16–18) is to begin to come face to face with the presence of God as enjoyed by Adam before the Fall."[24] God's command to "let there be light" is now the light of divine glory shining in the face of Christ.

The New Temple

Along with the glory-presence of God in Christ, the New Testament also identifies Christ as the fulfillment and replacement of the temple and all it represented.[25] As noted in the last chapter, the temple was God's designated location for his dwelling in the midst of his people. The temple and the mobile tabernacle disclosed the Lord's intimate nearness with Israel as well as his commitment to be present redemptively for salvation and judgment. Still, there were limitations and parameters to this Old Testament reality, particularly those associated with the law, the sacrificial system, and the architectural divisions built to ensure separation between God's divinity and his people's humanity.

But in Christ we have both full divinity and full humanity, and the divisions within the temple are no longer necessary. This is why the New Testament "portrays Jesus as not only revealing the divine presence in the midst of the Temple, but also replacing the Temple as the locus of divine presence."[26] As we touched on earlier, John 1:14 picks up on Christ's completion of the tabernacle/temple. There John explains that Christ "became flesh and dwelt among us, and we have seen his glory, glory as of the only Son from the Father, full of grace and truth."

---

[23] Donald Macleod, *Behold Your God*, 2nd ed. (Fearn, Ross-shire, UK: Christian Focus, 1995), 88–89.

[24] Hafemann, *2 Corinthians*, 181.

[25] See also Mary L. Coloe, *God Dwells with Us: Temple Symbolism in the Fourth Gospel* (Collegeville, MN: Liturgical Press, 2001), 23; Alan R. Kerr, *The Temple of Jesus' Body: The Temple Theme in the Gospel of John*, Journal for the Study of the New Testament—Supplement Series 220 (New York: Sheffield, 2002), 123.

[26] Bill Salier, "The Temple in the Gospel according to John," in *Heaven on Earth: The Temple in Biblical Theology*, ed. T. Desmond Alexander and Simon Gathercole (Waynesboro, GA: Paternoster, 2004), 125.

This prologue shows that the Word (another name for Jesus) who was God (John 1:1) is also the one who has come in the flesh to dwell in the creation. Verse 14 "presents Jesus as the dwelling place of God among his people . . . the fulfillment of and replacement for the Tabernacle and its successor, the Temple."[27] When we translate John 1:14 in a more literal sense, it reads, "the Word *tabernacled* [ἐσκήνωσεν] among us."[28] The verb "tabernacled" (σκηνόω [*skēnoō*]) is simply the verbal form of the Greek noun for tabernacle (σκηνή). This verb, Andreas Kösten-berger explains,

> commonly translated "dwelt," more literally means "to pitch one's tent." This rare term, used elsewhere in the NT only in the Book of Revelation (7:15; 12:12; 13:6; 21:3), suggests that in Jesus, God has come to take up residence among his people once again, in a way even more intimate than when he dwelt in the midst of wilderness Israel in the tabernacle (Ex. 40:34–35).[29]

This reminds us of God's presence in the wilderness. As with the tabernacle/temple of old, God is now with his people in the person of Jesus Christ. For those with ears to hear "the [verb "dwelt"] would call to mind the *skēnē*, the tabernacle where God met with Israel," imply-ing that "God has chosen to dwell amongst his people in yet a more personal way, in the Word-become-flesh."[30] As John 1:14 reveals, Christ is the true temple of God; he is the new and better location of God's presence with man. This passage, and the rest of the New Testament for that matter, makes it explicitly clear that God is present with his people in Jesus Christ.

The incarnation, therefore, makes way for the new temple. In Christ taking on flesh, "God's dwelling place among his people takes on a new

---

[27] Paul M. Hoskins, *Jesus as the Fulfillment of the Temple in the Gospel of John*, Paternoster Biblical Monographs (Eugene, OR: Wipf and Stock, 2006), 124.

[28] Koester argues that John's application of σκηνόω (*skēnoō*) in 1:14 is based upon the association found between "flesh" and "glory." He writes that this verb "resembles the noun σκῆνος, which can be connected with the idea of 'flesh' because it often refers to the tabernacle of the human body (Wis. 9:15; 2 Cor. 5:1, 4; Par. Jer. 6:6–7), as does the term σκήνωμα (2 Pet. 1:13–14). The verb σκηνόω can also be connected with the idea of glory, for it resembles the noun σκηνή, which the LXX uses for the Israelite tabernacle. The tabernacle was the place where God *spoke* with Moses (Ex. 33:9) and where he manifested his *glory* (Ex. 40:34). Therefore tabernacle imagery is uniquely able to portray the person of Jesus as the locus of God's Word and glory among humankind." Koester, *The Dwelling of God*, 102. In sum, he finds that John is using an analogy here that links Christ's flesh and the Hebrew tent/tabernacle/temple. See also Hoskins, *Jesus as the Fulfillment*, 117.

[29] Andreas J. Köstenberger, *John*, BECNT (Grand Rapids: Baker, 2004), 41.

[30] Carson, *John*, 127.

form, a human body."[31] In this simple yet critical passage, John identifies Jesus with the temple because he wants us to see that the Word-become-flesh is the new residence for the *shekinah* glory. According to the Evangelist, Christ is, one might say, the "more personal" dwelling place of God. Thus Gregory Beale contends, "Not only is Jesus identified with the temple because he is . . . the unique place on earth where God's revelatory presence is located. God is manifesting his glorious presence in Jesus in a greater way than it was ever manifested in a physical temple structure."[32] When we read John's prologue, we should be struck with the fact that Christ—the glory of God incarnate, the promised new temple of God—replaces the temple and completes its divine purposes and function.[33]

This temple fulfillment in Christ extends well beyond the implications of John 1:14. Take, for instance, Christ's cleansing the temple (Matt. 21:12–17).[34] Jesus, the new temple, enters the old temple— formerly a site of sacred worship and now a market for greedy street vendors looking to profit off Israel's "superstitions." Christ responds in righteous anger, overturning the tables and driving the merchants out of his Father's house. This shocking reaction seems to stem from more than just the economic exploitation of Israel's religion. Instead, we should take Christ's actions against these iniquities as "a parable of judgment against the temple . . . because it represented Israel's rejection of God's word and commandments and ultimately of Jesus himself."[35] Christ comes to remove the profiteers but also to correct the Jewish

---

[31] Hoskins, *Jesus as the Fulfillment*, 118.

[32] Gregory K. Beale, *The Temple and the Church's Mission: A Biblical Theology of the Dwelling Place of God*, NSBT 17 (Downers Grove, IL, InterVarsity, 2004), 178.

[33] As Hoskins notes: "John's phrase, ἐσκήνωσεν ἐν ἡμῖν ('dwelt among us') should be connected with God's promise to dwell among his people in a new Jerusalem. In the Septuagint of Zechariah 2:14 and Ezekiel 43:9, one finds an appealing linguistic parallel to John 1:14b ('I will dwell among'). Examination of the Hebrew Old Testament (MT) clarifies that Zechariah 2:10 and Ezekiel 43:7, 9 actually duplicate the wording of God's initial promise to dwell among the people of Israel in the consecrated Tabernacle (Ex. 29:45). This promise is later repeated with reference to the Jerusalem Temple (1 Kings 6:13). It is therefore not surprising that identical language is used when the promise is picked up again in Zechariah 2:10 and Ezekiel 43:7, 9 with reference to the new Temple of God to be established on Mount Zion. The repetition of this promise indicates that dwelling among his people is a consistent aspect of God's dealing with them. Furthermore, the expression of the promise with reference to the new Temple gives it a place within Israel's hopes for the future. Consequently, two significant points follow from the allusion to this promise in John 1:14b. First, John 1:14b suggests that the incarnation of the Word is an event that fulfills God's repeated promise to dwell among his people. Second, in doing so, the incarnate Word is fulfilling a promise whose most recent prophetic expression anticipated its fulfillment within a new Temple building." Hoskins, *Jesus as the Fulfillment*, 118–19.

[34] I am reliant upon G. K. Beale for this argument concerning the link between Christ's temple fulfillment and his cleansing the temple. For his position, see Beale, *Temple and the Church's Mission*, 176–80.

[35] Ibid., 179.

misinterpretations of the temple and relocate its eschatological purposes in himself.

To emphasize this, Christ recites the prophecy of Isaiah 56:7, claiming that the house of God will be a house of prayer. This passage has eschatological implications for the salvation of Gentiles and their inclusion in the temple presence of God (Isa. 56:3–8; see Mark 11:17, which adds to "house of prayer" the phrase "for all the nations"). In quoting this text from Isaiah, Jesus condemns the people and the temple itself for losing sight of the eschatological function of this "sacred space." Remember, this building was to be the point from which the presence of God would spread to the ends of the earth. But it did not, which meant that the temple now forecasts something better that was to come and had come in Christ.

So while he brings judgment, Jesus also tells us that salvation has come in him. Because Jesus is the new temple—the locus of God's presence in the midst of his people—the promises and objectives seemingly lost in this crowd of selfish money changers and merchandise can only be accomplished by the One who stands before them as their judge. What is more, Christ's coming actually inaugurates what Isaiah's prophecy foretells. On the heels of his corrective action, Christ opens the temple to all those once declared unfit and unclean for entrance. The lame and the blind come to him in the temple for healing (Matt. 21:14). In an ironic twist, Christ heals those once deemed unfit for salvation in the very place once identified with the presence of God. He is fulfilling the purpose of the temple right before the eyes of the chief priests and scribes (cf. Isa. 56:8). The restorative and reconciling work of Christ makes way for God's eschatological promises, all while the innocent voices of Israel's children—declaring, "Blessed is he who comes in the name of the Lord"—fill the air with the sweet song of his messianic fulfillment (Matt. 21:9, 16; cf. Ps. 8:2).

In the parallel account in John, Christ's recognition of himself as the new temple is even more apparent. Responding to the Jew's defiant challenges to his authority, Christ makes a yet bolder claim. He gives them a sign: "Destroy this temple, and in three days I will raise it up" (John 2:19). Missing the point altogether, the Jewish audience arrogantly balks at Jesus's prophetic declaration. In a literalistic way, they remind Jesus that it has taken forty-six years to build this (second-rate) temple. But to keep his readers from similar misconceptions, John clarifies that Christ "was speaking about the temple of his body" (John 2:21), not the temple of stone in Jerusalem. John continues to explain that when Christ rose from the dead, "his disciples remembered that he had said this, and they believed the Scripture and the word that Jesus had spoken" (2:22). James Hamilton writes, "As God formerly dwelt in the temple, now the Father dwells in Jesus: 'The Father is in Me and I am in the Father' (John 10:38; 14:10; see 1:14, 51; 2:19; 4:21–26; 10:30)."[36] From this Gospel account, then, it seems quite apparent that Christ understands himself to be the culmination and replacement of the temple and its purposes.[37] In his defeat of sin and death evidenced in the resurrection,[38] Christ both opens access to God's eschatological presence and expands God's dwelling place to all the nations. Christ "builds the new temple by fulfilling the function of the temple eschatologically, i.e. by offering his life for all."[39] So although the temple's eschatological role stalls in the sin and fall of Israel's covenant infidelity and lawbreaking, Christ, the new and better temple, does what the first temple could not, opening the way to the presence of God in eschatological fullness.

The Seed of the Woman and the Son of God

Coupled with the redemptive presence in Jesus is the culmination of the *protoevangelium*, that first gospel of Genesis 3:15. As early as Adam's

---

[36] Hamilton, *God's Indwelling Presence*, 153.

[37] This replacement and escalation of the old temple with the new temple of Christ is apparent in John 1:18 as well. In this text, John ends his prologue by declaring that Christ has made the invisible God manifest in a way that surpasses all other realities, including the limitations of the tabernacle/temple. As Hoskins concludes: "Previously no human being had ever seen God (1:18a). Even when God's glory appeared to Moses on Mount Sinai, Moses was only permitted a partial view of it (Ex. 33:19–23). Jesus, however, has not only seen the Father ([John] 6:46), but is himself God (1:1, 18). Consequently, he is uniquely qualified to enable humans to see and hear the Father (John 14:9–10; 3:34). In short, John presents the revelation that comes through Christ as the pre-eminent revelation of God and God's glory. It surpasses the revelation that was granted through previous events, persons, and institutions. This includes Moses, the Law, the Tabernacle, and the Temple." Hoskins, *Jesus as the Fulfillment*, 124–25.

[38] The work of Christ's death and resurrection is vital for the appropriate interpretation of the Old Testament and God's redemptive mission. N. T. Wright argues, "If Jesus has been raised, then this is how the Old Testament has to be read: as a story of suffering and vindication, of exile and restoration, a narrative that reaches its climax not in Israel becoming top nation and beating the rest of the world at its own game but in the suffering and vindication, the exile and restoration, of the Messiah—not for himself alone but because he is carrying the saving promises of God." N. T. Wright, *Surprised by Hope: Rethinking Heaven, the Resurrection, and the Mission of the Church* (New York: Harper, 2008), 237.

[39] S. Kim, "Jesus—The Son of God, the Stone, the Son of Man, and the Servant: The Role of Zechariah in the Self-Identification of Jesus," in *Tradition and Interpretation in the New Testament*, ed. Gerald F. Hawthorne and Otto Betz (Grand Rapids: Eerdmans, 1987), 143.

exile from the garden, God has been at work in redemptive history to save humanity from the fall and its consequences. Robert Reymond comments, "The promise [of Gen. 3:15] is given in 'seed-form,' true enough, but God clearly stated that someone out of the human race itself (the woman's offspring), although fatally 'wounded' himself in the conflict, would destroy the serpent (Satan)."[40] So even in its earliest expression, God declares to Adam and Eve that one of their descendants will deal righteously and punitively with the Serpent, an act that will bring forth redemption to God's people.

As shown earlier, this "seed" promise—though faced with great obstacles and threats at times—continues to advance through Israel's Old Testament story. From the lists of generations in Genesis to the lists in Chronicles, Yahweh has drawn near to move his promise forward in powerful and miraculous ways. In particular, the seed of redemption promised to the woman continues in the line of Abraham[41] and the royal house of David. Over time, however, the bright promise of Israel's future redemption begins to fade behind the ever-dimming history of Israel, especially in the nation's monarchy. The consistent sins of humanity, including those in the line of the promised seed, continue to raise issues concerning the validity of such a salvation and the place of Adam's line in this promise.

Yet with the dawning of the New Testament and the introduction of

---

[40] Reymond, *Jesus Divine Messiah*, 69.

[41] The New Testament makes the connection between the "seed" promise, Abraham, and its christological fulfillment in several places. For instance, per the apostle Paul, Christ is the promised seed of Adam because he is the fulfillment of the Abrahamic covenant. As T. Desmond Alexander argues, if we focus on the "announcement that 'all the nations will be blessed through you' (Gen. 12:3; 18:18) we will recognize Paul's argument is that Christ 'redeemed us in order that the blessing given to Abraham might come to the Gentiles through Christ Jesus, so that by faith we might receive the promise of the Spirit' (Gal. 3:14)." T. Desmond Alexander, "Seed," in Alexander et al., *New Dictionary of Biblical Theology*, 769. Later in Galatians, the apostle argues as well that "the promises were spoken to Abraham and to his seed. The Scripture does not say 'and to seeds,' meaning many people, but 'and to your seed,' meaning one person, who is Christ" (Gal. 3:16). Consequently, "according to Paul's reading of history, Christ is the true Heir of the promise, of the universal inheritance, and He determines the fellow-heirs." Ronald K. Fung, *The Epistle to the Galatians*, NICNT (Grand Rapids: Eerdmans, 1988), 156. These along with other New Testament writings (cf. Acts 3:17–26) demonstrate that Christ in his humanity is the culmination of the seed promise of Genesis 3. He is the one who has come to create an even greater dynasty through faith, a people who will inherit the new creation, which surpasses even the reality of the first paradise, and ultimately will restore humanity to the eschatological presence of God. Through Christ the curse of sin and death are broken. He pulls believers from the grip of sin through the vicarious nature of his own atoning sacrifice. He is the entry into the new nation of the redeemed, and he is the last king who is to sit on David's throne forever. In sum, "the New Testament presents Jesus Christ as the one who brings to fulfillment the divine promises associated with the unique line of seed descending from Abraham. Thus, through Christ God's blessing is mediated to the nations of the earth." Alexander, "Seed," 772. His conquest then as the seed of Adam, Abraham, and David procures both salvation and its teleological outcome. Christ defeats the Serpent to bring salvation to a new dynasty that he will usher into a new land filled with the glorious presence of God in full.

Jesus Christ, God responds to the question of sin in the line of Adam's redemptive seed. In his grace and mercy, Yahweh brings together that which was assumed to be mutually exclusive. In the coming of Immanuel (Isa. 7:14; 8:10; 9:6–7; Matt. 1:23) we have both the Son of God and the Son of Man. He is the promised seed of Adam, Abraham, and David (Matt. 1:1; Luke 1:32–33; 3:31–38; cf. Matt. 21:5, 9, 15); greater still, he is the divine presence in the midst of his people (Matt. 1:23), "the image of the invisible God" (Col. 1:15), "the exact imprint of [God's] nature" (Heb. 1:3). From this perspective, the Old Testament promises of a coming seed, a covenant king, and the future presence of God merge together in Jesus Christ. So while God's promise to make a people is very strong and reaches significant fulfillment, each expression points to Jesus Christ, the true seed. In being fully God and fully man, Christ fulfills both divine promises: he is the Serpent-crushing seed of Adam as well as the redemptive presence of God manifest to the world for salvation. For this reason, Jesus is the climactic end of all of the Lord's redemptive promises and goals.

These categories are quite significant for understanding who Christ is. They are so important that I would contend that the Gospel of Matthew builds its introduction around these dual realities. In Matthew 1:1, the Gospel begins with an emphasis on Christ's being a descendant of Adam. In particular, Matthew highlights that Christ is "the son of David, the son of Abraham," titles that associate him with the fulfillment of the *protoevangelium* (Gen. 3:15).[42] Christ's own genealogy, therefore, is wrought with references to the promises afforded Adam and his progeny. As the son of Abraham and David, Christ clearly represents the place of humanity in God's redemptive mission. Matthew underscores Jesus's pedigree and distinct family tree in order to tie Christ's humanity to the redemptive promises ringing in the ears of the long-suffering Hebrews. As they hear Christ's ancestry, they hear that their Messiah has come. Christ is a human king in the line of David,

---

[42] Matthew, therefore, illustrates the "Messiah's necessary lineage and royal rule (see 2 Sam. 7:11b–16)" in which Christ is revealed to be a "righteous warrior-king who establishes God's rule in Israel." Blomberg, *Matthew*, 52. Furthermore, the "son of Abraham" traces "Jesus' lineage back to the founding father of the nation of Israel, ensuring . . . the echoes of God's promises to Abraham that his offspring would bless all the peoples of the earth (Gen. 12:1–3)" (ibid.).

Abraham, and Adam who will conquer their enemies and defeat their oppressors once and for all (cf. Heb. 2:14–18).

But the promised seed of the woman is not the only promise fulfilled in Jesus Christ. Remember what Matthew does next. He tells us that Christ is God with us (Matt. 1:23). So not only is Jesus the human son of Abraham and David; he is also the very presence of God in history to redeem. It is in his being the Son of Man and the Son of God that Christ is able to bring a true salvation to his people. As the angel Gabriel foretells, "[Jesus] will be great and will be called the Son of the Most High. And the Lord God will give to him the throne of his father David, and he will reign over the house of Jacob forever, and of his kingdom there will be no end" (Luke 1:32–33). The prophecy reveals the means of God's redemption: Christ, the seed of the woman and the son of David, is also the Most High God who comes to secure the covenant objectives. Stephen Dempster summarizes:

> One of the most important [Gospel emphases] is that both meanings of the Davidic house merge in the person of Christ. He is the descendant of David who, by virtue of his resurrection, sits on the throne of David as the long-expected descendant of the Davidic house (understood as dynasty) (Luke 1:32; Acts 20:30–35). . . . But Jesus is also the Davidic house understood as temple, in which God's presence is incarnated, a presence that flows out of him like a surging river giving life to all (John 2:19–22; 7:37–39; cf. Ezek. 47:1–12).[43]

In other words, Jesus Christ, is the Son of Man and the Son of God. In being the Son of God, Jesus "is not simply representing the Father but in some fashion is bearing the Father's presence to the world."[44] The redemptive outcome accomplished in Christ's work is only available because Christ himself is the seed of Adam, Abraham, and David, as well as Immanuel, the full expression of God's divinity incarnated (e.g., John 1:1, 18; 20:28; Rom. 9:5; Titus 2:13; Heb. 1:8; 2 Pet. 1:1; 1 John 5:20; cf. Luke 1:35; Col. 2:9; 1 Tim. 3:16).[45]

---

[43] Stephen G. Dempster, *Dominion and Dynasty: A Theology of the Hebrew Bible*, NSBT 15 (Downers Grove, IL: InterVarsity, 2003), 233.

[44] Burge, "'I Am' Sayings," 356.

[45] As shown earlier, the introduction of Matthew's Gospel reveals that Christ is divine in nature. Thus, as Macleod concludes: "The birth narratives, especially Matthew's, contain clear hints of the absolute deity of Christ. He is Immanuel ('God with us') in Matthew 1:23. . . . Matthew's assumption is the same as Mark's who, at the beginning

Conclusion

So who is Christ? Jesus Christ is God present in human flesh for the redemption of God's people and God's place. His coming

> is not just another Christophany but something completely different—incarnation: "the same Son, our Lord Jesus Christ, the same perfect in Godhead and also perfect in manhood; truly God and truly man, of a reasonable soul and body; consubstantial with the Father according to the Godhead, and consubstantial to us according to Manhood."[46]

In this new temple of Christ, deity dwells in man and among men for the purposes of redemption and reconciliation (Col. 2:9). God has come among us, as one of us, in order to save us. By introducing the theme of divine presence and its fulfillment in Christ, the New Testament reinforces the Old Testament reality that salvation is *still* from the Lord and that his manifest work is *still* the agency of redemption (Isa. 9:7; cf. Pss. 37:39; 68:20; Isa. 40:9–11; 43:10–13; 59:15–20; Jer. 3:23; Jonah 2:9; John 1:1–18).[47] Simply put, God has come to complete his redemptive agenda by being present in Christ, who is the Messiah, Immanuel, the glory of God, the better temple, the seed of the woman, and the Son of God.[48]

---

of his gospel portrays the advent of Christ as the fulfilling of the Old Testament prophecy that the Lord would come to his temple (Mark 1:3)." Donald Macleod, *The Person of Jesus Christ*, CCT (Downers Grove, IL: InterVarsity, 1998), 34. Contra C. Meyers, *Binding the Strong Man: A Political Reading of Mark's Story of Jesus* (Maryknoll, NY: Orbis, 1988).

[46] Daniel Strange, "A Little Dwelling on the Divine Presence: Towards a 'Whereness' of the Triune God," in Alexander and Gathercole, *Heaven on Earth*, 225. This is a paraphrase of the Chalcedonian Creed.

[47] The name Jesus, which translates as "Jehovah saves," also places emphasis on God as the author of salvation.

[48] Moreover, the New Testament emphasis on the deity of Christ and his being the presence of God in this world answers the invalidity of the Adamic source of redemption. As all redemptive history has indicated and will indicate, sinners are unable to save sinners. For this very reason there is a sacrificial system put in place that requires the substitution of an *unblemished* animal in the place of the reprobate. The necessity of perfection in this atoning act points to the necessity of perfection in the once-for-all sacrifice of Jesus Christ. Thus, to save sinners, the Messiah cannot be a sinner himself. Instead, he must be holy as God is holy—he must be the perfect manifestation of God who fully meets the requirements of the law as only Yahweh himself could. So Christ, as the God-man, accomplishes what Adam could not because Christ is perfectly obedient (Matt. 4:1–11). Thus understood, Christ is not only fully man; he is also fully divine and thereby able to defeat the Serpent, death, and sin. Only through his sinless perfection as the Son of God can this Son of Man complete redemption and ready the world for the cosmological expansion of his divine presence. In sum, Christ fulfills the redemptive promises of God's presence by doing just that—making God present.

10

The Hero Takes His Throne

God Present to Redeem through
the Work of Christ

In the last chapter we saw who Jesus is, but now we must take a look at what the hero of our story does. Christ comes for a purpose: he enters human history to inaugurate and consummate the Father's redemptive agenda, which ultimately ends in the experience of God's eschatological presence. There is much at stake in the work of Christ. When Christ comes, he comes to be the presence of God in history *in order to redeem*. He comes to die on a cross to defeat sin and death, and to make the full experience of the presence of God available to his people (Matt. 20:28; Mark 10:45; 1 Pet. 2:24; 3:18).

Christ's redemptive work is best understood through his work as prophet, priest, and king. At the risk of oversimplifying, Christ the prophet enters history to proclaim redemption to us, Christ the priest enters history to accomplish salvation for us, and Christ the king enters history to complete the eschatological objectives for the Father's glory and our good. So, in replacing Moses the prophet, Christ, the incarnated presence of God, brings us a better deliverance from exile; as the Great High Priest, Christ provides us with the requisite once-for-all substitutionary and atoning sacrifice for salvation; and, finally, as the better David, Christ ushers in the new and greater kingdom that opens up the beauty of God's redemptive-historical objectives for us to enjoy. What should not be lost in all this is the fact that Christ's work as prophet, priest, and king is successful only because he is the very presence of God incarnate. Christ is still the means to salvation and its objectives, and his work of salvation is the way we can become a part of this glorious story ourselves.

Christ, Our Prophet

Christ's work begins with his coming as the better prophet. He is the final prophet who proclaims the arrival of the kingdom of God and works to bring us into that kingdom (Mark 1:14–15; Luke 4:16–21; Heb. 1:1–2). It has been said that "the whole work of Jesus in revealing the truth about God and the kingdom may be seen as the climax to the prophetic office of the Old Testament."[1] In particular, Christ is the new Moses who brings forth a better exodus so that we may be saved.

The Better Moses

To understand our place in the redemptive story we must understand our hero's role as the new Moses. Moses, we know, was the "human instrument through which God will act to redeem his people."[2] But, as the rest of the Canon demonstrates, the significance of leaders such as Moses lies "not primarily in the way they stand as examples of godliness and faith, but rather in the role they play in revealing and foreshadowing the nature of the work of Christ."[3] Christ is the better Moses because Christ is the one who finally saves.

Hebrews 3:3, for example, plainly states, "Jesus has been counted worthy of more glory than Moses." According to the author of Hebrews, Christ is greater than Moses because he accomplishes for us what Moses could not. Moses confessed in Deuteronomy 18, "The Lord your God will raise up for you [Israel] a prophet like me from among you, from your brothers. . . . And the Lord said to me, . . . 'I will put my words in his mouth, and he shall speak to them all that I command

---

[1] Graeme Goldsworthy, *According to Plan: The Unfolding Revelation of God in the Bible* (Downers Grove, IL: InterVarsity, 1991), 205.
[2] Ibid., 132.
[3] Ibid.

him'" (18:15, 17–18). Moses knew that one better than he was coming to bring a salvation greater than his own. Jesus understands that he himself fulfills this prophecy when he argues, "If you believed Moses, you would believe me; for he wrote of me" (John 5:46). Likewise, as the apostle Peter discloses, Moses's prophecy of "another prophet" finds its final completion in the ministry and redemptive work of Jesus Christ (Acts 3:22ff.).[4]

Christ is the superior prophet because not only does he speak the words of God; he *is the Word of God*. As John's Gospel puts it, Jesus "was the Word, and the Word was with God, and the Word was God" (John 1:1; see also John 1:2–3, 14–18; 14:6).[5] Jesus wields greater power than the prophets before him in that he not only announces the word of salvation but is the Word who saves. Christ's prophetic supremacy reflects the fact that he both proclaims deliverance and produces that deliverance. As Robert Letham contends, "Jesus transcends prophetism . . . for he himself is the truth to which the prophets bore witness. He is greater than a prophet, for he is the Son of God incarnate for us . . . and for our salvation."[6] In other words, while Jesus announces God's redemptive mission, he concurrently fulfills the Lord's mission and all the former prophecies concerning himself too (Luke 24:25–27, 44–47; John 5:45–47; 1 Pet. 1:10–12).

For example, when Christ comes to the synagogue on the Sabbath,

---

[4] Though Jesus does not reveal a specific Scripture where Moses refers to him, John's earlier interest in Deut. 18:15 would imply that it is a very probable reference (e.g., John 1:21; 4:19; 6:14; 7:40, 52). Yet, some have argued that "it is perhaps more likely that this verse [John 5:46] is referring to a certain way of reading the books of Moses than to a specific passage." D. A. Carson, *The Gospel according to John*, PNTC (Grand Rapids: Eerdmans, 1991), 266; cf. Carson, "John and the Johannine Epistles," in *It Is Written: Scripture Citing Scripture*, ed. D. A. Carson and H. G. M. Williamson (Cambridge: Cambridge University Press, 1988), 245–64 . Even so, this "Christocentric" reading of the books of Moses would show that Deuteronomy 18:15 is pointing to the coming of Christ. Reading the Torah, then, through the lens of Christ's fulfillment of the Torah would tell us the same thing: Christ is the fulfillment of this prophet whom Moses prophetically announces. Thus David Peterson comments on Acts 3:22: "A succession of prophets was raised up to follow Moses, but none was recognized as a prophet specifically like Moses himself (cf. Deut. 34:10). In time, Moses' words were interpreted as referring to one particular prophet who was yet to come and who would function as prophet-king and prophet-lawgiver in the end time. Moses' prophecy came to be regarded as messianic in its scope. Peter envisages Jesus as the eschatological prophet because he brings the ultimate revelation of God's will and leads God's people to final salvation (cf. [Acts] 7:35–38). Jesus functions for Israel now as Moses did at the time of the exodus." David G. Peterson, *The Acts of the Apostles*, PNTC (Grand Rapids: Eerdmans, 2009), 183–84.

[5] It is important to note that Christ's prophetic office did in fact contain a prophetic ministry. As Bruce Demarest maintains: "Jesus exercised a prophetic ministry verbally by speaking words from the Father (John 12:49; 14:24; 17:8). He proclaimed the requirements of the law (Matt. 5:17–18), preached the Good News of the kingdom (Luke 4:18–19), and infallibly predicted the future (Matt. 24:2–31; Luke 19:41–44). Bruce Demarest, *The Cross and Salvation: The Doctrine of Salvation* (Wheaton, IL: Crossway, 1997), 183. See also John Goldingay, *Old Testament Theology: Israel's Gospel* (Downers Grove, IL: InterVarsity, 2003), 826–28.

[6] Robert Letham, *The Work of Christ*, CCT (Downers Grove, IL: InterVarsity, 1993), 94.

he takes up the scroll and reads from Isaiah 61:1–2. Luke's Gospel quotes it this way:

> The Spirit of the Lord is upon me,
>   because he has anointed[7] me
>   to proclaim good news to the poor.
> He has sent me to proclaim liberty to the captives,
>   and recovering of sight to the blind,
>   to set at liberty those who are oppressed,
> to proclaim the year of the Lord's favor. (Luke 4:18–19)[8]

Christ follows his reading with the extraordinary and powerful declaration, "Today this Scripture has been fulfilled in your hearing" (Luke 4:21). What Isaiah could never be—and what therefore became a future and messianic reality—was standing before the crowd in the Nazarene synagogue. This is why the New Testament reveals that Jesus is the fulfillment of "all that the prophets have spoken" (Luke 24:25; cf. v. 27) and that in him "all the promises of God find their Yes" (2 Cor. 1:20). Christ surpasses all the prophets, including Moses, because he is the true revelation of God, the presence of God who has come to save us, and he is the one who both declares and completes the divine message and agenda.

The Better Exodus

Jesus's superior prophethood is tied to the "purification for sins" (Heb. 1:3). Christ rightfully understands himself to be the culmination of the prophets and their message, the one who completes the Old Testament promises through his ministry and work. One particular implication of Christ's office as the new Moses is his provision of a better redemption. Throughout the Old Testament, the "exodus set the mode of redemption as deliverance from oppression and reception into divine blessing. Redemption, the exodus shows, is a coming out and a going in, a coming out of the bondage of sin and going into the family and

---

[7] The use of "anointed" would easily conjure up ideas of Christ's messianic role and his fulfillment of the messianic mission in light of this particular passage. Furthermore, its usage in this text sheds light on the rest of Jesus's coming ministry, couching in a messianic light all that follows in Luke.

[8] Interestingly, Christ's reading abruptly ends in the middle of Isa. 61:2, thereby leaving off the declaration of judgment, "and the day of vengeance of our God." The reasoning behind this would seem to be in line with the inaugurated eschatology undergirding much of the time line of the New Testament. Specifically, in Christ's first coming he inaugurates and consummates the "year of the Lord's favor," whereas it is in his second coming that the day of vengeance is finally and fully brought forth on this earth.

presence of God."[9] In this context then, "leaving Egypt was only the first step towards the goal of Israel coming into God's presence. God's mighty act of delivering his people from Egypt and bringing them into a place of sonship and blessing in his presence sets the model of biblical redemption."[10] And, as we know from the progress of revelation, this redemption is never fully reached in the Old Testament. The New Testament reminds us that a final redemption, or a better exodus, awaits— an exodus inaugurated by the Messiah, the better Moses (e.g., Isa. 11:15; 43:2, 16, 19; 44:27; 48:21; 51:10–11; 52:12; Ezek. 20:33; cf. Ex. 13:21; 14:15–31). The New Testament answers the prophets' promise of a new exodus, linking Christ to the prophetic fulfillment of redemption and its outcome.[11] With the arrival of Immanuel in the New Testament epoch, "the God who in the past led a dispirited band of slaves out of Egypt was about to open a way into the future once again."[12] Christ, the presence of God in the world, makes final redemption available to the world.

Typifying Christ as the one who procures for us the new exodus,[13] the New Testament (and especially the Gospels) depicts Jesus as the one who rehashes Israel's and Moses's steps in Jesus's own ministry.[14]

---

[9] Michael D. Williams, *Far as the Curse Is Found: The Covenant Story of Redemption* (Phillipsburg, NJ: P&R, 2005), 22.

[10] Ibid.

[11] F. F. Bruce reports that the "word 'redemption' itself is drawn from the language of the Exodus and the return from exile: as the people of God were redeemed from slavery in Egypt and later from captivity in Babylon so in the fullness of time they were redeemed by the sacrifice of Christ from spiritual bondage under the 'elemental spirits of the universe' (Rom. 3:24; Gal. 4:3; Col. 4:15, 20)." F. F. Bruce, *The New Testament Development of Old Testament Themes* (Grand Rapids: Eerdmans, 1968), 33–34.

[12] Bernard W. Anderson, *The Unfolding Drama of the Bible*, 3rd ed. (Philadelphia: Fortress, 1988), 47. For further interaction with Isaiah's new exodus promise, see also Anderson, "Exodus Typology in Second Isaiah," in *Israel's Prophetic Heritage*, ed. Bernard W. Anderson and Walter J. Harrelson (New York: Harper & Row, 1962), 177–95.

[13] Mark Strom provides a helpful summary of Jesus's fulfillment of the exodus according to Matthew: "The Gospel of Matthew presents the early events of Jesus' life around a new exodus theme. Here are the highlights: (1) Jesus escaped Herod's attempt to kill all the male children (Matt. 2:13–15). Pharaoh had tried to kill Moses and the other Israelite children; (2) Jesus returned from Egypt to fulfill the prophecy of a new exodus (1:15; see Hos. 11:1); . . . (4) Jesus passed through the Jordan (Matt. 3:15–16); (5) Jesus was named God's Son (Matt. 3:17). This was the title God gave Israel before the exodus (Ex. 4:22); (6) Jesus went into the desert to be tempted for forty days (Matt. 4:1–11). He faced similar temptations to those Israel faced in the wilderness, and he quoted the scriptures which belonged to those original temptations; (7) Jesus gathered together his new people (Matt. 4:18–22) as the Lord had gathered Israel to himself; (8) Jesus went up on the mountain to give the new law (Matt. 5:1–7:29). He made direct comparisons to Moses on Mount Sinai." Mark Strom, *The Symphony of Scripture: Making Sense of the Bible's Many Themes* (Phillipsburg, NJ: P&R, 1990), 46–47.

[14] Goldingay adds: "Like Moses, Jesus exercises authority over the sea and the wind (Matt. 8:27; 14:24–33). Like Moses . . . he feeds people in miraculous ways—so profusely that there are twelve baskets of food left, enough for all twelve clans of Israel (Matt. 14:15–21). . . . He is like Moses, Elijah or Elisha but he is more than they were. He goes beyond Moses in walking on the sea despite the strength of the wind (John 6:16–21). He behaves more like God at the Red Sea than like Moses (see Ps. 77:19 [MT 20]; also Ps. 29). In manifesting the sovereignty over creation, Jesus manifests a characteristic of divinity." Goldingay, *Israel's Gospel*, 825. See also Richard Bauckham, *God Crucified: Monotheism and Christology in the New Testament* (Grand Rapids: Eerdmans, 1998), 25–42.

For example, in Matthew, "several aspects of the infancy account, such as the escape to Egypt and the killing of babies (2:13–23; see especially v. 15 and its citation of Hos. 11:1), also echo the exodus story of the Old Testament and help create the image of Jesus as a Mosaic figure who will save his people (cf. Ex. 3:10)."[15] So in his going to and coming from Egypt, Jesus is shown again to be the better Moses—the one who brings Israel from Egypt to the Land of Promise. In addition, "like Moses of old, the new Moses teaches on the mountain ([Matthew] chaps. 5–7, the sermon on the Mount; cf. Exodus 20–24, the giving of the law through Moses on Mount Sinai)."[16] Christ's ministry has to do with reenactment: when he comes, he re-creates the exodus to show that his messianic work is the final exodus because he is the one who brings final salvation.

In preparing the way for Christ, John the Baptist evokes the image and hopes of the exodus to describe the arrival of Israel's true Messiah (Matt. 3:1–3; Mark 1:1–3; Luke 3:1–6; John 1:19–23). Upon seeing the Christ, John proclaims, "Behold, the Lamb of God, who takes away the sin of the world!" (John 1:29). To John and every other educated Jew within earshot, this declaration would certainly recall the imagery of the Passover lamb. In identifying Christ with the sacrificial offering of the exodus, John

> connect[s] the whole system of Old Testament blood sacrifices in [the audience's] minds with the one who was being baptized. They may not have realized at the time, however, how radical the hope was that Christ would bring them, for he would in fact become their sacrifice and do away with the whole Old Testament system of sin sacrifices.[17]

As John's words foreshadow, the requisite sacrifices of the exodus and Sinai are made obsolete in Christ's redemptive work. His death, as the final sacrifice of God, is the true exodus, the final act of deliverance needed to remove sin and restore fellowship. This is obvi-

---

[15] Veli-Matti Kärkkäinen, *Christology: A Global Introduction—An Ecumenical, International, and Contextual Perspective* (Grand Rapids: Baker, 2003), 34.

[16] Ibid.

[17] Richard Patterson and Michael Travers, "Contours of the Exodus Motif in Jesus' Earthly Ministry," *WTJ* 66 (2004): 39.

ous when Jesus's sacrificial death occurs at the same hour that the paschal sacrifice was to die in the exodus ritual—an act that would remind all onlookers of John the Baptist's promise offered in John 1:29.[18]

In addition to the Baptist and the Gospels, Paul, in 1 Corinthians 5:7, applies similar language to Christ calling him "our Passover lamb." Peter also uses analogous exodus/paschal terminology when he describes "the precious blood of Christ, like that of a lamb without blemish or spot" (1 Pet. 1:19).[19] All that was once promised in the unblemished paschal lamb—that sacrifice that bears the wrath of God on behalf of his people—is now complete in the true and final Paschal Lamb, Jesus Christ.

We must not forget that the very heart of this new-exodus theme is the revelation that Christ is Immanuel, God with us. Christ is the very presence of God with his people for their salvation, just as God was earlier with his people leading them from Sinai to the Promised Land. When we hear the angel's announcement that Jesus shall be called Immanuel, not only should this recall the promises of Isaiah 7–9; it should also evoke the imagery and purpose of the exodus. Thus Robert Patterson and Michael Travers explain:

> With a simple declaration to a poor carpenter, the Lord promises the hope to his people that he would dwell among them. In exodus terms, it is as if they had been wandering in the wilderness and were now to enter the Promised Land. The New Testament presence of the Messiah brings to an end the sense of banishment the Israelites must have felt when God seemed to be ignoring them for all those years. . . . In effect, Jesus Christ brings to an end the exile [and exodus] of true Israel—those who would accept him as Messiah.[20]

---

[18] Picking up on a similar theme, George Balentine explains, "It is at the final Passover that Jesus dies as the true Passover Lamb of God, which according to the Johannine chronology is on the fourteenth of Nisan, the day of the Preparation of the Passover, at the time the paschal lambs were being sacrificed for the Passover." George L. Balentine, "Death of Jesus as a New Exodus," *Review and Expositor* 59 (1962): 34.

[19] As Balentine argues, 1 Pet. 1:19 is an allusion to Ex. 12:5, a text that speaks of the unblemished nature of the paschal lamb (ibid., 34). Furthermore, he quotes T. C. Smith: "While the blood of the Paschal lamb in itself did not effect deliverance but was a sign of deliverance (Ex. 12:13), the thought prevailed among the Jews that the deliverance from Egypt came about through the blood of the Paschal lamb. For Peter, release from Egyptian bondage by the blood of the Paschal lamb was a type of deliverance from the bondage of sin through Jesus Christ, the new Paschal lamb of the new Exodus." T. C. Smith, *Jesus in the Gospel of John* (Nashville: Broadman, 1959), 80–81.

[20] Patterson and Travers, "Exodus Motif," 38.

Christ, therefore, is like the manifestation of God in the wilderness of the first exodus. Just as God led his people from slavery to freedom, Christ brings people from their sin to the eschatological promises of the Lord (e.g., John 8:34; Gal. 5:1). Christ is the presence of God manifest in this world for deliverance, not merely from foreign oppression, but from the sin that separates the creation from the Lord's eschatological objectives.

Christ, Our Priest

Christ announces a true redemption—as his being the new Moses and the provider of the new exodus shows—and personally *accomplishes* that redemption. This work is set out in his priestly role and office. As we remember from chapter 4, the Israelite priest, coming from the tribe of Levi and the house of Aaron, administered the covenant, educated the people in God's law, and, most notably, offered sacrifices on behalf of sinners (Deut. 33:8–10; cf. Lev. 10:11; 2 Chron. 17:9).

Such acts, exemplified how the priests "served a mediatorial function between God and the covenant people. By offering sacrifices the priests represented the people before God, and by teaching the law they represented God before the people."[21] In other words, the central function of the priests was their mediation for Israel, in whose place they stood in the presence of God. This role of mediation was especially prominent on the annual Day of Atonement, when the high priest entered the Most Holy Place in the tabernacle/temple to atone for the sins of God's nation (Leviticus 16). As the priest's work of atonement illustrated, theirs was a privileged place: demarcating the priests' lives was an access to the presence of God unknown by the rest of Israel. But even in this place of privilege, the priesthood was only a shadow of what was to come when the Great High Priest would arrive.

The Great High Priest

As the Old Testament shows time and time again, the priesthood was not safe from the corruption of the fall. The infiltration of sin even in this office indicated a need for a better priest. God himself saw this

---

[21] Demarest, *Cross and Salvation*, 183.

need, and in responding to the insufficiency and broken nature of the priesthood, he promised, "I will raise up for myself a faithful priest, who shall do according to what is in my heart and in my mind. And I will build him a sure house, and he shall go in and out before my anointed forever" (1 Sam. 2:35). This promise was partially fulfilled in Samuel and the subsequent priests characterized by holiness. But even they looked forward to Jesus Christ, the Great High Priest, who administers salvation and offers *himself* as the atoning sacrifice so that the unrighteous may once again draw near to God.

To grasp Christ's priestly role let us turn first to the epistle of Hebrews, a letter that gives us great insight into the priesthood of Christ in both its fulfillment of and its superiority over Israel's priesthood and institutions (Heb. 3:1; 4:14–5:10; 7:24–10:25). According to the epistle, we find that Christ's supremacy extends over angels, Moses, *and* the Levitical priesthood. Utilizing the Old Testament promise of the enigmatic priest Melchizedek, cited in Genesis 14:18–20 and Psalm 110:4, the writer of Hebrews attributes the title of Great High Priest to Jesus Christ (Heb. 2:17; 4:14–5:10; 8:1–6). He is our Great High Priest because he comes from a better line—this priestly line of Melchizedek. In other words:

> By an irrevocable oath God appointed his sinless Son (Heb. 4:15; 7:26) to be high priest of a radically new order typified by Melchizedek, the godly priest-king of Salem (5:5–10). Because he came from the line of Judah he had no claim to an Aaronic priesthood but, as the author of Hebrews clarifies, Christ comes from a better line, the line of Melchizedek. This "king of righteousness" and "king of peace" exercised a priesthood that was superior to the Aaronic order (7:1–10) for several reasons: (1) Abraham, the ancestor of Levi, paid tithes to Melchizedek; (2) Melchizedek blessed the patriarch Abraham; and (3) Melchizedek "lives on" (NASB), whereas the Levitical priests all succumbed to death.[22]

Being a part of the line of this priest-king qualitatively sets Christ apart from the house of Aaron. He is the better priest because he belongs to

---

[22] Ibid., 184.

a priesthood not marked by sin and unrighteousness, and, as such, his priestly office can and will accomplish everything the former could not.

Building upon Christ's Melchizedekian lineage, the author of Hebrews demonstrates Christ's superior priesthood through an examination of his perfection. Unlike the priests of old, the sinless Christ does not need to offer sacrifice for himself before he atones for the sins of the people (Heb. 5:1–4; 7:23, 27). Nor does Christ require another priest to replace him, because sin and death do not reign over him as they did with the priests of old (Heb. 7:24). Instead, Jesus is the Great High Priest because his priesthood is perfect and eternal. It does not falter and it will not end.

Christ's priestly superiority is even greater in the context of his humanity. Jesus, as priest, experiences the same human struggle and temptations but overcomes them to remain the Great High Priest. He is, therefore, one who is fully able to "sympathize with our weaknesses" because he "in every respect has been tempted as we are, yet without sin" (Heb. 4:15). Jesus is superior not only because he is perfect and blameless, but also because he overcomes sin to remain holy. Because of his superiority as the Great High Priest, Jesus Christ "is able to save to the uttermost those who draw near to God through him, since he always lives to make intercession for them" (Heb. 7:25). As the perfect priest, then, Christ supersedes the Levitical priesthood, its mediation, its sacrifices, and its atonement (Heb. 7:26–28).

The Perfect Sacrifice

However, as the New Testament reveals, Christ is not only priest; he is simultaneously the final and effectual atoning sacrifice (Eph. 5:2). Simply put, Jesus is both sinless priest and spotless offering for sin. As Hebrews 2:17 reveals, part and parcel of Christ's becoming man is his intent to be the priest who would ultimately deal with sin: "Therefore he had to be made like his brothers in every respect, so that he might become a merciful and faithful high priest in the service of God, to make propitiation for the sins of the people" (cf. Heb. 5:9). But as the New Testament unfolds, we begin to realize that Jesus is both the "offerer" and the offering of atonement. He is, therefore, altogether the true priest and the one, perfect lamb (1 Cor. 5:7), the sinless offering for sin (2 Cor. 5:21; 1 Pet. 2:24). He is the superior sacrifice and thus the final sacrifice (Heb. 10:3). Though the blood of bulls and goats cannot take away sins it is his blood poured out on the cross that can and has redeemed the lost (Heb. 10:4; cf. Ps. 40:6–8). His priestly work is to take upon himself the curse which God declared on all who break his covenant (Deut. 11:26–28; Gal. 3:10–14).[23]

As the perfect High Priest and the perfect sacrifice, Christ completes all that the Old Testament sacrificial system promises.

Just as Christ made the temple obsolete, so Christ, as our Great High Priest, realizes all that the sacrificial system represented. Therefore, his "death supersedes the OT cultus, as reality supersedes a mere foreshadowing ([Heb.] 10:1–4); it effects in the conscience of the believer the forgiveness and purification that the OT cultus could effect only in an external manner (10:5–18)."[24] In Christ, sacrifices are no longer necessary because his death is the one and only atoning sacrifice that takes away the sins of the world (Heb. 7:27; 9:12, 24–28; 10:1–2, 10, 12, 14; 13:12).

Again, this is seen particularly in the context of the Day of Atonement. Here, Jesus "carries out on a cosmic scale the functions repeatedly and ineffectually performed by the high priest of the earthly sanctuary."[25] The workings and purposes of this Old Testament ceremonial ritual, great as it was, were incapable of dealing with the greater problem of internal sin. As a consequence, Israel's transgressions multiplied. This is why there was a constant need for cleansing and this annual shedding of blood. The yearly recurrence of the Day of Atonement highlights both the habitual nature of sin and, even more, the need for a better sacrifice. As the author of Hebrews contends, "It is impossible for the blood of bulls and goats to take away sins" (Heb. 10:4; cf. 1 Sam. 15:22ff.; Pss. 49:7–9; 50:7–15; 51:16–17; Isa. 1:11–20).[26]

---

[23] Goldsworthy, *According to Plan*, 205.

[24] Paul Ellingworth, "Priests," in *New Dictionary of Biblical Theology*, ed. T. Desmond Alexander et al. (Downers Grove, IL: InterVarsity, 2000), 700.

[25] Ibid.

[26] As Letham writes, "The most crucial difference of all [between Christ's priesthood and the Aaronic priesthood], of course, is that theirs were only animal sacrifices which had no intrinsic power to atone for human sins, *whereas his was the sacrifice of himself, the Son of God who was simultaneously sinless man.*" Letham, *Work of Christ*, 112, emphasis original.

It is Christ, our Great High Priest, who finally delivers the promises of the Old Testament Day of Atonement and the sacrificial system.[27] The Day of Atonement was provisional—a ritual established to point to something far greater than itself. As Hebrews and the rest of the New Testament unfold, this something greater is the sacrificial act of Jesus's death on the cross. Christ is the better sacrifice; he is the one who accomplishes what the animal sacrifices could not. Thus Vern Poythress states, "Because Christ had died, the animal sacrifices are ended, and we have access to God with freedom (Romans 5:1–2)."[28] By sacrificing himself, Christ removes all that stands between God and man. He is the Great High Priest who enters the heavenly temple and offers himself in the presence of God for our salvation in order to inaugurate the redemptive promises of God for his people. The author of Hebrews makes this clear:

> Christ has entered, not into holy places made with hands, which are copies of the true things, but into heaven itself, now to appear in the presence of God on our behalf. Nor was it to offer himself repeatedly, as the high priest enters the holy places every year with blood not his own, for then he would have had to suffer repeatedly since the foundation of the world. But as it is, he has appeared once for all at the end of the ages to put away sin by the sacrifice of himself. (Heb. 9:24–26)

In finishing what was promised in the Old Testament sacrificial system, Christ "surrendered his life and shed his blood once-for-all as the truly effectual sacrifice that frees from guilt and makes holy ([Heb.] 7:27; 9:15, 26, 28; 10:5–10, 12)."[29] As in the sacrifices offered in the earthly Holy of Holies, now upon Christ's head the sins of the people are transferred and finally removed (Lev. 1:4; 4:20, 26, 31; 6:7).[30] This

---

[27] Christ is the fulfillment of the Passover promises. He is the lamb without blemish offered in the place of his people (Ex. 12:5) whose life is poured out so that when Yahweh sees the blood, he passes over the people's transgressions, providing their deliverance (Ex. 12:13).

[28] Vern S. Poythress, *The Shadow of Christ in the Law of Moses* (Brentwood, TN: Wolgemuth & Hyatt, 1991), 13.

[29] Demarest, *Cross and Salvation*, 185.

[30] Leon Morris explains that the Old Testament act of the priest's laying his hands upon the sacrificial animal "was a symbolic transferral of the sins of the worshipper to the animal, so that when it died it was taking the punishment due to the worshipper for his sins. It was being treated as the sin it bore deserved. They [those seeing this act as the transferring of one's sin to the sacrifice] hold that this is the obvious symbolism and that it is supported by the fact that in later times at least there are passages which tell us that, as the worshipper laid his hands on the animal, he confessed his sins. It is not easy to see what the laying on of hands means if there is no symbolic transfer to the animal which was to die of the sins being confessed." Leon Morris, *The Atonement: Its Meaning and*

is the superiority of Christ's atoning sacrifice: unlike the Levitical high priests, who were many in number and temporary (Heb. 7:23–27)—needing daily and yearly atonement for their own sins (7:26–27) before they could mediate atonement for others through the insufficient blood of animals (7:27; 9:13)—Christ enters the presence of God through his own blood (9:11–12; 24) as the one, permanent, and eternal Mediator (7:23–24), who atones once and for all (7:27) through the sacrifice of himself (7:27; 9:11–14).[31]

The rest of the New Testament also emphasizes the priestly work of Christ, especially in his providing atonement for sin. The New Testament consistently shows us that Christ dies in the place of his people, taking upon himself their sin and their curse (Mark 10:45; Gal. 3:13).[32] As the Gospels assert, he is the one who "came not to be served but to serve, and to give his live as a ransom for many" (Mark 10:45; cf. Luke 22:19–20; John 10:11, 15; 2 Cor. 5:21; 1 Tim. 2:5–6). And as the epistles maintain, he is the one who "suffered once for sins, the righteous for the unrighteous, that he might bring us to God" (1 Pet. 3:18).[33] Robert Yarbrough summarizes the New Testament portrayal of Christ:

> Jesus is presented as having paid the penalty for sin (Rom. 3:25–26; 6:23; Gal. 3:13). He died in place of sinners so that they might become God's righteousness (2 Cor. 5:21). He redeemed sinners through his blood (Eph. 1:7). He paid the price for sinners to go free (1 Cor. 6:20; Gal. 5:1). He won the victory over death and sin, sharing with believers the victory (1 Cor. 15:55–57) that he paraded in spectacular fashion by his cross (Col. 2:15). He put an end to the hostility between warring human factions, most notably Jews and

---

Significance (Downers Grove, IL: InterVarsity, 1983), 47. This transmission of sins takes place with Christ on the cross as Jesus himself "suffered outside the gate in order to sanctify the people through his blood" (Heb. 13:12; cf. John 1:29; Acts 8:32; 1 John 3:5).

[31] The finality of Christ's sacrificial work is evident throughout Hebrews especially in those passages which tell of Jesus's "once for all" activity. We see therefore that Christ "has no need, like those high priests, to offer sacrifices daily, first for his own sins and then for those of the people, since he did this *once for all* when he offered up himself" (Heb. 7:27); "he entered *once for all* into the holy places, not by means of the blood of goats and calves but by the means of his own blood, thus securing eternal redemption" (9:12); by his "will we have been sanctified through the offering of the body of Jesus Christ *once for all*" (10:10); he also "offered for all time a single sacrifice for sins" (10:12); "by a single offering, he has perfected for all time those who are being sanctified" (10:14), and as a result, there is no longer a need for another sacrifice for sin (10:18).

[32] As O. Palmer Robertson explains: "Christ delivers from the curse of the covenant. No remission from guilty transgression could be gained without the shedding of blood. Christ therefore presented his body as the sacrificial victim of the covenant curse." O. Palmer Robertson, *The Christ of the Covenants* (Phillipsburg, NJ: P&R, 1980), 31.

[33] It should be noted that the purpose Peter gives for Christ's atoning death is "to bring us to God." In other words, Christ, the presence of God incarnate, dies on our behalf to open access to God himself. Christ, God with us, is the means to the Lord's eschatological presence.

Gentiles (Eph. 2:14–18), with implications for our ethnic divisions. His example of patient suffering according to God's will and the demands of his kingdom is a precedent for his people to follow (1 Pet. 2:21–23).[34]

Thus understood, Christ's priestly work is his work of atonement through which he redeems a people by his death in order that they may enter once and for all into the place of God's presence.

To understand his atoning work further, we must first recognize Christ's sacrifice as penal and substitutionary.[35] In other words, Jesus endures punishment (penalty) for the sins of others (substitution). The New Testament repeatedly emphasizes, "Christ himself willingly submitted to the just penalty which we deserved, receiving it on our behalf and in our place so that we will not have to bear it ourselves"[36] (e.g., Isa. 53:4–6, 10; Mark 10:45; John 10:15; 11:51–52; Rom. 4:23–25; Gal. 1:4; 2:20; 1 Tim. 2:5–6; Titus 2:11–14; 1 Pet. 1:18–19). As the substitute, Christ bears the sins of many when God makes him who has no sin to be sin for us (2 Cor. 5:21).

Moreover, Jesus's sacrifice is also expiatory, propitiatory, and redemptive in nature. Regarding his work of expiation and propitiation, this means that his penal-substitutionary work removes both the guilt of sinners and the righteous wrath of God. Like the scapegoat upon

---

[34] R. W. Yarbrough, "Atonement," in Alexander et al., *New Dictionary of Biblical Theology*, 391.

[35] Though it is a topic fiercely debated, I believe the purpose of the atonement centers on its penal-substitutionary nature. By no means am I arguing that the other aspects are lost in this emphasis; instead I contend that they stem from Christ's taking on the punishment of sin as our substitute. So Schreiner argues: "The riches of what God has accomplished in Christ for his people are not exhausted by penal substitution. The multifaceted character of the atonement must be recognized to do justice to the canonical witness. God's people are impoverished if Christ's triumph over evil powers at the cross is slighted, or Christ's exemplary love is shoved to the side, or the healing bestowed on believers by Christ's cross and resurrection is downplayed. While not denying the wide-ranging character of Christ's atonement, I am arguing that penal substitution is foundational and the heart of the atonement." Thomas R. Schreiner, "Penal Substitution View," in *The Nature of the Atonement: Four Views*, ed. James Beilby and Paul R. Eddy (Downers Grove, IL: InterVarsity, 2006), 67. For a sample of works that uphold the centrality and importance of this view, see Letham, *Work of Christ*, 125–94; Charles E. Hill and Frank A. James, eds., *The Glory of the Atonement: Biblical, Theological, and Practical Perspectives* (Downers Grove, IL: InterVarsity, 2004); Derek Tidball, *The Message of the Cross* (Downers Grove, IL: InterVarsity, 2001); Steve Jeffery, Michael Ovey, and Andrew Sach, *Pierced for Our Transgressions: Rediscovering the Glory of Penal Substitution* (Wheaton, IL: Crossway, 2007); J. I. Packer and Mark Dever, *In My Place Condemned He Stood: Celebrating the Glory of the Atonement* (Wheaton, IL: Crossway, 2007); Garry J. Williams, "Penal Substitution: A Response to Recent Criticisms," *JETS* 50 (2007): 71–86. For recent works that attempt to curtail the emphasis historically placed on this aspect of the atonement, see Steve Chalke and Alan Mann, *The Lost Message of Jesus* (Grand Rapids: Zondervan, 2003); Joel B. Green and Mark D. Baker, *Recovering the Scandal of the Cross: Atonement in New Testament and Contemporary Contexts* (Downers Grove, IL: InterVarsity, 2000); Alan Mann, *Atonement for a Sinless Society: Engaging with an Emergent Culture* (Milton Keynes, UK: Paternoster, 2005): Tom Smail, *Once and for All: A Confession of the Cross* (London: Darton, Longman, & Todd, 1998).

[36] Letham, *Work of Christ*, 133.

which the sins of Israel were transferred, Christ eliminates the guilt of sin through his own work outside the camp on Golgatha (Lev. 16:20–22; Ps. 103:12; Isa. 44:22–23; Mic. 7:19; Matt. 21:39; 27:32; John 19:17–20; Heb. 13:12). Furthermore, Christ's atoning sacrifice placates the wrath of God against those who find their hope in the death and resurrection of the Father's Son. Through his death, Christ finally and completely deals with sin and its implications, thereby removing the greatest obstacles that keep man from the presence of God.

The New Testament also emphasizes that God redeems, or ransoms, sinners from their bondage to sin in order that they may become God's own possession through the blood of Christ (Matt. 20:28; Mark 10:45; Eph. 1:7; Col. 1:13–14). The apostle Peter says that Christians' debts are paid "not with perishable things such as silver or gold, but with the precious blood of Christ, like that of a lamb without blemish or spot" (1 Pet. 1:18–19). As noted earlier, Christ is the Paschal Lamb who takes away the sins of the world. Through God's presence in Christ, the fallen return to God and his covenant promises. It is by way of Jesus's blood that the Lord finally redeems believers and restores his redemptive objectives.

As the divine presence in this world, Christ comes to bring fallen humanity back into relationship with the unrestricted presence of God once experienced in Eden and awaiting us in the new heaven and new earth. Reconciling his people so that we may again come before the Lord's eschatological presence is the great outcome of Christ's work in history. Through the blood of Immanuel, God is present to secure a future that will, in the end, be defined by eternal and unmediated access to the Lord. In dying on behalf of sinners, Christ moves us from children of wrath to God's adopted sons and daughters (Rom. 5:10–11; 2 Cor. 5:18–21; Eph. 2:11–22; Col. 1:19–20). It is his very real, very physical death that leads us out of a state of enmity with God into a renewed relationship marked by the future promise of being present with God.

In sum, the cross "is the goal of his mission, for through it he enables human beings to be reconciled to God."[37] The original fellowship that Adam enjoyed with God before the fall has been restored and

---

[37] T. Desmond Alexander, *The Servant King: The Bible's Portrait of the Messiah* (Vancouver: Regent, 1998), 147.

surpassed through the death, burial, resurrection, and ascension of Immanuel (cf. 1 Cor. 15:3, 22; Rom. 5:12–21). Leon Morris concurs:

> Our sins separate us from God (Isa. 59:2). We have no way to remedy the situation. But Christ has opened for his people the way into the very presence of God. . . . [Christians] need the mediation of no earthly priest. Indeed, now all of life is lived in God's presence. . . . Christ's fulfillment of the Day of Atonement ceremonies has opened up the way into the very presence of God for the humblest of his people.[38]

Jesus's atonement opens the doors to the completion of God's eschatological agenda; for through his blood, Christ provides safe access for fallen, finite creatures to the holy and transcendent covenant Lord. No longer are our sins counted against us. Instead, the Lord reconciles transgressors to himself through the shed blood of Jesus Christ (2 Cor. 5:18).

Christ, Our Servant-King

In his final office, Christ comes to the earth as king to rule and reign in such a way that ushers in a new kingdom and new creation where the eschatological objectives of God reach their culmination. For this reason, the New Testament casts Christ as the son of David, Israel's greatest king. In this role, Jesus completes all that David could not, owing to the earthly king's sin and death. As we remember, David and Solomon ushered in the golden age of Israel. The kingdom of David was the supposed end to which all the promises of God pointed. But this was not the beginning of Israel's climactic ascendancy; it was sadly its short-lived finale. After David's rule, the nation slipped deeper and deeper into sin and finally into exile. In the constant ebb and flow of Israel's sinful degeneration, all the promises of God were trampled under Assyrian, Babylonian, and Roman feet.

Still, Israel's downfall did not stop God; it was, in fact, part of God's greater plan to bring praise to himself and his presence to his people. All of this Christ accomplishes. God sends Christ into the world to pick

---

[38] Morris, *Atonement*, 87.

up the trampled pieces of God's redemptive agenda. He comes to be the better David. He comes to be our servant-king. He comes to die for sinners. And he enters history to establish the true kingdom through which all of God's redemptive agenda will culminate.

The Better David

To understand Christ's kingly office we begin with Christ as the son of David.[39] The New Testament takes pains to show Christ's Davidic lineage (e.g., Matt. 1:1; 9:27; 12:23; 15:22; 20:30; 21:9, 15; Mark 10:47–48; 11:10; Luke 1:27, 32–33; 2:4, 11, 26; Rom. 1:3–5; Rev. 5:5–6; 22:16).[40] This royal emphasis links Christ with the Davidic covenant as well as the promises of the psalmists and prophets who declare the coming of a better king, one of David's own descendants, who would fulfill the promises of God.[41]

For example, as touched on earlier, this is the point of Matthew's genealogy in chapter 1.[42] Matthew "affirms emphatically that Jesus is both an anointed one ('Christ') and a descendant of David ('son of David')."[43] Later in Matthew, the Christ-David "connection is made most explicit at Jesus' entry into Jerusalem, when Jesus is identified as the king and the 'Son of David' (21:5, 9, 15)."[44] Here in the midst of the Jewish authorities, the Hebrew crowd presses in on Jesus to take him as their king. They see him as the promised son of David who would bring them back into political prominence and punish their oppressors

---

[39] As Horton summarizes: "Christ is the son of David, the Messiah, whose origin is 'from of old,' and yet whose life will be unending, guaranteeing the security of David's house and throne forever. No thanks to his people, YHWH has himself ensured the fulfillment of his promise. It was this royal title to which the two blind men appealed, 'crying loudly, "Have mercy on us, Son of David!"' (Matt. 9:27; cf. Luke 18:35–40). And Luke's Gospel is eager to make this connection in the birth narrative (Luke 2:4). The Son of David theme is raised finally in Revelation 5. In this heavenly scene, no one is able to break the seals of the scroll and open it. Only one person—the Lamb who was slain, 'the Lion of the tribe of Judah, the Root of David'—is qualified to explain the mystery of history, because he is its fulfillment. The 'new David' becomes the catalyst finally for the unending 'new song' of the saints (vv. 8–10)." Michael S. Horton, *Lord and Servant: A Covenant Christology* (Louisville: Westminster John Knox, 2005), 265.

[40] T. Desmond Alexander contends: "It is possible to interpret several [Old Testament] passages as implying that the king is divine (Isa. 9:6–7; Jer. 23:5–6; cf. Ps. 45:6). While some scholars dismiss the significance of these references to the divine nature of the Davidic king as hyperbole, there can be little doubt that these passages support the New Testament belief that Jesus, as the promised Davidic king, is divine. What appear in the Old Testament as pointers to this reality are filled out and confirmed in the New Testament writings." Alexander, *Servant King*, 142.

[41] We saw this descendant promise explicitly in 2 Sam. 7:12–13. But as the New Testament advances the promise, Christ not only builds a house for God's name; he *is* the house of God's name.

[42] Or as Cleon Rogers has argued: "The promises to David in the Gospels show that Jesus came as the Son of David, with all the credentials necessary to demonstrate that He is the promised Messiah. He came from the family of David; He was born in the city of David; He was preceded by the forerunner of the Messiah, who was to prepare the way for the Davidic kingdom." Cleon L. Rogers Jr., "The Davidic Covenant in the Gospels," *BSac* 150 (1993): 478.

[43] Alexander, *Servant King*, 122.

[44] Kärkkäinen, *Christology*, 34.

once and for all. This, however, is not Christ's kingly mission. Instead, his royal way leads first to the cross, then to the throne.

Jesus also fulfills the Davidic promises of Psalms. This is made quite explicit in Peter's sermon at Pentecost (Acts 2:22–36; cf. 13:34ff.; Phil. 2:9–11). In confronting the scoffers and the cynics, Peter, like Paul in Acts 13,[45] picks up on Christ's superior kingship as compared with Israel's ideal king, David. Upon establishing the validity of the new covenant work of the Spirit (Joel 2:28–32; Acts 2:16–21), Peter addresses Christ and his place as the true messianic king of Israel. As we saw earlier, Peter shows how Christ completes all that David promised in Psalm 16:8–11. In exegeting the passage, Peter focuses on Christ's fulfillment of David's promise that the Lord's Holy One would not be abandoned to Sheol or see corruption of any kind (Ps. 16:10; Acts 2:22, 29–32).

As Peter reports, David both died and was buried. His audience knows this because they know the location of his tomb (Acts 2:29). What Peter wants us to see is that the promises of Psalm 16 are appropriated not by David, but by David's offspring Jesus Christ. Building off David's prophetic and covenantal status, Peter reveals that David "foresaw and spoke about the resurrection of the Christ" (Acts 2:30–31). By way of the resurrection, Christ conquers death, keeping his soul from being "abandoned to Hades" and "his flesh from [seeing] corruption" (2:31). Instead, God raises Christ from the dead to give him his rightful place on the greater throne, at the right hand of the Almighty, where he rules and reigns in a way that far surpasses the throne of the great but fallible King David.

David's prophetic words in Psalm 16 point to a better king—a king never to be defeated by death or to receive death's eternal consequences. Jesus Christ is the better king because he is *the* Davidic descendant who will rule in righteousness (Ps. 72:1–2; cf. 101:1–4) and complete the deliverance of his people (Pss. 72:4, 12–14; 101:6);

---

[45] In Acts 13:22–23, Paul clarifies that God responded to the Israelite demands for a king with David, the proper king who replaced Saul, and who the Lord said was "a man after my own heart, who will do all my will" (13:22). Yet, interestingly, Paul does not end with David. Instead, he uses David as a springboard to the fulfillment of David in Jesus Christ. The apostle declares, "Of this man's offspring God has brought to Israel a Savior, Jesus, as he promised" (13:23). To defend the truth of the gospel, Paul emphasizes Christ as the fulfillment of David, showing that through Jesse's line the messianic promises find completion. Through this old covenant reality of this former ruler, Paul introduces the new covenant reality of Jesus Christ, the better Davidic king (e.g., Luke 22:20; Hebrews 8). We can see the argument that Paul makes: Christ is the better David, the one who fulfills all of the Davidic promises and messianic expectations connected to the former king of Israel.

his reign will be limitless (Ps. 72:5, 15), and his kingdom will know no end (Ps. 72:8–11; cf. 86:9; Isa. 11:1–5, 60–62); and he is the one who expands the Lord's dynasty to its fullest potential (Ps. 72:16). In short, it is in Christ that we have "a transformed kingship—a human embodiment of the rule of Yahweh."[46] The presence of God in the Davidic king promises that the perfect reign and perfect redemptive plan of God would fully come in Jesus of Nazareth.[47] As Isaiah foresaw, "The LORD is our king; he will save us" (Isa. 33:22)—a reality that has taken place in Christ, the better David.

The Servant-King

Remarkably, it is suffering that defines Christ's kingship. Soon after exalting him as the son of David, the Jews put their king to death (Mark 15:32). In a horrific twist, the Roman soldiers, in ridiculing Christ, actually adorn him with mock symbols of royalty, an act that— reprehensible as it is—evokes the image of the servant-king. On the long climb up Golgatha, covered in the ragged robe of royalty and crowned with the crown of thorns, Christ becomes the real king of the Jews by becoming the suffering servant of God (Matt. 3:17; 8:17; 13:14–15; 23:37; 27:5–10, 27–31; Luke 23:11).

Recall the emphasis of the Old Testament prophets. As discussed in the last chapter, the prophets, particularly Isaiah, put forth two specific roles for the Messiah.[48] First, he would be the suffering servant. Second, he would be the royal seed of David. So not only was the Messiah going to be a reigning king from the line of David; he would also be the suffering servant who would atone for sin. Foretold by the prophets, these two realities combine in Jesus of Nazareth. And though Israel is closed-minded to the unification of these ideas, clinging desperately to the notion that the Messiah will politically and militaristically domi-

---

[46] Stephen G. Dempster, *Dominion and Dynasty: A Theology of the Hebrew Bible*, NSBT 15 (Downers Grove, IL: InterVarsity, 2003), 138.

[47] For the Gospels' accounts of Christ's Davidic descent and its redemptive promises, see, e.g., Matt. 1:1, 17; 2:2; 9:27; 12:23; 15:22; 20:30–31; 21:9, 15; 22:42–46; Mark 10:47–48; 11:10; 12:35–37; Luke 1:27, 32, 69; 2:11; 18:38–39; 19:38; 20:42–44; John 7:42; cf. 2 Sam. 7:12–16; Ps. 89:4; Jer. 23:5; Mic. 5:2.

[48] Central to the portrait of Jesus in the four Gospels is the belief that he fulfills the Old Testament expectations concerning a future Davidic king who would be God's Messiah and pour forth the Lord's blessing upon the nations. Jesus's messianic fulfillment lies at the heart of how the early church viewed him and is reflected in his titular designation as the "Christ." Χριστός, meaning "anointed one," is the Greek equivalent of the Hebrew word for Messiah. Accordingly, the name "Jesus Christ" is also a title and, to the first hearers, was most likely understood to mean "Jesus the anointed one" (e.g., John 1:41).

nate God's enemies, Christ fulfills both in his own time and on his own terms to conquer the real enemy of God's people: their sin. To the annoyance of many, Christ comes to initiate his kingdom through suffering and calls his own to follow him to do the same. He dies to prepare the way for his triumphant return as the warrior-king who comes to judge the world and fulfill all of God's "new creation" promises. Simply put, Christ is simultaneously the Davidic king and suffering servant. He is the king who hung on a cross. He is the servant-king who both atones for the sins of the world and ushers in the royal reign of God.[49]

What is more, Christ's suffering is vital for his kingly role, as it is through his sinless death that he is able to reign forever and bring cleansed sinners once again into his kingdom. From this perspective, Christ's death assimilates his kingship. In his suffering, his disciples

> were made whole, restored to health, "justified" or brought into a right relationship with one another. This is the most astounding testimony of the Bible: that God chose the way of humiliation, suffering, rejection, and defeat to make known divine glory and triumph in the world. And this is the truth which is fulfilled and "made flesh" in the New Testament.[50]

His being "crushed for our iniquities" (Isa. 53:5) forms the basis for his universal kingship and the inherent achievement of the eschatological agenda.

Christ's sacrifice ends in his glorification. This is most evident in the outcome of his suffering. When Jesus dies and is raised from the dead, he finally takes his rightful place of authority and rule at the right hand of God the Father.[51] Based on Christ's sacrificial suffering, God places him "at his right hand in the heavenly places, far above all rule and authority and power and dominion, and above every name that is

---

[49] What is more, it appears that the Gospels understand Christ's healing ministry in terms of Isaiah's servant songs as well. As Kärkkäinen asserts: "In Matthew 8:17, Jesus' healing ministry is seen as a fulfillment of Isaiah 53:4. 'He took up our infirmities and carried our sorrows,' while in Matthew 12:15–21, Jesus' withdrawal from public attention is understood in light of the first Servant Song (Isa. 42:1–4)." Kärkkäinen, *Christology*, 35.

[50] Anderson, *Unfolding Drama of the Bible*, 50.

[51] As the New Testament continues, we see that Christ's work has an intercessory element to it. On behalf of believers, Jesus intercedes in order that the elect may enter God's presence once and for all. In doing this, Christ continues to apply the benefits of his singular redemptive work to his people for eternity. So, for example, in Rom. 8:34, Paul reveals, "Christ Jesus is the one who died—more than that, who was raised—who is at the right hand of God, who indeed is interceding for us." Similarly, 1 John 2:1 states, "If anyone does sin, we have an advocate with the Father, Jesus Christ the righteous." This would also seem to be a purpose in Christ's going to heaven to prepare a place for us in the presence of God (John 14:2–3). See also Heb. 7:25.

named, not only in this age but also in the one to come" (Eph. 1:20–21; cf. Matt. 28:18; 1 Cor. 15:25).[52]

Christ is not ruled by death and disorder; instead, he is the ruler who brings eternal life and a new order so that his reign as the forever king starts at his resurrection. Following his death, Christ is raised by the Lord, and this, "after all, signifies the arrival of the age to come—the promised age of salvation and new creation that God had pledged. The new exodus and the new creation have arrived through the suffering and resurrection of Jesus."[53] Those who confess Christ to be their Savior, the one who has taken the penalty of their sin upon his back, will be inducted into the kingdom of God's eternal presence (Matt. 10:32; Col. 1:13–14).

The Coming Kingdom

What is this kingdom? The New Testament picks up on the importance of the kingdom theme right from the start. Matthew's Gospel opens Jesus's ministry with the declaration, "In those days John the Baptist came preaching in the wilderness of Judea, 'Repent, for the kingdom of heaven is at hand'" (Matt. 3:1–2). John's role, by his own admission, is to prepare the way for Jesus, who himself is the agent of the kingdom's completion. Though John has great insight into Christ's kingdom fulfillment, we also see that even the Messiah's forerunner is unsure of Jesus and his ministry, and how he fits into the broader categories of the Old Testament promises. To clarify Christ's messianic claims, John sends messengers to ask Jesus, "Are you the one who is to come, or shall we look for another?" (Matt. 11:3). As Schreiner understands this, "John the Baptist voiced doubts about Jesus, presumably because he languished in prison, and his expectations regarding the kingdom were not realized. We can think back to the words of his father, Zechariah, anticipating salvation, 'from our enemies and from the hand of all who hate us' (Luke 1:71)."[54] As John assesses Jesus's ministry in light of such

---

[52] This heavenly reign will yield to the fullness of Christ's kingship realized in his second advent when he comes to complete the Old Testament promises as the monarch over the cosmos and ruling warrior who finally and fully reclaims the world for God (Matt. 26:64; 2 Thess. 1:7–10; Rev. 19:11–16). In his second coming, then, Christ will consummate what it means to be king, and the world will recognize his reign, bowing every knee (Phil. 2:10) before the true King of kings and Lord of lords (Rev. 19:16).

[53] Thomas R. Schreiner, *New Testament Theology: Magnifying God in Christ* (Grand Rapids: Baker, 2008), 276.

[54] Ibid., 56.

a political-social emphasis, it is understandable that his own messianic expectations, as well as the rest of Israel's, are not being met in Christ's fledgling and—in the eyes of the world—insignificant ministry.

Christ's answer to John's question, though, is critical for our understanding of God's kingdom. To assuage John's doubts, Christ catalogs his works in a way that recalls the Old Testament promises of God's eschatological objectives. Jesus assures his herald by telling his questioners, "Go and tell John what you hear and see: the blind receive their sight and the lame walk, lepers are cleansed and the deaf hear, and the dead are raised up, and the poor have good news preached to them. And blessed is the one who is not offended by me" (Matt. 11:4–6). In his response, Christ turns John's attention from the political fulfillment of the kingdom to the inauguration of the "Edenic/new creation" nature of his ministry (Revelation 21–22). Christ's language would surely remind John and others of the broader prophetic imagery of Isaiah who—in portraying the work of the coming Messiah—announced that God's people

> shall see the glory of the LORD . . . .
>
> He will come and save you.
>
> Then the eyes of the blind shall be opened,
>   and ears of the deaf unstopped;
> then shall the lame man leap like a deer,
>   and the tongue of the mute sing for joy. (Isa. 35:1–10, quoting
>   vv. 2, 4–6; cf. 29:18; 40:9; 42:6–7; 52:7; 58:6; 61:1–2;
>   65:17–25; Luke 4:18–19)

The basis for Christ's kingdom work, according to the prophet and Christ, is that in Christ the glory of God is with his people to redeem and heal (Isa. 35:2). He strengthens the weak and makes firm the feeble because he is God present to redeem a people to reside in his presence forever (Isa. 35:3–4). The promise of Isaiah that "[God] will come and save you" (Isa. 35:4) finally reaches fruition in the kingdom of Christ.

Against the backdrop of Isaiah 35, Christ's portrayal of the kingdom details an exiled people entering into a land reminiscent of the former Eden—a land described in terms similar to the New Jerusalem, where the inhabitants see the presence of God in his full majesty through the Lord's coming to save. Schreiner observes:

> The remarkable thing about Isa. 35 is that it clearly speaks of a new creative work of God. The wilderness will become as beautiful and lush as a garden. The desert will flow with streams of water. No rapacious beast will destroy anyone, and when Israel returns to Zion with inexpressible joy, they will be blessed forever. Here we have the language of the new creation and the new exodus.[55]

Through his teachings and ministry, Jesus clarifies that his fulfillment comes in cosmic terms including, and even surpassing, the limited perceptions of Israel's own nationalistic messianic assumptions.

Christ, therefore, comes to save not predominantly from external oppression but from the bondage of sin in order to reconcile a people to the eternal joy of God's relational and eschatological presence. To be sure, this is a kingdom that surpasses the great powers of Egypt, Assyria, Babylon, and Rome, which line Israel's history of nationalistic suppression. This kingdom of God brings the reign of God's presence to all the earth, replacing the old earth with the new creation. In other words, the eschatological objectives of God are synonymous with the purposes of God's kingdom. Christ's kingly work appropriates a greater dynasty and a greater dominion, all so that the people of God can reside in the kingdom of God's eternal presence.

As the true king, Christ opens up a new kingdom for his people. To do this, the heavenly king comes to be the earthly king who does what his earlier vice-regents could not accomplish because of their pervasive sin. Thus understood, Christ comes to establish his dynasty and his dominion that his kingdom may flourish over the face of the earth. It is in the kingdom of heaven that the Lord gives his people a new land to be in the eternal presence of God under his good and sovereign reign.

Conclusion

Through his Old Testament prophet, Yahweh declares,

> The LORD your God is in your midst,
> a mighty one who will save;

---

[55] Ibid.

he will rejoice over you with gladness;
    he will quiet you by his love;
he will exalt over you with loud singing. . . .

Behold, at that time I will deal
    with all your oppressors.
And I will save the lame
    and gather the outcast,
and I will change their shame into praise
    and renown in all the earth. (Zeph. 3:17, 19)

The fulfillment of these prophetic words is the theological storyline of the New Testament. For in Christ, the Lord has truly come to be in the midst of his people to save. His arrival is the dawn of the new covenant age in which salvation's goals are finally accomplished. He is the prophet better than Moses, the priest better than Aaron, and the king better than David. He is the presence of God on earth, the climax of redemptive history, and the one who appropriates God's eschatological outcomes. Christ enters into history to heal the broken and save the lost in order to bring a people back into the relational glory-presence of God for all eternity. His mission is successful, and our lives as Christ's disciples are evidence of the success of his redemptive activity.

Part Four

Curtain Call

Good stories help us understand ourselves. Scripture is the best drama because it gives us a real picture of the world and a real picture of ourselves. It opens us up and interprets us. So all that we have seen thus far is not some distant fantasy; instead, it is our story. We have a place in it and a part to play. The question then becomes, What is our role and what is our direction?

To know this, we must remember that we are but one small chapter (or paragraph) of a much larger volume. So far we have seen that the unmediated and worldwide experience of God's eschatological presence has been the goal that motivates much of the Lord's redemptive plan. We have also seen that the only real and true way to that goal is by God's entering history to redeem his people.

The Lord's gracious decision to draw near for redemption shows us two things: (1) that God is not done with the world after the fall, and (2) that he will accomplish his eschatological objectives the only way they can be accomplished, namely, through his becoming present to redeem. So the story of Scripture quickly becomes the story of God's presence in the world to save his people and to secure his purposes for them. As we have seen, he comes to Adam, Seth, the patriarchs, Moses, and David. He becomes present to his people at Sinai to save, he brings them to Jerusalem, and he plants his temple in the middle of the city so that they may be his people and he may be their God. And yet, all these mighty acts promise something more; they point us to the greatest expression of God's presence with his people, Jesus Christ. In Christ,

God comes to bring perfect redemption and to reconcile humanity to himself once and for all. Through Immanuel we have access to God and all of his eschatological promises.

So we end our exploration where our story began. This is our part of the drama. We know what God has promised, and we know what God has done, but what we need to see is how the eschatological presence of God and the redemptive presence of God change *us*. Why do these things matter? Why should I care about the presence of God more than I already do? To answer this we must move from a description of God's presence to what this theme prescribes for the Christian life. The story of Scripture teems with emphasis on the presence of God, and as a result, our story should too.

11

Finding Our Place in the Story

The Presence of God for the Christian Life

How should we understand God's presence for us here and now? How do we move from the pages of Scripture to our own script? That is what I want to consider in this last chapter. I want to show that because we are in the presence of God now, our lives are by no means mundane. Instead, we should tie every aspect of who we are and what we do to the reality that God is with us. To do this, we will focus on three glorious outcomes of God's eschatological and redemptive presence *for us*. We want to see how the presence of God helps us understand our salvation, our church, and the future work of God. God is present to be relational and accomplish his purposes. He does this on the grand stage of redemptive history and even on the side stage of our lives. May we be encouraged and drawn to worship him because of what he has done for us through his presence.

The Presence of God for Our Salvation: Drawing Near to God and God's Drawing Near to Us

Christ comes into this world to save. He draws near to redeem us. Thinking back to our last chapter, Christ is our Great High Priest who offers himself in *our* place to take *our* penalty (penal substitution), remove *our* sin and guilt (expiation), placate God's wrath for *our* freedom (propitiation), and ransom *us* from *our* sinful bondage (redemption). And why does he do all this for us? Here is where an understanding of the presence of God helps. All of Christ's atoning work culminates in his reconciling man to God. The end product of all of his redemptive work is the reconciliation that takes place between God and sinners like us. God sends Christ *in order to* restore the relationship lost in Eden. Christ's work opens up access to God and offers to us the great eschatological promise that we can dwell with the Lord eternally.

So think of it this way: Jesus atones to remove the penalty of death and judgment, the two insurmountable obstacles keeping us from the eternal experience of God's presence (Matt. 25:46; Rom. 1:24–28; 2:16; 8:1). As our great atoning sacrifice, Christ saves us, unites us to himself, and re-creates us so that we may know life in the new Eden. In fact, as 2 Corinthians 5:17 shows, being in Christ means that he *has* re-created us. The old has passed away and the new has come in order that we may be with God once again. So, just as he remakes the world, he remakes his people so that we may eternally experience the presence of God in full.

What is telling in 2 Corinthians 5 is that God makes us new through the ministry of reconciliation. Paul tells us that our new standing before God is solely due to Christ's work on our behalf (2 Cor. 5:18). In dying on the cross, Christ takes the curses of the garden upon himself so that "in Christ Jesus the blessing of Abraham might come to the Gentiles" (Gal. 3:14). Jesus takes our place so that we may take upon ourselves his righteous works before God. Christ enters this world, and "for our sake [God] made him to be sin who knew no sin, so that in him we might become the righteousness of God" (2 Cor. 5:21). One of the main reasons Christ does this is to get us back into God's presence. Christ's reconciliatory work removes sin in such a way that our trespasses are no longer counted against us so that we, the ones who ran from God because of sin, may be the ones who run to God to dwell with him.

This is our great hope and joy. Christ's redemptive work will reconcile us to God and his covenant promises. We who were once enemies of God, separated from him in our rebellion and sin, are now able to partake of God's eschatological promises because of what God's redemptive presence in Christ has done on our behalf (Rom. 5:10–11). On the cross, Christ makes peace between the Creator and his creatures (Col. 1:20). Christ comes to make us—we who were alienated from God, hostile in mind, and doing evil deeds—holy, blameless, and above reproach. He makes us new so that we may stand before God dressed in Christ's righteousness (Col. 1:21–23).

Through Christ's priestly work we may now draw near to our Creator and Redeemer. The presence of God in Christ is our only way to receive God's covenant promises. We see this initially in the Gospels, when immediately following Christ's death, the temple veil separating the Most Holy Place from Israel is torn from top to bottom (Matt. 27:51; Mark 15:38; cf. Luke 23:45; Heb. 6:19; 9:3; 10:20). Here the division between the unrighteous world and our righteous God has been definitively removed through the cross. By Christ's blood, we are able to do the unthinkable: go behind the curtain of separation and enter into the holy places where God dwells. In other words, our salvation is about God becoming present in Christ to overcome the moral distance that separates us from him so that we may boldly approach the throne of grace, thereby entering into the presence of God in both this world and the world to come (Heb. 4:16; 1 John 2:1–2).[1]

Paul further develops this concept when, in speaking of the union of Jew and Gentile in Christ, he argues, "In Christ Jesus you who were once far off have been brought near by the blood of Christ" (Eph. 2:13). Through Christ's atoning sacrifice, we "have access in one Spirit to the Father" (Eph. 2:18). According to Paul, the redemptive action of Christ provides the reconciliation necessary for communion and fellowship between God and us.

This prophetic, priestly, and kingly activity is so conclusive that Paul explains that we not only have access to the Lord, but are also

---

[1] J. V. Fesko, *Last Things First: Unlocking Genesis 1–3 with the Christ of Eschatology* (Fearn, Ross-shire, UK: Mentor, 2007), 162. See also William Hendriksen, *Matthew* (Grand Rapids: Baker, 1995), 974; Donald A. Hagner, *Matthew 14–28*, WBC (Dallas: Word, 1995), 848–49. Fesko argues further that in the death and resurrection of Christ, the veil's tearing also represents the coming removal of the cherubim who guard the presence of God (Gen. 3:24). Fesko comments: "God placed two cherubim at the eastern entrance to the garden of Eden prohibiting entrance into the archetypal temple. In the subsequent tabernacle and temple these two cherubim were represented by embroidered figures on the veil or curtain that separated the outer temple from the holy of holies at will, unless it was the high priest at the appointed time (e.g., Lev. 16:1ff.). Now that the penalty for the curse was paid and the promise of the protoevangelium had arrived, at the dawn of the new creation the cherubim no longer stand guard at the entrance barring access under the penalty of death. Because the veil has been torn in two, the cherubim have withdrawn to their station before the throne of God (Rev. 4:6–8) and the new adamic humanity may once again enter into the divine presence." Fesko, *Last Things First*, 163.

being "built" together into a temple for God's dwelling (Eph. 2:20–22). In other words, God becomes present to save us so that we can experience that presence now. Christ dies on the cross to save us in order that we may gain access to God's full glory. Neither temple walls nor curtains separate us; and there is no ethnic division that keeps us from being with our Creator-Redeemer. In Christ, we can boldly and confidently access the Lord through faith (Eph. 3:12). Christ is "our blessed hope, the appearing of the glory of our great God and Savior Jesus Christ, who gave himself for us to redeem us from all lawlessness and to purify for himself a people for his own possession" (Titus 2:13–14; cf. Rom. 3:23; 7:4, 23). Here we see that Christ manifests God to save us. In this act, the redemptive presence of God makes a way for us to know and enjoy God's eschatological presence now and for all eternity (e.g., Rom. 8:19–23; 2 Pet. 3:10–13; cf. Isa. 65:17; 66:12; Rev. 21:1–22:5).[2]

Christ, therefore, has paved the way to God's eschatological objectives through his blood and resurrection (John 14:1–3; Heb. 6:20). As the author of Hebrews assures us, the certainty of Yahweh's covenant promises is grounded in the hope of Christ's going before the presence of God on our behalf. Christ's work of mediation as our High Priest fulfills the eschatological promises established at creation and graciously "re-presented" in the covenants. Christ secures this hope for us—the hope that God will fulfill his promises to bring a people to the place of his dwelling. For Christ enters the heavenly sanctuary to "appear in the presence of God" on our behalf in order to "put away sin by the

---

[2] As the prophetic voices of the Old Testament tell us, God's salvation brings a new creation (Pss. 98:7–9; 148:1–14; Isa. 44:23; 49:13). The Lord's people will return to a new land with the New Jerusalem, or new Zion, as its capital. At the center of the city and the promise is the new temple where God's presence dwells in the midst of his people in its eschatological fullness. Goldsworthy summarizes, "This is the new Eden, the land of fruitfulness and of harmony between all living things, and of perfect healing (Isa. 2:2–4; 11:6–9; 32:1–20; 35:1–10; 65:17–25; Ezek. 34:11–16, 25–31; 36:35–38; 47:1–12)." Graeme Goldsworthy, *According to Plan: The Unfolding Revelation of God in the Bible* (Downers Grove, IL: InterVarsity, 1991), 192. In the New Testament, Christ's death regenerates not only a people, but the cosmos as well. As we saw in Col. 1:20, Christ applies his reconciliation not only to his people but also to creation. He comes to "reconcile to himself *all things*, whether on earth or in heaven, making peace by the blood of his cross." This consummation takes place in the New Jerusalem detailed in John's eschatological vision in Revelation 21–22. Picking up on the imagery of Isaiah and other Old Testament passages, John reveals that Christ's work as the Lamb of God has appropriated this new land for the people who believe in him for salvation. In sum, Goldsworthy concludes, "There is a new heaven and a new earth, and a new Jerusalem coming out of heaven (Rev. 21:1–2). . . . That which the tabernacle and temple pointed to, the dwelling of God with his people, becomes a reality (Rev. 21:3). The regeneration is now complete (Rev. 21:5) and there is no longer any need of 'government outposts and agencies,' such as the temple, which is the symbol of God's presence, for he is present and is also the source of all light (Rev. 21:22–23). The old images of Eden are joined with those of the holy city and throne (Rev. 22:1–2; cf. Ezek. 47:1–12)" (ibid., 230). Christ's work as the redemptive presence of God appropriates this final goal of redemptive history as it provides access to the eschatological presence of God defining the New Jerusalem.

sacrifice of himself" that salvation and its blessings may be ours now and forever (Heb. 9:24, 26).[3]

Central to Christ's completion of the redemptive agenda is Jesus's work as our forerunner. He is the one who enters in to the presence of God for us so that we may follow him into the eternal, eschatological presence of the Lord. As our Great High Priest, Christ has faced our temptations and overcome them *so that* we may draw near (προσέρχομαι) to the throne of grace (Heb. 4:14–16).[4] By placing our confidence in the mercy and grace afforded to us by Christ's atoning work, we now have "confidence" to enter into God's presence (Heb. 10:19–25).

In Christ we have a better hope—a hope that accomplishes in full what the law failed to do (Heb. 7:19–25; 10:1ff.). As the apostle Paul makes clear, "When the fullness of time had come, God sent forth his Son, born of a woman, born under the law, to redeem those who were under the law, so that we might receive adoption as sons" (Gal. 4:4–5). Christ does it all: he is the fulfillment of the law, the better priest, and the guarantor of the new covenant (Heb. 7:22), who "holds his priesthood permanently" and is, therefore, "able to save to the uttermost those who draw near to God through him" (Heb. 7:24–25).

Let us take heart that the promises of the Lord are ours. We can be confident in what Immanuel has done for us through his death and resurrection. All that was lost in the fall is ours again in Christ. We no

---

[3] The sacrificial work of Christ is the means to God's eschatological presence because it is first the grounds for Jesus's glorification. Christ is the way to heaven because he has been there himself. Believers journey down a path that has already been cleared by the glorious justifying sacrifice of Christ. Being with him means we are made to be like him, and as a result, we too have access to the Father. As the shed blood of Jesus merits his position at the right hand of God, this same blood makes eternity in the presence of God available to his chosen. And as we receive our resurrection bodies because Jesus first received his, so too we meet the final objective of redemptive history because Christ's glorification attains it for us. The faithful will be in God's presence only because the object of their faith, Jesus Christ, first entered the presence of God both on our behalf and for his own glory.

[4] Remarkably, the verb προσέρχομαι (to "draw near"), applied in Hebrews to the believer's ability to enter into the presence of God, originally was used in relation to the temple and its sacrificial system (see Heb. 4:16; 7:19, 25; 10:1, 22; 11:6; 12:18, 22; cf. Ex. 16:9; 34:32; Lev. 9:5; Deut. 4:11). William Lane comments on Heb. 4:16: "The source of the terminology is cultic. The throne of Grace is the place of God's presence, for which grace emanates to the people of God. The only one who was permitted to 'draw near' under the provisions of the Mosaic covenant was the high priest, who could approach the altar in the Most Holy Place of the tabernacle once a year on the Day of Atonement. If his ministry was acceptable, the altar of judgment became the place from which mercy was dispensed to the people (cf. Lev. 16:2–34; Heb. 9:5). In bold extension of the language of worship the writer calls the community to recognize that through his high priestly ministry Christ has achieved for them what Israel never enjoyed, namely, immediate access to God and freedom to draw near to him continually." William L. Lane, *Hebrews 1–8*, WBC (Nashville: Thomas Nelson, 1991), 115. So in utilizing this "draw near" terminology, the author of Hebrews once again highlights the priestly work of Christ and his ability to remove the barriers of sin and judgment in order to grant Christians access to the Father's presence now and forever. In sum, through Christ's priestly work, believers have confidence to enter the sanctuary and draw near to God.

longer have to hide from our Creator, because our Creator has drawn near to also be our reconciler. So let us enter the holy places with confidence. And let us remember that we can enter the presence of God and know its future blessings only through the shed blood of Jesus Christ. It is he who opened this new and living way to God through his High Priestly work, and it is only because he became present to reconcile us that we have a real assurance of redemption and redemption's promises (Heb. 10:19ff.). So let us be reconciled to God; let us draw near to him.

The Present Presence

Not only does Christ's work of reconciliation call us to draw near to God; it also prepares the way for God to draw near to us. He does so most obviously in the coming of the Holy Spirit. In our current place in the story of redemption, God promises that he will not leave us or forsake us (John 14:18; cf. Deut. 31:6–8; Josh. 1:5; 1 Kings 8:57; 1 Chron. 28:20; Heb. 13:5). With Christ ascended to his rightful place of glory, God fulfills his new covenant promise to us by sending his Spirit to be with us and in us (Jer. 31:31ff.; 32:40; Ezek. 32:36–41; 36:22–32; 37:26ff.; Joel 2:28–32; cf. Luke 22:20; 2 Cor. 3:6; Heb. 8:8–12).[5] To us God extends himself in yet a more intimate way: he gives us the Holy Spirit—the presence of God for this (almost) final act of the redemptive drama.[6]

We must remember that before Christ ends his earthly ministry, he begins the new era of redemption with the promise of the Spirit. He declares, "These things I have spoken to you while I am still with you. But the Helper, the Holy Spirit, whom the Father will send in my name, he will teach you all things and bring to your remembrance all that I have said to you" (John 14:25; cf. vv. 16–17; 15:26; 16:7). The one the Father sends after Christ's departure continues Jesus's earthly mission

---

[5] For a helpful and comprehensive work on the Holy Spirit's roles in the Old and New Testaments see James M. Hamilton Jr., *God's Indwelling Presence: The Holy Spirit in the Old and New Testaments* (Nashville: Broadman & Holman, 2006).

[6] In what may otherwise seem a contradiction, the current and future aspects of the presence of God are completely consistent when represented in an "already, not yet" paradigm. This concept reveals that the kingdom of God is inaugurated in Christ's death and resurrection, is preserved and expanded by the indwelling Spirit here and now, and awaits full consummation that comes at Christ's return. Thus, the world is still under the effects and influence of sin, but through the work of the Spirit, the community of believers is sanctified for the experience of the presence of God in the new heavens and earth. In conclusion, the divine presence in the Spirit of God is a central means in the current preparation of the elect for the coming eschatological presence of God.

(Acts 16:7; Rom. 8:9; Gal. 4:6; Phil. 1:19; 1 Pet. 1:11; see also John 7:38; 19:30; 20:22; Acts 2:33; Heb. 9:14; Rev. 3:1; 5:6) and indwells us in order to apply Christ's reconciliatory work to us (John 14:16; see also 2:1). It is in the Spirit, then, that the presence of God resides with us for the consummation of what has begun in Christ's atoning sacrifice.

It follows that, just as with Christ, one of the central purposes of the Spirit is to help us experience the eschatological presence of God as we await Christ's consummating return. Even after the Messiah's ascension, the presence of God remains in the world in the Spirit to bring us the Lord's blessings. The Spirit is here to apply Christ's redemption to us and help prepare us for his eschatological presence (John 14:16–28; 16:7; Rom. 8:9ff.; 1 Cor. 6:17; 15:45; Eph. 3:16ff.; see also Rom. 1:4; 1 Tim. 3:16; 1 Pet. 3:18; Rev. 2–3).[7]

So with the ascension of Christ, there is another great shift in the way we experience God's presence. Before the new covenant, God's promise to be with us was only an external reality. God was out there. God was in the world redeeming. But with the coming of the Spirit, the presence of God now dwells *within* us. One of the fundamental purposes of the Spirit for us, then, is to dwell in us so that we may *"manifest the presence of God"* now and forever.[8] No longer is his presence just an outward expression; now, through the Holy Spirit, that once external reality of God's presence is an internal reality that we experience as we believe in the redemptive work of the Lord. The Spirit—the presence of God in this new act of the redemptive drama—now dwells within us to culminate the objectives of the Lord for his glory and our resultant joy (John 7:39; 14:18; 2 Cor. 3:17–18; Eph. 2:19–22; 1 Pet. 2:4–10).

The Need for Pentecost: Applying Christ's Redemption

So what does the presence of God in the Holy Spirit do for the Christian life? First, the Spirit makes the Christian life possible (Gal. 3:2). When we have the Spirit, we have Christ, for it is only through the actions of the Spirit that sinners like us are freed from the bondage of sin. He brings our justification (1 Cor. 6:11; Gal. 3:13–14; Titus 3:7). He applies

---

[7] This preparation also includes the readiness of the church to be a reflection of the presence of God in the world. This topic will be addressed in the next section concerning the church as the new temple.
[8] John M. Frame, *The Doctrine of God* (Phillipsburg, NJ: P&R, 2002), 96.

the work of Christ to us (Rom. 8:9) and unites us to our servant-king (1 Cor. 6:17). In other words, our

> union to Christ is inaugurated by the renewing work of the Spirit in which he begins the transformation into the image of Christ which will be completed at the eschaton. The ancient promise is thus fulfilled that God would give his people new hearts and spirits through the indwelling of his Spirit, resulting in a new lifestyle (Ezek. 36:24–27).[9]

The power of the Spirit is the power of redemption and regeneration (John 3:3–8; 1 John 3:9), for it is by his work of applying Christ's atonement to us that we are born again and reconciled to the Lord (John 6:63; 7:37–39). All that Christ has done is in the hands of the Spirit, and it is only through the Spirit's work that any of us can be saved.

The Holy Spirit shows us once again that God is present in the world for his redemptive purposes. Or as Grudem contends:

> *The work of the Holy Spirit is to manifest the active presence of God in the world, and especially the church.* . . . Scripture most often represents [the Holy Spirit] as being *present* to do God's work in the world. . . . After Jesus ascended into heaven, and continuing through the entire church age, the Holy Spirit is now the *primary* manifestation of the presence of the Trinity among us. He is the one who is most prominently *present* with us now.[10]

As the principal revelation of God's presence in our stage of redemptive history, the Holy Spirit, like Christ before him, has huge purposes for us. He is the one who makes us receivers and participants in the redemptive mission of the Lord. It is the Holy Spirit, working in us, who saves us and brings us back to stand before the presence of God.

To see just how this plays out in the New Testament, we need only to look to Pentecost, where the Spirit's full power is put on display. In Acts 1–2 the Holy Spirit is poured out upon the Messiah's disciples soon after his ascension. With the Spirit upon them, the disciples begin to confront the people of Jerusalem with the gospel, preaching and

---

[9] Sinclair B. Ferguson, *The Holy Spirit*, CCT (Downers Grove, IL: InterVarsity, 1996), 116.
[10] Wayne A. Grudem, *Systematic Theology: Introduction to Biblical Doctrine* (Grand Rapids: Zondervan, 1994), 634, emphasis original.

teaching in foreign languages understood by the crowd but unknown to the apostles. Viewing their astonishment and contempt at this fulfill-ment of Old Testament prophecy, Peter announces that God has raised Christ from the dead and sent the promised Holy Spirit to show the world and us that this one whom they crucified is the true Christ and Lord of lords (Acts 2:36). "Cut to the heart" by the disciple's words, many in the crowd follow Peter's instruction. They repent of their sin, are baptized in the name of Jesus Christ, and receive the Holy Spirit themselves (2:37–41). That day three thousand souls are added to the kingdom of God, three thousand souls who become a part of the dy-nastic promise through the activity of the Holy Spirit.

The redemptive means of the presence of God in the Holy Spirit is more apparent when Pentecost is understood in light of the Tower of Babel narrative (Gen. 11:1–10). If we remember, Babel was the place where a unified people sought entrance into the heavenly dwelling place of God through their own ingenuity for their own glory and praise. Their arrogance and pride induced God's wrath as the Lord came down to judge them by confusing their language and driving them out over the face of the earth.

At Pentecost, however, the exact opposite takes place. God comes down in the Spirit to redeem. Through his presence in the Spirit, God speaks to the nations in their own tongues in order that those once driven from him would return to their Creator. In Acts 2, we see that God is removing his judgment and is bringing the nations back to-gether again through the work of Christ by the power of the Spirit.[11] So when we read about Pentecost, we read about the reversal of what occurred at Babel. Instead of driving the nations from the presence of God, God has now indwelt us to bring us back to his presence. In the work of the Holy Spirit, the presence of God—the very thing the na-tions sought at Babel through their own pride—has come to the nations to make a better way to God's eschatological glory. This is our only way to God; it is the divine way appropriated by the Lord himself for his worship and praise.

The arrival of the Spirit at Pentecost signals that God is still pres-ent to act and redeem. As Pentecost and the rest of the New Testament

---

[11] David G. Peterson, *The Acts of the Apostles*, PNTC (Grand Rapids: Eerdmans, 2009), 136.

depict, it is through the Spirit that "the message [of salvation] will continue to go out into the world (Acts 1:8). The new era has begun with the promised Spirit's arrival. . . . The story [of salvation] is going out into the entire world. . . . God is powerfully present, directing his mission."[12] In applying Christ's reconciliatory work, the Holy Spirit brings us to salvation and salvation's promises.

The Indwelling Presence: Holy Spirit Sanctifying Believers

Not only does the Spirit bring us to salvation; he also keeps us in salvation. This is known biblically as sanctification, which very simply is the growth of the believer into Christlikeness (Rom. 8:29).[13] It is the "progressive work of God and man that makes us more and more free from sin and like Christ in our actual lives."[14] Being made into the image of Christ is a process. It is God's work of grooming us to be like our servant-king so that we can ultimately do what Jesus has done: enter into the presence of the Father. And it is the Spirit's presence in us that prepares us to do just this. The Spirit sanctifies us *in order to prepare us* for God's eschatological promises.

As we already know, the unholy cannot stand before the holy without penalty of death. Of course, Christ has dealt with this penalty by taking our curse of death upon himself. But the glorious thing about God's grace is that grace does not stop here. Rather, the Holy Spirit indwells us so that we might be made holy (John 14:16–17). The Spirit comes to make us like Christ so that we might experience the eschatological presence of God. The Spirit does what neither the Old Testament law nor the sacrificial system could do: he makes us holy as God is holy.[15]

Because Christ's righteousness is now ours, we are not our own but are being transformed into the likeness of our Savior (1 Cor. 3:18). We are called to live our lives as Jesus lived his. We are to follow the ethic of Christ and become personal expressions of the new covenant (Rom. 13:8–10; Gal. 5:14; 1 Thess. 4:9–10). In such internal transformation,

---

[12] Darrell L. Bock, *Acts*, BECNT (Grand Rapids: Baker, 2007), 106.
[13] Ferguson continues: "If the glory of God is the ultimate goal of all things, including our sanctification, conformity to Christ is the immediate goal of that sanctification. We are called to be like him. Our corresponding responsibility is to become like him." Ferguson, *The Holy Spirit*, 152.
[14] Grudem, *Systematic Theology*, 747.
[15] Ferguson, *The Holy Spirit*, 141.

we must set our minds on things that are above because we have died to this world and are now hidden with God in Christ (Col. 3:3). We, therefore, must kill the remnants of sin and worldliness in our lives (Col. 3:5). Through the power of the indwelling Spirit, we must remove ourselves from sexual immorality, impurity, passion, evil desire, covetousness—which is idolatry—anger, malice, slander, obscene talk, and lying (Col. 3:5–11). We should replace these sins with compassionate hearts, kindness, humility, meekness, patience, forgiveness, love, and the peace of Christ (Col. 3:12–14). We are responsible for these drastic changes, but we also know that true sanctification can be garnered in our lives only through the work of the Holy Spirit over time (Phil. 2:12; 2 Thess. 2:13).[16]

The progressive nature of sanctification shows us that we are being

---

[16] Recently, some have argued that the emphasis on sanctification in the New Testament is placed on positional sanctification rather than the historically held progressive understanding. For example, see David Peterson, *Possessed by God: A New Testament Theology of Sanctification and Holiness* (Grand Rapids: Eerdmans, 1995). Scholars such as Peterson contend that sanctification is "God's way of taking possession of us in Christ, setting us apart to belong to him and to fulfill his purpose for us" (ibid., 27). Those stressing this positional (or definitive) sanctification pick up on true characteristics of the doctrine. Philip Ryken claims that sanctification does have a sense in which it is defined "as being set apart for holiness," meaning that "we were sanctified when we first came to Christ." Richard D. Phillips, Philip G. Ryken, and Mark E. Dever, *The Church: One, Holy, Catholic, and Apostolic* (Phillipsburg, NJ: P&R, 2004), 56. This "sanctification as possession" is evidenced in such New Testament texts as 1 Cor. 1:30; 1 Thess. 4:3–7; 2 Thess. 2:13; Heb. 12:14; and 1 Pet. 1:2. For this reason, Peterson argues that the "moral aspect of sanctification is secondary to its soteriological reference." Peterson, *Possessed by God*, 103. Such an argument is helpful to highlight this aspect of holiness. However, the nature of sanctification is actually a balance of the positional and progressive perspectives. This can be clarified when the relationship between regeneration and sanctification is explained. As Ferguson rightly relates, "Union to Christ is inaugurated by the renewing work of the Spirit in which he begins the transformation into the image of Christ that will be completed at the eschaton." Ferguson, *The Holy Spirit*, 116. In regeneration, "the ancient promise is thus fulfilled that God would give his people new hearts and spirits through the indwelling of his Spirit, resulting in a new lifestyle (Ezek. 36:24–27)" (ibid.). In this mind-set, it is clear that "there is some overlap between regeneration and sanctification, for this moral change is actually a part of regeneration." Grudem, *Systematic Theology*, 747. The two aspects, then, should not be separated; regeneration is connected to transformation into the likeness of Christ. With this understanding, definitive and progressive sanctification should not be held at odds but, rather, united in the relationship between regeneration and purification. Paul views these redemptive realities in a holistic sense when he proclaims to the Corinthians, "You were washed, you were sanctified, you were justified in the name of the Lord Jesus Christ and by the Spirit of our God" (1 Cor. 6:11). This shows that the apostle and the rest of the Scriptures do not take the positional and progressive aspects of sanctification as contradictions; instead, they are two characteristics of a united act of God for the purpose of redemptive growth in Christ. Thus, in the end, the church is holy unto God in a positional sense and, simultaneously, the church's holiness "still need[s] to be brought to completion through the progress of sanctification." Phillips, Ryken, and Dever, *The Church*, 63. Once it is understood that the beginning of sanctification occurs at regeneration, it is obvious that the New Testament promotes the progressive transformation that continues throughout the life of the believer. The basis for such progress is Christ's freeing man from sin and the recognition that transgression still affects the lives of the regenerate. This is evident in Romans 6 where Paul states, "You also must consider yourselves dead to sin and alive to God in Christ Jesus. Let not sin therefore reign in your mortal body, to make you obey its passions. Do not present your members to sin as instruments for unrighteousness, but present yourselves to God as those who have been brought from death to life, and your members to God as instruments for righteousness" (vv. 11–13). This passage demonstrates both the victorious work of Christ and the believer's need for continued purification. Because of the ongoing battle with sin, the believer's growth through the work of the Spirit is still in process. Christians have not arrived and will never arrive at full sanctification until death or the return of Christ. Therefore, it is true that the idea of sanctification "has as its aim the elimination of all sin and complete conformity to the image of God's own Son, to be holy as the Lord is holy." John Murray, *Redemption Accomplished and Applied* (Grand Rapids: Eerdmans, 1993), 143.

made holy not for contemporary goals alone but for future purposes as well—purposes that include readying a people for an eternity in the presence of God. Simply put, we are made holy to enjoy the benefits of being holy, namely, to enter into the unlimited presence of God in the new heaven and new earth. From an eschatological standpoint, sanctification is the Spirit's work to transform us so that we may be with God eternally. The apostle Paul emphasizes this very point when he tells the church at Thessalonica that their sanctification is ultimately produced "so that [the Lord Jesus] may establish your hearts blameless in holiness before our God and Father, at the coming of our Lord Jesus with all his saints" (1 Thess. 3:13). Paul understands that sanctification is a preparatory act: it is a progressive work that continues in redemptive history for a future result. In other words, the Spirit works to prepare us in holiness so that we can stand in the presence of God now and when Christ returns in glory to usher in his kingdom.

To inherit the eschatological promises of God—specifically the promise of dwelling with God eternally—we must be in the process of sanctification. The apostle Paul once again makes this connection. In citing the objective of dwelling in the presence of God revealed in Leviticus 26:12, Paul calls on his audience to pursue true sanctification. As the apostle writes, "Since we have these promises, beloved, let us cleanse ourselves from every defilement of body and spirit, bringing holiness to completion in the fear of God" (2 Cor. 7:1). Our motivation for sanctification is the promise of dwelling with God eternally. We must be holy like God, and this is what the Spirit does for us: he works to make us into the likeness of our Messiah so that we may be with our Messiah forever.

The Presence of God in the Church:
What It Means to Be the New Temple

Let's be honest. We do not always "get" the church, do we? For many of us, the church is optional. Or when we think about church, we can only remember how people there hurt and betrayed us. It is true that the public image of the church has fallen on hard times, but I think a biblically grounded understanding of God's presence can relieve some of this tension. Specifically I want us to see that the church is not a human invention but a divine one. God gathers believers together to worship him and know him. Christ saves us and others so that we will gather together to fellowship with like-minded believers. The Spirit who applies Christ's work and sanctifies us to be like him ignites a desire to assemble together with other Christians.

But the presence of God shows us more about what the church is, or is supposed to be. Not only is the church the believers gathered; it is also a manifestation of God's presence to this world. The church is— in its own way, as rooted in Christ and made by the Spirit—a means to God's covenant promises. Granted, its power is not its own. The church does not save, but it does tell us how to be saved. So when God is present in Christ to save, he saves not just a person but a *people* who, through the work of the presence of God in the Spirit, reflect Yahweh's own character, glory, and presence to the world (2 Cor. 3:18). The identity of the church, therefore, has always been tied to God's presence. We are the people saved by God and marked out for God (Lev. 11:44–45; 19:2; 20:7, 16; cf. 21:8; 1 Pet. 1:16; 2:4–10). And this is not a stagnant reality.

One of our main purposes in the church, then, is to help others experience the presence of God. But how do we do this? First, we have the *external* work of the church through evangelism. In this, we invite others to be a part of God's people receiving salvation and its blessings. Second, we have the *internal* act of sanctification. Here, we help our brothers and sisters in the church be prepared for God's eschatological promise. These missional and transformative focuses are fundamental purposes of the church. The church becomes an instrument in the hands of the Spirit; it is the assembly of the redeemed moved by the presence of God to evangelize the lost and to play a sanctifying role among its members. In other words, the church is the gathering of indwelt believers come together to spread the redemptive presence of God through worldwide missions and to prepare each other for the eschatological hope of the new covenant. The church is an agent of the Spirit for God's own redemptive functions and eschatological agenda. As the Spirit indwells the church, his purposes become the purposes of the church, and as a result, we are called to be a part of God's work of salvation and sanctification. In short, the church—the temple of God indwelt by the Spirit—becomes an instrument of God through which he consummates his redemptive goals.

The Church as Temple

It should come as no surprise that the apostle Paul declares the church to be the temple of God. James Hamilton writes, "In the new covenant the people of God are the temple, and God dwells in them."[17] This particular designation is pertinent to our understanding of the means of God's presence in our current place in the redemptive story, for this temple metaphor describes the missional and sanctifying agency of the church (1 Cor. 3:16–17; 2 Cor. 6:14–7:1; Eph. 2:21–22; cf. 2 Thess. 2:4; Heb. 8:2; see also the true Zion and Jerusalem in Gal. 4:26; Heb. 12:22; Rev. 3:12; 4:18; 21:2).[18]

To be sure, this image finds its footing in the Old Testament locus of Yahweh's manifest presence. As we saw earlier, the tabernacle/temple was primarily the seat of God's reign, rule, and deliverance in the midst of his people. In the temple, God was manifest to work among his people for his redemptive objectives and the spread of his eschatological presence. But because of Israel's sin the temple failed, and it is in the dawning of the new covenant that this Old Testament type finds its completion. Rather than concluding with the glory of Solomon's temple, redemptive history moves forward to a better reality, executed ultimately in Jesus, in whom the presence of God tabernacles (John 1:14). However, the emphasis on the temple does not end with Christ; *it is also found in the church.*

This emphasis is seen throughout the New Testament, especially in the writings of the apostle Paul, who "develops this image of the church as the community of the redeemed which, through the sanctifying agency of the Holy Spirit, is constituted as the dwelling place of God."[19] Paul first utilizes this image in 1 Corinthians 3:16–17, where he

---

[17] Hamilton, *God's Indwelling Presence*, 160.

[18] Much of what the Spirit does is tied to the corporate assembly of God's people. The Spirit "possesses the church in divine Lordship," "leads the church in its mission (Acts 5:32; 13:2)," and "liberates the church from sin, death, and the condemnation of the law (Rom. 5–8; Gal. 4:2; 2 Cor. 3:17)." Edmund P. Clowney, "Church," in *New Dictionary of Theology*, ed. Sinclair B. Ferguson, David F. Wright, and J. I. Packer (Downers Grove, IL: InterVarsity, 1988), 141. The reason behind this activity is to bring redemption to its God-ordained ends. Therefore, much of what follows in Acts and the Epistles deals specifically with how the Spirit forms the church, its makeup, and its purposes.

[19] P. T. O'Brien, "The Church as a Heavenly and Eschatological Entity," in *The Church in the Bible and the World: An International Study*, ed. D. A. Carson (Grand Rapids: Baker, 1987), 99.

poses the question, "Do you not know that you are God's temple and that God's Spirit dwells in you?" The apostle continues, "If anyone destroys God's temple, God will destroy him. For God's temple is holy, and you are that temple." To be clear, the "you" in these verses is plural, revealing that Paul's audience is the whole Corinthian church. As New Testament scholar Thomas Schreiner writes, these verses do not "focus on the Spirit's indwelling believers individualistically"; rather "what Paul emphasizes is the Spirit's dwelling in believers corporately."[20] The church-wide "congregation is the temple of God and as such is holy."[21] Paul shows us that the presence of God in the Spirit dwells in and works through the assembly of the church.

The emphasis on the church as temple is also evident in Paul's second letter to the Corinthians. In a context similar to the first epistle, he again argues that the Corinthians should liken their church to the temple:

> What agreement has the temple of God with idols? For we are the temple of the living God; as God said,
>
> "I will make my dwelling among them and walk among them,
>   and I will be their God,
>   and they shall be my people.
> Therefore go out from their midst,
>   and be separate from them, says the Lord,
> and touch no unclean thing;
>   then I will welcome you,
> and I will be a father to you,
>   and you shall be sons and daughters to me,
> says the Lord Almighty." (2 Cor. 6:16–18)

As in 1 Corinthians, we see the corporate emphasis again in Paul's use of "we," a word "that clearly has as its primary reference the members of the congregation at Corinth."[22] Not only that, but Paul builds his argument on Old Testament references. When he writes about the temple, he quotes Leviticus 26:12, thereby making it abundantly clear that "the

---

[20] Thomas R. Schreiner, *Paul, Apostle of God's Glory in Christ: A Pauline Theology* (Downers Grove, IL: InterVarsity, 2001), 343.
[21] O'Brien, "Eschatological Entity," 99.
[22] Ibid., 100.

temple imagery of the Old Testament is fulfilled in God's dwelling with his people corporately."[23] Paul picks up the temple metaphor to show us that the church is to be sanctified for God's presence.

It is clear that the church is the fulfillment of the Old Testament institution of the temple. These "temple" texts reveal that the Holy Spirit, who resides in the church community, is at work to create a community defined by the presence of God. That presence, once confined to the temple, is now fulfilled by the Holy Spirit in the church. According to the New Testament, the gathering of the church is, in some sense, a new temple for God's presence in this world to continue the work of redemption and make way for the new heaven and new earth.[24]

The Church's Eschatological Mission: Presence to the Ends of the Earth

As the new temple of God, the church plays a vital role in the completion of God's eschatological objectives in the current era of redemptive history. In particular, one of the church's primary functions is the spread of the gospel. Practically speaking, the church executes this calling through the faithful practice of evangelism and missions. But in light of the presence of God, the external role of the church involves much more than rote obedience and duty. Instead, we are able to play a part in God's redemptive and eschatological plan. Through the efficacious work of the Holy Spirit acting through our evangelistic ministry, the dynasty and dominion of God increase exponentially, and the eschatological purposes of God near fulfillment. When we share the gospel, we offer others the opportunity to become part of God's people. In effect, each life saved loosens the grip of the prince of the power of

---

[23] Schreiner, Paul, 343.

[24] Consequently, the New Testament, in large part, seeks to describe, explain, and define the church in all its beauty, glory, and faults. To do so the New Testament authors employ numerous images and metaphors. "The Bible provides a rich kaleidoscope of imagery about the church composed of around one hundred metaphors and statements." "Church," in Dictionary of Biblical Imagery, ed. Leland Ryken, James C. Wilhoit, and Tremper Longman III (Downers Grove, IL: InterVarsity, 1998), 147. The power of these metaphors is that they vividly communicate truth about the reality and purpose of the assembly of God's people depicting the church to be the body of Christ (1 Cor. 12:12–31; Eph. 4:1–16), the household of God (Heb. 3:1–6), the Shepherd's flock (John 10:1–21; 1 Pet. 5:2–4), and the bride of the Messiah (2 Cor. 11:2; Rev. 19:7), each of which represents and articulates a unique ecclesiological reality. Interestingly, one of the main realities expressed in each of these metaphors is relationship. Central to the church, then, is the notion of being together, of being a community united in Christ. As this applies to holiness, there is no sanctification without relationship because the process of holiness in a corporate sense stems from relationships that, I would argue, are good and bad, difficult and easy. Thus, the church as impetus for sanctification is implicit in the ecclesiological images such as the body, household, flock, and even bride (we are one bride not many). The relational community of the church is a context where sanctification takes place.

the air on this age, causing his dominion to crumble and be replaced once and for all by the coming kingdom-dominion of God. To be sure, evangelism is about salvation, but it also concerns eschatology. It is about bringing people back into the garden-sanctuary filled with the all-satisfying presence of God.

Paul, in response to the Jewish rejection of the gospel, proclaims God's own missional purpose, declaring,

I have made you a light to the Gentiles,
   that you may bring salvation to the ends of the earth.
   (Acts 13:47)

N. T. Wright comments:

Jesus has now been raised from the dead as Israel's Messiah, and Israel's Messiah, as the psalms and prophets insist, is the world's true Lord. "His dominion shall be from one sea to the other, from the River to the ends of the earth." . . . And how is the [Lord] going to take command of his world-wide empire? His messengers, his emissaries, are going to go off into all the territories of which he is already enthroned as Lord and to bring the good news of his ascension, and his wise and just rule.[25]

The church, in this age between Christ's first and second comings, is to mediate God's redemptive presence in this world by telling the lost about God's salvation and his eschatological blessings (2 Cor. 5:20).

This is why the Gospel of Matthew starts with the fulfillment of the Immanuel promise in Christ but concludes with the reassurance that the presence of God will still function until he returns. Matthew shows us through the Great Commission that, in a way, the church's people are now the ambassadors of his redemptive presence. Christ tells us before he returns to the Father that he has transferred his mission to his disciples. The church, as a result, is called to "go therefore and make disciples of all nations, baptizing them in the name of the Father and of the Son and of the Holy Spirit, teaching them to observe all that I have commanded you" (Matt. 28:19). This is the purpose of the

---

[25] N. T. Wright, *Surprised by Hope: Rethinking Heaven, the Resurrection, and the Mission of the Church* (New York: Harper One, 2008), 242.

Great Commission: Christ gives his mission to his people to resume his eschatological purposes following his ascension. Notice that the Great Commission is accomplished only through Christ's presence, as seen when he declares, "I am with you always, to the end of the age" (Matt. 28:20).[26] Therefore, as the Spirit marks out the church as the temple of God, the Spirit also works through the church to bring about God's redemptive and eschatological ends.

So, on the basis of Christ's continued presence, we, the church, are ambassadors of his presence. We call nonbelievers out of their hopeless existence to the hope of the covenant promises secured by the work of our Savior. We are not bystanders in God's mission; rather, in God's grace, we are instruments of divine presence—limited as we may be— through whom God moves this world closer and closer to his redemptive ends. In other words, we are the church, the temple of God in this current redemptive age. As we point others to Christ, the way to God's eternal presence, we play a part in God's eschatological purposes. We know that we are "part of God's kingdom project which stretches out beyond 'me and my salvation' to embrace, or rather be embraced by, God's worldwide purposes."[27] Being in union with Christ means that we are united to Christ's mission; as the church we become an agency by which the gospel goes forth, securing more people for God's dynasty, thereby inducing the spread of God's covenant promises.

The Church as Sanctifying Agent

The external mission of the church (our calling to bring the gospel and its blessings to the lost world) is not the only role we play at this stage of the redemptive drama. As the New Testament depicts, the church is also driven by an internal mission in which we have a sanctifying role in the lives of the other congregants and the life of the church as a whole. In other words, there is a transformative objective central to the church whereby we, as members, work to sanctify, correct, and prepare one another for the eternal enjoyment of the new creation. The church,

---

[26] And according to the whole testimony of Matthew's Gospel, says Wright, "The closing line draws together the major themes of the gospel: the Emmanuel, the God-with-us, is now Jesus-with-us until the final end of the old age, the time when the new age, which has been inaugurated in the resurrection, has completed its transforming work in the world" (ibid., 235).
[27] Ibid., 229.

therefore, has an inward function by which it grooms the body—still struggling with sin and imperfections—for the eschatological kingdom of God.

Again, we find this sanctifying function of the church in the writings of the apostle Paul. The apostle makes it clear that his mission is the holiness of those who belong to Christ. This is evidenced in Ephesians 2:21–22, the final Pauline expression of the church-temple metaphor. Paul emphasizes the ongoing process of becoming the temple of God. For instance, in verse 21 he argues that "the whole structure, being joined together, *grows* into a holy temple in the Lord." To be more specific, the apostle continues to show this holy progression through the church when he insists that "in him you also are *being built together* into a dwelling place for God by the Spirit" (Eph. 3:22).

I believe this concept of "being built together" displays a corporate nature of sanctification happening in the ministry of the new temple. On the grounds of this communal growth, the church is not only the present dwelling place of the Lord, as indicated earlier; it is also a means through which the eschatological presence of the Lord is made available. In short, the present presence of the Spirit sanctifies us in order to prepare us for the Lord's eternal presence, and *one of the ways he does this is through the church*. The relationship between sanctification and the church is twofold: the church is both the *object* of sanctification and a *catalyst* of sanctification.

Take, for example, the New Testament Epistles as a whole. As mentioned before, these writings are "taken up with instructing believers in various churches on how they should grow in likeness to Christ."[28] Furthermore, "all of the moral exhortations and commands in the New Testament epistles apply [progressive sanctification], because they exhort believers to one aspect or another of greater sanctification in their lives."[29] The believers addressed in these letters hear the message through the perspective of the church. The church is the context for these moral exhortations. The Epistles are usually written to a corporate body of believers; and if they are written to individuals, they are often done so with their public reading in mind. What this shows us

---

[28] Grudem, *Systematic Theology*, 749.
[29] Ibid.

is that sanctification is always done in light of the church. The two are always connected.

We also see the sanctifying nature of the church within the church's practices. Take, for instance, the ministry of the Word and the work of church discipline. Both of these marks promote the corporate transformation of the community of Christ.

THE MINISTRY OF THE WORD

In the first place, the Holy Spirit uses the Word of God to bring regeneration and progressive growth in holiness. Jesus's high priestly prayer in John 17:17 petitions the Lord, "Sanctify them in the truth; your word is truth." Such a verse clarifies the purifying realities of the Word of God. And Paul, in Ephesians, associates the sanctification of the church with the Word of God when he writes, "Christ loved the church and gave himself up for her, that he might sanctify her, having cleansed her by the *washing of water with the word*" (Eph. 5:25–26). Not to mention 2 Timothy 3:16–17, where Paul tells us what Scripture is (the inspired Word of God), what it is good for (teaching, reproof, correction, training in righteousness), and why we need it (so that we may be made complete and be equipped for every good work). God's Word is for our growth in godliness. It is for our sanctification, and we hear Scripture taught and preached most often in the context of the church.

Such texts make it evident that the church "needs God's Word . . . to continually challenge and shape us" for "His word not only gives us life, it also gives us direction as it keeps molding and shaping us in the image of the God who is speaking to us."[30] This is why the act of preaching is so important for the internal sanctification of the church. Thus Donald Whitney concludes, "Spiritually robust Christians hunger for the proclamation of God's message. This is part of the nourishment God has planned for the soul."[31] But remember, preaching demands a corporate context. It demands an audience—one that is listening and hearing the Word of God and being conformed to the image of Christ by the Spirit's application of the preached Word.

---

[30] Edmund P. Clowney, "The Biblical Theology of the Church," in *The Church in the Bible and the World: An International Study*, ed. D. A. Carson (Grand Rapids: Baker, 1987), 37.

[31] Donald S. Whitney, *Spiritual Disciplines within the Church: Participating Fully in the Body of Christ* (Chicago: Moody, 1996), 73.

CHURCH DISCIPLINE

Another important (though often neglected) part of the church's sanctifying agency is its discipline. Throughout the New Testament there is continued command to be a holy and obedient community.[32] Much of what the church does is to bring about obedience in its congregants. This obedience is the reason for church discipline. Mark Dever rightly concludes that all of church life is "a part of discipline. It is positive, shaping, formative discipline."[33] So in a very real sense, the whole of the church is concerned with the positive aspects of church discipline.

But there is a type of negative discipline as well. This is the discipline that is addressed in Matthew 18:15–17, 1 Corinthians 5:1–11, Galatians 6:1–2, 1 Thessalonians 3:6–15, 1 Timothy 1:20; 5:19–20, and Titus 3:9–11.[34] It is a discipline aimed at church members who are in grievous sin, whose souls are at stake, and whose rebellion taints the whole community. This discipline is concerned primarily with correction. The New Testament makes it clear that "when Christians sin, their sin is to be confronted by the church in accordance with the pattern revealed in Scripture."[35] In such circumstances, the Bible explicitly states that action must be taken *corporately* in order to bring the backslidden back into fellowship. The goal of church discipline is the *sanctification* of believers and the retrieval of their souls from the impending reality of judgment. Church discipline, when it is accomplished biblically, displays a love deeper than any the world has known, because it pursues the holiness of rebellious people so that they may return to God's presence.[36]

---

[32] Heb. 12:1–14, for example, reveals that the ground for church discipline is God's work to train and instruct the church for the eternal hope set out before believers. In other words, "God Himself disciplines us and . . . He commands us to do the same for each other." Mark Dever, *Nine Marks of a Healthy Church* (Wheaton, IL: Crossway, 2000), 159. The church, therefore, reflects the sanctifying work of the Spirit in performing discipline upon its congregants.

[33] Ibid., 155.

[34] These texts on the relationship of the church to its discipline express the importance of this reality in the life of the community. More explicitly, these passages indicate the proper approach of church discipline and how it is to be accomplished. But why is church discipline important? In reply, it can be said that the whole of the church's existence is concerned with it. As indicated above, all that the church accomplishes is for the sanctification of believers.

[35] R. Albert Mohler Jr., "Church Discipline: The Missing Mark," in *Polity: Biblical Arguments on How to Conduct Church Life*, ed. Mark E. Dever (Washington, DC: Center for Church Reform, 2001), 55.

[36] To be sure, there are potential pitfalls the church must seek to avoid when disciplining correctively. Corrective church discipline is "never to be done out of meanness of spirit but only out of love for the offending party and the members of the church individually, and ultimately out of love for God Himself." Dever, *Nine Marks*, 173. This reveals that the main purposes of church discipline are for the good of the one being disciplined and for the growth of the congregation. The point of church discipline is to rescue the lost brother and bring him back into the fellowship of God so that the one being corrected will be restored to the covenant promises of God.

Church discipline benefits not only those who respond to the discipline, but also those of us in the congregation watching it unfold. When unrepentant sin is brought before the gathered assembly, we are faced with the weightiness of our iniquity and the personal need for repentance. Thus, corrective discipline is not only for the sake of the one in rebellion, but also for the health of all of us because we too have rebellious hearts. Church discipline, when done right, benefits the whole church.[37] It makes it clear that church membership is to be taken seriously and that life in the church is about corporate transformation. Through the Spirit's work in the church, church discipline brings disobedient hearts back to fellowship, strengthens the community, and glorifies God through increased holiness.

In the church, "the new creation has been decisively launched, and Jesus's followers have been commissioned and equipped to put that victory and that inaugurated new world into practice."[38] So it is through Christ that the church has a place in God's eschatological mission. We are the temple of God where his presence is specially located. God's presence goes out from it to the rest of the world through us. For this reason, the church has external and internal purposes. Through the Spirit God charges us to spread the presence of God to the ends of the earth and to help sanctify one another for the eternal enjoyment of the Lord's redemptive promises. The church is vital to the eschatological mission of God and to our being prepared for it. May we see the importance of the church in light of God's presence, and may we pursue the glory of God in our missional and sanctifying activity. May we be the body of Christ manifest for the lost world and for each other.

The Presence of God and Our Future Hope: The Return of Christ and the Consummation of All Things

Let's be honest again. How many of us are scared of eschatology? We have seen the weird billboards announcing the exact time and date of Christ's return, only to realize that this date came and went a few months ago. We all notice how strange people get when they talk

---

[37] Dever, *Nine Marks*, 175. For further reading on this issue, see Jonathan Leeman, *The Church and the Surprising Offense of God's Love: Reintroducing the Doctrines of Church Membership and Discipline* (Wheaton, IL: Crossway, 2010).

[38] Wright, *Surprised by Hope*, 204.

about the end times, and we have probably lost track of how many eschatological positions there really are out there. We are confused by the differences between amillennialism, premillennialism, and preterism—not too mention that some of these have subcategories (e.g., partial preterism). To be sure, all of this can be overwhelming, so much so that our conversation/debates can get downright nasty if we run into the wrong theologian with the wrong passions. So, many of us give eschatology a wide berth. We just avoid the end times like, well, the tribulation itself.

But here is where an understanding of the presence of God helps. Thinking about God's presence balances our conception of eschatology. What if eschatology is not only about when Christ will return but also, and maybe more importantly, about what Christ comes to accomplish in his return? Please do not misunderstand me. It is not that the dates and times of the millennium are unimportant; it's just that these debates should not overshadow the significance of Christ's eschatological work. With Immanuel as our lens, we cannot help but see the importance surrounding the christological focus of eschatology. We have already seen what Christ's first coming has accomplished, but we cannot grasp the fullness of our redemption without also understanding the second coming of Christ. So, may our hope be rooted, not on the basis of our figuring out dates and times, but because we know what God is coming to do and we long for him to fulfill these promises for his glory and for our eternal delight.

The Return of the King: Christ's Work in the Second Coming

As the New Testament makes clear, Christ has promised to return for the consummation of his redemptive purposes. Acts 1:11 tells us that immediately following Christ's ascension, two angels announce to the apostles, "This Jesus, who was taken up from you into heaven, will come in the same way as you saw him go into heaven" (cf. 1 Thess. 4:16). According to the author of Hebrews, "Christ, having been offered once to bear the sins of many, will appear a second time, not to deal with sin but to save those who are eagerly waiting for him" (Heb. 9:28). Again, in Revelation 22:7, Christ himself reminds us, "Behold, I am coming soon." All this tells us that Christ's personal and physical second coming is crucial to our own redemptive-historical hopes. For in his return, we see that Christ, the perfect manifestation of God, comes again into his world to finish what he started.

One of the first things we should recognize about Christ's second coming is his new role. No longer the servant-king, Jesus will one day enter the final act of redemptive history as the *great, conquering warrior-king*—the one who has come to judge his enemies and consummate the redemptive promises for his people. At the end of it all, Christ comes to complete the other half of Israel's messianic expectation. He finally comes as the royal commander of heaven's armies who will restore, surpass, and consummate God's eschatological goals first known to Adam, hinted at in David, and inaugurated in the coming of the suffering Messiah. He is now the rightful ruler over the entire world, and in his return he will take his place upon the throne.

Christ's conquering work is described in Revelation 19. Here he is cast as the divine warrior, the Son of God who removes everything that stands in the way of God's promises. To do so, he brandishes his swift sword and pours out his righteous fury upon all his enemies (see also Rev. 1:14–16; 2:12, 16, 18; 5:6; 6:16; 11:15; 12:11; 14:14; 17:14).[39] In Revelation 19:1, John shows us that, in the second coming, the presence of God in Christ is active in this world once more. We are told that the heavens open up in order that the Son may come and consummate the Father's end-time purposes. As Grant Osborne contends, "The thrust [of Rev. 19:1] is that the consummation of God's acts in human history has arrived. The eschaton is here."[40] Christ's return means that Christ comes again to complete the divine redemptive project.

As the warrior-king, Jesus is manifest to destroy his enemies to the extent that his white robe of righteousness is stained with their

---

[39] Christ is also shown to be the divine warrior through John's images of eyes ablaze with fire, the numerous diadems, and the name unknown (Rev. 19:12), as well as the title "The Word of God" (Rev. 19:13). As Poythress summarizes, these images "testify to his worthiness and authority for the task [of divine warrior-king]. The eyes like blazing fire, recalling Revelation 1:14 and 2:18, affirm Christ's ability to see and judge human hearts and not merely outward appearances (2:23; Isa. 11:3–5; 1 Sam. 16:7). The many crowns on his head indicate the legitimate kingly authority that he has from his Father. The name that no one knows (v. 12) indicates that the full and surprising aspects of his coming are still a mystery to all. It may also remind us of his transcendence, his deity (cf. Judg. 13:18, 22). The name Word of God, as in John 1:1, reminds us of his powerful role in creation (Gen. 1:3; Ps. 33:6) and providence (Ps. 147:15; Lam. 3:37–38; Heb. 1:3). By virtue of his divinity and his lordship over all, he has the ability to bring to a conclusion the history that he has ruled over from the beginning (Isa. 11:4)." Vern S. Poythress, *The Returning King: A Guide to the Book of Revelation* (Phillipsburg, NJ: P&R, 2000), 174.
[40] Grant R. Osborne, *Revelation*, BECNT (Grand Rapids: Baker, 2002), 679.

blood.[41] Following his lead and command is the army of heaven. Like their king, they too are pure, and they conquer those who stand against God's rule and reign. Yet, even their vital role is a reduced one. Christ alone, through the sword of his Word, triumphs over his foes. It is Christ alone, the very presence of God manifest before the world once again, who will receive the full glory of his victory (Rev. 19:13, 15–16; cf. Eph. 6:17; Heb. 4:12).[42] Through his rod of iron, Christ dashes his enemies into pieces (Rev. 19:15; cf. Ps. 2:9) and overthrows the rebellious nations (Rev. 19:19–21).

The only things left in the wake of this "King of kings and Lord of lords" are the bodies of those who opposed him. Instead of taking part in the marriage supper of the Lamb, those who stand against Yahweh become the food of birds (Rev. 19:17–18). As for Satan and his servants, Christ becomes present to cast them into hell, where they will be separated from God forever (Rev. 19:20–21; 20:7–10). The constant plea for the Lord to come and conquer his people's enemies is finally answered at the end of Revelation.

Christ's Return as Covenant Keeper: Consummating God's Eschatological Objectives

Not only does God come to remove his enemies, but he also comes to bless his people. Christ's final work, therefore, has major implications

---

[41] There is a debate as to whose blood stains the robe of Christ here in Rev. 19:13. Some argue that the blood belongs to Christ, the one who gave his life and his blood to save his people (cf. Rev. 1:5; 5:9; 7:14; 12:11). For example, see M. E. Boring, *Revelation*, Interpretation (Louisville: John Knox, 1989); Leon Morris, *The Book of Revelation*, rev. ed., Tyndale New Testament Commentaries (Grand Rapids: Eerdmans, 1987); M. G. Reddish, "Martyr Theology in the Apocalypse," *Journal for the Study of the New Testament* 33 (1988): 89; J. P. M. Sweet, *Revelation*, Westminster Pelican Commentaries (Philadelphia: Westminster, 1979). But others argue that the shed blood here belongs to the enemies of the Lord. See D. E. Aune, *Revelation 17–22*, WBC (Nashville: Thomas Nelson, 1998); R. H. Charles, *A Critical and Exegetical Commentary on the Revelation of St. John*, vol. 2, ICC (Edinburgh: Clark, 1920); G. A. Krodel, *Revelation*, Augsburg Commentary on the New Testament (Minneapolis: Augsburg, 1989); D. J. MacLeod, "The First 'Last Thing': The Second Coming of Christ (Revelation 19:11–16)," *BSac* 156 (1999): 214; H. B. Swete, *The Apocalypse of St. John*, 3rd ed. (London: Macmillan, 1911). I would argue that in the context of Revelation 19 the latter conclusion would seem to fit better. We see that the emphasis of this passage is on judgment and the destruction of the wicked. Again, as Osborne reports: "The context is a military one. . . . Thus Christ's robe is dipped in the blood of his enemies." Osborne, *Revelation*, 682–83. Furthermore, there are corresponding references in this text to Isa. 63:2–3, which depicts the Lord as the judging warrior whose clothing is also covered with the blood of those he tramples in the winepress (see also Rev. 19:15). It would, therefore, seem most likely that emphasis is on judgment just as in the rest of the pericope and as is foreshadowed in its Old Testament antecedents.

[42] Rev. 20:9 also emphasizes that the victory in this last battle belongs to God and Christ alone. We see that the satanic forces have been released and once again have surrounded Jerusalem, "the beloved city" (Rev. 20:9; cf. Pss. 2:1–2; 46:6; 48:4–6). However, these enemies never stand a chance in light of God's power and wrath. Accordingly, in one swift act God pours out fire from heaven to devour those who stand against him (Rev. 20:9). The victory is God's and Christ's, showing the world once again that salvation and its outcomes are the Lord's gift—a gift he has chosen to give by his presence to underscore the truth that it is his alone to give.

for our Christian life. In Revelation 20:4–6, we see that Christ will return to this earth to rule and reign with us. Christ comes to open God's eschatological presence to us. The promise of God's dwelling eternally with man, that promise undergirding the storyline of Scripture, will finally find fulfillment in the powerful, royal rule of Christ. As the presence of God, he will return to usher us into the glorious reality of God's new and final dwelling place, that temple-city of the New Jerusalem. As king, he will finally vanquish all of his foes; his conquering work will remove evil, sin, and its oppressive consequences.[43] Regarding the faithful, justice will prevail, and we will finally gain the promises for which we have waited so long.

In the eschatological achievement of the warrior-king, the goals of redemption are finally met: through his future victory, we are glorified. We will indeed enter into the new creation filled with the presence of God. We see that much of God's redemptive agenda will come to pass once Jesus has "put all his enemies under his feet" (1 Cor. 15:25), and "the kingdom of the world has become the kingdom of our Lord and of his Christ" (Rev. 11:15). Then

> the blessings of the new covenant—and, thus, the eternal blessings foreshadowed in all previous covenants—will come to ultimate fulfillment. . . . Then and only then—in the eschatological reality, the New Jerusalem—will the hope expressed in the age-old covenant formula be most fully experienced: "God's dwelling is now among the people, and he will dwell with them. They will be his people, and God himself will be with them and be their God" (Rev. 21:3).[44]

In this final act we receive our glorification. But let us not be deceived. Our glorification is ultimately God's glorification. The Lord is the giver; we are the recipients. God enters this world so that we may

---

[43] As touched on in chap. 3, evidence of the removal of evil is seen in Rev. 21:1, where the description of the new creation includes the negative statement "The sea was no more." Though it can seem odd at this juncture of redemptive history, once we realize that the sea according to the Old and New Testaments symbolized chaos and evil, it begins to make more sense. Thus we see that "echoing the divine warrior's victory over *yam* (the sea [and its beast]), there is no longer any sea (21:1). In the new creation, there is no death, pain, tears, or mourning (21:4); the old order has passed away and all things are new (21:4–5)." Tremper Longman III and Daniel G. Reid, *God Is a Warrior* (Grand Rapids: Zondervan, 1995), 191. In fact, in place of the sea as the archetype of cosmic evil, there is a "river of life" that flows from the throne of God, representing the new kingdom of God's presence and the removal of chaos that results from the former age of the Evil One (Rev. 22:1).

[44] Paul R. Williamson, *Sealed with an Oath: Covenant in God's Unfolding Purpose*, NSBT 23 (Downers Grove, IL: InterVarsity, 2007), 210.

reside with him in his. So even in the completion of our salvation, God takes center stage. He is present to secure our salvation and deliver our salvation. With Christ's return, the old creation will make way for a new and better creation—a place where we will enter into fellowship with God without limitations and in full delight.

This is why Revelation 21 and 22 follow Revelation 19 and 20. In John's structure, we see that Christ is present as the warrior-king to judge God's enemies but also to secure the promise of Christ for us. This eschatological vision of Revelation 21–22 shows repeatedly that "in the new heavens and new earth the presence of God will be unmediated once again."[45] In the new creation, the cosmological expanse of the Lord's presence will be finished, and the God of redemptive history will dwell among his people once and for all (Rev. 21:3). His presence will illuminate the New Jerusalem (Rev. 21:22–27) and his people will forever be before the face of God (Rev. 22:4).

Conclusion

"Behold, the dwelling place of God is with man" (Rev. 21:3). In this simple yet profound phrase, God's mission is complete.[46] It is what we as Christians all long to hear. It tells us that God's presence to redeem is successful; it has removed the barriers of Eden and reconciled us to his glorious, eschatological presence. At the center of this functional work is the presence of God in Christ. He comes to change us and prepare a way for us to draw near to God. But Christ does not leave us on our own. He sends his Spirit to apply his work of reconciliation and makes us holy. Not only that, but the Spirit unites us with other believers in the church. It is here that our place in the redemptive mission takes shape. We work corporately as the temple of God to tell others of God's presence and to prepare one another in the church for eternity with God. Finally we see that Christ has come to serve and save; he comes again to judge and destroy God's enemies and to make a way to the fulfillment of God's redemptive promises for his people. As the warrior-

---

[45] R. E. Averbeck, "Tabernacle," in *Dictionary of the Old Testament: Pentateuch*, ed. T. Desmond Alexander et al. (Downers Grove, IL: InterVarsity, 2003), 822. Thus, "Rev. 21:3, 'the tabernacle of God is with men'; Rev. 21:22–27, 'the glory of God' illumines the New Jerusalem and 'its lamp is the Lamb,' so that the nations will 'walk' by its light."

[46] As the discussion of the presence of God in heaven corresponds with the relational presence of God, chap. 3 expounds a more detailed and comprehensive analysis of the divine presence in the new heaven and new earth.

king, God will wage his final battle to culminate the goals of redemption (Ex. 15:2; Deuteronomy 20; Isa. 59:16–18; Ezek. 38–39; Hab. 3:8–15; Zech. 12:1–9; 14:3–5).[47]

So we marvel at God's work in redemption. We hope in God's eschatological promises. We wait for God's reclamation project to be finished once and for all. And with Christ's second coming, this will take place. As our eyes look back on what God's redemptive presence has done on our behalf, our hearts rejoice. And in looking back, we cannot help but also glimpse forward at what his redemptive presence promises. And what do we see? That beautiful garden-city filled with the presence of God. For those of us reconciled by Christ. Like John, we look in hope for Immanuel's return, and proclaim, "Come, Lord Jesus!" (Rev. 22:20). Come, be the means of our salvation. Come, usher us into the fullness of joy. Come, make our story your story.

---

[47] Poythress, *Returning King*, 173.

Bibliography

Articles

Abba, R. "The Divine Name Yahweh." *Journal of Biblical Literature* 80 (1961): 320–28.

Albright, W. F. "Contributions to Biblical Archeology and Philology." *Journal of Biblical Literature* 43 (1924): 363–93.

———. "The Names 'Israel' and 'Judah' with an Excursus on the Etymology of *Tôdâh* and *Tôrâh*." *Journal of Biblical Literature* 46 (1927): 154–68.

Alexander, T. Desmond. "The Passover Sacrifice." In *Sacrifice in the Bible*, edited by R. T. Beckwith and M. J. Selman, 1–25. Grand Rapids: Baker, 1995.

———. "Seed." In *New Dictionary of Biblical Theology*, edited by T. Desmond Alexander, Brian S. Rosner, D. A. Carson, and Graeme Goldsworthy, 769–73. Downers Grove, IL: InterVarsity, 2000.

Allison, D. C. "Eschatology." In *Dictionary of Jesus and the Gospels*, edited by J. B. Green, S. McKnight, and I. H. Marshall, 206–9. Downers Grove, IL: InterVarsity, 1992.

Anderson, Bernard W. "Exodus Typology in Second Isaiah." In *Israel's Prophetic Heritage*, edited by B. W Anderson and Walter J. Harrelson, 177–95. New York: Harper & Row, 1962.

Arnold, William R. "The Divine Name in Exodus iii. 14." *Journal of Biblical Literature* 24 (1905): 107–65.

Averbeck, R. E. "Offerings and Sacrifices." In *New International Dictionary of Old Testament Theology and Exegesis*. Vol. 4, edited by Willem A. VanGemeren, 996–1022. Grand Rapids: Zondervan, 1997.

———. "Tabernacle." In *Dictionary of the Old Testament: Pentateuch*, edited by T. Desmond Alexander and David W. Baker, 807–27. Downers Grove, IL: InterVarsity, 2003.

Balentine, George L. "Death of Jesus as a New Exodus," *Review and Expositor* 59 (1962): 27–41.

Basinger, Randall. "Evangelicals and Process Theism: Seeking a Middle Ground." *Christian Scholar's Review* 15 (1986): 157–67.

Beale, Gregory K. "The Eschatological Conception of New Testament Theology." In *Eschatology in Bible and Theology: Evangelical Essays at the Dawn of a New*

Millennium, edited by Kent E. Bower and Mark W. Elliott, 11–52. Downers Grove, IL: InterVarsity, 1997.

———. "Eschatology." In *Dictionary of the Later New Testament and Its Developments*, edited by P. H. Davids and R. P. Martin, 330–45. Downers Grove, IL: InterVarsity, 1997.

———. "The Final Vision of the Apocalypse and Its Implications for the Biblical Theology of the Temple." In *Heaven on Earth: The Temple in Biblical Theology*, edited by T. Desmond Alexander and Simon Gathercole, 191–209. Waynesboro, GA: Paternoster, 2004.

———. "Garden Temple." *Kerux* 18 (2003): 3–50.

———. "Revelation (Book)." In *New Dictionary of Biblical Theology*, edited by T. Desmond Alexander, Brian S. Rosner, D. A. Carson, and Graeme Goldsworthy, 356–63. Downers Grove, IL: InterVarsity, 2000.

Beale, Gregory K., and Sean M. McDonough. "Revelation 21:1–22:5." In *Commentary on the New Testament Use of the Old Testament*, edited by Gregory K. Beale and D. A. Carson, 1150–56. Grand Rapids: Baker, 2007.

Beckwith, R. T. "Sacrifice." In *New Dictionary of Biblical Theology*, edited by T. Desmond Alexander, Brian S. Rosner, D. A. Carson, and Graeme Goldsworthy, 754–62. Downers Grove, IL: InterVarsity, 2000.

Beilby, James. "Divine Aseity, Divine Freedom: A Conceptual Problem for Edwardsian Calvinism." *Journal of the Evangelical Theological Society* 47 (2004): 648.

Blomberg, Craig L. "The Unity and Diversity of Scripture." In *New Dictionary of Biblical Theology*, edited by T. Desmond Alexander, Brian S. Rosner, D. A. Carson, and Graeme Goldsworthy, 64–72. Downers Grove, IL: InterVarsity, 2000.

Bromiley, G. W. "Divine Presence." In *Evangelical Dictionary of Theology*. 2nd ed., edited by Walter Elwell, 951–52. Grand Rapids: Baker, 2001.

Brownlee, W. H. "The Ineffable Name of God." *Bulletin of the American Schools of Oriental Research* 226 (1977): 39–46.

Burge, G. M. "'I Am' Sayings." In *Dictionary of Jesus and the Gospels*, edited by Joel B. Green, Scot McKnight, and I. Howard Marshall, 354–56. Downers Grove, IL: InterVarsity, 1992.

Carson, D. A. "John and the Johannine Epistles." In *It Is Written: Scripture Citing Scripture*, edited by D. A. Carson and H. G. M. Williamson, 245–64. Cambridge: Cambridge University Press, 1988.

———. "Unity and Diversity in the New Testament: The Possibility of Systematic Theology." In *Scripture and Truth*, edited by D. A. Carson and John D. Woodbridge, 65–95. Grand Rapids: Baker, 1992.

Cartwright, Colbert S. "The Spiritual Nature of the Church." *Mid-Stream* 19 (1980): 322–33.

"Church." In *Dictionary of Biblical Imagery*, edited by Leland Ryken, James C. Wilhoit, and Tremper Longman III, 147–48. Downers Grove, IL: InterVarsity, 1998.

Ciampa, Roy E. "The History of Redemption." In *Central Themes in Biblical Theology: Mapping Unity in Diversity*, edited by Scott J. Hafemann and Paul R. House, 254–308. Grand Rapids: Baker, 2007.

Clements, R. E. "The Immanuel Prophecy of Isaiah 7:10–17 and Its Messianic Interpretation." In *Old Testament Prophecy: From Oracles to Canon*, 65–77. Louisville: Westminster John Knox, 1996.

———. "The Messianic Hope in the Old Testament." *Journal for the Study of the Old Testament* 43 (1989): 3–19.

"Cloud." In *Dictionary of Biblical Imagery*, edited by Leland Ryken, James C. Wilhoit, and Tremper Longman III, 157. Downers Grove, IL: InterVarsity, 1998.

Clowney, Edmund P. "The Biblical Theology of the Church." In *The Church in the Bible and the World: An International Study*, edited by D. A. Carson, 13–87. Grand Rapids: Baker, 1987.

———. "Church." In *New Dictionary of Theology*, edited by Sinclair B. Ferguson, David F. Wright, and J. I. Packer, 140–43. Downers Grove, IL: InterVarsity, 1988.

Cobb, John B., Jr. "Two Types of Postmodernism: Deconstruction and Process." *Theology Today* 47 (1990): 149–58.

Coote, R. "The Meaning of the Name Israel." *Harvard Theological Review* 65 (1972): 137–46.

Cross, F. M., Jr. "Yahweh and the God of the Patriarchs." *Harvard Theological Review* 55 (1962): 229–59.

Dean, William. "Deconstruction and Process Theology." *Journal of Religion* 64 (1984): 1–19.

Dempster, Stephen G. "Geography and Genealogy, Dominion and Dynasty." In *Biblical Theology: Retrospect and Prospect*, edited by Scott J. Hafemann, 66–82. Downers Grove, IL: InterVarsity, 2002.

Dumbrell, William J. "Genesis 2:1–17: A Foreshadowing of the New Creation." In *Biblical Theology: Retrospect and Prospect*, edited by Scott J. Hafemann, 53–65. Downers Grove, IL: InterVarsity, 2002.

Ellingworth, Paul. "Priests." In *New Dictionary of Biblical Theology*, edited by T. Desmond Alexander, Brian S. Rosner, D. A. Carson, and Graeme Goldsworthy, 696–701. Downers Grove, IL: InterVarsity, 2000.

Feinberg, Charles. "The Virgin Birth in the OT and Isaiah 7:14." *Bibliotheca Sacra* 119 (1962): 251–58.

Feinberg, John S. "Salvation in the Old Testament." In *Tradition and Testament: Essays in Honor of Charles Lee Feinberg*, edited by John S. Feinberg and Paul D. Feinberg, 39–77. Chicago: Moody, 1981.

Feinberg, Paul. "Bible, Inerrancy and Infallibility of." In *Evangelical Dictionary of Theology*, edited by Walter Elwell, 141–45. Grand Rapids: Baker, 1999.

"Fire." In *Dictionary of Biblical Imagery*, edited by Leland Ryken, James C. Wilhoit, and Tremper Longman III, 286–89. Downers Grove, IL: InterVarsity, 1998.

Freedman, D. N. "The Name of the God of Moses." *Journal of Biblical Literature* 79 (1960): 151–56.

Gaffin, Richard B., Jr. "Glory." In *New Dictionary of Biblical Theology*, edited by T. Desmond Alexander, Brian S. Rosner, D. A. Carson, and Graeme Goldsworthy, 507–11. Downers Grove, IL: InterVarsity, 2000.

———. "Last Adam, The Life-Giving Spirit." In *The Forgotten Christ: Exploring the Majesty and Mystery of God Incarnate*, edited by Stephen Clark, 191–231. Nottingham, UK: Apollos, 2007.

"Glory." In *Dictionary of Biblical Imagery*, edited by Leland Ryken, James C. Wilhoit, and Tremper Longman III, 330–31. Downers Grove, IL: InterVarsity, 1998.

Goitein, S. D. "YHWH the Passionate: The Monotheistic Meaning and Origin of the Name YHWH." *Vestus Testamentum* 6 (1956): 1–9.

Gordon, C. "Almah in Isaiah 7:14." *Journal of Bible and Religion* 21 (1953): 106.

Grenz, Stanley J. "Belonging to God: The Quest for Communal Spirituality in the Postmodern World." *Asbury Theological Journal* 54 (1999): 41–52.

Grogan, G. W. "Psalms." In *New Dictionary of Biblical Theology*, edited by T. Desmond Alexander, Brian S. Rosner, D. A. Carson, and Graeme Goldsworthy, 203–8. Downers Grove, IL: InterVarsity, 2000.

Gunton, Collin. "A Rose by Any Other Name? From Christian Doctrine to Systematic Theology." *International Journal of Systematic Theology* 1 (1999): 4–23.

Hafemann, Scott J. "Biblical Theology: Retrospect and Prospect." In *Biblical Theology: Retrospect and Prospect*, edited by Scott J. Hafemann, 15–24. Downers Grove, IL: InterVarsity, 2002,

———. "The Covenant Relationship." In *Central Themes in Biblical Theology: Mapping Unity in Diversity*, edited by Scott J. Hafemann and Paul R. House, 20–65. Grand Rapids: Baker, 2007.

Hamilton, James M., Jr. "Divine Presence." In *Dictionary of the Old Testament: Wisdom, Poetry, and Writings*, edited by Tremper Longman III and Peter Enns, 116–20. Downers Grove, IL: InterVarsity, 2008.

———. "The Glory of God in Salvation through Judgment: The Centre of Biblical Theology?" *Tyndale Bulletin* 57 (2006): 57–84.

———. "God with Men in the Prophets and the Writings: An Examination of the Nature of God's Presence." *Scottish Bulletin of Evangelical Theology* 23 (2005): 166–93.

———. "God with Men in the Torah." *Westminster Theological Journal* 65 (2003): 113–33.

———. "Theophany." In *Dictionary of the Old Testament: Wisdom, Poetry, and Writings*, edited by Tremper Longman III and Peter Enns, 817–20. Downers Grove, IL: InterVarsity, 2008.

Hammershaimb, E. "The Immanuel Sign." *Studia Theologica* 3 (1949): 124–42.

Hasel, G. F. "The Meaning of the Animal Rite in Gen. 15." *Journal for the Study of the Old Testament* 19 (1981): 61–78.

Hauser, A. J. "Linguistic and Thematic Links between Gen. 4:1–16 and Gen. 2–3." *Journal of the Evangelical Theological Society* 12 (1980): 297–305.

Horrell, J. Scott. "Toward a Biblical Model of the Social Trinity: Avoiding Equivocation of Nature and Order." *Journal of the Evangelical Theological Society* 47 (2004): 399–421.

Howell, Nancy R. "Feminism and Process Thought." *Process Studies* 22 (1993): 69–106.

Kim, S. "Jesus—The Son of God, the Stone, the Son of Man, and the Servant: The Role of Zechariah in the Self-Identification of Jesus." In *Tradition and Interpretation in the New Testament*, edited by Gerald F. Hawthorne and Otto Betz, 134–48. Grand Rapids: Eerdmans, 1987.

Krietzer, L. J. "Eschatology." In *Dictionary of Paul and His Letters*, edited by G. F. Hawthorne, R. P. Martin, and D. G. Reid, 253–69. Downers Grove, IL: InterVarsity, 1993.

Lattey, C. "The Term *'almah* in Isaiah 7:14." *Catholic Biblical Quarterly* 9 (1947): 89–95.

MacLaurin, E. C. B. "YHWH: The Origin of the Tetragrammaton." *Vestus Testamentum* 12 (1962): 439–63.

Marshall, I. Howard. "Acts 2:24–28." In *Commentary on the New Testament Use of the Old Testament*, edited by G. K. Beale and D. A. Carson, 536–39. Grand Rapids: Baker, 2007.

McCartney, Dan G. "*Ecce Homo*: The Coming Kingdom as the Restoration of Human Vicegerency." *Westminster Theological Journal* 56 (1994): 1–21.

McConville, Gordon. "Exodus." In *New International Dictionary of Old Testament Theology and Exegesis*. Vol. 4, edited by Willem A. VanGemeren, 601–5. Grand Rapids: Zondervan, 1997.

———. "Jerusalem in the Old Testament." In *Jerusalem Past and Present in the Purposes of God*, edited by P. W. L. Walker, 21–52. Cambridge: Tyndale House, 1992.

McDaniel, F. L. "Mission in the Old Testament." In *Mission in the New Testament: An Evangelical Approach*, edited by W. J. Larkin and J. F. Williams, 11–20. Maryknoll, NY: Orbis, 1998.

McKelvey, R. J. "Temple." In *New Dictionary of Biblical Theology*, edited by T. Desmond Alexander, Brian S. Rosner, D. A. Carson, and Graeme Goldsworthy, 806–11. Downers Grove, IL: InterVarsity, 2000.

Mohler, R. Albert, Jr. "Church Discipline: The Missing Mark." In *Polity: Biblical Arguments on How to Conduct Church Life*, ed. Mark E. Dever, 43–62. Washington, DC: Center for Church Reform, 2001.

Motyer, J. Alec. "Context and Content in the Interpretation of Isa. 7, 14." *Tyndale Bulletin* 21 (1970): 118–25.

Motyer, Stephen. "Israel (nation)." In *New Dictionary of Biblical Theology*, edited by T. Desmond Alexander, Brian S. Rosner, D. A. Carson, and Graeme Goldsworthy, 581–87. Downers Grove, IL: InterVarsity, 2000.

Mowinckel, Sigmund Olaf Plytt. "The Name of the God of Moses." *Hebrew Union College Annual* 32 (1961): 121–33.

Muller, W. "A Virgin Shall Conceive." *Evangelical Quarterly* 32 (1960): 203–7.

North, R. "Separated Spiritual Substances in the Old Testament." *Catholic Biblical Quarterly* 29 (1967): 419–49.

Obermann, Julian. "The Divine Name YHWH in Light of Recent Discoveries." *Journal of Biblical Literature* 68 (1949): 301–23.

O'Brien, P. T. "The Church as a Heavenly and Eschatological Entity." In *The Church in the Bible and the World: An International Study*, edited by D. A. Carson, 88–119. Grand Rapids: Baker, 1987.

Patterson, Richard, and Michael Travers. "Contours of the Exodus Motif in Jesus' Earthly Ministry." *Westminster Theological Journal* 66 (2004): 25–47.

Peterson, David. "Atonement in the Old Testament." In *Where Wrath and Mercy Meet: Proclaiming the Atonement Today*, edited by David Peterson, 1–25. Carlisle, UK: Paternoster, 2008.

———. "Worship." In *New Dictionary of Biblical Theology*, edited by T. Desmond Alexander, Brian S. Rosner, D. A. Carson, and Graeme Goldsworthy, 855–63. Downers Grove, IL: InterVarsity, 2000.

Pinnock, Clark H. "Systematic Theology." In *The Openness of God: A Biblical Challenge to the Traditional Understanding of God*, 101–25. Downers Grove, IL: InterVarsity, 1994.

Rehm, M. "Das wort 'almah in Is. 7:14." *Biblische Zeitschrift* 8 (1964): 89–101.

Reymond, Robert L. "Immanuel." In *Evangelical Dictionary of Theology*, edited by Walter A. Elwell. Grand Rapids: Baker, 1999.

Rogers, Cleon L., Jr. "The Covenant of David in the New Testament." *Bibliotheca Sacra* 150 (1993): 458–78.

Salier, Bill. "The Temple in the Gospel according to John." In *Heaven on Earth: The Temple in Biblical Theology*, edited by T. Desmond Alexander and Simon Gathercole, 121–34. Waynesboro, GA: Paternoster, 2004.

Sandmel, Samuel. "Haggada within Scripture." *Journal of Biblical Literature* 80 (1961): 105–22.

Schnabel, E. J. "Scripture." In *New Dictionary of Biblical Theology*, edited by T. Desmond Alexander, Brian S. Rosner, D. A. Carson, and Graeme Goldsworthy, 34–43. Downers Grove, IL: InterVarsity, 2000.

Schreiner, Thomas. "Penal Substitution View." In *The Nature of the Atonement: Four Views*, edited by James Beilby and Paul Eddy, 67–98. Downers Grove, IL: InterVarsity, 2006.

Scobie, Charles H. H. "Israel and the Nations: An Essay in Biblical Theology." *Tyndale Bulletin* 43 (1992): 282–305.

Seitz, Christopher. "Handing over the Name: Christian Reflection on the Divine Name YHWH." In *Trinity, Time, and Church*, edited by Colin Gunton, 23–41. Grand Rapids: Eerdmans, 2000.

Spina, F. "The 'Ground' for Cain's Rejection (Gen. 4): 'dāmāh in the Context of Gen. 1–11." *Zeitschrift für die alttestamentliche Wissenschaft* 104 (1992): 319–32.

Steinmueller, J. "Etymology and Biblical Usage of 'Almah." *Catholic Biblical Quarterly* 2 (1940): 28–43.

Strange, Daniel. "A Little Dwelling on the Divine Presence: Towards a 'Whereness' of the Triune God." In *Heaven on Earth: The Temple in Biblical Theology*, edited by T. Desmond Alexander and Simon Gathercole, 211–30. Waynesboro, GA: Paternoster, 2004.

Thomas, Gordon J. "A Holy God among a Holy People in a Holy Place: The Enduring Eschatological Hope." In *Eschatology in Bible and Theology: Evangelical Essays at the Dawn of a New Millennium*, edited by Kent E. Bower and Mark W. Elliott, 53–69. Downers Grove, IL: InterVarsity, 1997.

Vawter, B. "The Ugaritic Use of *glmt*." *Catholic Biblical Quarterly* 14 (1952): 318–22.

Vertin, Michael. "Is God in Process?" In *Religion and Culture: Essays in Honor of Bernard Lonergan*, edited by Timothy Fallon and Philip Riley, 45–62. Albany: State University of New York Press, 1987.

Waltke, Bruce K. "Cain and His Offering." *Westminster Theological Journal* 48 (1986): 363–72;

Ware, Bruce A. "How Shall We Think about the Trinity?" In *God under Fire*, edited by Douglas S. Huffman and Eric L. Johnson, 253–77. Grand Rapids: Zondervan, 2002.

———. "The New Covenant and the People(s) of God." In *Dispensationalism, Israel, and the Church: The Search for Definition*, edited by Craig A. Blaising and Darrell L. Bock, 68–97. Grand Rapids: Zondervan, 1992.

Weinfeld, M. "Sabbath, Temple, and Enthronement of the Lord—The Problem of the *Sitz im Leben* of Gen. 1:1–2:3." In *Melanges bibliques et orientaux en l'honneur de M. Henri Cazelles*, edited by A. Caquot and M. Delcor, 501–12. Kevelear, Ger.: Butzon and Becker, 1981.

Wenham, Gordon J. "The Coherence of the Flood Narrative." *Vestus Testamentum* 28 (1978): 336–48.

———. "Sanctuary Symbolism in the Garden of Eden Story." In *I Studied Inscriptions from before the Flood*, edited by Richard S. Hess and David Toshio Tsumura, 399–404. Winona Lake, IN: Eisenbrauns, 1994.

Whitaker, John. "Literal and Figurative Language of God." *Religious Studies* 17 (1981): 39–54.

Williams, Garry J. "Penal Substitution: A Response to Recent Criticisms." *Journal of the Evangelical Theological Society* 50 (2007): 71–86.

Williamson, Paul R. "Covenant." In *New Dictionary of Biblical Theology*, edited by T. Desmond Alexander, Brian S. Rosner, D. A. Carson, and Graeme Goldsworthy, 419–29. Downers Grove, IL: InterVarsity, 2000.

Wolf, Herbert Martin. "Servant of the Lord." In *Theological Dictionary of the Bible*, edited by Walter Elwell, 726–27. Grand Rapids: Baker, 1996.

———. "A Solution to the Immanuel Prophecy in Isaiah 7:14–8:22." *Journal of Biblical Literature* 91 (1972): 449–56.

Yarbrough, R. W. "Atonement." In *New Dictionary of Biblical Theology*, edited by T. Desmond Alexander, Brian S. Rosner, D. A. Carson, and Graeme Goldsworthy, 388–93. Downers Grove, IL: InterVarsity, 2000.

Books

Albertz, Rainer. *Israel in Exile: The History and Literature of the Sixth Century B.C.E.* Atlanta: Society of Biblical Literature, 2003.

Alexander, T. Desmond. *From Eden to the New Jerusalem: Exploring God's Plan for Life on Earth*. Nottingham, UK: InterVarsity, 2008.

———. *From Paradise to the Promised Land: An Introduction to the Pentateuch*. Grand Rapids: Baker Academic, 2002.

———. *The Servant King: The Bible's Portrait of the Messiah*. Vancouver: Regent, 1998.

Alexander, T. Desmond, and Simon Gathercole. *Heaven on Earth: The Temple in Biblical Theology*. Carlisle, UK: Paternoster, 2004.

Anderson, Bernhard W. *Contours of Old Testament Theology*. Minneapolis: Fortress, 1999.

———. *From Creation to New Creation: Old Testament Perspectives*. Minneapolis: Fortress, 1994.

———. *The Unfolding Drama of the Bible*. 3rd ed. Philadelphia: Fortress, 1988.

Barth, Karl. *Church Dogmatics*. Edited by G. W. Bromiley and T. F. Torrance. Vol. 2, *The Doctrine of God*. Part 1. Translated by T. H. L. Parker, W. B. Johnston, Harold Knight, and J. L. M. Haire. Edinburgh: T&T Clark, 1957.

Bauckham, Richard. *The Bible and Mission: Christian Witness in a Postmodern World*. Carlisle, UK: Paternoster, 2003.

———. *God Crucified: Monotheism and Christology in the New Testament*. Grand Rapids: Eerdmans, 1998.

———. *The Theology of the Book of Revelation*. Cambridge: Cambridge University Press, 1993.

Bauer, Walter. *A Greek-English Lexicon of the New Testament*. Edited and translated by William F. Arndt, F. Wilber Gingrich, and Fredrick W. Danker. 2nd ed. Chicago: University of Chicago Press, 1979.

Bavinck, Herman. *Reformed Dogmatics*. Vol. 1, *Prolegomena*. Edited by John Bolt. Translated by John Vriend. Grand Rapids: Baker, 2003.

———. *Reformed Dogmatics*. Vol. 2, *God and Creation*. Edited by John Bolt. Translated by John Vriend. Grand Rapids: Baker, 2004.

———. *Reformed Dogmatics*. Vol. 4, *Holy Spirit, Church, and New Creation*. Edited by John Bolt. Translated by John Vriend. Grand Rapids: Baker, 2008.

Beale, Gregory K. *The Book of Revelation: A Commentary on the Greek Text*. New International Greek Testament Commentary. Grand Rapids: Eerdmans, 1999.

———. *The Temple and the Church's Mission: A Biblical Theology of the Dwelling Place of God*. New Studies in Biblical Theology 17. Downers Grove, IL: InterVarsity, 2004.

Becker, J. *Messianic Expectation in the Old Testament*. Edinburgh: T&T Clark, 1980.

Beer, G. *Exodus*. Handbuch zum Alten Testament. Tübingen: Mohr, 1939.

Blocher, Henri. *In the Beginning: The Opening Chapters of Genesis*. Translated by David G. Preston. Downers Grove, IL: InterVarsity, 1984.

Block, Daniel I. *The Book of Ezekiel: Chapters 25–48*. New International Commentary on the Old Testament. Grand Rapids: Eerdmans, 1998.

———. *Judges, Ruth.* New American Commentary. Nashville: Broadman & Holman, 1999.

Blomberg, Craig L. *Matthew.* New American Commentary. Nashville: Broadman & Holman, 1992.

Bock, Darrell L. *Acts.* Baker Exegetical Commentary on the New Testament. Grand Rapids: Baker, 2007.

———. *Luke 1:1–9:50.* Baker Exegetical Commentary on the New Testament. Grand Rapids: Baker, 1994.

Boda, Mark J. *Zechariah.* NIV Application Commentary. Grand Rapids: Zondervan, 2004.

Boice, James M., ed. *The Foundations of Biblical Authority.* Grand Rapids: Zondervan, 1983.

Boyd, Gregory A. *God at War: The Bible and Spiritual Conflict.* Downers Grove, IL: InterVarsity, 1997.

———. *God of the Possible: A Biblical Introduction to the Open View of God.* Grand Rapids: Baker, 2000.

———. *Trinity and Process: A Critical Evaluation and Reconstruction of Hartshorne's Di-Polar Theism Towards a Trinitarian Metaphysics.* New York: Peter Lang, 1992.

Bray, Gerald. *The Doctrine of God.* Downers Grove, IL: InterVarsity, 1993.

Brother Lawrence. *The Practice of the Presence of God.* Translated by John J. Delaney. New York: Doubleday, 1977.

Bruce, F. F. *The New Testament Development of Old Testament Themes.* Grand Rapids: Eerdmans, 1968.

Brueggemann, Walter. *Theology of the Old Testament: Testimony, Dispute, Advocacy.* Minneapolis: Fortress, 1997.

Burns, J. Lanier. *The Nearness of God: His Presence with His People.* Explorations in Biblical Theology. Phillipsburg, NJ: P&R, 2009.

Caird, G. B. *The Revelation of St. John the Divine.* 2nd ed. Black's New Testament Commentaries. London: Black, 1984.

Calvin, John. *Institutes of the Christian Religion.* Edited by John T. McNeill. Translated by Ford Lewis Battles. Library of Christian Classics. Philadelphia: Westminster, 1985.

Carson, D. A. *The Difficult Doctrine of the Love of God.* Wheaton, IL: Crossway, 2000.

———. *Divine Sovereignty and Human Responsibility: Biblical Perspectives in Tension.* Grand Rapids: Baker, 1994.

———. *The Gagging of God: Christianity Confronts Pluralism.* Grand Rapids: Zondervan, 1996.

———. *The Gospel according to John.* Pillar New Testament Commentary. Grand Rapids: Eerdmans, 1991.

Carson, D. A., Douglas Moo, and Leon Morris. *An Introduction to the New Testament.* Grand Rapids: Zondervan, 1992.

Carson, D. A., and John D. Woodbridge, eds. *Hermeneutics, Authority, and Canon.* Grand Rapids: Zondervan, 1986.

———, eds. *Scripture and Truth.* Grand Rapids: Baker, 1992.

Chalke, Steve, and Alan Mann. *The Lost Message of Jesus.* Grand Rapids: Zondervan, 2003.

Childs, Brevard. *Biblical Theology in Crisis.* Philadelphia: Westminster, 1970.

———. *Biblical Theology of the Old and New Testaments: Theological Reflection on the Christian Bible.* London: SCM, 1992.

———. *Exodus: A Critical and Theological Commentary.* Philadelphia: Westminster, 1974.

Clines, David J. A. *The Theme of the Pentateuch.* Journal for the Study of the Old Testament 10. Sheffield, UK: Journal for the Study of the Old Testament, 1978.

———. *What Does Eve Do to Help? and Other Readerly Questions to the Old Testament.* Journal for the Study of the Old Testament 94. Sheffield, UK: Journal for the Study of the Old Testament, 1990.

Cobb, John B., Jr., and David Ray Griffin. *Process Theology: An Introductory Exposition.* Philadelphia: Westminster, 1976.

Cobb, John B., Jr., and Clark H. Pinnock. *Searching for an Adequate God: A Dialogue between Process and Free Will Theists.* Grand Rapids: Eerdmans, 2000.

Coloe, Mary L. *God Dwells with Us: Temple Symbolism in the Fourth Gospel.* Collegeville, MN: Liturgical Press, 2001.

Congar, Yves. *The Mystery of the Temple.* Translated by Reginald F. Trevett. Westminster, MD: Newman, 1962.

Craigie, Peter C. *Psalms 1–50.* Word Biblical Commentary. Waco, TX: Word, 1983.

Cranfield, C. E. B. *Romans 1–8.* Vol. 1. International Critical Commentary. Edinburgh: T&T Clark, 1975.

Daube, David. *The Exodus Pattern in the Bible.* London: Faber and Faber, 1963.

Davidson, Richard M. *Typology in Scripture: A Study of the Hermeneutical* τύπος *Structures.* Berrien Springs, MI: Andrews University Press, 1981.

Davies, W. D., and D. C. Allison. *The Gospel according to St. Matthew.* Vol. 1. International Critical Commentary. Edinburgh: T&T Clark, 1988.

Demarest, Bruce. *The Cross and Salvation: The Doctrine of Salvation.* Wheaton, IL: Crossway, 1997.

Dempster, Stephen G. *Dominion and Dynasty: A Theology of the Hebrew Bible.* New Studies in Biblical Theology 15. Downers Grove, IL: InterVarsity, 2003.

Dever, Mark. *The Message of the Old Testament.* Wheaton, IL: Crossway, 2006.

———. *Nine Marks of a Healthy Church.* Wheaton, IL: Crossway, 2000.

Driver, S. R. *The Book of Genesis.* Westminster Commentary. London: Methuen, 1904.

Duguid, Iain M. *Ezekiel.* NIV Application Commentary. Grand Rapids: Zondervan, 1999.

Dumbrell, William J. *Covenant and Creation: A Theology of the Old Testament Covenants*. Carlisle, UK: Paternoster, 1984.

———. *The End of the Beginning: Revelation 21–22 and the Old Testament*. Eugene, OR: Wipf and Stock, 2001.

———. *The Faith of Israel: A Theological Survey of the Old Testament*. 2nd ed. Grand Rapids: Baker Academic, 2002.

———. *The Search for Order: Biblical Eschatology in Focus*. Grand Rapids: Baker, 1994.

Durham, John I. *Exodus*. Word Biblical Commentary. Waco, TX: Word, 1987.

———. *Understanding the Basic Themes of Exodus*. Dallas: Word, 1990.

Edwards, James R. *Mark*. Pillar New Testament Commentary. Grand Rapids: Eerdmans, 2002.

Eichrodt, Walther. *Theology of the Old Testament*. Vol. 1. Trans. J. A. Baker. Philadelphia: Westminster, 1961.

Erickson, Millard J. *Christian Theology*. 2nd ed. Grand Rapids: Baker, 1998.

Farrer, Austin. *The Revelation of St. John the Divine*. Oxford: Clarendon, 1964.

Feinberg, John S. *No One Like Him: The Doctrine of God*. Wheaton, IL: Crossway, 2001.

Ferguson, Everett. *Church of Christ: A Biblical Ecclesiology for Today*. Grand Rapids: Eerdmans, 1996.

Ferguson, Sinclair B. *The Holy Spirit*. Contours of Christian Theology. Downers Grove, IL: InterVarsity, 1996.

Fesko, J. V. *Last Things First: Unlocking Genesis 1–3 with the Christ of Eschatology*. Fearn, Ross-shire, UK: Mentor, 2007.

Fitzmeyer, Joseph A. *The One Who Is to Come*. Grand Rapids: Eerdmans, 2007.

Frame, John M. *The Doctrine of God*. A Theology of Lordship. Phillipsburg, NJ: P&R, 2002.

———. *The Doctrine of the Knowledge of God*. A Theology of Lordship. Phillipsburg, NJ: P&R, 1987.

———. *Salvation Belongs to the Lord*. Phillipsburg, NJ: P&R, 2006.

France, R. T. *The Gospel according to Matthew: An Introduction and Commentary*. Downers Grove, IL: InterVarsity, 1985.

Franke, John R. *The Character of Theology: A Postconservative Evangelical Approach*. Grand Rapids: Baker, 2005.

Frei, Hans. *Types of Christian Theology*. New Haven, CT: Yale University Press, 1992.

Fung, Ronald K. *The Epistle to the Galatians*. New International Commentary on the New Testament. Grand Rapids: Eerdmans, 1988.

Gage, Warren Austin. *The Gospel of Genesis: Studies in Protology and Eschatology*. Winona Lake, IN: Carpenter, 1984.

Gamble, Harry. *The New Testament Canon: Its Making and Meaning*. Philadelphia: Fortress, 1985.

Geisler, Norman, ed. *Inerrancy*. Grand Rapids: Zondervan, 1980.

Glasser, Arthur. *Announcing the Kingdom: The Story of God's Mission in the Bible*. Grand Rapids: Baker, 2003.

Goldingay, John. *Old Testament Theology: Israel's Faith*. Downers Grove, IL: InterVarsity, 2006.

———. *Old Testament Theology: Israel's Gospel*. Downers Grove, IL: InterVarsity, 2003.

Goldsworthy, Graeme. *According to Plan: The Unfolding Revelation of God in the Bible*. Downers Grove, IL: InterVarsity, 1991.

———. *The Gospel in Revelation: Gospel and Apocalypse*. Carlisle, UK: Paternoster, 1984.

———. *The Lamb and the Lion: The Gospel in Revelation*. New York: Thomas Nelson, 1994.

Gorman, Frank J. *Leviticus: Divine Presence and Community*. Grand Rapids: Eerdmans, 1997.

Gowan, Donald E. *Theology in Exodus: Biblical Theology in the Form of a Commentary*. Louisville: Westminster John Knox, 1994.

Green, Joel B., and Mark D. Baker. *Recovering the Scandal of the Cross: Atonement in New Testament and Contemporary Contexts*. Downers Grove, IL: InterVarsity, 2000.

Grenz, Stanley J., and Roger E. Olson. *Twentieth-Century Theology: God and the World in a Transitional Age*. Downers Grove, IL: InterVarsity, 1992.

Grudem, Wayne A. *Systematic Theology: An Introduction to Biblical Doctrine*. Grand Rapids: Zondervan, 1994.

Gunkel, H. *Genesis*. Translated by Mark E. Biddle. Macon, GA: Mercer University Press, 1997.

Gunton, Colin E. *The Promise of Trinitarian Theology*. Edinburgh: T&T Clark, 1991.

Hafemann, Scott J. *2 Corinthians*. NIV Application Commentary. Grand Rapids: Zondervan, 2000.

Hagner, Donald A. *Matthew 14–28*. Word Biblical Commentary. Dallas: Word, 1995.

Hamilton, James M., Jr. *God's Indwelling Presence: The Holy Spirit in the Old and New Testaments*. Nashville: Broadman & Holman, 2006.

Hamilton, Victor P. *The Book of Genesis: Chapters 1–17*. New International Commentary on the Old Testament. Grand Rapids: Eerdmans, 1990.

———. *The Book of Genesis: Chapters 18–50*. New International Commentary on the Old Testament. Grand Rapids: Eerdmans, 1995.

Hartshorne, Charles. *The Divine Relativity*. New Haven, CT: Yale University Press, 1948.

Hartshorne, Charles, and W. L. Reese. *Philosophers Speak of God*. Chicago: University of Chicago Press, 1953.

Hendriksen, William. *Matthew*. New Testament Commentary. Grand Rapids: Baker, 1995.

Hill, Charles E., and Frank A. James, eds. *The Glory of the Atonement: Biblical, Theological, and Practical Perspectives*. Downers Grove, IL: InterVarsity, 2004.

Horton, Michael S. *Covenant and Eschatology: The Divine Drama*. Louisville: Westminster John Knox, 2002.

———. *Lord and Servant: A Covenant Christology*. Louisville: Westminster John Knox, 2005.

Hoskins, Paul M. *Jesus as the Fulfillment of the Temple in the Gospel of John*. Paternoster Biblical Monographs. Eugene, OR: Wipf and Stock, 2006.

Jeffrey, Steve, Michael Ovey, and Andrew Sachs, eds. *Pierced for Our Transgressions: Recovering the Glory of Penal Substitution*. Wheaton, IL: Crossway, 2007.

Kaiser, Walter, Jr. *The Messiah in the Old Testament*. Grand Rapids: Zondervan, 1995.

———. *Mission in the Old Testament: Israel as a Light to the Nations*. Grand Rapids: Baker, 2000.

———. *Toward an Old Testament Theology*. Grand Rapids: Zondervan, 1978.

Kärkkäinen, Veli-Matti. *Christology: A Global Introduction—An Ecumenical, International, and Contextual Perspective*. Grand Rapids: Baker, 2003.

Kerr, Alan R. *The Temple of Jesus' Body: The Temple Theme in the Gospel of John*. Journal for the Study of the New Testament—Supplement Series 220. New York: Sheffield, 2002.

Kidner, Derek. *Genesis*. Tyndale Old Testament Commentary. Downers Grove, IL: InterVarsity, 1967.

———. *Psalms 1–72*. Tyndale Old Testament Commentary. Downers Grove, IL: InterVarsity, 1973.

Kline, Meredith G. *Images of the Spirit*. Eugene, OR: Wipf and Stock, 1998.

———. *Kingdom Prologue: Genesis Foundations for a Covenantal Worldview*. Overland Park, KS: Two Age, 2000.

Köehler, L., and W. Baumgartner, eds. *Lexicon in Veteris Testamenti Libros*. Leiden: E. J. Brill, 1958.

Koester, Craig R. *Dwelling of God: The Tabernacle in the Old Testament, Intertestamental Jewish Literature, and the New Testament*. Catholic Biblical Quarterly Monograph Series 22. Washington, DC: Catholic Biblical Association of America, 1989.

Köstenberger, Andreas J. *John*. Baker Exegetical Commentary on the New Testament. Grand Rapids: Baker, 2004.

Köstenberger, Andreas, and Peter O'Brien. *Salvation to the Ends of the Earth: A Biblical Theology of Mission*. New Studies in Biblical Theology 11. Downers Grove, IL: InterVarsity, 2001.

Kulikovsky, Andrew S. *Creation, Fall, Restoration: A Biblical Theology of Creation*. Fearn, Ross-shire, UK: Mentor, 2009.

Kupp, David D. *Matthew's Emmanuel: Divine Presence and God's People in the First Gospel*. Society of New Testament Studies Monograph Series 90. Cambridge: Cambridge University Press, 1996.

Ladd, George Eldon. *A Theology of the New Testament*. Rev. ed. Edited by Donald A. Hagner. Grand Rapids: Eerdmans, 2001.

Lane, William L. *Hebrews 1–8*. Word Biblical Commentary. Nashville: Thomas Nelson, 1991.

Lee, Pilchan. *The New Jerusalem in the Book of Revelation: A Study of Revelation 21–22 in the Light of Its Background in Jewish Tradition*. Tübingen: Mohr Siebeck, 2001.

Letham, Robert. *The Holy Trinity in Scripture, History, Theology, and Worship*. Phillipsburg, NJ: P&R, 2004.

———. *The Work of Christ*. Contours of Christian Theology. Downers Grove, IL: InterVarsity, 1993.

Lindblom, J. *A Study of the Immanuel Section in Isaiah*. Lund: Gleerup, 1958.

Lints, Richard. *The Fabric of Theology: A Prolegomenon to Evangelical Theology*. Grand Rapids: Eerdmans, 1993. Reprint, Eugene, OR: Wipf and Stock, 1999.

Longman, Tremper, and Daniel G. Reid. *God Is a Warrior*. Grand Rapids: Zondervan, 1995.

Luz, Ulrich. *Matthew 1–7: A Commentary*. Translated by W. C. Linss. Minneapolis: Augsburg, 1989.

Macleod, Donald. *Behold Your God*. 2nd ed. Fearn, Ross-shire, UK: Christian Focus, 1995.

———. *The Person of Christ*. Contours of Christian Theology. Downers Grove, IL: InterVarsity, 1998.

Mann, Alan. *Atonement for a Sinless Society: Engaging with an Emergent Culture*. Milton Keynes, UK: Paternoster, 2005.

Martin-Achard, R. *A Light to the Nations: A Study of the Old Testament Conception of Israel's Mission to the World*. Edinburgh: Oliver & Boyd, 1962.

Mathews, Kenneth A. *Genesis 1–11:26*. New American Commentary. Nashville: Broadman & Holman, 2002.

———. *Genesis 11:27–50:26*. New American Commentary. Nashville: Broadman & Holman, 2005.

McGinn, Bernard. *The Presence of God: A History of Western Christian Mysticism*. 3 vols. New York: Crossroad, 1991–1998.

McGrath, R. A., and A. Galloway. *The Science of Theology*. Vol. 1. Grand Rapids: Eerdmans, 1996.

Merrill, Eugene H. *Everlasting Dominion: A Theology of the Old Testament*. Nashville: Broadman & Holman, 2006.

Mettinger, Tryggve N. D. *In Search of God: The Meaning and Message of the Everlasting Names*. Translated by F. H. Cryer. Philadelphia: Fortress, 1988.

Meyers, C. *Binding the Strong Man: A Political Reading of Mark's Story of Jesus*. Maryknoll, NY: Orbis, 1988.

Miles, Jack. *God: A Biography*. New York: Vintage, 1996.

Moberley, R. W. L. *At the Mountain of God: Story and Theology in Exodus 32–34*. Journal for the Study of the Old Testament—Supplement Series 22. Sheffield, UK: JSOT, 1983.

————. *The Old Testament of the Old Testament: Patriarchal Narratives and Mosaic Yahwism*. Minneapolis: Augsburg, 1992.

Moo, Douglas J. *The Letters to the Colossians and to Philemon*. Pillar New Testament Commentary. Grand Rapids: Eerdmans, 2008.

Morris, Leon. *The Apostolic Preaching of the Cross*. 3rd ed. Grand Rapids: Eerdmans, 1965.

————. *The Atonement: Its Meaning and Significance*. Downers Grove, IL: InterVarsity, 1983.

————. *The Book of Revelation*. Rev. ed. Tyndale New Testament Commentaries. Grand Rapids: Eerdmans, 1987.

Motyer, J. Alec. *The Prophecy of Isaiah: An Introduction and Commentary*. Downers Grove, IL: InterVarsity, 1993.

Mounce, Robert H. *Revelation*. New International Commentary on the New Testament. Grand Rapids: Eerdmans, 1998.

Murray, John. *Redemption Accomplished and Applied*. Grand Rapids: Eerdmans, 1993.

Nash, Ronald H. *The Word of God and the Mind of Man*. Grand Rapids: Zondervan, 1982.

Netland, Harold. *Dissonant Voices: Religious Pluralism and the Question of Truth*. Grand Rapids: Eerdmans, 1991.

Noth, Martin. *Die israelitischen Personennamen im Rahmen der gemeinsemitischen Namengebung*. Hildesheim: Olms, 1966.

Niehaus, Jeffrey J. *God at Sinai: Covenant and Theophany in the Bible and Ancient Near East*. Grand Rapids: Zondervan, 1995.

Ortlund, Raymond C., Jr. *Whoredom: God's Unfaithful Wife in Biblical Theology*. Grand Rapids: Eerdmans, 1996.

Osborne, Grant. *Revelation*. Baker Exegetical Commentary on the New Testament. Grand Rapids: Baker, 2002.

Otto, Rudolf. *Das Heilige*. Translated by J. Harvey. New York: Oxford University Press, 1950.

Packer, J. I., and Mark Dever. *In My Place Condemned He Stood: Celebrating the Glory of the Atonement*. Wheaton, IL: Crossway, 2007.

Pate, C. Marvin, J. Scott Duvall, Daniel Hays, E. Randolph Richards, V. Dennis Tucker Jr., and Preban Vang. *The Story of Israel: A Biblical Theology*. Downers Grove, IL: InterVarsity, 2004.

Peterson, David G. *The Acts of the Apostles*. Pillar New Testament Commentary. Grand Rapids: Eerdmans, 2009.

————. *Engaging God: A Biblical Theology of Worship*. Downers Grove, IL: InterVarsity, 1992.

————. *Possessed by God: A New Testament Theology of Sanctification and Holiness*. Grand Rapids: Eerdmans, 1995.

Phillips, Richard D., Philip G. Ryken, and Mark E. Dever. *The Church: One, Holy, Catholic, and Apostolic*. Phillipsburg, NJ: P&R, 2004.

Pinnock, Clark H., Richard Rice, John Sanders, William Hasker, and David Baringer, eds. *The Openness of God: A Biblical Challenge to the Traditional Understanding of God.* Downers Grove, IL: InterVarsity, 1994.

Piper, John. *God's Passion for His Glory: Living the Vision of Jonathan Edwards.* Wheaton, IL: Crossway, 1998.

Porter, Stanley E., ed. *The Messiah in the Old and New Testaments.* Grand Rapids: Eerdmans, 2007.

Powell, Mark Allen. *God with Us: A Pastoral Theology of Matthew's Gospel.* Minneapolis: Fortress, 1995.

Poythress, Vern S. *The Returning King: A Guide to the Book of Revelation.* Phillipsburg, NJ: P&R, 2000.

———. *The Shadow of Christ in the Law of Moses.* Brentwood, TN: Wolgemuth & Hyatt, 1991.

Pratt, Richard L., Jr. *He Gave Us Stories: The Bible Student's Guide to Interpreting Old Testament Narratives.* 1990. Reprint, Phillipsburg, NJ: Presbyterian and Reformed, 1993.

Rendtorff, Rolf. *The Canonical Hebrew Bible: A Theology of the Old Testament.* Translated by David E. Orton. Leiden: Deo, 2005.

Reymond, Robert L. *Jesus Divine Messiah: The New and Old Testament Witness.* Fearn, Ross-shire, UK: Mentor, 2003.

Richter, Sandra. *The Epic of Eden: A Christian Entry into the Old Testament.* Downers Grove, IL: InterVarsity, 2008.

Ringgren, Helmet. *The Messiah in the Old Testament.* London: SCM, 1956.

Robertson, O. Palmer. *The Christ of the Covenants.* Phillipsburg, NJ: Presbyterian and Reformed, 1980.

Ross, Allen P. *Creation and Blessing.* Grand Rapids: Baker, 1996.

———. *Recalling the Hope of Glory: Biblical Worship from the Garden to the New Creation.* Grand Rapids: Kregel, 2006.

Routledge, Robin. *Old Testament Theology: A Thematic Approach.* Downers Grove, IL: InterVarsity, 2008.

Rowley, H. H. *Israel's Mission to the World.* London: SPCK, 1939.

Sailhamer, John, *First and Second Chronicles.* Chicago: Moody, 1983.

Sanders, James. *The Old Testament in the Cross.* New York: Harper and Brothers, 1961.

Sanders, John. *The God Who Risks: A Theology of Providence.* Downers Grove, IL: InterVarsity, 1998.

Sarna, Nahum M. *Genesis.* JPS Torah Commentary. Philadelphia: JPS, 1989.

Saucy, Robert L. *The Case for Progressive Dispensationalism: The Interface between Dispensational and Non-Dispensational Theology.* Grand Rapids: Zondervan, 1993.

Schreiner, Thomas R. *1, 2 Peter, Jude.* New American Commentary. Nashville: Broadman & Holman, 2003.

————. *New Testament Theology: Magnifying God in Christ*. Grand Rapids: Baker, 2008.

————. *Paul, Apostle of God's Glory in Christ: A Pauline Theology*. Downers Grove, IL: InterVarsity, 2001.

————. *Romans*. Baker Exegetical Commentary on the New Testament. Grand Rapids: Baker, 1998.

Schultz, Samuel J. *Leviticus: God among His People*. Chicago: Moody, 1983.

Skinner, J. *A Critical and Exegetical Commentary on Genesis*. International Critical Commentary. Edinburgh: Clark, 1930.

Smail, Tom. *Once and for All: A Confession of the Cross*. London: Darton, Longman, & Todd, 1998.

Smith, T. C. *Jesus in the Gospel of John*. Nashville: Broadman, 1959.

Stein, Robert H. *Jesus the Messiah: A Survey of the Life of Christ*. Downers Grove, IL: InterVarsity, 1996.

Strom, Mark. *The Symphony of Scripture: Making Sense of the Bible's Many Themes*. Phillipsburg, NJ: Presbyterian and Reformed, 1990.

Sweet, J. P. M. *Revelation*. SCM Pelican Commentaries. London: SCM, 1979.

Terrien, Samuel. *The Elusive Presence: Toward a New Biblical Theology*. New York: Harper and Row, 1978.

Tidball, Derek. *The Message of the Cross*. Downers Grove, IL: InterVarsity, 2001.

Toon, Peter. *Our Triune God*. Wheaton, IL: Victor, 1996.

VanGemeren, William. *The Progress of Redemption: The Story of Salvation from Creation to the New Jerusalem*. Grand Rapids: Baker, 1988.

van Groningen, Gerard. *Messianic Revelation in the Old Testament*. Grand Rapids: Baker, 1990.

Vawter, B. *On Genesis: A New Reading*. Garden City, NY: Doubleday, 1977.

Von Rad, Gerhard. *Genesis*. Old Testament Library. Philadelphia: Westminster, 1972.

Vos, Geerhardus. *Biblical Theology: Old and New Testaments*. Grand Rapids: Eerdmans, 1948. Reprint, Carlisle, PA: Banner of Truth, 2000.

Waltke, Bruce K. *Genesis: A Commentary*. Grand Rapids: Zondervan, 2001.

————. *An Old Testament Theology: An Exegetical, Canonical, and Thematic Approach*. Grand Rapids: Zondervan, 2007.

Walton, John. *Genesis*. NIV Application Commentary. Grand Rapids: Zondervan, 2001.

Ware, Bruce A. *Father, Son, and Holy Spirit: Relationships, Roles, and Relevance*. Wheaton, IL: Crossway, 2005.

————. *God's Greater Glory: The Exalted God of Scripture and the Christian Faith*. Wheaton, IL: Crossway, 2004.

————. *God's Lesser Glory: The Diminished God of Open Theism*. Wheaton, IL: Crossway, 2000.

Webb, Barry G. *The Message of Isaiah*. The Bible Speaks Today. Downers Grove, IL: InterVarsity, 1996.

Weinandy, Thomas G. *Does God Suffer?* Notre Dame, IN: University of Notre Dame Press, 2000.

Wenger, Paul D. *An Examination of Kingship and Messianic Expectation in Isaiah 1–35.* Lewiston, NY: Mellen, 1992.

Wenham, Gordon J. *The Book of Leviticus.* New International Commentary on the Old Testament. Grand Rapids: Eerdmans, 1979.

———. *Genesis 1–15.* Word Biblical Commentary. Nashville: Thomas Nelson, 1987.

Westermann, Claus. *Genesis 1–11.* Translated by John J. Scullion. Minneapolis: Fortress, 1994.

Whitehead, Alfred N. *Process and Reality.* New York: Macmillan, 1929.

Whitney, Donald S. *Spiritual Disciplines within the Church: Participating Fully in the Body of Christ.* Chicago: Moody, 1996.

Williams, Michael D. *Far as the Curse Is Found: The Covenant Story of Redemption.* Phillipsburg, NJ: P&R, 2005.

Williamson, H. G. M. *Variations on a Theme: King, Messiah, and Servant in the Book of Isaiah.* Carlisle UK: Paternoster, 1998.

Williamson, Paul R. *Sealed with an Oath: Covenant in God's Unfolding Purpose.* New Studies in Biblical Theology 23. Downers Grove, IL: InterVarsity, 2007.

Wilson, Gerard H. *Psalms.* Vol. 1. NIV Application Commentary. Grand Rapids: Zondervan, 2002.

Wolf, Herbert M. *Interpreting Isaiah: The Suffering and Glory of the Messiah.* Grand Rapids: Zondervan, 1985.

Woodbridge, John D. *Biblical Authority: A Critique of the Rogers/McKim Proposal.* Grand Rapids: Zondervan, 1982.

Woods, Richard. *Christian Spirituality: God's Presence through the Ages.* Chicago: Thomas More, 1989.

Wright, Christopher J. H., *Deuteronomy.* New International Biblical Commentary. Peabody, MA: Hendrickson, 1996.

———. *Knowing Jesus through the Old Testament.* Downers Grove, IL: InterVarsity, 1992.

———. *Mission of God: Unlocking the Bible's Grand Narrative.* Downers Grove, IL: InterVarsity, 2006.

Wright, N. T. *The New Testament and the People of God.* Philadelphia: Fortress, 1992.

———. *The Resurrection of the Son of God.* Minneapolis: Fortress, 2003.

———. *Surprised by Hope: Rethinking Heaven, the Resurrection, and the Mission of the Church.* New York: Harper One, 2008.

General Index